Direct and Interactive Marketing

Adrian Sargeant

Douglas C. West

OXFORD

UNIVERSITY PRESS

OXFORD
UNIVERSITY PRESS

Great Clarendon Street, Oxford OX2 6DP

Oxford University Press is a department of the University of Oxford.
It furthers the University's objective of excellence in research, scholarship,
and education by publishing worldwide in

Oxford New York

Athens Auckland Bangkok Bogotá Buenos Aires Cape Town
Chennai Dar es Salaam Delhi Florence Hong Kong Istanbul Karachi
Kolkata Kuala Lumpur Madrid Melbourne Mexico City Mumbai Nairobi
Paris São Paulo Shanghai Singapore Taipei Tokyo Toronto Warsaw

with associated companies in Berlin Ibadan

Oxford is a registered trade mark of Oxford University Press
in the UK and in certain other countries

Published in the United States
by Oxford University Press Inc., New York

© Adrian Sargeant and Douglas C. West 2001

The moral rights of the authors have been asserted
Database right Oxford University Press (maker)

First published 2001

A catalogue record for this book is available from the British Library

Library of Congress Cataloging in Publication Data
(Data available)
ISBN 0–19–878253–5

10 9 8 7 6 5 4 3 2 1

Typeset by RefineCatch Limited, Bungay, Suffolk
Printed in Great Britain
on acid-free paper by
The Bath Press, Bath

Contents

3 Understanding Buying 71

List of Figures

List of Tables

Chapter 1

Direct Marketing: The Development of a Discipline

Contents

1.1 Objectives

By the end of this chapter you should be able to:

(a) define direct marketing;

(b) distinguish direct marketing from other forms of marketing;

(c) explain the benefits of direct marketing;

(d) distinguish between stand alone, integrated and peripheral direct marketing;

(e) describe the characteristics of direct marketing;

(f) explain how a direct marketing approach could be used to build customer relationships.

1.2 **What is marketing?**

In this initial chapter we begin by examining something of the role and history of marketing and in particular how 'classic' or 'mass' marketing might differ from the direct marketing we are primarily concerned with here. We will look both at what direct marketing is–and at what direct marketing is not, hopefully exploding some of the more common myths that surround our art. This chapter will also explore some of the benefits of direct marketing, both in terms of the short-term benefits it can deliver in enhanced marketing performance and also the longer-term benefits that accrue though the building of successful and profitable customer relationships.

However, no textbook on direct marketing would be complete without an initial exploration of the fundamentals of marketing. Marketing as a business discipline has been with us since the 1940s and many classic models have evolved in respect of how best to conceptualize it and to organize its activities. Pick up any standard textbook on marketing these days and you will undoubtedly find a plethora of different definitions. Two of the more popular of these are provided below:

Chartered Institute of Marketing

Marketing is the management process responsible for identifying, anticipating, and satisfying customer requirements profitably.

American Marketing Association

Marketing is the process of planning and executing the conception, pricing, promotion, and distribution of ideas, goods, and services to create exchanges that satisfy individual and organizational goals.

At the heart of these and other definitions of marketing is the idea that the ability to achieve organizational goals derives from a thorough understanding of the needs and wants of target markets and then setting about servicing these needs and wants more effectively and efficiently than competitors.

Both these definitions make it clear that marketing actually comprises two distinct elements. The first is the one that most people typically associate with marketing: that is, the notion of a functional department in an organization that is responsible for activities such as conducting research, designing products, and then promoting these products to consumers. These are some of the most visible aspects of marketing activity and might typically form part of the job descriptions of individuals working within a discrete marketing department. Indeed, one of the earliest typologies of this activity was provided by Neil Borden in 1964 who suggested that a marketing executive was in essence a 'mixer of ingredients'. His original list of these ingredients consisted of fourteen elements, including product planning, branding, pricing, channels of distribution, personal selling, advertising, promotions, packaging, display, servicing, physical handling, fact finding and analysis. It was left to McCarthy (1960) to reduce this list down to the now famous four Ps of marketing, comprising:

Product—specifying the product design, features, composition of the product range, product portfolio management, etc.

Price—the price that will be charged for the product or service, whether different types of customer will be charged differentially, what the discount and credit policies might be, etc.

Place—the channels of distribution that would be used to reach each customer group. This would include a detailed analysis of the types of outlet to be used and a consideration of the physical distribution methods to be employed.

Promotion—the mix of promotional tools that would be used to communicate with the customer–e.g. advertising, sales promotion, public relations, personal selling, direct marketing, and exhibitions/trade fairs.

An example of a typical marketing mix is provided in Figure 1.1. Although the list of four Ps might appear a little simplistic, it seems to have endured the test of time. It is still impossible to study marketing these days without at least a passing reference being made to this classical mix. More recently, numerous authors have tried to extend or adapt it in an attempt to make it relevant to a variety of other contexts, including the provision of services. Notable amongst these is the work of Booms and Bitner (1981) who proposed a seven P mix, where the additional three Ps are:

Physical evidence—often services can be completely intangible, with little or no evidence as to the quality of what is being provided. The telephone banking service provided by First Direct is one such example. In a bid to build up ownership of intangible services such as this, many companies provide tangible evidence of the existence of the service, tactfully reminding consumers of the quality thereof. In the case of our example, First Direct provides a file for storing statements, wallets to hold credit and debit cards, and regular branded mailings that project a consistent image.

Process—this dimension of the mix refers to the process that consumers go through in enjoying a service. In taking a flight on British Airways, for example, the traveller encounters a series of interactions with BA and airport staff. They have to find somewhere to park their car, they then take transport to the terminal, check in, and off-load their baggage. They may then enjoy duty free shopping or a rest in an airport lounge. They will also experience a programme of in-flight service and hopefully be reunited with their baggage having passed through immigration at their final destination. By mapping out

Product:

(a) Tangible
- Fast food
- Standardized
- Small range
- Consistent (across outlets)
(b) Augmented
- Children's entertainment
- Additional leisure time
- 'Buy-in' to brand image

Price:

Standardized
Consistent (across outlets)
Value deals / Promotional pricing

Place:

(a) Channel
- Franchise
(b) Location
- Widely accessible
- High traffic locations
- Major centres of population

Promotion:

(a) Advertising
- National TV
- National/regional press
- Billboards
- Radio
(b) Sales Promotion
- Free children's toys
- Competitions
- Coupons
- Promotional meals
(c) Direct Marketing
- Website
- Direct mail
- Direct response TV
(d) Public Relations
- Support of charity
- Sponsorship of events

Fig. 1.1 Typical marketing mix – fast food retailer

the process in this way, service marketers can think about what might be important to customers and engineer additional value in those areas that are perceived as most important. They can also (perhaps) look to cut costs in those areas that do not appear to add value.

People—The final dimension of the extended marketing mix is arguably the most important of all. In a service context, it could be argued, the 'people' are the service. This would certainly be true of the hotel marketplace, for example, where the lion's share of satisfaction from a visit probably derives from the interaction a guest might have with staff such as receptionists, porters, cleaners, waiters, etc. Service marketers need, therefore, to be mindful of the characteristics of the people they employ and ensure that only those motivated to provide the highest possible quality of service are recruited and retained.

Marketing is, however, much more than the mere ingredients of these mixes. It is much more than just advertising, research, sales promotion, or many of the other things that marketers actually do. There is a second facet of marketing and it follows from the idea of 'process' alluded to in both the definitions we cited earlier.

Genuinely marketing led organizations begin the planning of their operations by developing a thorough understanding of customer needs and then gearing up everything that the organization does around satisfying these needs. Marketing is therefore much more than a narrow organizational function. It is a philosophy, or total approach to business, that puts the customer right at the centre of everything the organization does. Thus, marketing should not be regarded as the preserve of the few individuals that happen to be working in the marketing department. Rather, it should permeate the thinking of every individual working for the organization. All staff should have a clear knowledge of customer needs and understand how their own role assists in the satisfaction of those needs. Value can then be created at every contact the customer has with an organization. In short, all an organization's procedures and systems can be designed with the simple goal of delivering the maximum possible value to the customer.

1.3 What is direct marketing?

So now we have an idea of what 'classic' marketing is and how it might be applied at both a philosophical and a functional level within an organization. Direct marketing differs from this classic model only in the sense that it is one approach that might be adopted to marketing. The classic four Ps of marketing are all very well, but their weakness is that they tend to focus the effort of the organization on the nature of the product, the price that will be charged, how it will be distributed, etc. Direct marketing, by contrast, focuses organizational attention on the customer, an approach much more in keeping with the philosophy of marketing described above. What do customers actually want, how do we know we are providing it, how should we communicate? Direct marketing can provide some of the answers. It achieves this by drawing on information stored in customer records held on a database. It is these records that guide the thrust of subsequent marketing activity, rather than the nature of the product per se.

Indeed, as we shall demonstrate later, the customer database is at the heart of all direct marketing activity. Data about known customer behaviours is stored and manipulated to provide profiles of the best prospects to receive particular communications. Higher value customers are identified and treated with an especially optimized standard of care. Customers are offered products/services in which they are known to have an interest and the focus of communication generally moves away from 'intrusion' to 'invitation' as marketing messages are targeted only at those that are likely to receive them positively.

Direct marketing is also characterized by a focus on retention. Traditional mass marketing of the type conducted in the 1950s and 1960s was focused very much on the attraction of ever larger numbers of new customers. Little or no thought was given to how these customers might be kept loyal, except perhaps through the building of a strong brand that consumers might choose to identify with. Communication was generally a monologue with messages issuing forth from a variety of companies competing in a given product category. Direct marketing, by contrast, is about 'closing' this communication loop: building a 'dialogue' with customers and using the ensuing information to refine the nature of the marketing offer to keep customers loyal.

Direct marketing is thus an approach to marketing that treats customers as individuals and defines them, not only by their individual characteristics, but also by how they have behaved in the past. Thus, for example, organizations engaged in direct marketing will tend not to view all 30–40 year-old customers as alike. They will endeavour to identify subtle differences in behaviour each of which could potentially be used to inform the development of a uniquely tailored customer relationship. In short, database information about historic behaviours is integrated into the marketing decision-making process and utilized to ensure that all customers receive a marketing mix specifically adapted to their own requirements.

This contrasts sharply with the days of the traditional 'mass marketing' approach when organizations treated all customers alike. A standard campaign was developed to address everyone regardless of individual preferences or whether they had been a customer in the past. Fortunately, the death knell for this form of marketing was sounded over three decades ago. It was 1970 when Alvin Toffler introduced the term *demassification* into marketing vocabulary, noting that mass markets were gradually eroding and with them went the need for mass marketing approaches. By the mid 1970s consumers had started to become more discerning, thoughtful and individualist–what the Henley Centre (1995) later described as 'thoughtful butterflies'. Indeed, in the modern era consumers have come to expect greater choice and products/services that are ever more tailored to their own individual requirements. For evidence of the impact of this new thinking it is worth remembering that it is not so very long ago that bathtubs were white, telephones were black, and cheques were green. Marketing has certainly come a long way in the past 30 years!

This increasing consumer choice has also been reflected in a proliferation of communication channels. In the late 1940s it was possible to reach half the adult population of the

UK with a single ad in the Radio Times. The early days of commercial television offered similar opportunities for mass marketing. Brands could be created almost instant-aneously with high profile campaigns and market shares could be doubled virtually over-night. With the onset of the new millennium and the proliferation of communication media, mass advertising is loosing its appeal. Highly focused channels now exist that can reach a customer group much more cost effectively than would previously have been the case. Indeed, the profile of individuals using particular media can be carefully compared with the known profile of a particular organization's customers and the closest match identified. Media can now be selected with a high concentration of customers possessing very specific characteristics. Advances in targeting and database technology have greatly facilitated this process and media wastage is being rapidly eliminated.

One of the pioneers of mass marketing, William Hesketh Lever, famously remarked that he knew half the money he spent on advertising was wasted, but that he didn't know which half. Even at the time he was making this comment one group of marketers had a pretty good idea how their advertising was working. For some time, early direct marketers had been testing customer responses to various media and using this information to tailor both their media selection and the creative approach employed. Direct marketing activity has the advantage of being infinitely measurable! Whilst marketers can only make educated guesses about the impact of a traditional advertising campaign, the customer response to most forms of direct marketing can be measured to two or even three decimal places. Opportunities for testing abound and direct marketers rolling out expensive campaigns are now in a position to predict with a high degree of accuracy the consumer response that will ultimately be achieved.

This characteristic of measurability is reflected in the Direct Marketing Association's definition of direct marketing:

> Direct marketing is an interactive system of marketing which uses one or more advertising media to effect a measurable response and/or transaction at any location.

Although this is a definition now widely supported by leading practitioners such as Stone (1996) and Nash (1995), it does perhaps lack an emphasis on the collection and manipu-lation of customer data that characterizes so much of direct marketing activity. The definition developed by the UK's Institute of Direct Marketing makes this additional dimension clear. Direct marketing is:

> the planned recording, analysis and tracking of customers' direct response behaviour over time . . . in order to develop future marketing strategies for long term customer loyalty and to ensure continued business growth.

In the modern era, this process of recording, analysing, and tracking customer behaviour is made possible by database technology. Customer information can now be easily captured, processed, and used to inform the development of strategy. Advances in com-puting power have made it much easier for organizations to process vast quantities of information and hence to develop more personalized relationships with their customers. We will explore later in this text exactly how this might be achieved.

1.3.1 Some common misconceptions

Having already focused on what direct marketing is, it will also be instructive to consider what it is not. As Tapp (1998) notes, too many marketing texts continue to regard direct marketing as a mere sub-section of the communications mix. Such a label not only lowers the perceived importance of the direct marketing function, it also ignores the fact that direct marketing should be seen as an alternative to traditional marketing approaches, based on a genuine dialogue with consumers.

Ask any class new to the study of the subject what direct marketing is–and a whole set of negative stereotypes will undoubtedly be offloaded. Many students and, indeed, consumers continue to see direct marketing as synonymous with direct mail. Worse still, many see it as synonymous with junk mail. It is important to be clear that whilst direct marketing can include direct mail as a potential communications tool, there are a variety of other media options that may be employed including: direct response television (DRTV), door-to-door distribution, direct response press advertising, magazine inserts, telephone, radio, personal selling, and the internet. Direct marketing is therefore much broader in scope than mere direct mail.

The perception of direct mail as junk is also fallacious. Rapid developments in database technology now make it easier than ever before for companies to ensure that their communications are targeted only at those individuals who might have an interest in the products/service on offer. The days of gardening catalogues being sent to folks living at the top of high-rise apartment buildings are long since past. Opportunities now exist to segment a customer database much more explicitly and thus to ensure that specific offers can be targeted at specific groups of customers. That is not to say, of course, that some companies do not still adopt a 'shotgun' approach to marketing, sending all their communications to everyone whose name happens to appear on their list. It is probably fair to say, however, that the incidence of such activity is now much lower. The fact that poorly targeted activities will inevitably underperform and end up costing offenders money, is ultimately the most effective control mechanism. Thus, whilst it seems fashionable to grumble these days about direct marketing, the quality of the activity improves daily.

1.4 The benefits of direct marketing

From the preceding discussion it will already have become clear that a number of benefits can accrue from adopting a direct marketing approach. These derive from the fact that direct marketing media are, by their very nature, direct response. Direct response press ads, for example, typically invite readers to fill in a coupon to make contact with a company, or offer a freephone number to call to place an order or to request product details.

Similarly, direct response television ads (DRTV) are designed to compel viewers to pick up the phone and call to place an order. In short, there are clear opportunities to link 'cause with effect' making it easier to calculate campaign ROI (Return On Investment). Accountable results of marketing activity undertaken in various media can easily be compared and an optimal communications strategy designed.

The fact that a direct response is generated also makes it possible for direct marketers to control the timing of what they do. Whilst a mass marketer could control the timing of the placement of their advertising, for example, they would be unlikely to be in a position to control the timing of the response. With mass marketing it is all but impossible to link a sale to the advertisement that initiated it. The actual response may follow some time after the original ad was placed, and/or the effect of an ad can be impacted by a variety of other marketing mix factors such as sales promotion, point of sale displays, etc. Mass marketers are rarely able to identify exactly which of their diverse activities actually stimulated a sale. Direct marketers, by contrast, know exactly which ad generated a sale and the duration over which these sales will be generated (most responses will be back within three days). This makes it possible to manage the consumer response and ensure that, for example, a company is not swamped by requests for service at a particular time of the day, month or year.

It is also the case that direct marketers have access to a wider range of media than their mass marketing counterparts. This opens up additional creative opportunities. A recent charity mailing initiated by Help The Aged, for example, to raise money to fund cataract operations in the third world, comprised a simple letter detailing the nature of the cause and a response device including a credit card facility and a reply envelope. What made the mailing unusual, however, was the fact that it also included a sheet of frosted Perspex. The prospective donor was invited to look through the perspex to see exactly what it might be like to have one's vision impaired by cataracts. Try achieving the same degree of involvement and empathy with a mass marketing campaign!

The characteristics of direct response also facilitate multi-media planning and many direct marketing campaigns are now run in a series of different media. A particularly memorable campaign was run in the late 1990s for Tango, a fruit flavoured carbonated drink. The ad campaign ran primarily on television (although supported by other media) and the content reflected the generally zany nature of the brand. Interestingly however, the commercials also featured a direct response device which allowed the manufacturers to add substantial value to the Tango brand. Specifically, consumers were invited to call in and 'pass' a series of Tango challenges. If they were not put off as the telephone call progressed they were finally rewarded for their persistence with the opportunity to leave their name and address and receive their very own Tango doll (see Figure 1.2). Keen not be swamped with demand the contact telephone number only appeared on screen for a short period of time. Sufficient numbers of sharp-eyed viewers called in, however, for the Tango promotion to become the UK's first self-liquidating telemarketing campaign.

The Tango example also serves to illustrate a further feature of direct marketing, namely the use of a database. In the case of Tango, the manufacturers were able to build up a database of respondents and generate a useful profile of a typical Tango drinker as a result. Indeed, many direct marketing campaigns are designed with the gathering of relevant

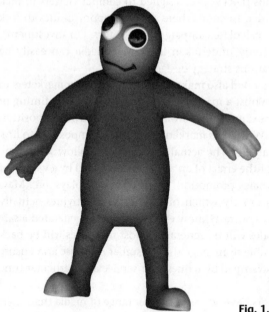

Fig. 1.2 Tango man

marketing data in mind. Much of loyalty marketing operates on this basis. Consumers exchange information with the organization in return for a series of benefits that accrue to them over time. The supermarket Tesco's had data capture high on its list of priorities when it started its revolutionary new loyalty scheme. By enrolling in the scheme consumers shared information about themselves with the company. Initially, this consisted of a relatively simple demographic profile which was then stored on the company's database. As the consumer then used their loyalty card each time they visited a store, data in respect of each cardholder's purchase pattern was stored in the Tesco database. The company was thus soon in a position to be able to profile typical users of specific product categories, distinguish higher value customers from lower value customers, and to recognize immediately when a customer appeared to have lapsed. In return for supplying all this information, the consumer was rewarded with a regular newsletter, discounts, and money off coupons for products that were likely to be of interest.

1.5 Four cornerstones of direct marketing

Closely allied to the features described above are what Holder (1998) regards as the four cornerstones of direct marketing. These are illustrated in Figure 1.3. At the top of the pyramid is the concept of continuity. In a mass marketing approach the 'contact' with the customer is standardized and regarded merely as a series of one-off exchanges. All customers are treated alike and very simple 'product' based messages are employed

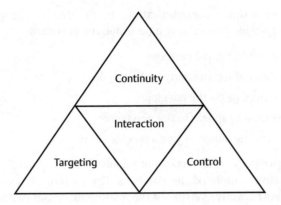

Fig. 1.3 Cornerstones of direct marketing
Source: Holder (1998)

stressing the desirability of making a particular purchase. The emphasis lies in making a profit on each sale and budgets and communications strategy are developed accordingly.

In direct marketing, the goal is to use customer information to develop an ongoing, continuous relationship with each individual on the database. Direct marketers recognize that it is not essential that the organization makes a profit on each transaction with the customer, provided that over the full duration of their relationship a respectable ROI can be obtained. Thus, the costs of recruitment are less of an issue for direct marketers as they recognize the future potential (or lifetime value) that will accrue from each customer. Indeed, the concept of customer lifetime value lies at the core of successful direct marketing activity and drives both what the organization is prepared to spend on recruiting each new customer and what it is prepared to spend on developing a relationship with them over time.

At the base of the pyramid is the concept of interaction. Direct channels afford marketers numerous opportunities to engage the customer, with creative opportunities far superior to those that would be available through traditional channels. A recent RNID (Royal National Institute for the Deaf) Xmas mailing to its donors, for example, included a newsletter, donation form, an audio cassette featuring a Xmas message from the charity's chief executive, and even a festive party whistle in keeping with the 'celebratory' nature of the season.

Direct marketing activity is also characterized by a unique ability to target customers with relevant communications. Modern geodemographic and lifestyle lists make it possible to target consumers with increasingly relevant marketing offers. Once recruited, information in respect of past-purchase behaviour can be used to develop ever more refined communication strategies. Customers ordering baby clothes from a mail order catalogue today, for example, are likely to be in the market for 'toddler toys' in 18–24 months. Database information can thus be used to ensure that they receive relevant product information at the appropriate time.

Finally, direct marketing is characterized by control. It is possible to pre-test almost every dimension of a direct communication. In the case of the RNID mailing, for example, the charity could conceivably have tested the impact of:

- including, or not including, the cassette;
- including, or not including, the party whistle;
- the presence of a message on the envelope;
- the choice of colour(s) to appear in the newsletter;
- the impact of asking the donor to give a specific sum;

In practice, perhaps three or four versions of a mailing might be developed and mailed to a small representative sample of the database. The pattern of response can then be assessed and the most effective version of the mailing rolled out to the remainder of the customer base. Not only does this allow an organization to select the most appropriate mailing, it also allows it to predict with a high degree of accuracy the performance of the overall campaign.

It is these four elements together that combine to make direct marketing a unique discipline within marketing. At its core, however, is the concept of customer lifetime value, since it is this that will shape the strategy to be adopted.

1.6 The development of a discipline

Many people assume that direct marketing is a new phenomenon. This could not be further from the truth. Direct marketing has its roots in the mail order industry and as the chart in Figure 1.4 makes clear, the basic ideas have been around for centuries (McCorkell 1997). Indeed, these early pioneers would have adopted many of the same distinctions between categories of customer that their contemporaries do today. Most, for example, would have recognized the distinction between active/lapsed customers and unconverted enquiries. Certainly, from the middle of the nineteenth century a separate marketing approach would have been adopted for each distinct customer group.

Most of the organizations listed in Figure 1.4 constitute early examples of stand-alone direct marketing. In fact, this is only one of three categories of approach to direct marketing now commonly adopted. Each is described briefly below:

1.6.1 Stand-alone direct marketing

In many ways this might best be regarded as the 'ultimate' direct marketing approach. Organizations that employ stand-alone direct marketing employ no other means to manage the relationship with their customers. Companies such as First Direct and Direct Line Insurance clearly fall within this category. Customers are typically recruited via direct response press advertising, direct mail and/or the internet. Thereafter, the relationship is managed using a combination of telephone, mail, and email. Both organizations

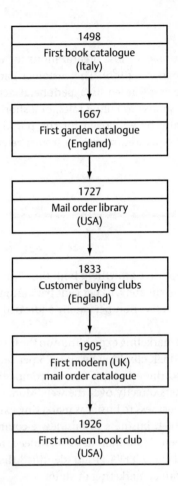

Fig. 1.4 The history of direct marketing
Source: Adapted from McCorkell (1997)

pride themselves on the degree of service provided and both maximize the benefit they can provide for their customers through a careful manipulation of their database.

1.6.2 Integrated direct marketing

A second approach is to employ direct marketing as part of an integrated marketing mix. Here, direct marketing may be viewed as complementing the other marketing activities undertaken. Organizations such as the AA, or a major charity such as Save the Children, can be classified as adopting this general approach. The AA, for example, recruits new customers through its kiosks at motorway service areas, through press advertising, mass television advertising, and direct mail. The organization also has a network of retail outlets situated in many high street locations. Once recruited, direct marketing is employed to develop the value of these customers to the organization, perhaps through cross-selling other product lines, or even asking them to 'recommend a friend'. In such cases, direct marketing is an integral part of a very broad mix.

1.6.3 **Peripheral direct marketing**

The final category of direct marketing activity embraces those organizations for whom direct marketing is only an occasional tactical marketing tool. The customer database may be poorly developed and direct marketing is regarded as a peripheral activity. Indeed, it may often be initiated as a knee-jerk response to falling sales, or a short-term response to competitive pressures. It will typically be employed for the purposes of customer recruitment and the second side of the equation, namely customer retention and development, will be all but ignored.

1.7 **Reasons for growth**

In recent years direct marketing has undergone explosive growth. In both the US and the UK, direct mail volumes continue to grow by approximately 10 per cent per annum (see Table 1.1). Expenditure on door-to-door distribution (i.e. non-personally addressed mail) and DRTV is climbing at a similar rate.

Perhaps the greatest growth, however has been in marketing expenditure on the internet, with total annual expenditures in both the US and UK climbing by circa 25 per cent per annum. This growth has historically been due to the efforts of various companies to communicate with and do business with consumers directly over the web. More recent years have seen a correspondingly steep climb in business to business marketing expenditures with Goldman Sachs estimating that,by 2004, business to business e-commerce revenue will reach $1.5 trillion climbing from a mere $39 billion in 1998. Indeed, recent research by the Direct Marketing Association and the WEEFA group identified that the iternet is the fastest growing business to business direct marketing medium.

There are five key reasons for this rapid growth in direct marketing expenditures:

1.7.1 **Changing demographics and lifestyles**

In the 1950s and 60s, the structure of society was radically different. Simple variables such as gender, race, income, and social class were generally good indicators of the

Table 1.1 Direct mail expenditures by year and country

	1994	1998	1999	2000
Direct mail US	$29.6bn	$39.7bn	$42.2bn	$44.6bn
Consumer	$18.8bn	$24.6bn	$26.0bn	£27.1bn
Business to business	$10.8bn	$15.1bn	$16.2bn	£17.5bn
Direct mail UK	£1,050m	£1,665m	£1,897m	£2,004m
Consumer	£787.5m	£1,299m	£1,498m	£1,603m
Business to business	£262.5m	£366m	£399m	£401m

products/services a given individual might buy. The nuclear two-parent family was the household norm and patterns of behaviour were correspondingly uniform. Consumers generally bought the same few newspapers and magazines, bought the same branded products, watched the same television channels, and had the same predominantly class-based aspirations.

Society has certainly come a long way since then, fragmenting to the point where almost 30 per cent of us now live alone. The capacity for individual expression has been heightened and consumers generally now expect a much greater degree of choice than would hitherto have been believed possible. The talk is now of consumer lifestyles; lifestyles that define small percentages of the population, yet serviced by a plethora of media channels offering an even more diverse set of product and service choices. It is no longer enough for manufacturers to simply ply their wares with broad based messages designed to appeal to all. Consumers increasingly expect that the communications they receive will have a direct relevance to them and reflect their new-found individuality.

Similarly, new markets have started to emerge. We are all living longer. It is estimated, for example, that by the year 2010 there will be three million Americans aged 110 or over. Markets for healthcare, investments, and leisure have developed alongside an ageing population looking for ways both to plan and enjoy their retirement. Indeed, one well-known agency refers to this emerging segment as the 'Silver Surfers', reflecting the fact that not only are people living longer, but they are also healthier, opening up opportunities for them to pursue their hobbies and interests with renewed vigour.

We have therefore experienced over the past thirty years a period of unprecedented change and it would be puerile to suggest that the pattern of consumer marketing should not also change to reflect this. Direct marketing has seen an explosion of growth because it is the one form of marketing capable of handling such a diverse range of consumer needs, wants, and aspirations. Only direct marketing can allow organizations to develop a 'one-to-one' dialogue with their customers–a dialogue tailored exactly to the needs of the individual.

1.7.2 Media fragmentation

In the middle of the twentieth century there were only a few hundred specialist magazines catering for the needs of both genders and a few of the more popular lifestyle interests. By January 2000, the number of specialist magazines had climbed to over 6,000 separate titles in the UK alone. In the US the figure is closer to ten times that amount.

Aside from the proliferation of print media we now have access to digital TV networks offering households the choice of over 100 different channels with the promise of more to come. The government also has plans to extend community based television targeted at specific societal groups; what some observers now refer to as 'narrowcasting'. Consumers seeking movies can already chose the films they want to watch and the times they want to watch them.

Indeed, as channels have proliferated, costs have generally declined. Advertisers can no longer reach mass TV audiences, unless they advertise during the Super Bowl in the US or a major sporting fixture such as the World Cup in the UK. Generally, audiences are smaller and defined to a greater degree by the channels they watch as they indulge their respective interests. This makes it easier for direct marketers to tailor the nature of their communications to target audiences statistically more likely to have an interest in the products on offer.

There are also home shopping channels on both cable and satellite television that do nothing other than sell goods and services to consumers. Amazingly, these channels are proving popular with the public as people elect to do a greater share of their shopping from home.

1.7.3 Increasing salesforce costs

The *Financial Times* currently estimates the cost of an on-site visit by a company sales-person to be of the order of £190. This is obviously an average figure and includes both salary and 'on the road' costs such as samples, promotional materials, and training. When one considers that a high proportion of such visits are speculative, not resulting in a sale, it is easy to why for many companies the costs of employing a direct sales force are prohibitive. Direct marketing offers a low-cost alternative and even more sophisti-cated products requiring higher degrees of explanation are now sold routinely over the web.

1.7.4 Alternative distribution channels

As we shall later demonstrate, direct marketing has also experienced growth because of the increasing range of media opportunities it offers. Aside from the more common media of direct mail, door-to-door distribution, and DRTV, other potential media now include the internet, e-mail, fax, teletext, statement stuffers (direct marketing included with your bank and credit card statements!), and interactive terminals such as bank cash dispensers which have now been adapted to carry interactive marketing material.

1.7.5 Changing business focus

The final reason for the rapid increase in direct marketing's popularity is the fact that businesses are slowly beginning to change the focus of their activity. For many years, businesses were overly concerned with the recruitment of ever larger numbers of new customers. It would not have been unusual for an organization to devote some 80 per cent of its effort and expenditure to this purpose. By the mid 1990s, the folly of this strategy had been recognized and businesses were increasingly keen to focus on the other side of the equation, namely customer retention. Direct marketing designed to retain and reward existing customers has therefore enjoyed particular growth.

1.8 Towards relationships not transactions

Already in this chapter we have seen some of the advantages and features of direct marketing, notable amongst which is the capacity of direct marketing to close the communications loop, gather data from customers, and then use this data to refine the nature of the marketing approach. Direct marketing can therefore be used to foster direct one-to-one relationships with customers. Indeed, some would argue that this is its greatest strength.

Whilst this might sound a little obvious, much early direct marketing activity was poorly applied. Mail, press, and television communications were not adapted to reflect the needs of each group of customers and the majority of direct marketing activity was aimed at customer acquisition (i.e. bringing new customers into the organization) rather than looking after them once they arrived. Indeed, few organizations took a long term view of relationships with their customers and managed each 'relationship' as a series of one-off transactions, rather than as an ongoing relationship per se.

The relationship bandwagon has certainly been rolling for a number of years now, Having originated in the service marketing arena, it is now gaining widespread acceptance in direct marketing circles. The 1992 publication of Peppers and Rogers' 'One To One Marketing' has certainly fuelled the drive, further encouraged by a range of other texts on the subject. What the best of these have in common is an invocation to deal with customers on a one-to-one basis, recognizing each customer as unique in terms of their purchase history, their level of expenditure, and the overall standard of care that they expect to receive from the organizations they do business with. A transaction based approach takes no account of this variation. The interaction with customers is standardized and regarded merely as a series of one-off exchanges. All customers are treated alike and very simple 'product' based messages are employed stressing the need to make a particular purchase. In a relational approach, by contrast, the entire relationship with a customer is viewed holistically and marketing decisions are taken in the light of the perceived value of that overall relationship.

Such a change in emphasis is long overdue and more accurately reflects real market behaviour. In the commercial marketplace comparatively few purchase decisions are, for example, taken on a 'once only' basis. Real market behaviour consists of a series of exchanges rather than purely one-off transactions (as has been argued effectively in the economics literature, see, for example, MacNeil 1980, or Williamson 1981). Whilst it is certainly true that some customers do elect to make only one purchase from a given supplier a significant percentage of customers recruited by a particular campaign or mechanism will elect to make a second purchase. It was well worth asking the question 'if we were better at managing relationships with customers, would we succeed in attracting more repeat business?'

Whilst for the uninitiated the transition from a transaction to a relationship approach to marketing may seem little more than a play on words, the differences in terms of the impact on marketing strategy and performance are profound. If we consider for a moment the transaction based approach, marketing strategy would typically be driven by the initial returns that might be expected from each campaign a particular organization might run. This would be true, even of customer recruitment activity. Thus, marketers adopting this stance will concentrate their efforts on attempting to achieve as near as is practicable a break-even position at the end of even this latter category of campaign. In subsequent customer development campaigns they will also endeavour to maximize the returns generated by each individual campaign they run. Their strategy will be based on achieving the highest possible ROI when the costs and revenues of a particular campaign are calculated. Marketers following such a strategy tend to offer customers little choice. They can't afford to–to do so would merely add to the cost. Little segmentation takes place and customers typically receive a standard approach. The emphasis of the content is usually on the urgency and immediate desirability of a particular purchase. They may then be approached in a few months time with a further seemingly 'must have' series of messages. The customer is thus bombarded with a series of very similar communications each designed with an eye to achieving the maximum possible short-term ROI.

A relationship approach, by contrast, recognizes that it is not essential to break even on the first communication with a customer, or even the second or third. The relationship approach recognizes that, if treated with respect, customers will want to buy again, and marketers are therefore content to live with somewhat lower rates of return in the early stages of a relationship. They recognize that they will achieve a respectable ROI, but anticipate that this will follow naturally in the longer term. Whilst the costs of acquisition and development are still strictly controlled, the initial costs of acquisition are less of an issue since the organization concerned recognizes it will make a return on this investment over the full duration of the relationship. Relationship marketers are therefore not afraid to spend slightly more on recruitment than their transaction based counterparts, as even those relationships with customers with a comparatively high acquisition cost may generate perfectly respectable returns over time. Indeed, it is this longer-term perspective which has prompted many organizations, particularly those using the internet, to establish service centres that were forecast to take several years to break even. Amazon.com is a classic example of this, breaking even only after several years of operation.

Relationship marketing is characterized by customer choice. Recognizing the benefit of future income streams, marketers are not afraid to invest in their customers and to allow them greater flexibility over the content, nature, and frequency of the communications they receive. As Jackson (1992) notes, this makes people feel important thereby fulfilling a basic human need. Whilst the initial costs of implementing such a strategy are undoubtedly higher, the benefits in terms of enhanced patterns of customer loyalty and therefore future revenue streams far outweigh this investment.

Moreover, the advent of modern technology has created what *Business Week* recently referred to as an opportunity to create a 'silicon simulacrum' of the relationships that people used to have with tradesmen such as butchers, bakers, etc. Tailoring the approach to dealing with different categories of customers no longer means doubling the marketing cost. Modern relational software can greatly facilitate the identification of discrete customer segments and suggest contact strategies that would be beneficial for both customer and direct marketer alike.

At the heart of this relational approach to marketing is the concept of 'lifetime value'. Once marketers understand how much a given customer might be worth to them over time, they can tailor the offering to that customer according to the individual's needs/ requirements, and yet still ensure an adequate lifetime Return on Investment.

These differences between the transaction and relational approaches are summarized in Table 1.2.

Relationship marketing may therefore be defined as:

> An approach to the management of the customer exchange process based on the long term value that can accrue to both parties

From a customer's perspective, this style of approach addresses how an organization:

- finds you;
- gets to know you;
- keeps in touch with you;
- tries to ensure that you get what you want from them in every aspect of their dealings with you; and
- checks that you are getting what they promised you.

Naturally, as Stone et al. (1996, p. 676) point out, this depends on the effort being worthwhile to the organization concerned.

The concept of benefit accruing to both parties is also quite fundamental. Customers do have expectations of how they will be treated by an organization. The problem for most organizations though, lies in recognizing what these expectations might be when often even the customers themselves aren't aware of them. As Levitt (1981, p. 100) notes:

'the most important thing to know about intangible products is that the customers usually don't know what they're getting until they don't get it. Only then do they become aware of what they bargained for; only on dissatisfaction do they dwell'

Whilst it would be quite ridiculous to suggest that an organization should strive to service every potential customer need, there is no earthly reason why they should not strive to meet the most basic of these across the board and thereafter concentrate on developing the specific ingredients that appear to be attractive to each discrete customer group. There are clearly very elementary requirements in respect of service that will undoubtedly be common to all the customers on the database. These may legitimately be regarded

Table 1.2 Relationships versus transactions

	Transactional	Relational
Focus	Single sales	Customer retention
Key measures	Immediate ROI, revenue, response rate	Lifetime value
Timescale	Short term	Long term
Orientation	Purchase	Relationship
Customer service	Little emphasis	Major emphasis

as the minimum standard of service that even those organizations insisting on following a simple transactional approach may wish to adopt.

By contrast, relational marketing departments make every effort to segment their customer base and to develop a uniquely tailored service and *importantly* 'quality of service' for each of the customer groups or 'segments' they identify. The relational approach to marketing recognizes that not all customers are created equal and bases decisions in respect of segmentation not only on the product category preferred by a particular customer, but also on their expected lifetime value. It is this which drives the nature of the contact strategy, the dimensions of the relationship and the initial investment that an organization might be prepared to make to recruit its customers in the first place.

Of course, to achieve this, a company needs to capture, store, and leverage data in respect of customer needs and preferences. This data driven approach is at the heart of direct marketing and we shall explore in later chapters exactly how this might be achieved.

1.9 **Summary**

In this chapter we began by distinguishing direct marketing from traditional marketing, noting that direct marketing should in fact be regarded as a different approach to marketing rather than as merely one component of a communications mix. Direct marketing, we argued, was characterized by a focus on the needs and preferences of individual customers and ensuring that these needs and preferences were catered for by the marketing organization. Direct marketing also differed from traditional marketing approaches by virtue of its use of the customer database. Direct marketers closed the communication loop by inviting a response from consumers, the details of which could then be recorded on a database. Over time, this data could be leveraged to ensure that subsequent contacts with a customer reflected their own needs and preferences.

That is not to say, of course, that a direct marketing organization will necessarily wish to meet the needs of all its customers. The degree of tailoring that might take place in the design of marketing strategy will hinge on whether or not a reasonable return could be generated by the additional investment. If not, it may be more appropriate to consider adopting a mass marketing approach.

In the remainder of this text we will look in considerable detail at the development of direct marketing strategy and specifically at how it might be utilized for the purposes of both customer acquisition and customer development. Throughout the text, however, a relational approach will be adopted, stressing how the tools and techniques of direct marketing can be used to facilitate the management of enduring and profitable customer relationships.

Further reading

Booms B. H. and Bitner M. J. (1981) 'Marketing Strategies and Organization Structures for Service Firms' in Donnelly J. and George W. R. (eds) *Marketing of Services* (Chicago: American Marketing Association).

Borden, N. H. (1964) 'The Concept of the Marketing Mix', *Journal of Advertising Research*, June, pp. 2–7.

Henley Centre for Forecasting (1995) *Dataculture 2000*, Henley Centre, Henley-on-Thames, Oxon.

Holder D. (1998) 'The Absolute Essentials of Direct Marketing', IDM Seminar, Bristol.

Jackson D. R. (1992) 'In Quest of the Grail: Breaking The Barriers To Customer Valuation', *Journal of Direct Marketing*, March.

Levitt T. (1981) 'Marketing Intangible Products and Product Intangibles', *Harvard Business Review*, Vol. 59, May/June, pp. 94–102.

MacNeil F. E. (1980) *The New Social Contract: An Inquiry into Modern Contractural Relations* (Connecticut, New Haven: Yale University Press).

McCarthy E. J. (1960) *Basic Marketing: A Managerial Approach* (Illinois: Richard Irwin).

McCorkell G. (1997) *Direct and Database Marketing* (London: Kogan Page).

Nash E. (1995) *Direct Marketing Strategy: Planning, Execution*, 3rd edn (New York: McGraw Hill).

Stone B. (1996), *Successful Direct Marketing Methods*, 5th edn (Chicago, Illinois: NTC Business Books).

Stone M., Woodcock N. and Wilson M. (1996), 'Managing the Change from Marketing Planning to Customer Relationship Management', *Long Range Planning*, 29(5).

Tapp A. (1998) *Principles of Direct and Database Marketing* (London: FT/Pitman Publishing).

Williamson O. (1981), Markets and Hierarchies: Analysis and Anti-Trust Implications (New York: Free Press).

Case study: Nike: an integrated campaign

Nike Inc was founded in 1962 by Bill Bowerman and Phil Knight as a partnership under the name Blue Ribbon Sports. Their early aim was to distribute low-cost high quality Japanese athletic shoes to American consumers, attempting to break Germany's hold on the domestic industry. So successful has the organization been that by January 2000 Nike Inc now manufactures and distributes athletic shoes across the whole spectrum of market price to a global market worth in excess of $8.8 billion in revenue. Nike has also developed both traditional and non-traditional distribution channels for its goods, utilizing over 20,000 retailers, factory stores, Nike stores, and internet based Web sites to both promote and distribute its products. Globally, the company now defends a 33 per cent market share in the athletic footwear industry.

Despite fierce competition in the home US market Nike continues to perform well and still maintains a lead over its competitors. In 1999, Adidas held 15.5 per cent of the market, whilst Reebok held 11.2 per cent. The remaining competitors, including Fila, Timberland, Converse, New Balance, and Asics, each held around 3–5 per cent of the market. By late 1999, Nike remained confident that it could maintain its leadership position given its planned sponsorship of the summer Olympics in Sydney and the 2002 World Cup in Japan and Korea.

Nike is particularly noteworthy since it was amongst the first in its sector to market through its e-commerce web site. It launched a trading site in April 1999 and offered 65 styles of shoes to US consumers. It also took the decision to increase its presence in November 1999 by launching NIKEiD, a facility which now allows consumers to design certain key elements of the shoes they purchase.

It was in keeping with this spirit of innovation that the company decided to generate higher levels of awareness of its internet presence and to seek to integrate the various elements of its communication strategy, historically developed separately for each medium.

The result of this deliberation was the Nike 'Whatever' Campaign which first aired in the winter of 1999/2000. It combined the medium of television with the use of the internet for the first time. At its launch it caused something of a storm since many of the major TV networks refused to run it.

The campaign was designed to promote the Air Cross Trainer II. The ads were designed to drop the viewer into specific situations such as racing Marion Jones, the fastest woman in the world. They built to a climax and asked the viewer 'what do you do?' The strapline 'continued at nike.com' then appeared on the screen. When viewers then visited the website they could choose how the ad would end.

The network TV operators balked at the line 'continued at nike.com' as they feared that viewers would desert their television sets and log on to Nike's website. Initially, Nike were therefore forced to run without the link, although when one of the media operators broke ranks it became possible to integrate the advertising with the company's web strategy. The initial flap almost certainly worked in the company's favour as the coverage undoubtedly stimulated additional viewer interest.

The nature of the campaign was designed to emphasize the personality it was intended that the shoe project. The Air Cross Trainer had versatility as a core value and hence the idea of allowing viewers to chose the end the commercial neatly reinforced this message. Viewers could elect to choose from six or seven possible endings for the ad, read information on the various sports and athletes featured, or actually purchase the shoes. The site also allowed users to view the shoes from several different angles, thereby allowing visitors to interact with the brand. Athletes featured in the commercials included Marion Jones, Mark McGwire, and Rod Kingwell.

The company also ran a series of on-line ads designed to target the same young audience as the TV commercials. The on-line ads mirrored the TV slots and ran on bolt.com and MTV's WebRiot site, amongst others. Each ad was run in Superstitial format which, unlike static web banners, plays like a mini commercial, thus retaining the feel of the original TV ads.

When the commercial was run, sales of the shoe immediately rose to overtake the company's second most popular design by a ratio of 10–1. Visitors to the website also rose dramatically, climbing from 589,000 in January 2000 to 852,000 in February when the campaign reached its peak. The campaign won the Interactive Marketing Award in the category Best Integrated Campaign.

Chapter 2
Marketing Planning

Contents

2.1 **Objectives**

By the end of this chapter you should be able to:

(a) Describe a framework for marketing planning;

(b) Understand the relationship between direct marketing and overall marketing planning;

(c) Develop marketing objectives and strategies;

(d) Develop a marketing mix for a product or service;

(e) Develop a communications mix for a product or service;

(f) Delineate communications strategy.

2.2 **Introduction**

It is the purpose of this chapter to provide a framework for direct marketing planning. It will specify the key headings that would normally be utilized and explain specifically how communications planning integrates within this framework.

In reading this chapter it is important to be aware that the nature of direct marketing planning will depend on the organization's general approach to direct marketing. In the previous chapter we demonstrated how direct marketing can be a stand-alone activity in the sense that it is the only marketing the organization does and the only contact with customers is via direct channels. We also illustrated how direct marketing in some organizations can be regarded as little more than a single component of their communications mix, alongside mass advertising, personal selling, etc.

In the case of stand-alone activity it is likely that the organization will approach direct marketing planning utilizing a framework similar to that depicted in Figure 2.1. It should be noted that there is no one right way in which to write a direct marketing plan and the style and format will hence vary considerably from one organization to another. Indeed, there are almost as many different formats as there are authors of marketing texts! Nevertheless the process outlined in Figure 2.1 has the merit of including what are considered to be the key ingredients of a typical marketing plan, namely, an analysis of where the organization is at present, where it would wish to be in the future; and the detail of how it proposes to get there.

The figure also illustrates the utility of a key facet of direct marketing activity, namely feedback. The use of direct media allows an organization to obtain immediate and ongoing feedback from its customers and to use this to refine the precision and quality of the activities undertaken. The figure, therefore, includes a feedback loop making it clear that one planning period's data can be used to inform the marketing strategy/tactics developed in another.

Fig. 2.1 Marketing planning framework

However, for those organizations for whom direct marketing is merely an ingredient of their communications mix, the extent to which such a formalized planning process will be undertaken by direct marketers is likely to be minimal. The direct marketing department is likely simply to be given a number of communications objectives to fulfil and designs its approach accordingly. In reading this text you should therefore be aware that for many organizations the direct marketing process begins with the delineation of such objectives and works from there.

In this chapter we will consider both approaches and begin by describing the steps undertaken in the general planning process depicted in Figure 2.1.

2.3 **Mission**

Many organizations find it helpful to begin the marketing planning process by restating their mission and organizational objectives. This helps focus the minds of those responsible for marketing on the issues that are considered to be of paramount importance for the organization as a whole. It also assists them in delineating those aspects of the organization's role which warrant further investigation in the detailed marketing audit which follows. Missions are shaped by society, the resources and skills of a company, its key competencies and the values and objectives of its management. They describe the overall value system applied by the company and relate to all stakeholders, not just the target market. When most companies start up, the mission is so obvious and shared that it rarely needs writing down. However, over time, as a company's activities change and develop and new markets and products are added to the portfolio, it becomes increasingly useful to re-state the mission. Missions should be focused, sustainable, measurable, and capable of inspiring the creative team. For example, Pepsi has stated that its mission is to be 'the badge of a generation'.

General advice on mission statements is that they should be short on numbers and long on rhetoric while remaining succinct. Three areas should be covered:

- customer group to be served;
- customer needs that will be met;
- technology to satisfy those needs.

Here is an example from Marks & Spencer to illustrate:

'We offer our customers a selective range of high-quality, well-designed and attractive merchandise at reaonable prices using the most modern techniques of production and quality control.'

Mission statements should address what the organization wishes to achieve, but in such a way that the mission can be adopted consistently for a reasonable period of time. It should not be necessary to readdress the mission on an annual basis, since it should serve only to provide the most general of signposts.

2.4 Organizational objectives

The specific detail of what an organization seeks to achieve within the planning period would normally form part of the content of the organizational objectives. Drucker (1955) isolated what he believed to be eight aspects of operations where organizational objectives could be developed and maintained:

- market standing;
- innovation;
- productivity;
- financial and physical resources;
- manager performance and development;
- worker performance and attitude;
- customer needs to be served;
- public/shareholder responsibility.

It would also be normal at this very general 'helicopter' level of organizational performance to outline the financial performance that the organization wishes to attain and in particular the revenue targets and return to shareholders that will be generated.

Restating both the mission and the organizational objectives assists marketing planners in ensuring that the direct marketing plan will move the organization forward in the manner envisaged.

2.5 The marketing audit

From here on in the marketing planning process can be conceptualized as having three main components:

- Where are we now?
- Where do we want to be?
- How will we get there?

The marketing audit addresses specifically the first of these issues. As such, it is arguably the most crucial stage of the whole planning process since without a thorough understanding of the organization's current position it will be impossible for planners to develop any kind of vision of what they would wish to accomplish in the future. The marketing audit is essentially a detailed review of any factors which are likely to impinge on the organization, taking into account both those generated internally and those emanating from the external environment. The marketing audit is thus a systematic attempt to gather as much information as possible about the organization and its environment and, importantly, how these might both be expected to change and develop in the medium and long-term futures. A typical framework for a marketing audit is given below:

2.5.1 PEEST factors

It is usual to begin the audit process by examining the wider environmental influences which might impact on the organization. Often, these may be factors over which the organization itself has little control, but which will nevertheless crucially impact on it at some stage in the future. The framework utilized for this analysis is typically referred to as a PEEST analysis and is comprised of the following elements:

- Political;
- Economic;
- Environmental;
- Socio-cultural;
- Technological.

In each case the aim is to accumulate a list of all the pertinent factors and how these are expected to change over the planning period. It is best at this point in the process not to spend too much time deliberating about the impact that these factors might have on the organization, but rather to note them, detail how they might change, and move on. The danger of precipitating a discussion at this stage, is that other clues as to the impact these PEEST factors might have will tend to emerge as the audit process progresses. It is therefore better to consider potential impacts 'en masse' when the audit itself is complete. A sample PEEST analysis for an internet bookstore is presented in Figure 2.2.

2.5.2 **Market analysis**

The second stage of the audit involves conducting a thorough analysis of the markets in which the organization perceives itself and, importantly, is perceived by its customers, as operating. Data such as the size or each market, relative growth rates, and current trends will all clearly be of value.

Political

- Attitude of world governments to foreign trade
- Legislative frameworks
- Degree of political risk/uncertainty in each country of operation

Economic

- Performance of economy in each country of operation
- Exchange rates
- Interest rates in home and other countries

Environmental

- Packaging considerations
- Attitudes/behaviours of suppliers/distributors

Socio/Cultural

- Demographics in each country of operation
- Trends in Internet take-up and usage
- Cultural/religious norms in each country of operation
- Literary/lifestyle interest in each country of operation

Technological

- Penetration of home computer use
- Penetration of domestic telephone usage
- Quality and reliability of postal/freight networks

Fig. 2.2 Sample PEEST analysis: Internet bookstore

2.5.3 **Competitor analysis**

To be able to compete successfully in their chosen markets organizations need to have a sound understanding of the behaviours of organizations who might be regarded as competitors and attempt to determine what their future strategies might be. It is also helpful to understand something of the capabilities of each major player and to define clearly their individual strengths and weaknesses. The following checklist could therefore be used as the starting point for analysis, although it should be noted that the specific factors an organization will need to examine are likely to vary considerably from case to case.

- contact details of each competitor;
- size and geographic location(s);
- financial performance;
- resource capabilities;
- past strategies;
- tactical marketing mixes employed;
- key alliances formed;
- major strengths and weaknesses.

2.5.4 **Customers**

Clearly, a key component of the marketing audit will be an analysis of the key customer groups with whom an organization is doing business. Some information may need to be conducted in advance of dealing with a particular customer group, whilst other information can be gleaned post hoc by analysing the organization's database. Typical categories of data gathered include:

- identification of each key customer group;
- requirements/needs/wants of each group;
- basis (if any) for market segmentation;
- buying behaviours;
- attitudes;
- media exposure;
- patterns of change in any of the above.

2.5.5 **Analysis of own organization**

Having now analysed every important component of the external environment it is important to conclude with an examination of the capabilities of the focal organization. A detailed audit should be undertaken of the organization's current marketing activity and its overall performance in respect of previous marketing goals. The following checklist is indicative of the categories of information that might typically be regarded as relevant, but in no sense should it be regarded as exhaustive.

- revenue (subdivided by customer segment);
- profit (subdivided by customer segment);
- sales (subdivided by channel/segment) and margins achieved;
- customer satisfaction;
- marketing procedures;
- marketing organization;
- marketing intelligence systems;
- marketing mix;
- market share analysis;
- cost effectiveness of services being provided.

Clearly, conducting a marketing audit can be a very time-consuming process and given that it is good practice to conduct an audit each year, it can place considerable demands on organizational resources. Nevertheless, the benefits that the audit can offer in terms of enhanced management decision making far outweigh the costs that might be incurred. Indeed, if the auditing process is instituted on an annual basis, most of the necessary mechanisms for the gathering of data will have been put in place in the first year, and hence the costs in both time and effort should subsequently fall substantially.

Regrettably, however, many organizations continue only to take the trouble to complete this exercise when they are facing a crisis. Faced with decreased demand for their services, or a dramatic reduction in profitability, organizations begin to panic and only then seek the reasons for these occurrences. Had a systematic approach to environmental scanning been adopted, not only would they have been less likely to have been taken by surprise, but the development of suitable strategies to counter the problems might already be well under way.

2.6 SWOT analysis

Clearly, at this stage, the output from the marketing audit may be regarded as little more than a collection of data and in this format it is as yet of little value for planning purposes. What is required is a form of analysis which allows the marketer to examine the opportunities and threats presented by the environment in a relatively structured way. Indeed, it should at this point be recognized that opportunities and threats are seldom absolute. An opportunity may only be regarded as an opportunity, for example, if the organization has the necessary resource strengths to support its development. For this reason it is usual to conduct a SWOT analysis (i.e. Strengths, Weaknesses, Opportunities, and Threats) on the data gathered during the marketing audit. This is simply a matter of selecting key information from the audit and presenting it under one of the four headings. The important word here is 'key'. It is important that some filtering is undertaken of the data gathered at this stage so that the analysis is ultimately limited to the factors of most relevance for the subsequent development of strategy.

The principal aim of the SWOT analysis is to allow the organization to find a fit between its internal capabilities and the opportunities and threats presented by the external environment. This idea is represented diagramatically in Figure 2.3. It can also assist managers by focusing their attention on areas where there are either gaps in their knowledge or high levels of uncertainty. In the case of the latter it may prove necessary to make a series of assumptions about the manner in which the environment will change to facilitate the SWOT analysis. If so, these should be kept to a reasonable minimum and made as specific as possible. This will aid planners in subsequently estimating outcomes from the strategies ultimately prescribed.

On completion of the SWOT analysis the organization should be in a position to develop strategies which maximize the potential offered by the market opportunities (drawing on organizational strengths), whilst at the same time looking to minimize the likely effects of any weaknesses or perceived threats in the environment. The output from the SWOT analysis should also help inform the development of appropriate marketing objectives since it should at this stage be clear what the most appropriate means of achieving the organizational objectives (stated earlier) will be.

2.7 **Setting marketing objectives**

As their name implies, marketing objectives are focused on the interaction between the company or organization and the marketplace. They can be largely grouped into four types:

- profits;
- market share;
- sales;
- customer satisfaction.

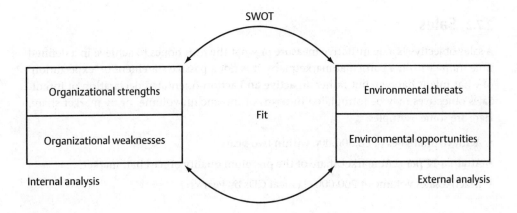

Fig. 2.3 SWOT analysis

2.7.1 **Profits**

Marketing is often linked to profitability, given investment costs are incurred in marketing plans. Here are some examples:

- Produce net profits of £480,000 before end of April next year.
- Earn an average return on investment of 7 per cent over the next three years.
- Produce a contribution of £90,000 within six months.

Any statement of profitability must be linked to the company's or institution's cost-volume relationship and any restraints on capacity. In the case of new products, issues around fixed and variable costs should be carefully considered as well as any extraordinary marketing investments before launch.

Multi-product firms have the possibility to carefully evaluate their products and lines and remove those that are making a poor contribution and have no prospect of being turned around. This must be conducted carefully in cases where cross-selling is involved or wherever products are interlinked. For example, an insurance company might remove unprofitable house contents sets of policies, but in the process lose the ability to cross-sell a profitable car insurance policy to those abandoned customers.

2.7.2 **Market share**

Many organizations also develop market share objectives. For each of the markets in which the company is competing a target figure for share can be identified. This is frequently the case where some specific benefits might accrue from having an enhanced or leading market share. Aside from the benefits in increased revenue that might result, it is often the case in many markets that economies of scale result from a higher output of product. This allows the organization to take advantage of a lower cost base to either heighten profitability, or to reduce the selling price of its products. Thus, in markets where such economies of scale are available it would not be unusual for an organization to set aggressive share targets.

2.7.3 **Sales**

A sales objective is a quantitative measure of what the firm hopes to achieve in a defined time frame within a particular marketplace. It is not a passive statement of 'expectation' of what might happen, but rather an active and action-orientated declaration of intent. Sales objectives may be formulated in terms of income, in volume, or by market share. Here are some examples:

- Achieve total sales of £2,500,000 within two years.
- Attain a 17 per cent market share of the premium quality office chair market.
- Reach a sales volume of 200,000 classical CDs by year-end.

2.7.4 **Customer satisfaction**

Customer satisfaction objectives describe the types of customer behaviour and/or attitudes the firm intends to engender in line with its sales and profit objectives. They relate to the overall strategy being pursued and are normally developed interactively along with targeting and positioning. Satisfied customers are the primary source of profits, shareholder value, and sales. Companies such as British Airways, Holiday Inn, and Xerox regularly monitor satisfaction. Here are two examples of customer satisfaction objectives:

- To raise the average scoring of a hotel from '4-out-of-5' to '5-out-of-5' for comfort.
- To increase the percentage of customers extremely satisfied with a bank's chequing account service from 35 to 55 per cent.

A related objective to satisfying customers amongst many companies is to set objectives for the satisfaction of employees. The logic is that in many organizations, particularly in service sectors such as restaurants, financial advice, and hotels, the employees are the generators of profits, shareholder value, and sales through their impact on customer satisfaction.

2.7.5 **Not-for-profit and interest group objectives**

Not-for-profit (NFP) organizations also develop marketing objectives, but the nature of profits, sales, and customer objectives needs to be slightly modified.

Profit to an NFP organization, at first sight, appears to be an anathema. However, it may be modified to make sense by having an objective to achieve net revenues of a certain level to make contributions to the chosen cause, for example the treatment of blindness. Return on investment and contribution can be similarly applied.

Sales objectives can be angled towards measures such as donations, response rates, and number of donors.

Customer objectives may be based upon levels of satisfaction amongst donors.

Some examples of nonprofit marketing objectives are:

- To achieve a 20 per cent increase in student attendance at all performances between October 15th and December 10th 1997.
- To attract £200,000 in voluntary income from individual donors by the end of the calendar year.

2.8 **Key strategies**

Having specified the objectives it is intended that the plan will achieve, it is now possible to address the means by which these will be accomplished. The 'means' is termed marketing strategy and it is useful to consider this in relation to the following four categories

- overall direction;
- segmentation strategy;
- positioning strategy;
- branding.

Each will now be considered in turn.

2.8.1 Overall direction

There are essentially four key strategic directions that an organization could follow if it is looking to achieve growth. All the options involve making decisions about the range of products/services that will be provided and the markets into which they will be delivered. Each strategic option will now be considered in turn.

(a) Market penetration

This option involves the organization in attempting to gain a greater number of sales in its existing markets. The existing range of services continues to be marketed to the existing market segments and no changes are planned to either. There are many ways in which an organization could look to penetrate the market, including finding some way to reduce the price charged for the product, enhancing promotional activity, improving distribution facilities, etc.

In cases where demand is less buoyant, however, or where the organization has a comparatively low level of awareness amongst its target audience, the organization may have to resort to intensifying its marketing activity to stimulate the additional demand that it requires. If there are competitors in the market this may prove to be no easy task as additional sales may have to be gained at their expense. This is perhaps less of a problem in an expanding market as there may be sufficient increases in demand per annum to allow all competing organizations to realize their growth objectives without having to compete directly with others in the sector. In static or declining markets however, the reverse is true and additional sales will only be generated by 'stealing' them from others competing within the same market.

(b) Product development

Product development will be an attractive option where the organization does not perceive sufficient opportunities for growth by continuing merely to supply its existing products. The demand for product development may also be driven by demands from customers. Faced with such a situation an organization may decide that it is appropriate to develop other products which the members of its existing markets may utilize. It should be noted, however, that product development is inherently more risky than market penetration since substantial investment is often required to develop new products and there is no absolute guarantee that once developed they will be favoured by the organization's current customer groups.

(c) **Market development**

Market development involves the organization in continuing to provide its current range of products, but extending the range of markets into which they will be delivered. The organization can hence elect to target additional market segments, to exploit new uses for the product, or both. A strategy of market development may be most appropriate where a given organization has distinctive expertise which it can offer. In such cases it may make more sense to target other segments rather than dilute the available expertise by attempting to broaden the range of products on offer.

(d) **Diversification**

This is perhaps the most risky of all the four potential growth strategies. It involves the organization in beginning to deliver products of which it has no experience and supplying these to completely new groups of customers. The degree of risk the organization is subjecting itself to will depend on whether the diversification is related or unrelated.

In the case of related diversification the organization is continuing to operate within broadly the same sector but is attempting to do something new for the first time. The coach operator 'Stagecoach', for example, was pursuing a strategy of related diversification when it first bid for one of the UK's new rail franchises. Unrelated diversification is perhaps less common since this would involve an organization in a radical departure from its existing products/markets.

(e) **Are there other strategic directions?**

For the sake of completeness it is worth noting that not every organization may wish to achieve growth. Other strategic options include:

Do nothing—where the organization takes a conscious decision not to alter current strategy.

Withdraw—where the organization decides to sever its links with a particular service/market.

Consolidation—which involves the organization in seeking strategies that will allow it to maintain its current market position. This should not be confused with the 'do nothing' option since the strategies necessary to support a current strategic position are unlikely to be identical to those that allowed an organization to create it in the first place.

2.8.2 **Segmentation**

The second key strategy that must be decided upon is how the markets in which the organization is operating will be segmented. Segmentation involves breaking down a market into increasingly homogenous sub-groups of customers each with very specific needs. Looking at segments of customers rather than the market as a whole can often allow an organization to develop a clearer view of customer needs and preferences and to tailor its offerings accordingly. It would thus be usual at this stage in the marketing plan to specify the exact nature of the customer groups (or segments) that will be served. The criteria that may be used for the purposes of segmentation are developed in detail in Chapter 4. Aside from specifying those segments that the organization is already addressing, if a strategy of market development or diversification has been decided upon, it will also be necessary to identify new segments to be targeted. Marketing planners can then ensure that a coherent marketing plan is developed which will capitalize on any potential synergies that might be gained from the strategy/tactics used to develop each segment.

2.8.3 **Positioning**

According to Ries and Trout (1972): 'Positioning is not what you do to a product. Positioning is what you do to the mind of the prospect.' A position is not a slogan, a mission statement, or an objective. A positioning statement emphasizes the product's place in the market in relation to rival products—it represents the point of distinction. Coca-Cola, for example, has communicated itself as the 'real thing'. Positions that establish market presence are especially effective and helpful for market leaders or those in the number two position. Strategically, the aim of the positioning communications process is to establish in the buyer's or influencer's mind what distinguishes one product from another and to establish a defensive 'ring'. Sometimes, companies or institutions adopt positions that provide safety. Just like buyers, competitors notice positions and can retaliate if they feel threatened. Thus, companies may develop positions that do not overtly challenge competitors to ensure their safety. If the world were dominated by cheap chocolate, a relatively safe place to occupy would be the luxury end of the market. Given these points, positioning statements need to be concrete and focused—there is no room for abstract meandering words. The last point to bear in mind with positioning is that 'less is more'. Companies with one or two points of differentiation have a much better chance of establishing their positions than those with many.

In developing a positioning strategy in a new market it is often helpful to conduct research to specify the location of existing players in the minds of consumers against the key criteria for purchase. A series of perceptual maps such as the one in Figure 2.4 can thereby be developed and marketers can identify whether any potential gaps might exist in the market. This tool may also be used by companies already competing in a market to examine how they are perceived in relation to the competition. By developing a perceptual map marketers can identifying whether they are perceived 'appropriately' by consumers, or whether some form of corrective action might be necessary.

2.8.4 **Branding**

Organizations can also offer considerable value to the customer through an association with their 'brand'. The American Marketing Association defines a brand as:

> a name, term, sign, symbol, or design, or a combination of them, intended to identify the goods or services of one seller, or group of sellers and to differentiate them from those of competitors.

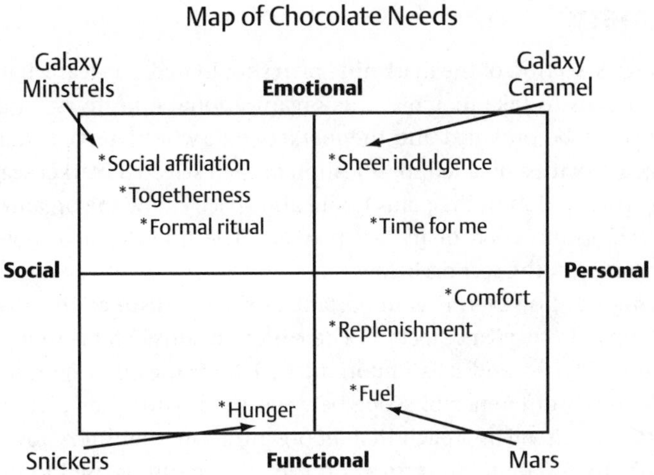

Map of Chocolate Needs

Fig. 2.4 Perceptual map

A brand, therefore, has the capacity to convey considerable meaning to a target group and an association with specific tangible or emotional benefits. They are, therefore, a form of shorthand in that they create a set of expectations in the minds of consumers about purpose, performance, quality, and price (Wilson et al. 1994). A brand can thus be used to aid differentiation from the competition, a fact which ensures that leading brands such as Coca-Cola, Rolex, Cartier, etc. are all now of immense value.

Four approaches to brand strategy are possible:

(a) Corporate umbrella branding

Heinz, Kellogg's, and Cadbury's utilize the name of the organization as an umbrella to cover a wide variety of specific products. Cadbury's, for example, produces Cream Eggs, Flake, Milk Tray, and Roses.

(b) Family umbrella branding

In this case, the brand is used to cover a range of products in a variety of markets. The brand Persil, for example, has come to be synonymous with cleaning and the brand has been extended into washing powder, dishwasher tablets, washing up liquid, etc.

(c) Range branding

Here, the brand is used to cover a range of products that have a clear link to a specific market. Lean Cuisine, for example, is a brand used to cover a range of low fat, low calorie food products.

(d) Individual branding

The final approach involves the development of separate brands for each of the products in an organization's portfolio. Sometimes, the brand may be extended to different sizes, flavours, etc. but the product remains essentially the same. Examples of this include: Heineken, After Eights, Lottery Instants, Dyno-Rod.

2.8.5 **Summary**

The 'Key Strategies' section of the marketing plan should make it clear what direction the organization intends to take to achieve its organizational objectives. In particular, the products/services to be provided and the markets that will be served should be clearly identified, together with a detailed specification of each selected market segment and the needs thereof. This section of the plan should also specify how the organization intends to position itself within each of its key markets. The fine detail of how this will be achieved is provided in the section below.

Before moving on, however, it is important to draw a distinction in our discussion between the terms 'strategy' and 'tactics'. There is often considerable room for confusion between these two terms and it is important that their meaning be fully understood. Essentially, there is a difference of scope between them with the term 'strategy' being used to refer to the general approach that an organization might take towards the fulfilment of its objectives. The term 'tactics', on the other hand, is used to denote the fine detail of exactly how the strategy will be implemented.

The marketing mix detailed below is considered generally to offer a description of tactical detail. It should be noted, however, that a number of the issues we discuss may be strategic for some organizations in the sense that the decisions taken pervade the whole of the organization's approach to market. The test of whether it is a strategy or a tactic requires a consideration of the implications of the decision and determining the scope thereof. For the sake of convenience, however, we have grouped the relevant strategic and tactical marketing models and frameworks under the general headings of the marketing mix below.

2.9 **The marketing mix**

2.9.1 **Product/service**

(a) **The components of products and services**

The starting point for examining this component of the marketing mix lies in determining the requirements of the target market. What needs do the target segments have and how can they best be satisfied? Armed with this knowledge marketers can then ensure that the products and services their organization provides are tailored appropriately to the needs of each of their customer groups.

The marketing literature presents a variety of frameworks for the analysis of the components of a product/service and these provide a useful guide for examining and defining the market entity that the organization is looking to provide. Kotler for example, distinguishes between the core, tangible, and augmented aspects of a product whilst Levitt focuses on a product's generic, expected, and augmented components. In each case, the analysis is based on the idea that any product can be seen as offering a basic set of features from the point of view of the consumer. Beyond this, products are augmented by a variety of additional features which associate it with a particular supplier, differentiate it from competing products, and make it in some way distinctive.

Kotler's perspective is presented in Figure 2.5.

The core dimension of the product or service is simply that dimension that may be obtained from any supplier in the market. It is the generic product offering that the consumer might reasonably expect as a base from whoever they choose to do business with.

The tangible component of the product relates to the physical nature of the product purchased. The design features, the packaging, and the overall appearance can convey value to a consumer. This dimension is particularly important in the service context since, for example, recent research indicates that consumers are more likely to purchase and re-purchase a service if they can take away something tangible from the experience. Enhancing the tangible nature of the service can also serve to reduce risk from the perspective of the purchaser (see, for example, George and Berry, 1991, or Palmer, 1994) and act as a useful reminder of their experience that can assist in word-of-mouth advertising amongst friends and colleagues.

The reader will therefore appreciate that giving consideration to the tangible components of their product or service may be one way in which an organization could look to differentiate their market offering from that supplied by potential competitors. Given that the core component is widely available, however, it is unlikely that simply adjusting the tangible dimension will in itself be enough to create and sustain an advantage over the competition. The augmented part of the product/service is the real key to this issue. Whilst the consumer is paying for a certain core experience and will doubtless be happy if he/she receives it, the augmented component goes in some way beyond what the

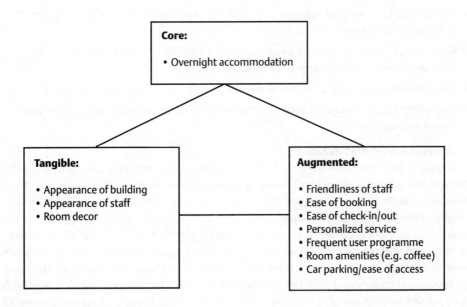

Fig. 2.5 Dimensions of hotel service

consumer was expecting. It may be thought of as value added which can be used to draw a distinction in the minds of consumers between the product/service provided by one organization and that provided by another. Clearly, augmenting the service in any of the ways described in Figure 2.5 would be costly, but the rewards in terms of enhanced customer satisfaction and hence loyalty to the organization could well be worth the initial investment.

Together, these three components form the basis of the market offering. Each component should be considered both in isolation and as a part of the complete market offering. This latter point is of particular significance since all three aspects of the product/service have the capability to communicate a message to the customer and it is hence essential that each of the three dimensions reinforces the message communicated by the other two. Whilst a useful starting point in the analysis, however, a consideration of the mere components of a market entity will in itself not be enough. In the case of many businesses, the organization is offering much more than merely one or more product/service offerings to the market.

(b) Product lifecycle

Returning to the issue of the product/service offering, however, one of the most fundamental concepts in marketing is the idea that a market entity will pass through several discrete stages from the moment it is first introduced until it is ultimately withdrawn from the market. An understanding of these stages can greatly aid a marketer as the appropriate tactics for the successful management of the product/service will often vary greatly between each stage of its life. Wilson et al. (1992, p. 274) summarize the implications of the life cycle concept thus:

- Products have a finite life.
- During this life they pass through a series of different stages, each of which poses different challenges to the seller.
- Virtually all elements of the organization's strategy/tactics need to change as the product moves from one stage to another.
- The profit potential of products varies considerably from one stage to another.
- The demands upon management and the appropriateness of managerial styles also vary from stage to stage.

The idea is illustrated in Figure 2.6

During the introductory stage of the lifecycle the product will take time to gain acceptance in the market and sales will hence be relatively low. At this stage, the organization will be unlikely to have recouped its initial set-up and development costs and profitability remains negative. Over time, as the product begins to gain acceptability in the market, sales will experience a period of sustained growth and provision of the product should at this stage become profitable. With the passage of time, the level of sales will eventually begin to level off as the market becomes saturated, until ultimately the product becomes obsolete and sales begin to decline. At this stage, the organization may wish to consider discontinuing the product, as with the lower volume of sales, the costs of provision may prove prohibitive.

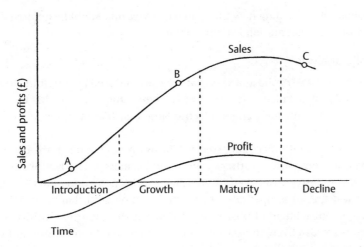

Fig. 2.6 Product life cycle

The lifecycle concept has been much criticized over the years but it can still offer marketers considerable utility in that it can help to define the form that the marketing mix might take at each stage. As an illustration of this point, consider the role of advertising in the marketing mix. At point (A) in Figure 2.6 the role of advertising would almost certainly be to inform the potential market that the product exists and the potential benefits that it might offer. Raising awareness would hence be a key objective at this stage. As the product moves to point (B) in the lifecycle, however, the nature of the market has changed. If the new product has been particularly innovative it will be unlikely that competitors have stood idly by watching developments. Instead, they will probably have entered the market with their own version of the product at this stage and the objectives of the advertising will thus need to change. A continual emphasis on raising awareness would be inappropriate since it would only serve to increase the overall level of demand in the market and thus benefit the advertiser and all the competition alike. Instead, a rather more useful objective might be to differentiate the product offered from those provided by the competition. The emphasis would change to identifying a clear positioning in the minds of target consumers. By the time that the product moves to point (C) in its lifecycle advertising support may be withdrawn altogether to reduce costs, or additional moneys may be spent to 'prop up' ailing demand in the market.

Whilst we have focused solely on how the model can assist the planning of advertising, it is clear that equal utility could be offered to any other ingredient of the marketing mix.

Organizations normally have more than one product available at any one time and the lifecycle concept has the significant drawback that it tends to focus management attention on each product individually without viewing the organization's portfolio as a coherent whole. Indeed, most organizations may be viewed as a set of activities or projects to which new ones are added intermittently and from which older ones may be withdrawn. These activities and projects will make differential demands on, and contributions to, the organization as a whole. Hence, some form of portfolio analysis might prove a useful tool in deciding how the product/service mix might be improved given the resource constraints that are valid at any one time.

(b) **Portfolio analysis**

There are a variety of portfolio analyses that may be employed to determine the health of a firm's portfolio. A detailed consideration is beyond the scope of this text, but as an example, one such tool, the General Electric Nine Cell Matrix, is described below (see Figure 2.7).

To utilize the model it is necessary to begin by examining in detail the components of the two axes, namely industry attractiveness and business strength. If we consider first the question of industry attractiveness, this may well be a function of market size, its rate of growth, the degree of competition, the pace of technological change, and the extent to which government regulation places constraints on the industry. Historic or forecast profit margins are also likely to be a key concern. Similarly, business strength is likely to be a function of market share, product quality, brand reputation, production capacity, and customer satisfaction. In using this matrix the firm must decide what determines industry attractiveness and business strength in its specific case and then develop its own list of factors accordingly.

Once the factors have been defined, the reader will appreciate that not all the factors identified could be seen as having equal importance to a given organization. For this reason it is important to weight the factors according to their relative importance. This is illustrated in Table 2.1. The reader will note that the weights for the components of each axis should all add up to 1. In the example given the market size is seen as being a more important determinant of industry attractiveness than the degree of competition.

The next step is to take each activity in which the organization is engaged and give it a score from 1 (Very Poor) to 10 (Excellent) in terms of how it measures up against each of the components listed. To make this process clear a fictional example (let us call it Activity A) has been worked through in Tables 2.1 and 2.2. Considering first the question of how attractive this industry might be, it is clear that the market size for this activity is relatively high. For this reason, a relatively high rating of 7 has been awarded against this factor. The activity does face rather severe competition, however, and for this reason a somewhat lower rating has been given to this factor. Multiplying the weights by the ratings assigned produces a value for each factor. Summing these values gives an overall score for (in this case) the industry attractiveness axis of 6.7.

Similarly, in the case of the business strength axis, each factor is assigned a weight. Each activity in which the organization is engaged is given a rating according to its performance in respect of each factor. Once again 1 = Very Poor, 10 = Excellent. Returning to our analysis of activity (A) Table 2.2 makes it clear that the organization has only moderate production capacity to offer and the activity has suffered from consistently mediocre customer satisfaction ratings. When combined with scores for the other dimensions the result is an aggregate score of 3.5 on the business strength axis.

These figures can now be plotted on the matrix in Figure 2.7b, where the position of activity (A) has been clearly indicated. If it is conceptually useful, some organizations choose to progress the analysis one stage further and draw a circle around the plotted position, the diameter of which is directly proportional to the percentage of a firm's

a

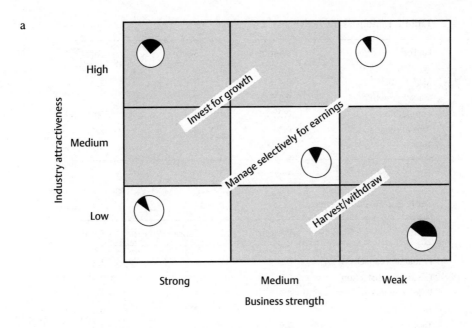

b

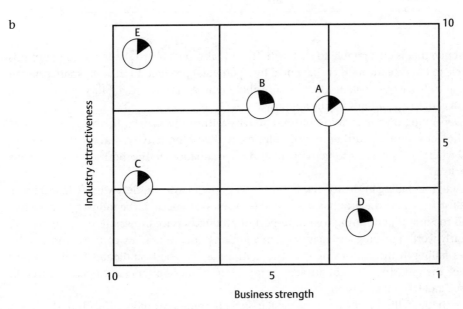

Fig. 2.7 General Electric: 9 cell matrix

Table 2.1 Industry attractiveness

Factor	Weight	Score	Total
Market size	0.4	7	2.8
Market growth rate	0.1	7	0.7
Competition	0.2	4	0.8
Pace of change	0.3	8	2.4
Total	1.0		6.7

Table 2.2 Business strength

Factor	Weight	Score	Total
Production capacity	0.3	4	1.2
Customer satisfaction	0.3	3	0.9
Brand reputation	0.2	5	1.0
Market share	0.2	2	0.4
Total	1.0		3.5

revenue that is attributable to each activity. It is also possible to shade a segment of this circle to indicate the market share held by a particular product. In this way managers can see at a glance how 'balanced' their portfolio might be and the desirability of continuing with certain operations may be appraised.

Depending on the location of each activity within the matrix, the organization can either look to invest further in its development, divest the activity, and use the resources elsewhere, or subject the activity to further evaluation if the position still remains unclear.

Activities falling in the top left hand corner of the matrix are clearly those in attractive industries, where the firm has considerable business strength. If the industry is attractive and the firm is performing well in respect of product/service provision, the activities are clearly worth pursuing and may warrant additional investment. By contrast, those activities falling in the bottom right of the matrix may be good candidates for divestment since the industries are not attractive and the firm does not appear to perform well in respect of its own provision.

Activities falling within the centre diagonal are somewhat more difficult to develop a prescription for. The designers of the matrix suggest that activities falling in this sector should be appraised carefully to determine whether indeed they are worth continuing and whether additional investment might be warranted to improve their standing in the portfolio.

2.9.2 **Price**

The second of the ingredients of the marketing mix concerns issues connected with price. Factors typically determining the price of a product or service include:

- production costs;
- costs of distribution;
- costs of marketing;
- the price charged by the competition;
- the value perceived by the customer in the market entity;
- government influence/regulation;
- sales volume targets which the organization might have set.

(a) **Setting the price**

There are a variety of ways in which an organization can go about setting price, namely:

Cost Plus—identifying what it costs to provide the service and adding on an appropriate profit margin.

What they can afford—setting the price to match the organization's expectations of what the customer segment can afford to pay.

Competitor matching—identifying what competitors are demanding for their products/ services and setting the organization's own price accordingly.

Pricing to achieve organizational objectives—price can also be used as a tool to achieve a certain level of return, market share, level of profitability, or sales volume.

(b) **Price discrimination**

The methods of price setting outlined above all make the assumption that all the organization's customers will pay a set price. This is not necessarily the case. Often, organizations will have quite different categories of customers with widely ranging abilities to pay. The rail operators, for example, recognize that certain customers will want to pay more for a higher degree of comfort. They, therefore, draw a distinction between first and standard class. They also recognize that some groups, such as the elderly or university students, have a lower ability to pay. They therefore offer a range of railcards and charge less for some seats which may be booked only in advance of the date of travel. This is known as 'price discrimination' and there are a variety of bases on which such discrimination can be based:

By market segment—as in the example above, the organization charges different segments of customers different prices for the service provided. Hence, rail operators might offer discount packages to students, OAPs, family groups, schools, etc.

By place—theatre tickets are usually sold according to the desirability of their location. Customers will therefore pay very different prices for the same performance depending on where they elect to sit.

By time—discrimination by time could take may forms. For example, prices could vary at different times of the day; entrance fees could vary by season to encourage off-peak demand; last minute discounts could be offered on unsold theatre tickets to fill the auditorium, etc.

By service category—often, an organization will elect to offer several grades of service, many of which could be perceived as exclusive—the first night of a show, for example, or a celebrity opening. Although the additional costs associated with the creation of such an exclusive event will clearly need to be taken into consideration when pricing, organizations often charge well in excess of what it actually costs them to provide these 'add-ons'. Certain categories of customers are often prepared to pay for the prestige of being able to take advantage of this exclusivity.

2.9.3 **Place**

The 'place' element of the marketing mix is concerned with the channels of distribution that will be employed, how the product/service will be distributed to customers, the level of control required over any intermediaries that might be used and the geographical coverage for the product/service that is desirable.

In a direct marketing context, if the approach to direct marketing is stand-alone, with the whole organization's approach being 'direct' in nature, many of these considerations will not be applicable. The channels of distribution employed by an organization will be identical to those employed for the purposes of communication and may therefore be considered under the general heading of 'promotion' (see below). If, however, the organization is only employing direct marketing as part of its overall communications mix, it is likely that it will be employing a range of other channels such as:

- retailers;
- wholsesalers;
- agents; or
- distributors.

Marketers would therefore need to consider how the various members of the channel were to be motivated and the specific functions that might be performed by each intermediary. These typically include:

- the provision of information about the product/service;
- the promotion of the product/service;
- order negotiation;
- order taking;
- financing (if required);
- taking payment;
- title.

The latter point is worthy of some elaboration since channels such as agents never take 'title' to the goods that are being supplied. Legally, this means that they never become owners of the goods. Rather, they simply arrange the sale on behalf of the supplier and are paid on commission. Channels such as distributors, by contrast, usually purchase the goods and sell them on to the end customer, adding on their own profit margin or mark-up.

Choosing between the various channel options available is usually a function of three evaluative criteria:

Economic criteria—it would clearly be favourable to select those channels of distribution that offered the highest sales volumes, revenues, or profitability.

Control criteria—it would also be usual to select those channels that afforded the supplier the greatest degree of control over how the product would be portrayed and handled by the intermediary.

Adaptive criteria—in electing to pursue particular channels, organizations are likely to be committing themselves to a long-term arrangement. It may be difficult to withdraw from a channel or to make significant alterations to the terms of trade once it has been established. For this reason the degree of flexibility that might be offered for alteration and/or termination may well be an issue for firms to consider in their initial selection.

2.9.4 **Promotion**

The promotional element of the mix is responsible for the communication of the marketing offer to the target group. Promotion is (Delozier, 1976):

'the process of presenting an integrated set of stimuli to a market with the intent of evoking a set of responses within that market set . . . and . . . setting up channels to receive, interpret, and act upon messages from the market for the purposes of modifying present company messages and identifying new communication opportunities.'

It can be used for a variety of purposes within the marketing mix, typically:

- to inform potential customers of the existence and benefits of the service;
- to persuade potential customers that the benefits offered are genuine and will adequately meet their requirements;
- to remind members of the target group that the service exists and of the key benefits that it can offer;
- to differentiate the service in the minds of potential customers from the others currently on the market, i.e. to clearly define the positioning of the service;
- e) in the direct marketing context—to generate orders.

2.10 **Communications objectives**

It is often the case that organizations elect to develop specific objectives for the communications they undertake. There should obviously be a clear relationship between the marketing objectives alluded to earlier and the communications objectives that are developed, but on many occasions they differ in terms of the level of detail provided.

Communications objectives can be written in terms of:

• sales;

• recall (of the communication);

• enquiries;

• awareness;

• attitudes (towards the brand or product).

2.10.1 **Modelling communication**

Before moving on, however, to examine the elements of the communication mix and how they can be utilized to achieve the purposes outlined above it will be instructive to begin by a short analysis of the communication process. Figure 2.8 illustrates a simple model of communication.

The source of the communication message is simply the organization that intends to communicate with its market. To enable it to do so, it must decide on the message that it wishes to convey, i.e. what does it want to convey about itself and what action (if any) would it like members of the target group to take on receipt of the message. In the case of Gevalia Coffee this might involve the organization in trying to persuade potential customers to change their purchasing habits and to look to purchase their coffee from a direct supplier.

However, the reader will appreciate that simply transmitting this message to the target market would be unlikely to be successful. To begin with, people may be very happy to continue purchasing their coffee from the supermarket and see no rationale for change, simply because the organization is offering to ship coffee to them through the mail.

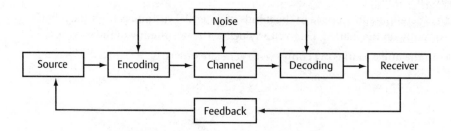

Fig. 2.8 A simple model of communication

Others might not perceive the message as being relevant to them because they perceive one coffee as pretty much like another, or because they feel that buying from a direct supplier might add substantially to the cost. It is normal, therefore, for communications messages to be encoded.

Encoding involves the source in deciding what the communications will actually contain to get across their message to consumers. In essence, this is the creative treatment that is applied to the message to ensure that when it arrives at the receiver he/she decodes it as being of relevance to them and acts on it. This may be done for example, by portraying the coffee as part of an overall 'quality' lifestyle using images in advertising or direct mail that reflect this. It may also be achieved by the use of a premium incentive which reduces the cost of trial for consumers wary of the price. In Gevalia's case, they offer a selection of premiums in each of the direct response ads that they run (See Figure 2.9). New subscribers can qualify for promotional merchandise such as Gevalia coffee mugs, bath robes, or coffee makers.

Of course, there is no guarantee that when the message is received it will be decoded in the manner in which the source had originally intended. There are a variety of factors which can interfere with a communications message and these are typically referred to as 'noise'.

Noise acts to distort the message or to prevent its reception by the receiver. It can thus take many forms, including:

- a lack of attention on the part of the receiver;
- heavy promotional spending by other competing organizations;
- selection of inappropriate media;
- poor creative treatment, resulting in ambiguous messages;
- poor perception of source—if it is not regarded as credible the message may be ignored;
- environmental distractions—the message may be received under conditions that make it impossible for the recipient to concentrate.

It is thus important for an organization to try to minimize the effects of noise by selecting the most appropriate communication channels available to reach their target market. They can also help reduce noise by giving adequate thought to the encoding process and making sure that the promotional budget allows the organization to gain access to an appropriate audience at a time/place most conducive to response. Clearly, this is not an easy process to manage and it is hence essential to ensure that there are mechanisms in place to gather adequate feedback from the target market. If messages are either not being received, or are being decoded and 'wrongly' interpreted, it will be essential for the source organization to take corrective action immediately. Indeed, it would be usual to test all forms of marketing communications prior to exposing them to the market, although even this is no guarantee of success. There is hence a need for the monitoring of marketing communications to be ongoing.

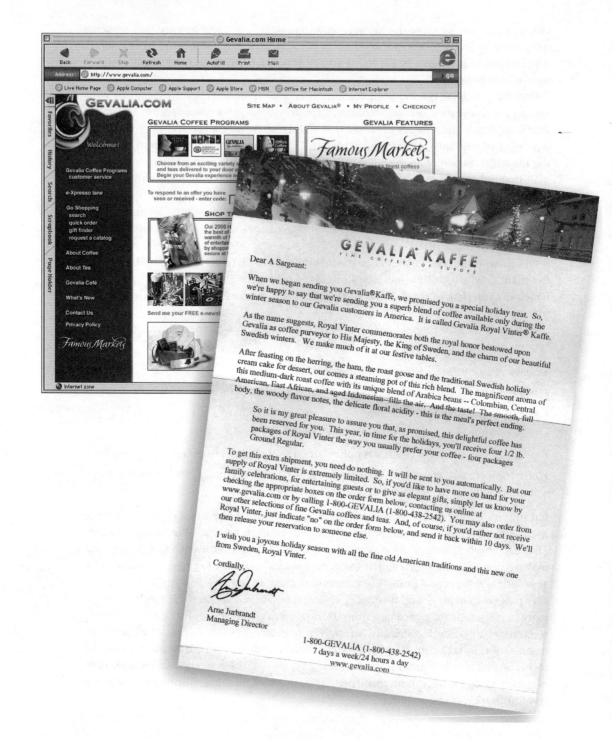

Fig. 2.9 Gevalia direct response advertising

2.10.2 **Communications and branding**

Underlying all great communications strategies is a clear and concise understanding of buyer behaviour in the marketplace. At the core, all buying is a blend of rational and emotional motivations. People buy cars for rational reasons such as commuting, shopping, and leisure pursuits, but there is also a degree of emotion in terms of image, prestige, and status in the choice. The degree and balance between the rational and emotional may vary across product types and people. Strategically, it is important to determine the best product image plus the best emotional image and to integrate the two seamlessly.

A popular approach is to find the prime prospect's problems. For example, when it comes to dog food the benefit approach would suggest that owners want nutrition and good taste in dog food. However, from a problem-solving approach it might be best to focus on the fact that owners hate their dog's bad breath and dislike the smell of dog food. The former is a benefit is for the category, whereas the latter solves a personal problem.

2.10.3 **Some more examples**

(a) **Pepsi**

- rational stance is 'tastes best';
- emotional stance is 'contemporary' and 'in';
- resultant combination: 'Pepsi: The Choice of a New Generation'.

(b) **Crispy Crunch (a North American chocolate bar)**

- Research showed rational reasons to buy:
  - Different taste based on texture combination of flaked crispy toffee blended with roasted peanuts and chocolate.
  - 86 per cent of regular chocolate bar buyers liked the taste.
- However, the emotional research showed several emotional factors such as a sense of anticipation when taking it home, and the pleasure of slowly unwrapping the bars. This was *not* an experience to share. It was a hoarding feeling, primal and selfish. Typical comments were, 'if anybody tries to get a piece of my bar they will be in trouble'.
- The resulting communications strategy was: 'There's nothing like a Crispy Crunch (rational). It's so delicious you'll want to keep it all for yourself (emotional)'.

Thus, in branding, it is important to understand the emotional needs of consumers, or business-to-business customers as distinct from the traditional performance-based appeals. The trick in communications strategy is to marry the performance image with the emotional image of the product.

One other important factor in communications strategy and branding is the extent to which buyers 'wear' products. 'Wearing', in this sense, refers to the importance of image amongst reference groups and/or self indulgence. Examples of the types of products that people 'wear' would be chocolates, cigarettes, beer, newspapers, and laptop computers.

For example, people often buy cheap beer for home consumption while buying up-market beers in restaurants and bars.

Strategically then, communications must support the chosen brand, positioning the dual needs of rational and emotional buying behaviour. As such, brands offer an emotional overlay, generally in terms of values or personality, to the more functional and rational reasons to purchase. A prestigious car, such as BMW, must maintain this throughout the mix. Therefore, the communications and the rest of the mix must all work towards prestige on both a rational and emotional level. Particularly important aspects would be product design and features and 'feel' of the car (product), premium pricing (price), status direct marketing (communications), appropriately located show-rooms (place), and well trained and professional personnel dealing with customer satisfaction issues (people). The major reward for implementing the communications strategy and mix to support the strategy in an integrated manner is brand equity (the overall worth of the brand).

2.10.4 Communication strategy

Direct communications strategies can take a number of different forms. Here are some key examples:

Product definition—make the central benefit salient.

Performance superiority—solve a problem or better fulfill a desire.

Emotional—help brand matter to the buyer.

Cultural identification—make the brand part of consumer's world.

Paradigm shift—alter the consumer's definition of category.

There are also a number of specific themes that can be utilized in any strategy. Here are some examples:

Product characteristics—ingredients, texture, performance in use, packaging, availability (or rarity), disposable/refillable, country of origin.

User characteristics—celebrities use it, snobs use it, experts use it, most people use it, only a few people use it.

Ways of using the product—sharing, giving, self-indulgence.

How the product is made—surprising points about the product, user or usage.

Price characteristics—lasts longer, money off, cheaper, more expensive.

Image characteristics—quality, good value, friendly, bigness, contemporary.

Satisfying psychological/physiological needs—thirst, hunger, social status, self-confidence etc.

Product heritage—established in 1920, quality of yesteryear, founders of the firm.

Disadvantages of non-use—resultant suffering, resultant damage, missed opportunity.

Direct comparisons with rivals.

Product comparison—parodying competitors' advertising, 'knocking' copy.

Newsworthiness—new/improved, anniversaries, topical events.

Generic benefits—appropriating characteristics of all brands to yourself, e.g. 'refreshment'.

The key issue to consider with the development of any direct communications strategy is 'How does it fit in with the overall marketing strategy?'. Always bear in mind that the communications strategy is a sub-set of marketing strategy.

2.10.5 **Competitive roles and communication strategies**

(a) **Market leader**

Dominant market leaders need to expand the total market as much as possible as they are the ones most likely to benefit given their leadership position. They can achieve this with communications strategies to support market usage and new applications as well as considering developing any niche markets previously neglected. The best defence of market share for leaders is the continual communication of product innovation, service, and brand building, to ensure buyer loyalty as practised by companies like Gillette or Hewlett Packard. Other communication strategies might be used to directly attack; for example the Esso 'Price Promise'. Once attacked, a leader is generally advised to 'take stock of the situation' before deciding on the best form of communication counterattack. Normally, market leaders have enough strength to wait and decide on the best communication response, which is rarely a direct counter-attack, as market leaders have to ensure the continuation of their 'above the rest' position.

When it comes to declining markets, market leaders have several attacking or defensive communication options. As leaders, they have the greatest visibility in the market and by tactics such as communicating reductions in their prices and increasing their media spends they can encourage rivals to exit rapidly from the market place. Alternatively, they may decide to milk their position, withdraw steadily and re-allocate their resources to other markets where they consider they have better prospects.

(b) **Market challengers**

Market challengers are organizations that vie for 'control' of a market. They therefore have little alternative but to attack leaders either directly or indirectly with their communications. Unlike the leaders, they are not positioned at the top of the pedestal and the consumer knows this. Better use of the communications than the leader is the preferred route to success. In order to do this they need to 'out innovate' the leader's communications and attack its strengths or its weaker spots. A concentrated all-out communications attack on a leader may be the best way forward to take the high ground. Attacking other challengers, followers, or smaller niche players in the market place is a more discrete option. Such tactics will result in the challenger building share discreetly without going head-to-head in its communications with the leader by picking-off weaker geographic markets or segments in so-called 'bypass' attacks. Thus, Swatch managed to outmanoeuvre Seiko in the fashion market. Relatively smaller challengers may adopt 'guerrilla' communication tactics by picking off smaller markets intermittently. But unless backed-up by some wider and deeper campaign at some later point, small-scale communication tactics will never dismount a leader.

(c) Market followers

By definition, a market follower needs to stick to its title. They need to follow leaders and challengers and not launch overt communication attacks. If they launch communication attacks, they will become challengers and will need the requisite resources and skills to survive. As a follower they can clone with look-alike communications and products (e.g. Casio Palm-type personal organizers), imitate the core product with a few superfluous variations, or offer some modest adaptations, but if they are too innovative they run the risk of being seen as a challenger (e.g. Sony and Samsung televisions).

(d) Market niche

The basis of the market niche communications strategy, be it a sole strategy or one adopted by leaders or challengers, is to specialize. Market niche communictions strategies may be based upon goods or services, segments, channels, or promotional images. Best practice for sole nichers is to develop more than one market niche so that the company or institution is less vulnerable to communications attack from a rival. It is essential that a sole nicher be not seen as a potential rival to a leader or challenger, which might lead to a direct attack. An ideal communications position for a sole nicher would be one where just about everyone else in the market place regards their niche as too much effort to bother with. A company marketing organic non-dairy chocolate products is unlikely to have much trouble from the Cadburys! Turning to leaders or challengers, they can use niches either to entrench their positions or as a form of attack. As discussed above, in the hands of leaders or challengers a niche can provide a basis for market growth or to attack a rival's market position indirectly.

2.10.6 The promotional or communications mix

The techniques of communication that may be employed by an organization are collectively known as the promotional or communications mix. These are essentially advertising, sales promotion, public relations, personal selling, and direct marketing. We will now give a brief consideration to each of these elements in turn.

(a) Advertising

Kotler (1994, p. 627) defines advertising as 'any paid form of non-personal presentation and promotion of ideas, goods or services by an identified sponsor'. Advertising can be placed in a variety of media including, television, radio, cinema, newspapers, magazines/

trade press, and outdoor (poster and transport advertising). With an ever increasing number of promotional media becoming available it is becoming ever more difficult to identify those media which offer the most appropriate use of promotional resources. Essentially, one is looking to find the media which can reach the largest number of members of the target market at the lowest price. Thus, the measure of 'CPT' or 'Cost Per Thousand' is used by many organizations to compare between the use of various media. CPT is calculated very much as you would expect. If a full page advertisement in a national newspaper circulated to 3 million readers is £9,000, the cost per thousand is £3. This figure can then be used to compare between the various media options available. It is, however, a very simple measure and it is necessary to be very clear about the profile of the media audience. If the profile does not match your requirements exactly (and it rarely does), you may be under-estimating the CPT figure since you could be communicating with a large number of people who are not in your target market.

Media can also be selected on the basis of how many competitors use the medium, since if a large number of competitors are present the returns accruing to each advertiser are likely to be less than they would be in a publication where it is possible to enjoy a wider 'share of the voice'. It may also be important to consider the environment of the medium. Does the medium offer an environment that is appropriate for the message being conveyed? There would be little point, for example, in placing an advert for an alcoholic drink in a publication whose editorial was generally critical of such products. Similarly, the term can be applied to the environment in which the message is received. Some media demand a lot of concentration of readers, such as specialist trade journals, making it possible to provide much more detailed information about the product/service in advertisements. Television advertising, on the other hand, offers little opportunity in this regard since it commands little attention. Indeed, many people leave the room, perhaps to make a coffee, when the commercial break begins.

(b) **Sales promotion**

The term sales promotion refers to:

'any immediate stimulation to buy that might be provided at or near the point of sale.'

The purpose of sales promotion is hence to prompt the customer to engage in a transaction with the organization. It is thus more immediate in its effects and hence favoured in times of budgetary constraint since an immediate return on the investment can be demonstrated. The same, regrettably, cannot be said of advertising, whose effects are considerably less tangible and certainly longer term. Sales promotion activity includes the provision of free gifts, discounts, premiums, leaflets, contests, display material, or demonstrations. The key to the selection of successful sales promotion activities undoubtedly lies in selecting something which reflects the needs and wants of the customer group and offers them something which they will find intrinsically to be of value. This may be as simple as an introductory discount on a service to tempt customers into sampling, or it may be something altogether more elaborate.

(c) **Public relations**

Public relations is often confused with publicity, crisis management, lobbying, etc. In fact, PR can embrace all these elements, but it should in itself be regarded as a somewhat wider function within an organization. One of the most frequently used definitions of PR is as follows (Public Relations News, 27 October 1947):

'Public relations is the management function that evaluates the attitudes of important publics, identifies the policies and procedures of an individual or an organization with the public interest, and executes a program of action to earn understanding and acceptance by these publics.'

It is hence concerned with the development of each of the organization's publics and might typically involve an organization in proceeding through the stages outlined in Figure 2.10.

The process begins with an analysis of the current perceptions of each of an organization's publics. Those perceptions are then assessed to see how desirable they might be from the organization's perspective and, where weaknesses/ambiguities are identified, a programme of PR can be developed to address them. The process Kotler and Fox advocate also makes it clear that it is important for an organization to plan for potential crises, however unlikely it may be that these might occur. If an organization has plans to deal with all potential contingencies, should the unthinkable happen it will be well placed to implement a cogent response.

There are a variety of PR tools that an organization could utilize to develop the desired perceptions amongst its target publics. These include:

Production of written material—this might include, leaflets, flyers, magazines, annual reports and newsletters.

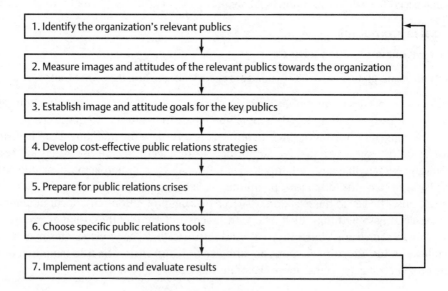

Fig. 2.10 The public relations strategic planning process
Source: Kother and Fox, *Strategic Marketing for Educational Institutions* © 1985. Adapted by permission of Prentice Hall.

Organizational identity media—most businesses today have some form of corporate identity which features prominently in the organization's stationery, brochures, signs, and business cards. These are what might be referred to as organizational identity media and it is essential that through the careful use of design, logos, etc. that all these media conform to a standard format and convey a consistent message to the publics targeted.

Publicity—the PR department can often identify newsworthy activities within the organization and seek to promote these amongst the various media. The problem with such 'free advertising' is that there is no guarantee the media will elect to cover it. Unlike advertising, which must be sent to the media and paid for, publicity must be sent to the media and prayed for!

Telephone helplines—many commercial organizations now offer a telephone helpline which consumers can call for further information or advice about the product. Given that it now costs very little to provide a toll-free or Freephone number many organizations are now prepared to cover the costs of this activity in their marketing budget as part of a co-ordinated PR strategy.

Businesses generally have very complex audiences to whom they must communicate their message. This audience may be made up of government officials, pressure groups, shareholders, employees, current and potential customers, the media, and the business and local community. Given this complexity it is not surprising that public relations takes such a prominent place in the marketing mixes of many organizations. Unfortunately, PR has a much less obvious price tag than media advertising and its results are even more difficult to assess. It remains, however, an important tool for many organizations, primarily because of the impact it can have on the market. Messages carried through third parties are perceived by the public as having greater credibility than messages conveyed in advertising where the organization, perhaps, has a tendency to portray itself in an overly positive light.

(d) **Direct marketing**

The key direct marketing media that can be used both to communicate with the customer and to solicit orders are listed below:

- direct mail (i.e. personally addressed mail);
- door-to-door (unaddressed mail);
- telemarketing;
- direct response press advertising (DRPA);
- direct response radio advertising (DRRA);
- direct response television advertising (DRTV);
- e-mail;
- magazine and media inserts;
- internet web-sites.

The use of each of these media and the issues that must be considered in employing them for both customer recruitment and customer development will be explored in detail in later chapters.

(e) **Personal selling**

The final element of the communications mix is usually considered to be the use of a salesforce. Organizations with customers of particularly high value, or whose customers are few and concentrated in certain geographic areas, may well find it appropriate to engage a salesforce to promote and sell their range of goods and services. Organizations deciding to adopt this route to market need to consider issues such as the design of appropriate sales territories and the recruitment, retention, and motivation of their sales personnel.

2.10.7 **People**

In the case of service organizations, the four P marketing mix is felt to be inadequate. Authors such as Booms and Bitner (1981) have suggested extending it to include people, process, and physical evidence. To an organization providing a service to clients, the people element of the marketing mix is arguably the most important. After all, it may reaonably be argued that the people ARE the organization.

Ensuring that all staff, whatever their status, deliver a service of the highest quality is a key issue for all organizations. The inseparability of services makes it impossible to distinguish between service production and service delivery and it is the people of the organization who are, therefore, responsible for both. In this section of the marketing plan the organization must, therefore, give consideration to the people skills that it will need to provide its service and, indeed, to deliver every component of the marketing plan. This can then be matched against the profile of the existing human resource and appropriate gaps identified. The organization can then ensure that those 'gaps' are represented in the staff recruitment programme and that the appropriate person specifications are in place.

It is, of course, usually much easier to develop and retain existing staff than it is to attain new ones. The second focus of this section of the plan is hence to identify what steps need to be taken to retain existing personnel. By far the easiest way of achieving this is probably to survey those who decide to leave and having discovered the reasons for dissatisfaction implement any changes that may be necessary to ensure that problems are corrected. One can also ensure that an ongoing dialogue is maintained with existing staff so that they do not feel compelled to leave in the first place!

2.10.8 **Process**

When marketers talk of process, they are talking about the process that a particular client group must go through to purchase and enjoy the service being provided. Clearly, for a service organization every aspect of the encounter that a customer has with staff will be important. Each stage of the service will be evaluated by customers and many will have the capability of having a substantial impact on the overall level of satisfaction experienced. The question is, however, which elements of the process are deemed by the customer to be most important. To answer this it is often useful to draw a flow chart of the various components of the service that the customer experiences. An example is shown in Figure 2.11.

Although this is a gross simplification of the process that one might go through in purchasing and enjoying an evening at the theatre, it does at least serve to illustrate that the process consists of a number of specific encounters with the organization. Each of these may, of course, be broken out into a number of sub-encounters. Take, for example, the telephone reservation process; there are a number of components to this including the length of time you would have to wait to have your call answered, the efficiency and friendliness of the operator, and the accuracy with which he/she performs his/her role. For the moment, however, we will stick with the general process depicted in Figure 2.11. The reader will appreciate that not every aspect of the service will be equally important. The provision of a cloakroom, clean toilets, and the existence of a bar may be relatively unimportant for the segment of customers addressed. If research is conducted which identifies those aspects of the service that the customer places most importance on, the organization can invest in those areas, ensure that they are of the highest quality, and hence enhance overall customer satisfaction. Conversely, in those areas that are considered unimportant, the organization can look to minimize cost and perhaps even remove that aspect of the service altogether, utilizing the resource saved in other areas that are perceived as being important. The idea of engineering customer value in this way was first suggested by Porter (1985) who referred to the concept discussed above as the Value Chain. In his view, it represents an essential tool for organizations to use in appraising their service process with a view to enhancement.

2.10.9 Physical evidence

The final ingredient of the service marketing mix is physical evidence. Since the service product is largely intangible it is important for the organization to focus on those

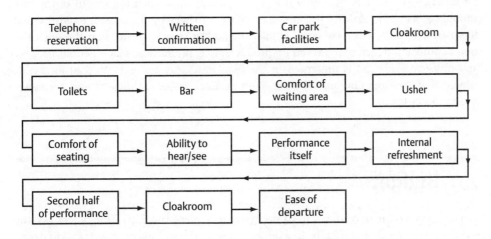

Fig. 2.11 Flow chart of a visit to the theatre

tangible cues that do exist and to ensure that they convey appropriate messages to the consumer about the quality of the service he/she is purchasing. As has already been identified above, in the absence of a physical product consumers will use tangible cues to make their judgements in respect of service quality. In a typical organization these cues may include:

Premises—customers may infer quality by the presentation of the channel. In the retail context, they may infer quality from the design, style, and layout of a store.

Facilities—the appearance of the facilities on offer is also important. In selecting a school for example, parents are unlikely to rely totally on the reputation that a school has in a given area. They are also likely to inspect the facilities that it has to offer for themselves and may ask to see the sports, library, and IT provisions.

Dress—the presentation of the staff can help reinforce the corporate image that the organization is looking to project. Smart, attractively presented staff can infer quality, in the absence of other cues, and may reassure potential customers of the professionalism offered by a particular organization.

Reports—the written communications of the organization may also be regarded as tangible cues. The annual report and the 'sales' brochure could all be used to evaluate the service.

2.10.10 Summary of the tactical marketing mix

We have now examined each of the ingredients of a typical marketing mix. In developing a marketing plan an organization will need to give careful consideration to each of these seven elements, whilst at the same being careful not to fall into the trap of viewing each ingredient in isolation. The mix should be viewed as a collective whole and opportunities for synergy will only be exploited if it is regarded as such. Each ingredient of the mix should consistently reinforce the 'message' being conveyed by the others. To ensure that the plan does represent a coherent whole, the author should ensure that the organization's approach to each of the seven Ps (product, price, promotion, place, people, process, and physical evidence) is presented in the plan in a clear and easy to read format. It should then become obvious whether flaws or ambiguities are present and corrective action can be taken.

2.11 Budget

Having detailed the steps that will be necessary to achieve the marketing objectives, the writer of the plan should then be in a position to cost the various proposals and to derive an overall marketing budget for the planning period. Of course, in reality, life is just not that neat. Cost will undoubtedly have been in the minds of marketing planners even before they commenced the marketing audit. At the very least, the development of a suitable budget is likely in practice to have been an iterative process, with proposals being re-evaluated in the light of budgetary constraint.

There are a variety of ways of determining the marketing budget. The ideal would clearly be to specify the strategy and tactics that are felt necessary to achieve the marketing objectives, and then to cost these to arrive at an overall budget. This is usually referred to as the 'task method' of setting a marketing budget. Of course, in reality, this method is seldom employed since financial pressures from senior management, the budgeting/ accounting practices of the organization, and uncertainty about resource attraction all hamper the derivation of an appropriate budget. In practice, therefore, budgets tend to be set by the following methods:

Percentage of last year's sales—there is a danger with this method, however, in that if the organization has been suffering from poor performance of late, reducing the marketing budget in line with sales could actually serve to worsen the situation. Clearly, when sales fall there is a strong case for enhancing, not reducing, the marketing budget.

Percentage of budgeted year's sales.

Competitor matching—estimating the amounts spent on marketing by the competition and matching their resource allocation.

What can be afforded—perhaps the least rational of all the methods of budget calculation, this method involves the senior management of the organization deciding what they believe they can afford to allocate to the marketing function in a particular year. Little or no reference is made to the marketing objectives, nor to the activities of competitors.

Irrespective of the method actually used, in practice it would be usual to specify how the eventual budget has been allocated and to include such a specification in the marketing plan itself. It would also be normal for an allowance to be made for contingencies in the event that monitoring by the organization suggests that the objectives will not be met. Sufficient resources should then exist for some form of corrective action to be taken.

2.12 Scheduling

The reader will appreciate that a large number of tactics will have been specified in the main body of the plan. To ensure that these tactics are executed in a co-ordinated fashion over the duration of the plan, it is usual to present a schedule which specifies clearly when each activity will take place. This would often take the form of a GANTT chart (an example, for a direct marketing campaign, is given in Figure 2.12). If the responsibilities for various marketing activities are split between different departments/sections of the organization, the schedule will act as an important co-ordination mechanism. Indeed, if responsibilities are split in this way it would be usual to add an addition section to the plan specifying the individual postholder who will have responsibility for the implementation of each component of the plan.

Activity	Jan	Feb	March	April	May	June	July	Aug	Sept	Oct	Nov	Dec
Direct mail		x	x							x	x	
Press advertising	x			x			x			x		x
Inserts											x	x
Telemarketing		x			x			x			x	x

Fig. 2.12 GANTT chart

2.13 **Monitoring and control**

As soon as the plan has been implemented, marketing management will then take responsibility for monitoring the progress of the organization towards the goal specified. Managers will also need to concern themselves with the costs that have been incurred at each stage of implementation and monitor these against the budget. Thus, control mechanisms need to be put into place to monitor:

- the actual sales achieved, against the budget;
- the actual costs incurred against those budgeted;
- the performance of individual services against budget;
- the overall strategic direction that the organization is taking—i.e. will the overall corporate objectives be achieved in a manner commensurate with the organization's mission?

If variances are detected in any of these areas, corrective action can then be initiated, if necessary by utilizing resources allocated for contingency in the budget.

2.14 **Summary**

In this chapter we have outlined a framework that may be used for the purposes of marketing planning. Given the diverse perspective on direct marketing adopted by organizations, it is likely that direct marketers are likely to have more or less responsibility for aspects of this plan depending on the extent to which direct marketing dominates their organization's approach to market. In cases where direct marketing is a stand-alone and dominates the organization's approach to marketing, many of the tactical ingredients of the marketing mix alluded to above will be of no relevance.

In cases where direct marketing is simply one of a number of 'promotional' techniques employed by an organization it is likely that marketing planning is likely to involve each of the stages alluded to above. It is also significantly less likely that direct marketers will have responsibility for the development of marketing strategy, since under these circumstances direct marketing is more likely to be regarded as a short-term tactical tool.

We have thus provided an overall framework and explained how direct marketing fits within an overall marketing plan, irrespective of the approach adopted. We can therefore now move on to an examination of how and why people buy and how direct marketing can be used to influence that process. The specifics of using direct marketing for customer acquisition and development are left for later chapters, as is a consideration of the tactical detail.

Discussion questions

1   In your role as the marketing manager of an internet bookstore prepare a presentation to your team, on the role and components of a typical marketing audit. You should also specify the specific information you perceive as being relevant to your organization.

2   Describe the relationship between corporate, marketing, and communications objectives.

3   A manufacturer of computer games that have been selling well in the US through conventional stores and computer warehouses is considering entering the UK market for the first time. In your role as a consultant appointed to advise the organization, specify the marketing strategy and tactics that they could adopt in entering the new market and promoting the range of games they produce.

4   Floralart, a nationwide distributor of floral bouquets, wreaths, and baskets has recently recruited a marketing agency to design an appropriate communications mix for the next 12 month period. In your role as the client director for Floralart, develop a communications mix which should include a balance of printed and electronic media. You should also give consideration to an appropriate schedule and budget.

Further reading

Booms B. H. and Bitner M. J. (1981) 'Marketing Strategies and Organization Structures for Service Firms, Marketing of Services', in Donnelly, J. and George W. R. (eds) *Marketing of Services* (Chicago, IL.: American Marketing Association).

Delozier M. (1976) *The Marketing Communication Process* (New York: McGraw Hill).

Drucker P. (1955) *The Practice of Management* (London: Heinemann).

George W. R. and Berry L. L. (1991) 'Guidelines for the Advertising of Services', *Business Horizons*, Vol. 24, July–August.

Kotler P. (1994) *Marketing Management: Analysis, Planning, Implementation and Control*, 8th edn (Englewood Cliffs, N.J.: Prentice Hall).

Palmer A. (1994) *Principles of Service Marketing* (Maidenhead: McGraw Hill).

Porter M. E. (1985) *Competitive Advantage: Creating and Sustaining Superior Performance* (New York: Free Press).

Trout J. and Ries A. (1972) 'Positioning Cuts Through the Marketplace', *Advertising Age*, May 1.

Wilson R. M. S, Gilligan C., and Pearson D. (1994) *Strategic Marketing Management* (Oxford: Butterworth Heinemann).

Case study: The power of the brand — Virgin Direct

Background

Richard Branson has amassed a billion-dollar fortune by doing things that business strategists suggest he shouldn't: he targets well-established industries with entrenched competitors — airlines, records, retailing and then attacks head on. In the process, the affable balloonist garners huge amounts of publicity from an unending assortment of goofball stunts and daredevil deeds.

Despite the risk Virgin usually wins through because Branson manages to do the mundane exceptionally well. He also has considerable ability to connect directly with consumers, particularly younger ones. His personality is projected into the Virgin brand and he finds it easy to motivate the people who work for him, offering them the same enjoyable, rewarding experience that he seems to be seeking for himself.

The Virgin organization is a conglomerate of nine divisions and more than 100 companies. The extension of the brand into such diverse product categories as vodka and insurance works because the values it espouses are generic. Consumers understand that the values that apply to one product in their portfolio can equally apply to others, namely: good service, style, quality, value, and fair dealing. It is this latter characteristic that appears to drive much of Branson's selection of new industries to target.

'If it's something that interests me. If I think it is done badly by other people and feel I could do it better. If we can shake up an industry — and have fun doing it . . . we do it'

There can be little doubt that the financial services industry in the mid 1990s offered consumers a raw deal. Products were generally bland, undifferentiated, and out of touch with real consumer needs. There was also a problem with public trust since confidence had been shattered by a number of well-publicized cases of individuals being mis-sold pensions and other investment/insurance products by commission-hungry sales staff. Branson therefore decided to ask his colleague Rowan Gormley to create Virgin Direct, a straightforward, jargon-free alternative to the rest of the industry, with 'no hidden catches'.

Right from the outset the aim was to provide consumers with products designed by marketers to meet their specific needs, a radical switch from the historical approach adopted in the industry where products were designed by actuaries largely for the benefit of their respective service providers. To achieve this, Rowan deliberately assembled a team from Virgin's partner Norwich Union that comprised largely 'activists' known for criticizing and challenging the current way the organization did business.

On 3 March 1995 Virgin Direct launched and, in doing so, initiated a sea-change in the way in which people in the UK thought about money. It is interesting to note that at the launch the company offered only one product—the Virgin Growth PEP (Personal Equity Plan). Within only a month over £40 million had been invested and the product was to go on to become the most successful retail financial services product ever offered in the UK.

By September 1995, the Virgin Income PEP was added to the company's portfolio and in November the association with Norwich Union was brought to a close, with the Australian Mutual Provident Society (AMP), one of the world's largest insurers, joining Virgin Direct as a partner.

As both products continued their rapid growth Virgin saw an opportunity in the early weeks of 1996 to capture an even greater share of the market, encouraging investment in PEPs before the end of the tax year in March. To achieve this goal an aggressive DRTV campaign was launched featuring Richard Branson and reinforcing the characteristics of the brand. This was also supported by a range of direct response press ads, such as the one depicted in Figure 1. The essential proposition was 'the PEP that likes to say NO—no salesmen, no commission, no jargon, no hassle'

1996 also saw more product introductions, including Virgin Life and Survival Plan. In addition, the organization introduced a personal pension. By the end of the year the company was looking after over £500 million for over 100,000 customers. A further £300 million was invested by the end of the tax year in March 1997.

The end of 1997 saw the creation of another partnership—this time with the Royal Bank of Scotland. The aim here was to launch a radical new way of banking in the guise of the Virgin One account. What made this product so unique was the way in which it combined savings and borrowing into one account. In essence, the customer establishes a single account borrowing whatever they need to consolidate existing loans and mortgages at one new low rate of interest. The customer then pays in whatever they earn to reduce the balance outstanding, interest being charged on a daily basis for the amount outstanding. It thus allows consumers to repay their debt at a lower rate than they would

Case Study Fig. 1 Virgin direct

be likely to achieve elsewhere, with almost complete flexibility. The only requirements were clearly that the customer could afford to borrow the amount requested and that they schedule the repayment of the amount outstanding to be completed before the date of their retirement. A particular benefit that this flexibility offered was a way around the early repayment penalties that many mortgage lenders were charging their borrowers for the early redemption of their mortgage.

The end of the tax year in 1998 saw a considerable cause for celebration. The Virgin Growth PEP showed growth of over 100 per cent in just three years. As the news arrived at the same time as the organization's third birthday, Branson had ten tons of sand shipped in to create a limbo party for guests and staff. More products were also launched that year including a new deposit account. At the end of 1998, the organization was thus able to meet most of the basic needs for managing money that people might have. Given the now broad portfolio the company decided the time was right to introduce the Virgin Money Manager Service, which offered expert advice and guidance in respect of all of Virgin Direct's Products.

1999 saw a number of changes to the UK's financial service arena. PEPs and TESSAs were finally bought to an end and replaced with ISAs. With the general confusion that the changes created, Virgin capitalized on what it saw as a major opportunity and provided a free guide authored by Branson entitled 'Branson's Guide to PEPs, TESSAs and ISAs'. The book proved to be an enormous hit and was quickly followed up by the launch of Virgin's own ISA (Individual Savings Account). To assist in educating the public a series of advertorials appeared in the national press. The aim here was to provide information, but also to reinvent the advertorial tool to become a combined brand and sales building medium.

Why the success?

There are a number of reasons why the organization has been so successful. First, the strong Virgin brand values, alluded to earlier, were clearly applicable to this sector. It was also clear that Virgin could offer a level of service that would be clearly differentiated from the competition.

In 2000, Virgin Direct won the prestigious Diamond Award for the third time at the Teleperformance Grand Prix held in Paris. After 2,000 mystery shopper calls to over 100 UK companies the judges decided that Virgin Direct remained very much the industry leader. They answer their calls quickly, are courteous, helpful, and thoroughly briefed about all the organization's products. They also went further and offered real 'value-added' by being proactive in their approach to dealing with clients. Whilst the judges concluded that all the call centres they approached were capable of providing a high level of service, only Virgin Direct was able to offer this consistently.

Unencumbered by a long history, Virgin Direct was able to support its call centre activity with a unique set of documentation that was simple for the customer to understand, both in words, style, and format. Central to the success of the literature was its relevance to what had been discussed on the phone between Virgin Direct and the client and its ability to distil information in an easy-to-read way. Furthermore, Virgin was to do this in one form, so all the customer had to do was read, sign, and return it.

'With many of our competitors, if a customer asks for two products, the details often arrive in separate envelopes. We wanted to get away from this traditional approach which meant that the customer had to do the hard work of sifting reams of irrelevant information before making a choice. We wanted to rationalize and simplify the process as far as possible so that the customer got only one document and that related directly to what had been discussed over the phone'

In achieving this level of service there were many technological issues for the company to wrestle with. On the one hand, Virgin could have computerized a whole series of standard letters that could have been selected by the operator according to the information needs, or transaction details associated with a particular customer. There were difficulties with this approach, however, since to meet the needs of all its customers adequately a large number of standard letters would have needed to be created. The second alternative was that the customer service operators be required to type in the whole letter manually following their conversation with the customer. Neither option was particularly attractive.

The solution was to employ Geneva Digital's Autograph, document composition solution. It allows Virgin to hold a relatively small number of standard letters, yet be able to modify them easily to tailor content to a specific customer's needs at the touch of a button. It can also fulfil the standard customer responses to an advertisement and capture documents electronically for archival use and viewing, an essential feature for a direct selling organization. Utilizing its document viewing service (DVS), Autograph makes an archival copy of all documents sent out. These are then viewable by operators taking subsequent calls, thus preventing the need for lengthy explanations on the part of the customer. A customer phoning up with a query can have the matter dealt with quickly and promptly irrespective of the operator who might answer the call. Interestingly, the system also recognizes which operator has generated a particular document and appends that individual's signature to the bottom of the customer's letter.

Virgin has also made clever use of marketing research data. It regularly conducts its own research into buying motives and the needs and aspirations of its customer groups. Recently, for example, it identified the 'dreams' of customers who might be looking to retire in 20–30 years' time. These are cited in Table 1.

A knowledge of these factors allows the organization to tailor the nature of its promotional message in both traditional print media and over the web. As an example of the latter the Virgin Direct Pension website features an interactive consumer-friendly guide to pensions for individuals and companies. The site www.virginpension.com includes a pension calculator and allows on-line applications. The calculator allows visitors to see how much they need to start saving now to retire on their chosen income and at their chosen retirement age. The calculator also shows the cost of delaying a pension and what the projected retirement fund would be worth in today's money.

Case Study Table 1 Aspirations of tomorrow's pensioners

Dream	% Citing
2 foreign holidays a year	55
Eating out several times a month	47
Bankrolling granchildren's education	29
Wintering abroad every year	26
Having money to invest in the stock market	26
Driving a sports car	16

Case Study Table 2 Attitudinal/demographic segments

Category	Attitude to retirement	Pension/ISA mix
Early birds	Want to retire early	50–50
Twilighters	Looking to retire after 55	90/10
Regimented investors	Needing to lock money away	85/15
Floating voters	Unable to commit	10/90
High rollers	Maximizing higher rate tax relief	80/20

The website also recognizes that not everyone is unique and that the needs for particular categories of product might vary by customer segment. The advice given will differ according to the profile of needs a given saver or investor might have. For example, the company identifies the following five segments of savers (see Table 2).

The recently revamped website now includes full online service, valuations, bill payments, and direct debit facilities. The site also features its Golden Rules of Money consisting of several simple principles of savings. To help bring these principles to life Virgin has created some simple fun calculators to demonstrate how the golden rules can work for an investor. These reflect the attitudinal research the organization has garnered and include:

Millionaire-o-meter—which illustrates how a user might become a millionaire and that it might be quicker than they think.

Beat the system—which shows how users can beat the banks at their own game. Virgin reveals how UK banks manage to create hefty profits at their customers' expense.

Tiny acorns—a demonstration of how compound interest can turn regular small savings into a sizeable portfolio.

Dreams—which allows the user to see how their dreams could be turned into a reality.

The new look site is both practical and pragmatic. The self-discovery approach using personalized calculators allows users to recognize immediately how saving can work for them.

New customers

The company is also targeting potential customers of the future by supporting a new education initiative. The website www.young-money.co.uk presents an on-line game-show created by kids for kids. The UK Government, the Financial Services Authority (The Regulatory Body for Financial Services), and Virgin Direct—the initiative's sponsors are attempting to educate young people about financial services so that by the time they leave school they are financially literate.

'The game strikes a balance between the discipline of managing money and the fun of spending it. We think the internet is a great way of helping young people learn about money. A lot of teenagers find out the financial facts of life the hard way once they leave school. With this game if you make a mistake your house may get evaporated by aliens, but at least you can go back to the start and have another go'.

Media stance

Virgin has traditionally adopted an aggressive stance in the media, never losing an opportunity to reinforce the values of its brand appropriately. On occasion, it has publicized the findings of its own research which it believes will be of interest, such as the study of employee motivations (see Table 3).

On others, it has proactively addressed any concerns that the public might have in respect of issues of the day. At the time of writing, research into the human genome looks set to transform the whole life-insurance industry. It should shortly be possible to test an individual to see if they may be susceptible to particular disorders in their later life. Whilst this is good news in terms of the possible prevention of certain complaints there are currently fears that the life-insurance industry could use such tests to discriminate against certain individuals. Virgin was amongst the first to respond to this issue, issuing a statement in respect of how the company would respond to the taking of such tests and how (if at all) it might affect insurance premiums. The policy is outlined below:

- The company will NOT ask customers if they have taken a test
- Virgin will continue to underwrite policies over the phone on the basis of medical history
- If a customer's family history shows risk of an inherited medical condition their insurance will be underwritten on that basis
- If a customer volunteers information about a test it will only be used to the customer's advantage, e.g. if a customer with a family history of inherited disease tells Virgin about a genetic test that shows they do not have the condition they will lower their premiums accordingly
- If a customer with a family history of inherited disease tells Virgin they have taken a genetic test which does show there is evidence of the likelihood of an inherited condition, they will underwrite solely on the basis of family medical history.

Case Study Table 3 Desired benefits and current provision

Benefit	What's important to employees, %	What employers offer, %
Pension contribution	81	26
Flexible working	71	54
Bonus	64	43
Health insurance	64	17
Life Insurance	64	14
Paternity leave	55	21
Crèche	53	3
Company car	45	25
Gym membership	29	3
Luncheon vouchers	18	2

In setting out this policy Virgin was keen to stress that the organization feels it has a duty not to deter people from taking tests which may one day save their life because of fears that they may lose out financially.

Human resources

Branson has also focused on his staff, recognizing that highly motivated individuals were likely to provide the highest possible standard of service. The organization undertook a detailed review of the needs of employees and the needs that were currently being catered for in the workplace. A comparison of the two suggested to Virgin how it might attract and retain the highest quality individuals with the skills it required. The remuneration and benefits package was designed accordingly (see Table 3).

The future

In the UK in 1999 Virgin became an internet service provider (ISP) and offered customers for the first time a route through the Virgin organization to the internet. Whilst still in its fledgling stages of development, Branson intends to invest heavily in the site's development with the ultimate goal of offering consumers everything from cars and CDs to electricity. To this end he is now launching two to three new e-businesses per week.

In the US, the aim is to open up the group's businesses to a mass consumer audience. Virgin will offer internet access and aim to beat existing operators such as AOL by linking its internet service to technologies other than just PCs. Branson aims to offer access to his organization's products over cell-phones in the very near future and has already forged the links necessary to allow this to happen.

Discussion questions

1   Describe the marketing strategy adopted by Virgin Direct in the late 1990s.

2   Explain how Virgin was able to take advantage of an extended (7P) mix to offer a superior service to its clients.

3   Explain how the expansion of the Virgin group to the internet might influence the strategy adopted by Virgin Direct in the future.

Chapter 3
Understanding Buying

Contents

3.1 **Objectives**

By the end of this chapter you should understand:

(a) how customers purchase;

(b) how customers evaluate, acquire, use or dispose of products;

(c) the physical behaviour of customers—the overt act of buying;

(d) The buying decision process: the mental activities pre and post purchase.

3.2 **Introduction**

Consumer and organizational buying behaviour may be defined as:

> The environment and decision process affecting individuals and groups when evaluating, acquiring, using or disposing of goods, services or ideas.

In both consumer and organizational buying contexts there are a plethora of different environment and decision related variables that can impact on the decision of whether or not to initiate a purchase (Loudon and Della Bitta, 1993). In this chapter we consider each in turn and discuss the specific marketing implications.

Before moving on, however, it is important to recognize the importance of a detailed understanding of buying behaviour since it can help delineate:

• market opportunities;

• target market selection;

• product—size, shape, features, and packaging;

• price—initial price, discounts, awareness and sensitivity to price;

• appropriate promotion messages.

3.3 **Culture and sub-cultures**

Culture is defined as the beliefs, attitudes, goals, and values held by most people in a society. However, the content of a culture also includes the physical and social environment (Quelch and Hoff, 1986). Sub-cultures contain distinctive groups of people within the culture that share common cultural meanings (Herbig, Koehler, and Day, 1993; Schaninger, Bourgeois, and Buss, 1985).

3.3.1 **Patterns of beliefs and behaviour**

A large and important part of any culture is the set of knowledge, meanings, and beliefs that are shared by a group, including symbolic meanings. Characteristic patterns of behaviour are also part of culture, such as drinking wine with meals, or not drinking any alcohol at all, or taking afternoon siestas, or working a nine to five day.

3.3.2 **Physical environment and social institutions**

Another aspect of culture includes the physical objects and social institutions constructed by a society and the meanings that these have for most people. Examples would be dominant architectural styles, sizes of homes and configurations, traffic laws, art, household artefacts, and products.

3.3.3 **Cultural change**

'Charge It' was the slogan for many consumers in the 1980s. Average real disposable incomes only rose by a few per cent, but the credit boom fuelled consumer spending and personal debt mushroomed (as did corporate debt). The 1990s proved to be a watershed era replacing consumer concerns for 'prestige' with 'value' and 'prudence' which has continued into the turn of the century. There are underlying demographic and attitudinal changes going on:

- 'Upscale' is out and 'downscale' is in. Flaunting money is frowned upon: if you have it—keep it to yourself or give it away! In place of materialism people are spending more time with family and friends, rest, recreation and 'good deeds'. People have been awakened to many personal issues such as the plight of a homeless neighbour or the loss of a job.
- Middle-aged 'baby boomers' now have older families and more financial responsibilities.
- People are not pessimistic, just 'realistic' about job opportunities and income growth.
- There is a general trend towards recycling, environmentalism, and spirituality.

3.3.4 **Specific applications**

(a) **Values**

There is a wide body of research and analytical approaches attempting to link values and consumer behaviour. Various studies have linked values of ownership and household appliances, recreational activities, giving to charities, media usage, etc. Examples include the Rokeach Value Survey (RVS) which uses 18 'instrumental' and 18 'terminal' values and the University of Michigan's list of Values (LOV). SRI International has combined value and lifestyle (VALS and, more recently, VALS 2) identifying eight categories of consumers based on their value orientation and available resources (Novak and MacEvoy, 1990):

1. Actualizers	5. Strivers
2. Fulfilled	6. Experiencers
3. Believers	7. Makers
4. Achievers	8. Strugglers

Fig. 3.1 VALS

The argument is that consumer behaviour will be modified to a lesser or greater extent depending on the category into which an individual falls.

(b) **Multinational business**

Marketers operating abroad need to have a good understanding of cross-cultural differences. The kinds of issues focused upon in research include:

- M-Time (monochronic) where punctuality is desired and P-Time (polychronic) where time is more loosely defined;
- low-context communication, where everything is explicit and high-context where verbal and non-verbal dominate;
- customs and standards;
- degree of competitiveness and individuality.

(c) **Sub-cultures**

Sub-cultures are large groups or segments of people who share common values, goals, beliefs, attitudes, norms, and behaviour patterns. Individuals may belong to several sub-cultures at the same time. Typically they are defined by:

- race:
- nationality;
- religion;
- location.

Direct marketers often target sub-cultures because they have distinguishable purchasing patterns; they may be large in spending terms and are often concentrated in identifiable locations.

3.3.5 **Examples of culture and buying behaviour**

- Society's concerns over health and personal responsibility have hit the alcohol industry over the past ten years. Hard alcohol consumption has declined steadily in face of a shift to lighter beverages, bottled water, and soda.
- Increasingly pro-active views of health have led to a boom in sales of sportswear and equipment.
- Cocooning and home values are rising trends that have affected all mass outdoor

entertainment industries and benefited take-home drinks and food and home entertainment.

- Greater emphasis on stress reduction has led to an increased focus on relaxing and travel.
- Marlboro re-positioned itself from a feminine cigarette in the 1950s to a rugged masculine one in the 1960s through the use of cultural symbolism.
- People generally dress according to cultural norms and expectations, such as for work or going out for an informal party.
- Price haggling may be an important cultural ritual.
- North American commercials tend to have a hard-sell focus compared to British ones.
- Coca-Cola sells mainly as a mixer in Spain.

3.4 **Social groups**

Social groups may be classified as either primary or secondary. A primary group would be your family and friends. A secondary group would be your doctor, work colleague, or teacher.

- Groups can assign status to individuals according to an ascribed position. The position will normally have rights and obligations.
- Groups to regulate behaviour apply norms.
- People are allocated roles in groups and these roles are dynamic.
- New group members normally have to go through a period of formal or informal socialization.
- Groups have the power to control their members' behaviour by rewards, coercion, legal rights, or expertise.

3.4.1 **Reference group behaviour**

Other members within groups are known to affect the behaviour of members. This is known as reference-group influence. Reference group buying influence is strong because people find other members of their group credible and because purchases enhance group acceptance.

3.4.2 **Issues**

The nature of the product category and the brand concerned are important factors in reference-group influence. People do not phone their parents to ascertain whether or not to buy a bar of chocolate. On the whole, group product symbols or high-risk products (e.g. cars) are subject to the greatest reference-group influence. There will also be variability in influence depending on the nature of the group and the individual concerned (e.g. their strength of character).

3.4.3 **Direct marketing and reference groups**

One of the key issues in reference group influence relates to direct marketing strategies. It is difficult for direct marketers to know which celebrities to use as influencers and whether it would be better to use 'ordinary' members of the representative group instead. The trend in the 90s has been to move away from celebrities whose image may turn sour (e.g. Michael Jackson). In addition, people have tired of the 80s celebrity emulation and are returning to more home-spun simple values in all kinds of groups.

3.4.4 **Examples of groups and buying behaviour**

- Cars are the quintessential product representing social class. Mercedes, BMW, Jaguar, Volvo, Honda, Audi, Toyota, Renault, Vauxhall, and Ford all have different symbols.

- People throughout social classes use furniture, but brands have developed narrow social class targets with different styles and price levels. These range from museum level antiques, to designer furniture, regular antiques, popular brands, self-assembly, and used furniture shops.

- Levi-Strauss experienced significant drops in profitability from the mid-1980s onwards owing to the decline in the teenage market.

- By contrast, personal savings have risen owing to the growth in proportion of older people.

- Generation X has rejected many of the values of the baby boomers and has defined a new value system of work and almost 60s culture. The economy and the threat of AIDS have fostered a different outlook.

3.5 **Family and opinion leadership**

The family is a primary group involving intimate face-to-face interaction (Spiro, 1983). It is also a reference group with members referring to particular family values and norms of behaviour. Its scope has largely moved from the extended family to the more common nuclear one of today.

A household is a housing unit and may include families (where at least two people are related) or non-families. Direct marketers are concerned with families because they have such strong bonds between each other. These bonds affect purchasing and families often function as the ultimate consumers. Families are the relevant decision-making unit for many products (e.g. cars, home furnishings, vacations, and appliances as well as a great number of cheaper everyday items). Rather than study a single consumer, it makes more sense to try and understand the complex interaction of family decision-making.

Surprisingly little is known about the complexity of family decision-making. The traditional two-adult/two-children family is a minority, with new kinds of families, such as gay/lesbian couples and single-parent households entering the accepted definition in society.

Opinion leadership relates to the issue of who consumers get their information from. It is recognized that consumers do not just ask anyone for advice, but choose particular people. People who are knowledgeable about products, and whose advice is taken seriously, are called opinion leaders.

3.5.1 Family life cycle

There are felt to be various stages in the traditional family lifecycle (Wells and Gubar, 1966; Gilly and Enis, 1982). These include:

Traditional stages	Modern stages
• Bachelor	• never married
• Newly married	• divorced
• Full nest I (married no children)	• separated
• Full nest II (married with young children)	• widowed
• Full nest III (married with older children)	• no children
• Empty nest I	
• Empty nest II	
• Solitary survivors	

Fig. 3.2 Lifecycles

3.5.2 Purchasing decisions

(a) Roles

Different members of the family tend to perform different roles in the recognition of need and the taking of purchase decisions. Typical roles include:

Instrumental—leaders who fulfil the task in hand. Men tend to fill this role and concern themselves with functional attributes and participate most actively in making the actual purchase.

Expressive—fulfil the need for morale and cohesion. Women tend to fill this role and are more concerned with aesthetic attributes and with suggesting the purchase.

Purchasing—

– Initiator

– Influencer

– Information gatherer

– Decision maker

– Purchaser

– User

(b) **Power structure**

The balance in power within a family will typically vary from one purchase situation to another. These can be:

Male dominant—(e.g. lawnmower, power tools).

Female dominant—(e.g. child's clothing, toiletries, and some groceries).

Joint—in which both partners share decision-making (e.g. holidays, major appliances, and furniture).

Autonomic—where the relative influence of both partners varies (e.g. males dominate stereos and cameras, whereas women dominate jewellery and toys).

Gender role power in decision-making varies significantly across product categories. In particular, equal decision-making occurs most frequently for expensive outlays or where the purchase affects all members together. Conflict may arise when the family members diverge or disagree on a decision. Such conflict may be explicit or implicit and different strategies may be adopted to resolve the problem.

3.5.3 **Situational influences**

Culture is a powerful influence. In Europe and North America there is a tendency to equality in many decisions. In Latin America women are subordinated in many ways, but quite free in others. In Moslem and many other cultures wives are rigidly subordinated. In Europe, research indicates that joint decision-making is most likely:

• amongst higher social classes and particularly middle;

• in the early stages of the life cycle;

• where families have geographic mobility;

• in rural areas;

• in families with children;

• where couples are married.

3.5.4 **Changes in families**

A variety of changes have occurred in family set-ups, values, and purchasing behaviour over the past 30 years, including:

- fewer children;
- women spending more time outside the family;
- more female professionals;
- tendency for women to be more individualistic than collective in their decisions;
- shopping as a shared male–female activity;
- evening and weekend shopping trips;
- New Breed Husbands willing to share housework;
- growth in single households and one-parent families owing to either the postponement of marriage, of divorce, or death;
- time becoming a critical resource for many families.

3.5.5 **Children**

Families transmit the cultural meanings of society to their children and thereby influence their children's behaviour. 'Consumer socialization' is the term behaviourists give to this process of how children acquire knowledge about goods and services and the buying-process, such as bargaining. Amongst others, as well as the family, friends, teachers, and television participate in this process. Children undoubtedly have a say in what their parents buy, especially for products like cereals, clothing, toys, and ice cream. Research indicates they have a lesser influence on more expensive items such as computers or health or 'moral' related items such as toothpaste or videos. On a personal basis, some parents will allow their children to participate actively in purchasing and others will be more restrictive. As children age they tend to get what they want more often, but this can be explained by their own growing maturity in deciding what they want.

Psychologists have argued that children go through different stages of development. Piaget believed that between the ages of 2 and 7 children are largely preoperational with low cognitive structures whereas by the age of 11 they can think in abstract ways and are much more sophisticated. Roedder has argued, alternatively, that children simply have different information-processing capabilities namely, limited (2–6), cued, respond to prompts (6–12) and strategic (12+). Children have a surprisingly high degree of knowledge about goods and services. Their behaviour mirrors a great deal of adult consumption. For example, the lunch box has been found to be the child's equivalent to the adult car as a status symbol. Children undoubtedly need protection from the potential activities of direct marketers until they can reason-out decision-making alone.

3.5.6 **Opinion leadership**

An opinion leader is someone who is frequently able to influence other people's attitudes or behaviours. The media can create opinion leaders with celebrities or leading experts in a product field. For example, double glazing or bathroom renovation companies sometimes offer key homeowners cheap deals in an area with the proviso that they allow others to see the finished product. Using the average person-on-the-street has become a common appeal in direct advertising.

Opinion leaders often find that telling other people about products, and offering advice, makes them feel good and re-affirms their status. Their influence is based on a number of factors:

- seen as experts in their field;
- views are unbiased, unlike direct marketing;
- often socially active and influential in a community;
- similar in social status and beliefs and empathetic to the consumers that they are advising;
- often the first to buy new products and, thus, they absorb the risk of the less courageous consumers;
- tend to have influence in products that are highly visible (e.g. fashion), expensive and/ or complex.

3.5.7 Traditional views of OLs

Early views of opinion leaders (OLs) assumed that they had influence over all product categories. It was also argued that opinion leadership was a static process, much like a lecture. It was also argued that opinion leaders soaked-up the majority of product information and then disseminated it to other consumers.

New research has indicated that OLs tend to be monomorphic—experts in a limited field rather than polymorphic—experts in several fields. Thus, they are more likely to offer advice for cosmetics and receive advice on microwaves, than know about both. Polymorphic OLs are sometimes called 'market mavens'. OLs are also likely to seek information from others. They are generally more involved in a product category and to want information from a variety of sources.

Contrary to the static view of OLs, most product related discussion is not in a lecture format where one person talks and the other listens. Most discussions are prompted by particular circumstances or situations and are casual rather than formal. People being given advice by OLs are also likely to seek product information as well, such as from trade journals and advertising and not simply rely on their friends' advice.

3.5.8 How can direct marketers find OLs?

It is possible to write direct marketing for OLs for any field, particularly technical products, but finding OLs in the community is a difficult task. For example, athletic shoe manufacturers seek out inner city youths, because urban kids represent hard-core experience and authenticity in this marketplace. To curry favour with inner city kids, Reebok has a policy of repaving inner-city basketball courts in the US.

Because of the problems of reaching OLs, many companies simply undertake small exploratory studies to determine their basic characteristics and aggregate them to society at large. Thus, financial influentials are known to use computers, watch financial programmes on TV, manage their own finances, and read a great deal.

3.5.9 **Methods to track OLs include:**

Self-designation—probably the most common technique whereby consumers fill out a questionnaire detailing how much and what kind of advice consumers give. As many people inflate their own importance, or have their views ignored, this is a weak method.

Sociometry—tracing communication amongst group members by interviews. It is a precise method, but it is expensive and best used in restrictive networks like hospitals and prisons.

Key informants—may be identified by product usage or product enquiries, or some such, and asked who their OLs are in their group.

3.6 **Personality and self-concept**

Many products, from cars to perfume, are bought, in part, because people want to express their personalities. The 1980s were called the Me decade because many people were largely absorbed with themselves. It is hard to remember that the importance of self is relatively new in terms of social history. The idea that each person is unique, rather than part of a group or tribe, only developed during the Renaissance. The focus on self in recent years is a further development of the phenomenon and has occurred mainly in western societies rather than elsewhere (particularly the Far East) where the importance of the social group remains strong.

Self-concept refers to the attitude that a person holds towards him/herself. Overall self-attitudes are normally positive. However, people are often critical about aspects of their personality. For example, someone might feel good about their professional life, but feel the social side is lacking something.

3.6.1 **Towards a definition**

Personality is generally defined as: 'The fact or state of being an individual with a distinctive or well-marked character' (Loudon and Della Bitta, 1993). The concept of a personality is essentially integrative in nature. People share common characteristics, but different mixes of these characteristics, and people's own experiences, interact to give people unique personalities.

3.6.2 **Measurement of personality**

Over the years researchers have attempted to measure personality in a variety of ways. These include:

Rating methods—involve one or more evaluators assessing predetermined characteristics of a person on standardized scales.

Situational tests—provide a topic or scenario for several people in a group and observe the frequency or intensity of their behaviour.

Projective—people are presented with visual images, such as inkblots (Rorschach Test) or pictures of vague situations (Thematic Apperception Test) and directed to explain the meaning of the images. Such tests are said to uncover the basic organization of a personality and the conflicts and motives held.

Inventory—respondents answering banks of standardized questions with optional answers that reveal personality types which are linked to appropriate jobs, such as 'artistic' (e.g. writer), 'investigative' (e.g. surgeon) and 'enterprising' (e.g. marketer). Well-known ones are the California Personality Inventory, Edwards Personal Preference Schedule, and the Minnesota Multiphasic Personality Inventory (MMPI) which all have several hundred questions. You may have experienced some of these methods with personality inventories used by career advisors.

3.6.3 **Major personality theories**

(a) **Psychoanalytic**

Freud proposed that everybody's personality is the result of a struggle amongst the 'id' and the 'superego' with mediation by the 'ego'.

- The id is the source of drives and urges, is unconscious and seeks immediate pleasure.
- The superego is the moral component based on society's values.
- The ego is more reality based and only releases tension when the environment is appropriate. It develops through learning and experience.

Freud argued that slips of the tongue, when people say things that they later regret, represent the id. He also argued that people have personality problems in relating the various tensions between the id, ego, and superego and that this manifests itself in dreams. Freudian-based marketers emphasize social symbolism in their marketing activities, as compared to function.

Psychological motivation theory was in vogue in Madison Avenue during the 1950s and early 1960s, with researchers exploring the hidden meaning of consumption. However, it is rarely used nowadays. Freudian theory remains controversial and should not be taken literally. After all, the bulk of Freud's insights were based on his own patients—a limited and restricted sample of affluent Viennese women. Also, bear in mind that he assumed that women were inferior to men.

Freudian market researchers have highlighted the importance of so-called 'unconscious' motives. The implication is that consumers cannot consciously tell researchers of their true motives in purchasing. It also suggests that the ego relies on symbolism in products to compromise between the demands of the id and the prohibitions of the superego. A person might channel their unacceptable desires into acceptable outlets by using particular products that signify these desires. Product symbolism could, therefore, motivate consumers if you believe in the ideas of Freud.

Sexual symbolism is the most prevalent kind, with phallic symbols said to abound in direct marketing. Bear in mind that the whole field originates in Freud's analysis of dreams, which he interpreted as communicating repressed desires.

(b) Social theories

Social theorists have reinterpreted Freudian ideas to form their own distinctive branch. They regard individuals as striving to overcome feelings of inferiority and searching for ways to obtain love, security, and brotherhood. Karen Horney's three clusters are (Cohen, 1968):

Compliant—people who like other people and need love, approval, and affection.

Aggressive—people who dislike other people and need power, strength, and to manipulate others.

Detached—people who wish to distance themselves from others and need freedom, independence, and self-reliance.

Researchers have attempted to relate certain product and brand preferences and knowledge to each type.

(c) Trait theories

Trait theorists believe that people share common behavioural tendencies, such as the need for achievement and aggression or to be socially outgoing, but differ to the degree to which they possess them. By using techniques such as inventories they believe that they can correlate single personality traits with personality clusters. Consumer behaviourists have attempted to link personality traits with the consumption of certain brands or products. For example, cigarette smoking has been linked to a need for achievement amongst young men and women. Specific traits that are relevant to consumer behaviour include innovativeness (degree of liking new things), materialism, and self-consciousness.

3.6.4 Issues to consider

Personality theories have a number of applications to direct marketing. The notion that consumers buy products as extensions of their personalities certainly makes intuitive sense, and many direct marketers have created personalities for their brands.
   However, the main drawbacks are:

- Inventory scales are not reliable and have mixed results over time.
- Most tests are borrowed from social scientists and not tailored to the needs of direct marketers.
- Untrained staff often administer tests.
- One of the main problems is that the personality tests tackle big issues such as introversion or emotional stability. These are then applied to the more mundane issues of choosing brands of toothpaste or cooking oil.

- A final problem is that much of personality research is random. Researchers often have no idea what they are looking for, but hope to find something interesting.

3.6.5 **Self-concept**

Related to the study of personality is self-concept. Here, individuals provide descriptions of themselves in a socially pre-determined context, rather than described by outside observers. Self-concept research has gained in popularity in recent years. Self-concepts have been shown to be quite consistent over time, but will alter in the long-run like anything else. The four components of the self are:

Ideal—how you want to be.

Social—how you think others perceive you.

Ideal social—how you want others to perceive you.

Expressive—how you want to be in particular situations.

It has been argued that products shape the self—you are what you consume. Furthermore, products can be used to fill holes in the self, such as cigarettes for macho teenage boys and ostentatious consumption for the nouveau riche. In a reverse way, it is possible to lose the self by removing possessions. Thus, prisons confiscate all possessions on entering the establishment.

The main aspects of self-concept involve:

Self-appraisal—people label their own behaviour by what they envisage as socially acceptable.

Reflected appraisal—in essence, people build-up an idea of their self-concept by how others appraise them. However, the appraiser must be credible and take a personal interest in the person being appraised. People build their self-concepts from a consistent pattern of appraisals.

Social comparison—people's self-concepts only have meaning when compared to others, e.g. in one social situation a person might be an achiever, but in another they might not. Related to this is the idea of 'biased scanning' or selective perception, where individuals scan the environment selectively to confirm their chosen self-concept.

3.6.6 **Congruity theory**

Direct marketers have applied self-concept theory in a variety of ways, particularly in advertising. At a base level, it has been shown to influence what particular goods and services people buy to enhance their self-concept. One area of particular interest is congruity theory which holds that the greater the brand/self-image congruence, the more a brand will be preferred. Congruity theory holds that people construct a mental image of themselves using the product and decide if they like the image. They build an image of their extended self and see if the brand fits or not. There is mixed evidence that people buy and prefer brands in line with their own self-concept. For example, BMW drivers see themselves as more active and risky than Volvo drivers. Of course, you need the resources to follow all your brand preferences through to purchase.

It cannot be assumed that consumers will buy products just because the brand personality matches their own. Few brands, especially in commodity products, e.g. toasters, have distinctive human-like personalities. Psychologically, a further problem is that people often assume that the personality of the things that they buy are similar to their own simply because they have bought them.

3.7 **Motivation and involvement**

A **motive** is a consideration or emotion that excites someone to action. Some believe that instincts provide most of the motives that people have today. However, the prevalent view is a cognitive one that suggests that motives are more typically directed by mental processes. This view is more popular because the existence of instincts is hard to prove. Also, to explain motives by instinct makes the whole discussion tautological. To say a consumer buys an expensive status car because he or she wants status is hardly earth shattering. Motives guide people's behaviour in achieving their goals.

Involvement refers to the level of perceived importance and/or interest evoked by a stimulus. It will differ according to the interests of consumers and the situation. One person who likes computers might read a direct mailing on the subject, while a friend receiving the same mail shot does not bother. Involvement is the motivation to process information, ranging from simple and inert, to elaborate and intense processing.

3.7.1 **Nature of motives**

(a) **Drive theory**

This focuses on biological needs that produce tension (e.g. your stomach rumbles with hunger). According to the theory, satisfying the problem may reduce tensions. The difficulty is that people often ignore biological needs. For example, if your stomach rumbles, but you are going out to dinner in two hours, you will most likely ignore the problem in the knowledge that it might be better to remain hungry.

(b) **Expectancy theory**

Behaviour is largely pulled by expectation of positive outcomes rather than pushed from within. For example, a person might choose one brand of toothpaste over another because they believe it fights cavities better.

3.7.2 **Classifying motives**

Motives have direction, as well as strength—a consumer who needs a pair of jeans can choose between a variety of brands to project a desired image, be it Levis, Wranglers, Guess, or Calvin Klein.

Motives can be positive or negative—many products have negative motives, such as deodorants and mouthwashes.

The specific way in which a motive might be satisfied will vary according to the consumer concerned—a health conscious consumer who is hungry might buy a salad, while another might buy a cheeseburger and chips. Hunger is a need whereas salads and cheeseburgers are wants. On the whole, direct marketers have had more success in channelling wants than creating needs.

3.7.3 **Structuring motives**

Purchase decisions often involve more than one source of motivation, and consumers find themselves in a position of conflict. Consumers have to structure the types of choices that they face and decide on the degree of motivation accordingly:

Approach–Approach—a person must choose between two desirable alternatives, for example choosing between two CDs. In general, people content themselves with a snap decision and resolve the conflict after the purchase.

Approach–Avoidance—many goods and services have negative consequences attached to them like ice-cream. People try to overcome guilt by convincing themselves that they are deserving of luxuries.

Avoidance–Avoidance—sometimes consumers face two undesirable choices. For example, spending a great deal of money repairing an old car or buying a new one. Often, consumers may be weighed by options that reduce the pain, e.g. a new car purchase with low interest and long-term repayments.

Maslow's Hierarchy is worth a mention at this point because it is valuable in assessing the hierarchy of motives (Maslow, 1954) (see Figure 3.3).

3.7.4 **Motivational research**

Motivational research was developed and pioneered by a Vienna-trained psychologist, Ernest Dichter, who studied over 230 different products with in-depth interviews. Amongst others, Dichter was responsible for the Freudian-symbolic 'Put a Tiger in Your Tank' for Esso.

Motivational research has been attacked on two fronts. There are those who believe it does not work, given that so much of the material is open to subjective interpretation. Also, there are those who believe it works too well, and manipulates consumers. Overall,

Physiological
Staple items, generics

Safety
Insurance, security systems, investments

Belongingness
Clothing, clubs, drinks, grooming

Esteem
Cars, furniture, credit cards, wines,
country clubs

Self-actualization
Hobbies, travel, education   **Fig. 3.3** Maslow's Hierarchy

the motivational researchers' over-emphasis on Freudian, and therefore, sexual symbolism, makes much of its explanation of behaviour too simple.

On the positive side, motivational research is cheap and often seems to focus intuitively on the deep-seated needs of consumers, such as coffee being associated with companionship. Whether women baking cakes associate the activity with giving birth is doubtful! Nevertheless, the phrase 'bun in the oven' seems to relate to this. Overall, motivational research should only be used in conjunction with other standard techniques if the budget allows.

3.7.5 Involvement

Involvement may take many forms depending on the nature of the product and the individual concerned:

Purchase involvement—relates to the consumer's level of interest in the buying process and is triggered by the nature of the need.

Message involvement—the processing of direct advertising and promotions. TV has traditionally been considered low involvement compared to print.

Ego involvement—importance of the decision to the person's self-concept.

3.7.6 Measuring involvement

A variety of ways have been experimented with to measure involvement. Two French researchers, Laurent and Kapferer, have suggested a way that recognizes that there is no single way of measuring involvement. They have advocated a profile based on four aspects:

Importance and risk—importance of the product and risk of a bad buy.

Probability of making a bad choice

Pleasure value of the product—hedonistic.

Sign value—self-concept.

Direct marketers can use this profile to develop appropriate strategies. For example, a product may be low on signage, but strong on pleasure.

3.8 Information processing

Information processing focuses on the way in which sensations are absorbed by people and used to interpret and attribute meaning to the marketing environment (Tybout, Calder, and Sternthal, 1981). Like computers, people undergo stages of information processing in which stimuli are input, stored, and manipulated. Only a relatively small number of stimuli in the environment are noticed. Of these, an even smaller amount enters the conscious to be processed objectively.

3.8.1 Aspects of information processing

Personality—information processing (IP) is strongly influenced by a person's personality. Such considerations as attitudes, attributes, experiences, learning, and motives will alter the select perception of each person accordingly.

Stimuli—the stimuli involved are colour, smell, sound, touch, and taste.

Processing—information may be processed directly a stimulus is received or it may be stored in memory for later use.

Pro-active—personality affects the selective perception of stimuli. In turn, stimuli, once processed as information, have a pro-active affect on personality. In other words, IP will affect beliefs, attitudes and behaviour.

Observable—IP cannot be observed, however, the outcomes can be monitored and evaluated.

3.8.2 Stimuli

(a) Colour

Colours have a variety of symbolic meanings. Red and white are patriotic colours, black is sophisticated (Johnny Walker), green is natural (frozen vegetables), yellow is fun (boxes of cereals), red is also sexy and gold is valuable (boxes of chocolates). Marketers make careful colour choices when it comes to packaging, advertising, and shop design. Research has even indicated that colours can affect other stimuli. For example, manufacturers have found that by darkening the shade of orange on an orange drink, consumers ascribe the taste to be sweeter than when a lighter colour is used.

The choice of colours has not always been such an important issue. For example, the familiar Campbell's Soup can came about because a company executive liked the red and white uniforms of Cornell University. In rare instances companies have been granted copyright over colour combinations used in their packaging in order to avoid confusion with rival products. For example, Eastman Kodak has successfully protected its use of yellow, black, and red.

Colour research has yet to establish whether the impact of colour is a cultural issue or one of nature. The evidence suggests that both 'nurture and nature' have a role to play. It is clear that both personality and class differences in colour exist. Researchers have found that the top three per cent of wealthy North Americans prefer 'forest green' and 'burgundy' to all other colours. By contrast, lower income people prefer 'sky blue' and 'grass green.' In any year certain colours are 'hot' and dominate fashion choices for each season. People say, 'red is in this year' or 'purples are the thing this spring'. In reality, a cluster of fashion trade groups and consultants selects hot colours. Hot seasonal colours are often decided up to ten years ahead by analysts. As part of the trend, colour analysts have emerged to guide consumers on colour co-ordination and decor in their homes.

(b) **Smell**

Smells can stir emotions like anger, or calm people down, or evoke memories. Smells play an important role in interpersonal attractions and feelings. The perfume industry is a direct beneficiary, and is valued at around $3 billion. Home fragrance products have also benefited from the rise in cocooning. Home fragrance products include potpourri, room sprays, atomisers, drawer liners, sachets and candles. Computerized systems for 'fragrancing' buildings have been shown to increase productivity and mitigate the effects of sick building syndrome. Lavender and lemon have proved to be the smells of preference.

(c) **Sound**

Music and the spoken word are integral parts of most people's lives. One survey published in *Psychology Today* reported that 96 per cent of respondents said that they found music gave them thrills.

One way that marketers use music is with muzak in shops, shopping malls, and offices to relax or stimulate people. Muzak has been found to stimulate people at work in the mornings and has been linked to reductions in absenteeism.

Advertisers have experimented with time compression to examine how fast a voice can be speeded-up before it becomes unintelligible. Such time compression enables some advertisers to increase the amount of information communicated in short commercials. About 120 to 130 per cent of normal is as far as it has been shown to go.

(c) **Touch**

Very little research has been done on the impact of tactile stimulation on consumer behaviour. However, common sense tells us that touch is an important stimulus, as with a cold or warm wind or the feel of the sun. Touch can be relaxing or invigorating. Consumers certainly use touch to judge how a car 'feels' when they take it for a test drive and detergent companies continue to advertise 'baby soft' soap powders. Fabrics are either literally or symbolically linked with different stimuli, as with 'smooth as silk.' Researchers have demonstrated certain male/female characteristics of fabrics such as wool and denim (male) and silk and cotton (female).

(d) **Taste**

Taste is the pre-occupation of food and drink companies. Millions of pounds are spent every year to maintain the consistency of tastes and to find new ones. However, taste cannot be viewed in isolation. Many people bring back wines from abroad, for example, only to find that in their homes, the taste is somehow not as good. A similar mistake was made with the new Coke formulation. The new formulation was preferred to Pepsi in blind taste tests, but produced howls of protest when Coke decided to change the product. People do not buy Coca-Cola for its taste alone.

3.8.3 **Stimuli/awareness thresholds**

There is a limit to the amount of stimuli that a person can perceive. Key concepts here include:

Absolute threshold—the lowest intensity of a stimulus that a person can register is a threshold. The 'absolute threshold' is the minimum amount of stimulation that a person can detect. For example, a dog whistle is below a human's auditory threshold. The print on a poster may be too small for the visual threshold of passing motorists to read it.

Differential threshold—this relates to the ability of the sensory system to detect changes or differences between stimuli. A TV commercial produced intentionally in black and white might be noticed on a colour television, but not on a black and white one. The point is that the difference is relative rather than absolute. For example, a whispered conversation cannot be heard in a busy shopping mall, but could be heard in a quiet room.

Noticing change—sometimes, marketers might want consumers to notice a change, such as during a sale. However, sometimes marketers may not wish customers to notice, such as with price increases, detrimental changes to ingredients, smaller pack sizes, or changes to packaging or symbols. The minimum change in a stimulus that can be noticed is called the JND: 'just noticeable difference'. Ernst Weber, a nineteenth century psycho-physicist (the study of the integration of stimuli) found that the amount of change necessary to be noticed is systematically related to the intensity of the stimulus. The stronger the initial stimulus, the greater the change must be for it to be noticed: Weber's Law. The formula is $\Delta s/S = K$, where:

S = initial stimulus value
Δ = JND
K = constant

Fig. 3.4 Weber's Law

The formula says that if we know the value of K and S, we could predict how large a change in a stimulus is necessary before consumers perceive a change. For example, a test may show that you can add 50ml ($\Delta s = 50$) to a 250ml litre of ketchup ($S = 250$) before a change is noticed. This would yield a constant of K = 50/250, which equals 0.2. This means we could predict that a manufacturer of an economy bottle of ketchup of 1000ml could add or remove 200ml of ketchup without a change being noticed.

There are many difficulties in applying the law, yet it has gained widespread support amongst marketers. It is used widely amongst food manufacturers, particularly for private labels and brand names and in pricing. It has been shown that price reductions of at least 10 per cent are needed to gain attention and about 30 per cent to be motivating.

3.8.4 **Perception**

The brain's ability to process information is limited and consumers are extremely select-ive about what they pay attention to. Consumers practice a form of 'psychic economy' picking and choosing among stimuli that they will pay attention to, particularly in rela-tion to advertising clutter. People can attend to five to seven pieces of information at one time. The amount varies according to whether the stimuli have to be processed or not (familiar information does not need much processing). In one case reported in *Time*, the North-Western National Bank distributed a leaflet to 120,000 customers, at considerable cost, to provide legally required information relating to ATMs (Automated Teller Machines). Out of 120,000 leaflets no one found a sentence amongst all the legal jargon that offered a $10 reward just for finding that sentence!

The two key elements in perception are exposure and attention:

Exposure—is the degree to which people notice a stimulus within their perception. People notice some stimuli and either are unaware of or ignore others. Personal experi-ence and preferences are important variables in exposure. A sports enthusiast is likely to notice sports commercials more than someone who is indifferent to sport. Closely related to this is *perceptual vigilance* that indicates that consumers relate to stimuli that concern their current needs. For example, when you are looking to buy a car you are much more likely to notice car advertisements. *Adaptation* is another element in exposure. Adapta-tion relates to the degree to which consumers notice a stimulus over time. When stimuli become too familiar, consumers no longer pay attention.

Attention—is the degree to which consumers focus on stimuli within their range of exposure. Creative advertising and packaging are often required to gain attention amongst the 'clutter'. Key factors in gaining attention are novelty, relevance, size, colour, and repetition.

3.8.5 **Encoding**

The final stage of IP is encoding the stimuli. As people differ in the stimuli that they perceive, they also differ in the meaning that they attribute to stimuli. In one advertising test students at Princeton and Dartmouth in the US viewed a film of a violent football game between the two universities. Everyone saw the same film, but the degree of blame attributed to each university depended on the student's affiliations. Consumers assign meaning to stimuli based on their beliefs. Hi-fi manufacturers have found that Japanese sounding brand names perform well in the marketplace, regardless of country of origin. If a stimulus is ambiguous in meaning, then consumers have more freedom to use their own beliefs to interpret it.

3.8.6 Gestalt

People do not perceive a stimulus in isolation. On the whole, they tend to view it in relation to other stimuli and their own experiences. Gestalt theory holds that people gain meaning from the totality of a set of stimuli rather than any individual one. A German word, 'gestalt' basically means a pattern or configuration. There are three elements to gestalt perception:

Closure—people tend to fill-in gaps in stimuli, e.g. people have no trouble reading words even if several letters are missing. Advertisers often capitalize on this tendency such as 'ingle ells, ingle ells—The holidays aren't the same without J&B'.

Similarity—consumer's group together objects that share similar physical characteristics.

Figure-ground—one part tends to dominate a stimulus, while other parts recede into the background. For example, loud music can be the figure of the commercial or soft music the ground.

3.9 Learning and memory

Learning is a permanent change in knowledge or behaviour as a result of a stimulus. Learning may involve motor actions (e.g. how to write) and mental processes. People store their beliefs, attitudes, knowledge, and experiences in their memories. Building a memory involves the process of acquiring information and storing it over time so that it will be available when needed (Kellaris, Cox, and Cox, 1993; Lammers, 1991).

3.9.1 Types of learning

(a) Classical conditioning

You will have heard of Pavlov's experiments in which he conditioned a dog to salivate at the sound of a bell. He did this by first pairing the sound of a bell with sprays of meat powder. Eventually, Pavlov found that he could eliminate the meat powder and the dog would salivate at the sound of the bell alone. This research provided the basis for classical conditioning.

Classical conditioning is a sequential process in which:

• a previously **neutral stimulus** (the bell) . . .

- is paired with an **unconditional stimulus** (the meat powder) . . .
- and comes to elicit an **unconditioned response** (salivation) similar to the original unconditional stimulus.

Classical conditioning can be accomplished with previously conditioned stimuli, and not just unconditioned ones. For example, most people are conditioned to jump up at the sound of the phone ringing or a doorbell. This device is used to attract consumers' attention in many commercials, such as for Avon. Another point to note about classical conditioning is that the behaviours are controlled by stimuli that occur *before* the behaviour. Also, the behaviours are largely involuntary.

Emotions can often be linked to classical conditioning. As such, classical conditioning has important implications for direct marketers. Individuals may wish to obtain, avoid, or be indifferent to a wide variety of goods and services through classical conditioning. For example, research has shown that when a product, for which people have neutral feelings, is advertised between an exciting television event (such as the FA cup or Wimbledon), it may eventually generate excitement on its own—from the pairing with exciting events. Sports personalities attempt to provide the same role when they are seen or heard in advertisements. Another example is that by playing patriotic music in a commercial, political candidates can elicit patriotic feelings.

(b) Operant conditioning

Unlike classical, operant conditioning refers to behaviours that are under the individual's control and are elicited by stimuli that occur *after* the behaviour. For example, if you responded to a direct TV commercial for a furniture shop and in negotiating for an item were offered a bigger discount than you expected, the probability that you will shop there again is increased. Probabilities that certain behaviours will result from particular situations can be compared in operant conditioning. If all the possible behaviours were arranged in descending order of probability, this would form a response hierarchy.

There are four operant conditioning consequences:

Positive reinforcement—this is the most common consequence used by direct marketers. In general, it is argued, the greater the reward for behaviour and the sooner it is given, the greater the possibility that behaviour will be repeated. For example, a £2 off coupon placed in a mail-shot for a shop will be more likely to lead to a purchase than a £1 coupon that has to be redeemed via the post.

Negative reinforcement—this is where purchase leads to the removal of adverse stimuli. Perhaps a pushy salesperson is pressuring someone to buy something. Many people may refuse to buy altogether, but some people may buy the product with the reinforcement that they are removing the problem salesperson. In future, when they are thinking of buying something, a pushy salesperson may continue to trigger a sale.

Extinction—this is where stimuli are arranged in such a way that there is no reinforcement. For example, if you buy a gift for somebody who does not give any reaction to you, positive or negative, then you are less likely to buy that person a gift again. It is argued that without any reaction, the behaviour will eventually become 'extinct'.

Punishment—the probability of performing an action is likely to diminish if a response is followed by a noxious event. An obvious example would be to phone a shop in response to an ad and be spoken to by a rude salesperson.

(c) Cognitive learning theory

In contrast to conditioning theories of learning, based on automatic reactions to stimuli, the emphasis in cognitive theory is on mental processes. The argument is that people actively use information to understand the world around them and make decisions on the basis of their findings. The cognitive school says that expectation of a stimulus (which requires mental activity) forms part of the outcome, so that even apparent conditioned learning is cognitive. For example, in operant conditioning, the offer of a 20 per cent price reduction should lead to a greater probability of returning to a clothes shop.

However, the cognitive school would argue that consumers' expectation would affect the outcome. If you had anticipated a 10 or 30 per cent reduction, your response to the stimulus might be different. Observational learning is a sub-set of cognitive theory and occurs when people watch the actions of others and note the reinforcements that *they* receive for their behaviour. People store these observations in memory and use their accumulated knowledge later to guide their own behaviour. The process of imitative learning is, therefore, cognitive, and called modelling.

3.9.2 Modifying learning and behaviour

A variety of direct marketing techniques can be used to modify consumer behaviour.

(a) Reinforcement schedules

A variety of ways can be developed to reinforce positive behaviour. Direct marketers might try continuous schedules, where every element of the sale is reinforced. For example, Apple is currently offering top quality computers at competitive prices with good service contracts.

Most companies find continuous schedules too difficult to implement in the long run and too expensive, so fixed ratio schedules provide another option. Here, reinforcement is given at a fixed rate. Thus, airlines cannot perform on price and service constantly (bad weather, delayed flights, etc.) and so the air miles plan offers a fixed reward for purchases. As people accumulate air miles, they can eventually gain a reward at fixed points and this may outweigh any difficulties along the way. Some very interesting research has shown that a variable ratio schedule can perform just as well as a constant one. With a variable ratio the reinforcement is random, such as with gambling on a slot machine. Direct marketers have found that competitions, sweepstakes, and give-aways can work as well as more expensive continuous schedules.

(b) Shaping

Shaping involves arranging reinforcement behaviours so that the probability of *other* behaviour will occur. For example, a shop may offer extremely low prices on a particular group of brands. The aim may be to sell other brands once people are in the shop rather than to sell the brands concerned. Or a car dealer may set-up a 'carnival' in a parking lot close to a shopping centre in order to shape behaviour (catch people who would not normally go to the dealership). Similarly, a casino might offer a free trip to gamblers.

Shaping may occur throughout the shopping process. To cite car dealers again, they might offer free coffee and biscuits to anyone who comes in, £20 for a test drive and £500 cash-back on a sale.

(c) Discriminative stimuli

A discriminative stimulus is where, in the process of learning, consumers realize that the same response to two similar, but different stimuli, leads to different consequences. Discriminant stimuli include brand names, logos, and trademarks.

(d) Observation

Rather than reward individuals, marketers can use observational learning to modify behaviour. For example, a deodorant commercial may show a wearer being given flowers. In a cognitive way, this message may be processed and acted upon.

3.10 Memory

Modern approaches to the study of the memory employ an information processing approach. This implies that the mind is, in some way, like a computer:

Encoding—where information is entered in a way that the mind will recognize. Incoming data is easier to encode when it is more concrete than abstract. For example, 'Sani-Flush' toilet bowl cleaner makes sense and 'Tide' detergent can be visualized.

Storage—knowledge is then integrated with the current information and retained until needed.

Retrieval—the information is later found when needed.

3.10.1 Types of memory

Sensory—a stimulus processed simply by its sensory meaning, e.g. colour or shape.

Abstract—a meaning based on an idea, e.g. rich people drink champagne.

Episodic—memories triggered by events that are personal and relevant. Hearing a particular song, a smell or seeing a particular event may trigger these.

3.10.2 **Memory systems**

Memory system research suggests that there are five stages to long-term memory storage:

Sensory memory—the temporary storage of sensory information. The memory capacity at this stage is huge, but lasts for less than one second for vision and about two seconds for hearing.

Attention—if a person decides to investigate the sensation further, the information may be retained for further processing. It will be transferred to short-term memory.

Short-term—the information may be stored here only for a limited amount of time because the capacity of the short-term memory (STM) is restricted. It might best be described as a 'working memory'. Verbal information may be stored by how it sounds or in terms of its meaning. The duration in short-term memory is about 20 seconds. Originally, it was thought that STM was capable of processing about five to nine chunks of information at a time (hence phone numbers were designed to have seven units). However, it is now known that the optimum efficiency is three to four chunks (hence phone numbers are 'chunked' into two codes).

Elaborative rehearsal—elaborative rehearsal then occurs with deeper processing to decide if the information is worth keeping.

Long-term memory—long-term memory (LTM) has unlimited storage capacity for an endless amount of time. LTM can retain conditioned, cognitive, abstract and skill-based knowledge.

3.10.3 **Memory relationships**

Ideas on the relationships between the types of memory remain controversial. The traditional perspective is that STM and LTM are separate systems. Recent research has challenged this view and instead focuses on the inter-dependence of the two. The research indicates that, depending on the nature of the processing task, different levels of processing occur that activate some aspects of memory rather than others. The deeper the processing required the more likely that the information will be placed in LTM.

These new models of memory propose that incoming pieces of information are stored in associate networks containing bits of related information organized according to certain relationships. From the consumer behaviour perspective it implies that there is an organized system relating to goods and services. Initially, information is analysed in a simple way and is then further processed in with ever more complexity and linked to ever more pieces of other information. When asked to list perfumes, a consumer will recall only those brands contained in an associate category. This group is called the *evoked set*. The task of a new entrant would be to provide cues to the consumer to facilitate its placement in the relevant category.

Different levels of knowledge may be built up in the memory. 'Meaning concepts' are individual nodes (e.g. sophisticated) which may be combined with beliefs. A belief links two or more nodes together to form a more complex meaning: e.g. a Mercedes is a sophisticated car. Propositions are, in turn, integrated to produce a complex unit known as a *schemata*, which is a cognitive framework developed with experience. Information that fits with an existing schemata will, of course, be encoded more readily. For example, some people have a lot of trouble coping with changes in the marketplace when the schemata is challenged such as with automatic bank machines.

3.10.4 Factors affecting memory

A number of factors are known to affect the ability of the memory to retrieve and shop information:

State—the internal state of the mind is an important factor. For example, it has been shown that people remember commercials more readily during fast-paced programmes rather than during stop-start ones like chat shows and baseball.

Familiarity—as a rule, prior familiarity with an item enhances its chance of being placed in the memory. Sometimes, over familiarity to a brand may lead consumers to pay less attention because they feel that they have enough information already.

Salience—refers to prominence or the novelty of a stimulus. Anything that improves salience will generally improve memory processing.

Visuals—evidence shows that pictures outperform speech in recall. However, the research also indicates that cognitive processing of information does not improve with a picture. For example, research on television news items showed that recall of items was improved with pictures, but that the comprehension of the issues remained unchanged.

Forgetting—as the brain ages, information is forgotten. Forgetting also occurs as new information displaces the older, less relevant, material.

Prior learning—can sometimes inhibit the ability to learn new information in a node. Since pieces of information are stored in nodes in the memory that are linked together with other nodes, these larger groupings are more likely to be retrieved than the new.

Products—can be 'memory makers'. For example, surveys show that the three types of products most valued by consumers are furniture, visual art, and photographs (which are also external memory banks for people). Direct marketers can use nostalgia to enhance recall.

3.11 Attitudes

An attitude, in buyer behaviour terms, is a lasting, general, evaluation of products and ideas. Attitudes are formed by personal usage or trust in the attitudes of other influential users (beliefs may be formed without product experience). When you have an attitude towards anything, be it a bar of chocolate or democracy, it is called an 'attitude object' (Ao).

3.11.1 Measuring attitudes

Their direction and degree may measure attitudes:

Direction—whether the Ao is favourable or unfavourable.

Degree—rates the Ao by the extent of liking or disliking.

3.11.2 Why do people form attitudes?

The formation of attitudes is linked to a basic survival and coping requirement. Attitudes help us make sense of the world at large and maintain our self-image:

Knowledge—attitudes guide us towards what we feel we need to know. The seemingly inexhaustible amount of information in the world would be hard to cope with unless people formed attitudes. For example, if your attitude is that computers are an important part of your life, you will seek out and store knowledge on the subject. If your attitude is that they are not, you do not have to bother with computer information.

Self-image—attitudes may also enable us to protect our self-image when we receive set-backs. If you buy that computer, and it does not quite live up to your expectations, then you may console yourself with the attitude that you made the most informed decision possible at the time.

Rewarding—as attitudes are largely based on personal experiences, they serve to guide people towards products that they like and away from ones that they dislike.

Values—attitudes enable people to express their innermost values. Consumers can express values such as modern and trendy, by developing favourable attitudes towards products that express such values (e.g. modern furniture/trendy clothing etc.).

Social—there is a social component in holding many attitudes. Attitudes are formed individually, but there is an interaction with other people in their formation, particularly family and friends. Attitudes enable people to rebel or integrate (identify) with their groups and society at large and attitudes towards products are part of this process.

3.11.3 Consistency theories

(a) Balance theory

The psychologist Fritz Heider developed Balance theory. He considered the elements a person perceived as belonging together. There are always three elements to the attitude structure, according to Heider, called *triads*. Each triad contains: (1) a person's perceptions, (2) an Ao, and (3) some other object or person. Heider argued that people alter their perceptions in order to make relations between the three elements consistent: people seek harmony. The triad may link together as a *unit* relation, where one element belongs to a part of the other or as a *sentiment* relation where two elements are linked because of the person's like or dislike of the other.

This might seem a little confusing, so an example may help. Direct marketers may attempt to establish a unit relation for a product so that a consumer can establish a sentiment relation when they were previously neutral. Take the case of the US beef industry that has used famous celebrities to endorse the product. The idea was to establish a unit relationship between the celebrity and beef and hopefully establish a positive sentiment by consumers. The strategy can cause problems if the unit relationship is challenged. For example, in the US, Cybill Shepherd did promotions for the beef industry and then subsequently admitted publicly that she never ate red meat of any kind! If this produces sufficient tension amongst some consumers of beef, they may question their attitudes to the product. Others may simply downgrade Shepherd's credibility to restore the unity of the message and their sentiments.

(b) Congruity theory

Congruity theory is another consistency theory that specifically examines how attitudes are affected when a person is linked to an object. Its advantage over balance theory, from a direct marketing perspective, is that it enables measurement of attitudes. The theory points out that there is a risk in associating objects and/or people for which consumers have different attitudes. One of the earliest studies using congruency theory evaluated the decision by the top US fashion designer Halston (upscale image) to create a clothing line for the clothing retailer J.C. Penny (downscale image). The study concluded that the decision would slightly improve J.C. Penny's image, but severely diminish Halston's. According to congruity theory, attitude change is rarely proportional. The results tend to indicate that the Ao with the more extreme attitude will change less than the one with the more moderate attitude. Thus, getting Saddam Hussein to endorse Pepsi might slightly improve his image, but will have an awful effect on Pepsi!

(c) Cognitive dissonance

Leon Festinger from his research on students getting engaged developed cognitive dissonance. He discovered that getting engaged upset the 'mind's equilibrium' because it was such a risky decision. This meant that people felt dissonance and in order to regain their balance sought dissonance reduction. To do so they rationalized their choice of partner in every way possible, including distorting their views of previous partners. The women would comment how 'Bill was a total slob—look how he has turned out—I am happy I am marrying Harry'. Likewise, the men would distort the negative aspects of their previous partners in order to enhance the image of their fiancées.

Madison Avenue first translated the theory into advertising strategies when it was realized that the theory explained post-purchase dissonance. The purchase of expensive and involving products (e.g. cars or cameras) often leads consumers to experience dissonance immediately after purchase. As consumers actively seek information to reduce dissonance, direct marketing may be an important source. Direct marketers can reduce post-purchase dissonance by advertising to consumers in a way that congratulates. The main point is that companies want long-term customers. Car companies want consumers to come back again in the years ahead, so post-purchase dissonance reduction is an important issue.

3.11.4 **Multiattribute models**

Multiattribute attitude models attempt to address the complexity of attitude components.

(a) **ABC model**

The ABC model of attitudes has widespread support amongst behaviouralists. It has three components:

Affect—how consumers feel about an Ao.

Behaviour—relates to a person's intentions to *do* something with an Ao (conative).

Cognition—the knowledge a person has about an Ao.

The ABC model is useful, because it reminds us that, from a behavioural perspective, it is important to establish the relationship between feelings, intentions, and knowledge. For example, a consumer may know that a car has all the right specifications and feel that it is the car for them. However, they may have no intention of buying it because of a variety of circumstances.

(b) **Fishbein**

The most influential multiattribute model in marketing is the Fishbein, named after its primary developer (Fishbein, 1967). The model has three components:

Beliefs—cognitive beliefs about an Ao.

Affective—an evaluation of each of the important attributes.

Importance—importance of the attributes.

The formula is:

- Aijk = BijkIik

  where

- A = consumer k's attitude for brand j

- i = attribute

- j = brand

- k = consumer

- B = consumer k's belief on extent to which brand possesses attribute i

- I = importance given to attribute (i) by consumer k

Overall attitudes are found by deriving a person's beliefs and feelings about various attributes of the Ao. The method is to multiply the belief scores by the importance ones.

It should be noted that it is difficult to adequately specify all the relevant attributes of a brand. Nor is it likely that consumers would approximate to the Fishbein model when making purchase decisions, i.e. people do not make such calculations. Another point is that it takes no account of the influence of other influences on a purchasing decision. Finally, consumer intentions may change over time, so the Fishbein model provides only a snapshot of the process (see Figure 3.5).

3.11.5 Low-involvement

Low involvement theories may be more relevant to much of purchasing behaviour than the models considered above. It might be argued that an attitude is too strong a description in the first place, and that consumers only hold opinions about some products, e.g. do people have attitudes about chewing gum?

Low involvement theories stress the haphazard nature of purchases, the chances people take and that fact that many attitudes are at an extremely low level and easily altered or changed. Put simply, a more realistic view of purchasing would recognize that consumers do not care much about many of the decisions that they make and do not pay much attention to the stimuli for many products, e.g. a consumer purchasing cling film may simply look for the best value for money rather than anything else.

Ironically, the less important the decision and the lower the involvement and intensity of attitude, the greater the role of marketing strategies may take in the decision, e.g. packaging and advertising.

Example of Measuring Attitudes Towards Watches Using the Basic Fishbein Model

Attribute (i)	Importance (I)	Beliefs (B)		
		Brand X	Brand Y	Brand Z
accuracy	9	9	3	3
waterproof	7	8	6	9
price	5	5	6	9
features	6	3	5	1
stylish	8	6	7	9
Attitude Score		228	185	213

Note: These hypothetical ratings are scored from 1 to 10—where higher numbers equal a better standing on an attribute. Thus, higher scores on price indicate the attitude that a brand is cheaper. Attitude is obtained by multiplying a consumer's rating of each attribute for all the brands considered by the importance rating for that attribute.

Fig. 3.5 Basic Fishbein

3.11.6 **Attitude towards the advertisement**

Linked to low involvement theories is the observation that consumers' affective reactions to a brand are influenced by their evaluations of the advertising itself, sometimes above their feelings about the brand. This is known as attitude towards the advertisement (Aad).

Determinants of Aad include attitudes towards the advertiser, evaluations of the advertisement, the mood evoked, and arousal levels. The effects demonstrated by Aad emphasize the importance of an advertisement's entertainment value and creativity. The kinds of feelings that can be generated by advertisements, particularly commercials, are positive (amusement, delight, play), warmth (affection, contemplation, hope), and negative (criticism, defiance, and offence). The essential point is that Aad can effect the Ao (attitude to the brand).

3.12 **Problem recognition, search, and evaluation**

It is now worth considering the process of purchasing (Engel, Blackwell, and Miniard, 1993; Nicosia, 1966). Classically, consumer decision making involves initially going through a series of three steps (Alpert, 1993; Hayer, 1984; Simonson, 1992):

- problem recognition;
- information search;
- evaluation of alternatives.

Some problems are more or less important than others, so the amount of effort put into solving them will vary. Problem solving may take weeks, with consumers mulling over product or brand choices at night whereas others (the majority) are based on quick judgements.

3.12.1 **Approaches to decision making**

There are several approaches to consumer decision making:

Rational—consumers carefully integrate as much information as possible with what they already know, weigh up the negatives and positives, and then make the best decision. In reality, if consumers did this for all their purchasing decisions they would have little time left over for anything else in life.

Low involvement—consumer decision making is a learned response to environmental cues, for example, a direct marketing promotion for a supermarket.

Gestalt—there are problems to which the rational approach does not lend itself. For example, how can the rational process explain a person's choice of art, music, or theatre? The gestalt approach stresses the totality of the good or service, emphasizing effective (emotional) responses.

3.12.2 **Type of decisions**

One helpful typology for decision making is to examine the amount of effort that goes into the decision. Researchers offer a continuum. At one end is 'extended problem solving' and at the other 'routine problem solving'. Many decisions fall in the middle and are called 'limited problem solving'.

Extended Problem Solving (EPA)—this corresponds most closely to traditional decision making. A relatively important issue initiates the process with the decision perceived as carrying a degree of risk. Most consumers will try and collect as much information as possible both from memory (internal search) and the environment (external search). Each brand's attributes will be carefully evaluated.

Limited Problem Solving (LPS)—a straightforward and simple decision-making process. Buyers do not search extensively for information but instead use 'decision rules' to choose among alternatives. Such 'cognitive shortcuts' enable consumers to fall back on general guidelines rather than having to start from the beginning each time.

Routine Problem Solving (RPS)—whereas both EPS and LPS involve problem solving with varying degrees of information, RPS uses little cognition. Purchases are made automatically with little or no thought. RPS is used by consumers to minimize the time and effort devoted to familiar purchasing decisions.

3.12.3 **Problem recognition**

The motive to undertake a decision can only begin when consumers perceive a problem has to be solved, be it small or large, simple or complex. Problem recognition starts when consumers see a significant difference between their current situation and their 'ideal' state. For example, a person who hears someone else's new hi-fi system may return home and decide that their old system is out of date and needs replacing (this is called opportunity recognition). Or the same person may wake up in the morning and realize that he or she has run out of cornflakes (called need recognition). In both examples, a gulf occurred between the actual situation and the ideal.

Direct marketers may attempt to modify primary problems, e.g. the introduction of internet banks. Or secondary problems, let's say internet banks, are now well established in the market place, so the consumer problem becomes, which bank? A well-known structure for direct advertisements is 'problem-solution'. Consumers are shown problems that the advertised product will solve. This form of appeal is prevalent in the cosmetics and drug industries with such products as dandruff shampoos and aspirins.

3.12.4 **Information search**

Once consumers have recognized that they have a problem, they realize that they need information to solve it. Consumers have to engage in information search, surveying their own and external information to make an informed decision. 'Prepurchase search' is when a consumer explicitly searches the market place for specific information. 'Ongoing search', however, is the consumer behaviour term for 'browsing'. This involves people who like hunting for information and keeping track of product developments for the fun of it or for future use.

Thus, information sources may be categorized in two ways: internal and external:

Internal—experience of a consumer society and purchasing inevitably leaves everyone with a degree of knowledge about products. Internal search involves scanning memory to assemble product information about different alternatives. Knowledge may be built-up cognitively or incidentally and passively through exposure to such things as advertising or shop displays.

External—if consumers feel their knowledge is inadequate, they may undertake an external search (going outside themselves for information). The sources may be friends and family, trade magazines, advertising, and retailers.

3.12.5 **Amount of search**

The traditional view of information search is based on utility theory. This states that consumers will search for information to the extent that the rewards of doing so equal the costs incurred. Rewards include such aspects as making an informed choice, getting greater product satisfaction, being knowledgeable, and saving money. Costs include the time and effort, frustration and forgoing social activities. Once the cost of searching for information exceeds the benefits, then consumers will cease to search. Obviously, the most valuable pieces of information will be sought first, and then there will be a diminishing return to the effort-information reward as the search continues.

Research, however, indicates that people do not invest much time in search at all, even for expensive items. Consumers often make decisions on surprisingly small amounts of information. Forty to 60 per cent of shoppers visit only one shop before making a purchase. Even decisions on expensive durable goods indicate that consumers make decisions quickly with little information. In a study of Australian car buyers, it was found that more than one third made only one or two trips to inspect cars prior to buying one. Another interesting finding is that low-income shoppers, who have more to lose with a bad choice, search less than affluent ones.

3.12.6 **Buyers tend to search more when:**

- the purchase is important. This is often characterized by decisions that involved a degree of risk: where the product is expensive, complex, hard to understand or socially visible (i.e. there is a risk of embarrassment it the choice is wrong).
- information can be easily obtained;
- they are younger;
- they are better educated;
- they enjoy shopping;
- they place greater value on their self-image;
- they lack confidence.

3.12.7 **Novices and experts**

There has been a considerable amount of research on whether novices or experts search the most. On the one hand, novices, who know little, have the motivation to search. On the other, experts may be more familiar with the product category, so they should be more familiar with the product sources and better understand the information. The evidence on who searches the most turns out to support an inverted 'U' relationship. Neither novices or experts search the most—the ones that search the most are those with moderate knowledge about a product category. Novices often feel that they are incapable of searching extensively and may not even know where to start. They tend to rely upon the opinion of others and to focus on non-functional attributes like brand name and price to distinguish between brands. Information, for novices, is often processed in a 'top-down' manner, concentrating on details rather than the overall picture. For example, a novice is more likely to be impressed by all the functions on a hi-fi system rather than what those functions do. At the other extreme, experts can use an extensive memory search and may not need much external information. When they do search it tends to be highly selective and focused on functional product attributes.

3.12.8 **Alternative evaluation**

Much of the effort in consumer decision making involves evaluating alternative brands in a product category. Most people buy brands that they are familiar with and the alternatives that are actively considered during choice are known as a consumer's evoked set. When thinking of buying a laptop computer, a consumer might think of Dell, Toshiba, Compaq, IBM, and Gateway 2000, but struggle to think of any more. The evoked set would comprise those brands that the consumer considers buying.

Brands that consumers are aware of, but would not consider buying, are known as the inept set. For example, from the list above a consumer might include Compaq and Gateway 2000 in their inept set. Brands not entering the list of alternatives at all, say, in our example, Tiny and Fujitsu computers, would consist of the inert set.

Evoked sets are often small in number and vary culturally. For example, Canadian consumers typically have an evoked set of seven beers compared to two for Americans. Whereas Norwegian car buyers tend to hold about two brands in their evoked set compared to about five or six for North Americans.

Much as you cannot win the National Lottery if you do not play, direct marketers have trouble 'winning' in the marketplace if they are not in a consumer's evoked set. As you can imagine, it is even more difficult to place an existing brand into the evoked set from a consumer's inept set than it is to place a new brand that has yet to be placed in any set at all.

Brand groupings are particularly important to marketers in entering evoked sets. Consumers tend to group brands that they consider to be similar and evaluate them according to these criteria. Thus, when Toyota and Nissan launched their high-end cars they gave them the distinctive brand names of Lexus and Infiniti. Additionally, they used advertising to compare them to BMW, Mercedes, and Jaguar in order to separate them from the grouping of cheaper/reliable Japanese cars.

3.12.9 **Brand or attribute?**

'Compensatory' and 'non-compensatory' models are used to explain how consumers make choices amongst brands. Compensatory means that consumers will compensate between attributes whereas non-compensatory models do not allow attributes to compensate—brands are compared to each other and eliminated.

Choice by processing attributes (CPA) involves evaluating single attributes across brands. On the other hand, choice by processing brands involves evaluating one brand at a time (CPB) which is non-compensatory.

(a) **Compensatory**

Compensatory decision rules allow a brand to make up for its shortcomings. For example, if someone only believes in buying brand baked beans, they may not allow own-label beans into their evoked set. However, if they are willing to let good and bad points to be taken into account, they might try some own-label brands. With the simple additive rule consumers choose the brand with the largest *number* of positive attributes. A slightly more complex version is the weighted additive rule, based on multi-attribute modelling, where consumers multiply brand ratings by importance weights (e.g. Fishbein, above.)

(b) **Non-compensatory**

This is where consumers are *not* willing to upgrade a brand that has a low standing on one particular attribute. For example, someone who does not like soft drinks that contain caffeine would be unlikely ever to place a caffeine brand into their evoked set. Consumers may eliminate brands in a variety of processes:

Conjunctive rules—are where minimum levels of acceptability are established for each attribute. For example, in choosing a lawn mower, only brands in the evoked set satisfying cost, ease of operation, and lightness standards would be chosen. The brand satisfying all three or all three the best, would be the one chosen.

Disjunctive rules—are where minimum standards are set. For example, a consumer might have an evoked set of lawn mowers. If low price were the minimum standard, then the cheapest brand in the acceptable evoked set would be chosen.

In the lexicographic rule—brands are eliminated on a hierarchical attribute by attribute basis (an extension of the disjunctive rule.) If two or more brands are equally good on one attribute, the consumer then compares them on the second attribute, and so on, until a choice is made.

The aspect rule—is where a consumer has a primary attribute, and all brands are evaluated by the degree to which they fulfil it. For example, quality of sound may be the primary attribute for someone purchasing a hi-fi and this may be the one way that all brands are evaluated.

(c) **Heuristics**

Heuristics are mental 'rules of thumb' that lead to speedy decisions. They might be quite general, such as 'higher priced products have better quality' or specific: 'buy Oral B toothbrushes, they are the best'. Heuristics may develop in a variety of ways:

Availability heuristic—is where people use personal knowledge to outweigh the evidence. For example, a car with an excellent reliability record may not be in someone's evoked set because they know of someone who has experienced problems with the model.

Market beliefs—consumers may be led by a number of heuristics based on a person's belief about the marketplace. Examples would be beliefs based on when a company was founded, price, and certain brand names.

Purchase pals—consumers also use family and friends to act heuristically and give help or advice in purchasing. In some markets, such as finance or diet, consumers often turn to counsellors for advice.

3.12.10 **Choosing**

When moving from alternative evaluation to choice, consumers move through evaluative criteria, beliefs, attitudes, and intention (see Figure 3.6):

Evaluative criteria—are the personal standards by which people rate products. In choosing a computer, some people have a primary requirement for speed, others want storage more than anything, and others may be more concerned by the monitor than anything else.

Beliefs—are what people think a product will deliver. Someone who has an evaluative criterion that they like strong tea may be tempted to buy a packet of tea that is advertised as the 'strongest in the marketplace'. However, if the tea is weaker than they expected, and certainly not as strong as other teas that they have drunk, they will now have an attitude that the tea is weak. It will now be virtually impossible for the 'strong tea advertising' to work on this consumer again, unless there is a change in the product formulation.

Intention—is the result of beliefs or attitudes, and represents the purchasing goal of the consumer. However, intention may not lead to choice because of a lack of resources or other intervening variables that may stop a consumer making a purchase.

Fig. 3.6 Choosing

As relatively few products in the marketplace are completely new to most consumers, there is often no belief stage (see Figure 3.7):

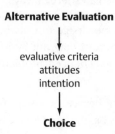

Fig. 3.7 No belief stage

3.12.11 **Direct marketing implications**

- positioning;
- defining competitors;
- prototypicality—leading brands in an evoked set get to make the marketing 'rules';
- niche marketing;
- influencing attributes and brands in evoked sets;
- research.

3.13 **Purchasing and post-purchase behaviour**

Shopping is an activity that preoccupies many people. It has been calculated that we spend about 6–10 per cent of our waking hours shopping. Shopping is part of the culture, as evidenced by phrases such as 'born to shop', 'shop till you drop', and 'when the going gets tough, the tough go shopping'.

3.13.1 **Shopping**

The primary motive for most shopping trips is obviously to acquire goods and services Lewis, 1993; Munk, 1994; Phillips, and Bradshaw, 1993; Putsis and Srinivasan, 1994). However, there are some important social aspects to shopping:

Sharing—speciality shops offer people the ability to discuss with sales staff, or other consumers, common interests, such as computers and records.

Social—shopping malls and centres have replaced many of the old town squares as community gathering places. Many people have few other places to go to spend their time, especially in inclement weather. For many teenagers 'hanging-out' in malls is an easy way of boy–girl watching, and for seniors, the mall offers a controlled and safe environment.

Status—shopping often helps self-esteem when interacting with salespeople. When playing the role of 'shop customer' people can experience being waited on, and having their opinions valued and pandered to, whether they want to buy something or not.

Trends—shopping enables consumers to keep up with trends in the marketplace.

Sport—haggling and bargaining is a thrilling experience for many people.

Surveys show that people are finding shopping less and less pleasurable. This may be part of the trend towards placing greater emphasis on time, the home and 'spiritual values'. In practice, approaches to shopping differ according to person, product category, and the shop concerned. For example, it is hard to equate the experience of grocery shopping with spending money on a gift for yourself. Stone has identified five shopping types (Stone, 1954):

Economic shopper—rational and goal-orientated and wanting to maximize value.

Personalized shopper—a shopper who forms strong personalized bonds to shops.

Ethical shopper—supporter of local shops and/or environmental products.

Recreational shopper—someone who likes to spend their leisure time shopping.

Apathetic shopper—finds shopping a necessity and an unpleasant chore.

The activity of shopping may be either planned or spontaneous. Planners know what products and brands they want before entering the shop. Partial planners know what products they want before getting to the shop, but have not made up their minds about brands. Impulse purchasers do no advance planning whatsoever (these people should not be confused with impulse shoppers, those with an uncontrollable urge to buy something).

3.13.2 **Shops**

Shop location, image, and layout provide important elements in choosing shops. At its most simple, the closer the shop, the better the image and layout, the greater the likelihood of shopping there. Other obvious criteria in shop choice are price, value, variety of products, cleanliness, and the attitude of the sales staff. The relative importance of different attributes will vary according to shop type. For example, department store shoppers want value, choice, and hassle-free shopping and warranties. Whereas grocery shoppers want a mix of own-labels and brand names, cleanliness, and ease. Several factors are worthy of closer attention.

(a) **Entertainment**

Shopping malls have tried to gain more traffic and spending by incorporating entertainment into their mix. Many malls have become mini amusement parks, where the shopping is almost an afterthought.

Many shops also incorporate entertainment into their mixes with such things as offering shop-wide promotions based on the culture of a selected country. A specific example would be the Cabbage Patch Dolls that do not have sales staff, instead they have 'doctors', 'nurses', and 'adoption officers': dolls are adopted rather than bought.

(b) Shop image

Consumers evaluate shops on their specific attributes and on their global evaluation or 'gestalt'. The gestalt has much more to do with interior design (e.g. Ralph Polo Lauren) than the quality of the brands. The atmosphere is carefully designed to enhance shop image. Light colours and classical music can impart spaciousness and serenity, and bright colours and rock music can create excitement. For example, restaurant studies have proven that when customers are played classical music, they eat their food more slowly and eat less than when listening to rock music.

(c) Sales staff

In many shops, the salesperson is a critical factor in shopping and buying behaviour. Exchange theory can be applied to the salesperson, as each participant gives something to the other in shopping and hopes to receive something back in return. Most customers look to sales people for expertise to make shopping easier. In general, research shows that sales staff who appear as experts tend to be more successful in selling than those that do not. The key variables in effectiveness are age, appearance, educational level, motivation, and adaptability of the salesperson.

Adaptability is a key trait in salespeople. Consumers vary in their degrees of assertiveness in shopping from the non-assertive, who may be highly intimidated by shopping, to the assertive, who are firm in their decisions, to the aggressive who may be rude or threatening.

Finally, salespeople, if they develop their 'own' group of customers, may employ one-to-one relationship marketing. Techniques may include phoning someone after a purchase to inquire about satisfaction or to recommend an item or even writing to thank a customer for shopping at the shop.

3.13.3 Situation effects on purchasing

The knowledge of what consumers are doing or feeling at the time of brand choice can be an important factor in direct marketing. For example, someone trying to impress someone else over dinner may suggest an up-market restaurant and select fine foods and wine from the menu, whereas they would make different choices for a lunchtime meal with a close friend.

The situational factors include:

Physical—shop location, decor, sound, and lighting.

Co-consumers—the groups or social settings of purchasing. For example, an empty bar can have a depressing effect on purchasing (however, an overcrowded bar may have the same effect). The type of consumers may also play a role, hence some restaurants insist on a certain dress code and 'hot' clubs often hand pick who they will let in.

Temporal—time has become a sought-after commodity. Speed of delivery has become an important attribute for such services as optometrists, photograph processors, car repairs, and fast food deliveries. One Chicago funeral home even offers a drive-through service. Eating habits have changed drastically, and it is now recognized that you are no longer what you eat, but what you 'heat'. Many people find opening a tin of soup too time-consuming!

Task—the specific reason or the occasion for which it is intended may affect purchasing. Gift giving is one aspect of task and a good example of task is when people drink cheap alcohol on a regular basis but save premium to entertain friends.

Antecedent states—these are momentary moods such as pleasure or hostility that can effect purchasing (never shop at a supermarket if you are hungry!).

3.13.4 Brand loyalty

Brand loyalty is the 'Holy Grail' sought by shops, brands, and direct marketers, because loyalty is the best way to increase market share and sales, rather than seek new customers. Consumer attachments to certain shops like the Co-op, or brands like Coca-Cola, or direct marketers like Boden or Lands End, can be powerful. Many people buy the same brands in certain categories at the same shops on a regular basis. Such consistency may be linked simply to inertia where a brand is bought simply out of habit. Brand switching is easier when the main reason for purchase is inertia, because inertia provides little reason for loyalty. However, this is not brand loyalty. Brand loyalty is a cognitive decision to repeat purchase based on an underlying positive view of the brand. Sometimes, brand loyal customers can be passionate in defence of their brands, as with New Coke.

Brand loyalty is undoubtedly on the wane as many brands have reached parity in consumers' minds and there has been a flood of new brands using competitive direct marketing. A recent survey showed that only 2 per cent of people were brand loyal in more than sixteen categories. Brand loyalty is particularly low in categories such as canned vegetables and shoes and is highest for ketchups, cigarettes, drinks, and some electrical brands.

While it may be on the wane in general, it is still a potent force in purchasing behaviour. Brands are symbols of 'quality' (however defined) and consistency. They can be particularly powerful in markets where consumers are confused. For example, when faced with buying hi-fi, many consumers stick to brand names like Sony, because the multitude of offerings can be bewildering. See Figure 3.8 for a summary of the stages in consumer buying.

3.13.5 Post-purchase behaviour

Consumer satisfaction or dissatisfaction (CS/D) can be measured by the attitude someone has after a product has been purchased (Donnelly and Ivancevich, 1970). There is a constant process of evaluation. The two primary things people want from products are quality and value. The two are inter-linked and the concept of 'quality' has become so

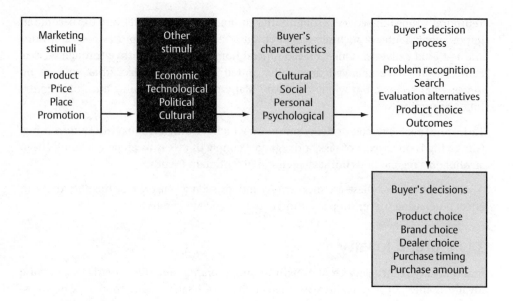

Fig. 3.8 Summary of consumer buying

vague as to become completely meaningless today. Nevertheless, quality remains an important aspect in the analysis of post-purchase behaviour.

Post-purchase CS/D is related to prior expectations of a product. The expectancy disconfirmation model proposes that people form attitudes based on prior experience of the product. Consumers tend to feel satisfied if a product exceeds expectations. They do not think about it when a product performs as expected. However, negative effect results from a worse performance. Consequently, it is particularly important not to over inflate a brand's attributes prior to purchase. For example, people accept waiting a relatively long time for a bus, but have higher expectations of airlines. Of particular relevance here is the previously discussed behavioural theory of cognitive dissonance.

There are three courses of action for a consumer who is dissatisfied with a good or service:

Vocal—an appeal directly to the retailer.

Private—tell friends and/or boycott the shop—negative word of mouth.

Third party—taking legal action against the merchant, write to the press or complain to the Better Business Bureau.

Product disposition is an important aspect of post-purchasing behaviour. It is impossible for people to keep everything that they are given or buy in their lifetimes—there is just too much to cope with. Additionally, there are environmental concerns about waste that has made product disposition a public policy issue.

The three options in post-purchase are (1) to keep it (use it, convert it to a new purpose, or shop it), (2) get rid of it permanently (throw it away, give it away, trade it or sell it), and (3) get rid of it temporarily (rent it or loan it).

The most important market in post-purchase involves selling. Garage sales, flea markets, classified, bartering, hand-me downs, and the black market represent a significant alternative distribution system to shops and direct marketing. Figure 3.8 provides a summary of the various stages in purchasing discussed above.

3.14 **Organizational buyer behaviour**

Organizational buying refers to the process by which firms and institutions purchase goods and services (Howard and Sheth, 1969). It may be defined as the decision-making process by which organizations establish their needs for products and services and then search, identify, evaluate, and choose amongst the alternatives.

Similar to consumer behaviour, purchases are made by individuals in organizational buying. However, there are several differences compared to consumer buying, which place organizational buying on a different point on the buying spectrum. That is to say that organizational buying shares many characteristics with consumer buying, but that taken as a totality, it is significantly different and worth viewing as such:

- Groups typically control purchasing in organizational markets. These groups generally buy directly from suppliers and form relationships. Individuals within groups have varying degrees of influence and particular roles when joining together to make purchases.

- Buyers tend to be competent and rational because organizational buying often involves the purchase of complex products, or large quantities of simple products, or both. That is not to say that emotional and impulsive factors do not come into play. Rather that there are numerous constraints in organizational buying, and irrational behaviour tends to be minimized. In particular, organizations look for value, innovation, and responsiveness from suppliers and service has become a key benefit to organizational buyers.

- In most markets there are a few large industrial buyers with great power. Large organizational buyers have policies of multiple sourcing and can make significant but infrequent purchases (e.g. airlines purchasing aeroplanes).

- Markets tend to be horizontal or vertical or a combination of both. Horizontal markets cross industries (e.g. Xerox photocopiers), whereas vertical markets cut through specific industries (e.g. Shimano bike accessories).

- Organizational markets are based on derived demand, i.e. the ultimate market demand comes at a later stage. For example, military aircraft component manufacturers ultimately satisfy government demand and cotton weavers ultimately satisfy consumer demand for clothing items such as jeans.

- The economic cycle tends to be far more pronounced in organizational markets than in consumer markets owing to the multiplier effect.

- Formality is important in organizational buying, with elaborate systems of checks and balances and written proposals and contracts. Negotiations over contracts can be lengthy.

3.14.1 **Decision process**

The organizational buyer decision process is similar to the consumer one:

Problem recognition—someone or some people in the organization perceive a need, e.g. machinery may break down or a rival may be seen to be using a more efficient service. The nature of the need is qualified and agreed within the organization.

Specification—next, detailed specifications of the product are drawn-up.

Supplier search—the organization will use its evoked set of suppliers or seek information outside this set.

Proposals—suppliers will be requested to bid for the contract.

Selection—a supplier or suppliers will be chosen on the basis of the criteria originally established, e.g. price, suitability, adaptability, etc.

Post-purchase evaluation—many organizations conduct a post-purchase audit to assess how well the purchase worked out.

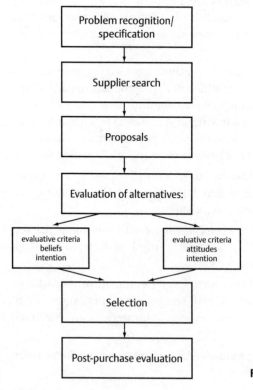

Fig. 3.9 B2B buying process

3.14.2 **Organizational buying process**

In order to assess the underlying dimensions of the supplier-buyer relationship it must first be noted that, owing to the complexity of buyer organizations, direct marketers are rarely able to communicate directly with all the relevant 'stake-holders', even if they were able to identify them.

Normally, direct marketers have most contacts with top management, senior directors, and professionals/buyers but rarely interact with others involved in the wider relationship. It makes sense, from an effective use of resources perspective, for suppliers to narrow the channels of communication to top management and senior managers. However, the underlying reason for the narrow focus is often political. Top managers, and senior directors generally regard buying as solely within their spheres of influence.

(a) **Buying tasks**

Webster and Wind's (1972) industrial-buying tasks of 'new buy', 'modified re-buy', and 'straight re-buy', are widely accepted by marketers to describe organizational buying tasks:

New task—completely new purchase, (e.g. a computer network).

Modified task—familiar buying decision, but there is a need to modify, (e.g. new computers).

Straight re-buy—repetitive replacement of products (photocopying paper).

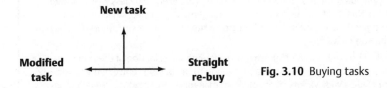

Fig. 3.10 Buying tasks

The nature of the task may be an important factor in the supplier–buyer relationship:

Buyers involved in **new tasks** are likely to enjoy a close relationship with their supplier as the need to reduce perceived risk will be paramount—particularly when the client is launching a new product and/or entering a new market.

Modifying purchases gives the supplier a moderate role, with the buyer having a greater role over the decision-making process.

With the **straight re-buy**, perceived buyer risk is minimal because the task is characterized by the repetitive replacement of products and so the buyer tends to be more 'powerful'.

(b) **Buying centre**

Sustaining a longer-term supplier-buyer relationship requires developing a close personal bond between both parties and, thus, the nature of the buying centre is another key organizational buying issue.

Developing a bond is easier to achieve with a small buyer than a corporate one, given the number of parties and possible influences involved. The importance of this for direct marketers is clear. Direct marketers may liaise regularly with a distinct and small group of senior managers and/or professionals/buyers. However, in large companies the decision to select, continue, or terminate the good or service is typically the result of a joint decision-making process within the buying organization involving a large number of decision makers and influencers. Furthermore, with Total Quality Management (TQM) and increasingly decentralized management structures amongst buyers, many suppliers find that they are increasingly isolated and marginalized as they were too closely associated with the 'old' management structure before changes are made.

From the perspective of the marketing literature the buying centre incorporates the five roles of (Webster and Wind, 1972):

Users – people who use the product on a regular basis. Users are the most easily identified by a supplier.

Buyers – people who are authorized to negotiate with the supplier. Buyers, i.e. senior managers, may be easily identified, but can be more conspicuous than their 'real' importance to buying decisions.

Influencers – people who influence the selection (e.g. define selection criteria.) Influencers may cover a wide group of people such as finance directors, production managers, and lawyers who may help establish relationship criteria and direction.

Deciders – people who determine and approve the final selection of the supplier. The decider may be the 'buyer' but in many organizations may involve someone removed from the day-to-day business activities – principally top management. Their criteria are likely to be less well informed and far more subjective than those of the more junior management or professionals and may involve issues of prestige or making judgements based on a supplier's other customers (e.g. buying IBM computers for prestige reasons).

Gatekeepers – people who guide flows of information regarding the selection of the supplier. Gatekeepers, who control the access of information through to the buying centre (either positively or negatively), may include a wide variety of people from managers, professionals to secretaries and receptionists. Senior and top managers are likely to channel information on suppliers that they have gathered externally.

Fig. 3.11 Buying centre

Individuals within the buying organization may assume one or more of these roles and have direct or indirect influence on the supplier-buyer relationship.

3.15 **Summary**

This chapter has examined the key aspects of buying (culture, social groups, family, opinion leadership, personality, motivation and involvement, information processing, memory, and attitudes) as well as the process of buying from problem recognition through to post-purchase. A comparison between consumer and organizational buying was made. An understanding of buying behaviour is fundamental to formulating direct marketing strategy and tactics. If you fail to understand why and how people buy, the chances are high that your direct marketing activities will have little success.

Discussion questions

1   Identify the major population changes taking place in the UK. Explain the implications of these changes for the direct marketers of: (a) banking, (b) wine, (c) clothing.

2   Analyse the extent to which the concepts of family and opinion leadership might help direct marketing strategies for retailers of women's fashion clothing.

3   What role do you think personality plays in the purchasing decision by consumers of up-market furniture? Illustrate your answer with examples of your choice. What are the implications for direct marketing?

4   Evaluate the contributions (negative or positive) made by followers of Freud to our understanding of consumer motives in direct marketing. Illustrate your answer with examples of your choice.

5   Explain the relationship and differences between personality and self-concept. Argue a case for using either or both concepts in the direct marketing of computers.

6   How does an understanding of the buying process help direct marketers develop (a) strategies and (b) tactics in marketing?

7   To what extent is B2B buying different to B2C?

8   How might an understanding of B2B buying roles help direct marketers?

Further reading

Alpert F. (1993) 'Consumer Market Beliefs and Their Managerial Implications: an Empirical Examination', *Journal of Consumer Marketing*, 10 (2) 56–70.

Cohen J. B. (1968) 'Towards an Interpersonal Theory of Consumer Behaviour', *California Management Review*, 10, 73–80.

Donnelly, J. H. and Ivancevich J. M. (1970) 'Post-Purchase Reinforcement and Back-Out Behavior', *Journal of Marketing Reseach*, 399–400.

Engel J. F., Blackwell R. D. and Miniard P. W. (1993) *Consumer Behavior*, 7th ed. (Chicago: Dryden).

Fishbein M. (1967) 'A Behavior Theory Approach to the Relations Between Beliefs About An Object and the Attitude Toward the Object' in Fishbein M. (ed.) *Readings in Attitude Theory and Measurement* (New York: John Wiley).

Gilly M. C. and Enis B. M. (1982) 'Recycling the Family Life Cycle: A Proposal for Redefinition' in Mitchell M. (ed.), *Advances in Consumer Research*, 9 (Ann Arbor, MI.: ACR).

Hayer W. D. (1984) 'An Examination of Consumer Decision Making for a Common Repeat Purchase Product', *Journal of Consumer Research*, 11, 822–29.

Herbig P., Koehler W., and Day K. (1993) 'Marketing to the Baby Bust Generation', *Journal of Consumer Marketing*, 10 (1) 4–9.

Howard J. A. and Sheth J. N. (1969) *The Theory of Buyer Behavior* (New York: John Wiley).

Kellaris J. J., Cox A. D., and Cox D. (1993) 'The Effect of Background Music on Ad Processing: A Contingency Explanation', *Journal of Marketing*, 57, 114–25.

Lammers H. B. (1991) 'The Effect of Free Samples on Immediate Consumer Purchase', *Journal of Consumer Marketing*', 8, 31–7.

Lewis G. (1993) 'The Impulse Zone', *National Petroleum News*, April, 24.

Loudon D. L. and Della Bitta A. J. (1993) *Consumer Behavior: Concepts and Applications* (New York: McGraw-Hill).

Maslow A. (1954) *Motivation and Personality*, (New York: Harper & Row).

Munk N. (1994) 'Shopping in Peace', *Forbes*, March 14, 94–6.

Nicosia F. M., (1966) *Consumer Decision Processes: Marketing and Advertising Implications* (Englewood Cliffs, NJ: Prentice-Hall).

Novak, T. P. and MacEvoy B. (1990) 'On Comparing Alternative Segmentation Schemes: The List of Values (LOV) and Values and Life Styles (VALS)', *Journal of Consumer Research*, 17, 105–9.

Phillips, H. and Bradshaw R. (1993) 'How Customers Actually Shop: Customer Interaction with the Point of Sale', *Journal of Market Research Society*, 35 (1) 51–62.

Putsis, W. P. and Srinivasan N. (1994) 'Buying or Just Browsing? The Duration of Purchase Deliberation', *Journal of Marketing Research*, 393–402.

Quelch, J. A. and Hoff E. J. (1986) 'Customizing Global Marketing', *Harvard Business Review*, 59–68.

Schaninger C. M., Bourgeois J. C., and Buss W. C. (1985) 'French-English Canadian Subcultural Consumption Differences' *Journal of Marketing*, 49, 82–92.

Simonson I. (1992) 'The Influence of Anticipating Regret and Responsibility on Purchase Decisions', *Journal of Consumer Research*, 19, 105–18.

Spiro R. L. (1983) 'Persuasion in Family Decision Making', *Journal of Consumer Research*, 393–402.

Stone G. P. (1954) 'City Shoppers and Identification: Observations on the Social Psychology of City Life', *American Journal of Sociology*, 60, 36–45.

Tybout, A. M., Calder B. J., and Sternthal B. (1981) 'Using Information Processing Theory to Design Marketing Strategies', *Journal of Marketing Research*, 73–9.

Webster F. and Wind Y. (1972) *Organizational Buying Behavior*, (Englewood Cliffs, NJ: Prentice-Hall).

Wells, W. D. and Gubar G. (1966) 'Life Cycle Concept in Marketing Research', *Journal of Marketing Research*, 3, 355–63.

Chapter 4

Customer Acquisition

Contents

4.1 Objectives

By the end of this chapter you should be able to:

(a) distinguish between customer acquisition and customer retention activities;

(b) develop customer acquisition objectives;

(c) segment consumer and industrial markets;

(d) profile and target appropriate prospects;

(e) implement a customer acquisition campaign;

(f) analyse and interpret the response.

4.2 **Introduction**

It is now widely accepted by members of both the academic and professional communities that it costs five times as much to conduct business with a new customer than
an existing one. An organization's existing customers have, after all, demonstrated their
interest in the available products/services by virtue of their past purchase and are therefore considerably more likely to purchase again. Thus, for example, a supplier of garden
seeds is likely to generate a much higher response from mailings to its past customers,
than it will ever achieve using a cold list of prospects, because inevitably its catalogues
could be sent to some individuals who have little or no interest in gardening, or who are
perfectly happy buying from a competitor.

Indeed, there is a world of difference in response rates between cold mailings (i.e. those
to prospective customers) and warm mailings (those to existing customers). It would be
usual for the former to achieve a response rate of between 0.1 and 5 per cent, whilst
response rates to the latter have been known to exceed even 50 per cent.

In practice, direct marketers draw a distinction between four distinct groups of
customers, each of which possesses it's own unique response characteristics. This is
illustrated in Figure 4.1. As one works along the continuum from repeat sales to the
generation of completely new business, the attainable response rates worsen considerably.

It isn't only response rates, though, that make targeting existing customers a particularly attractive option. Organizations generally know more about the needs and wants of
their existing customers, if only by virtue of their purchase history. This makes it possible
to tailor the market offerings more precisely to those customer needs, quite possibly
allowing the organization to charge a premium for the enhanced quality of service that
results.

Existing customers can also be cross-sold different product lines and be encouraged to
generate referrals of other individuals who might have a similarly enhanced interest in
the organization's products. There is therefore, a world of difference between the likely
profitability of customer acquisition activity and customer retention activity. Indeed,
many organizations aspire only to break even from acquisition activity, but are content

Response Rate			
High			**Low**
Repeat sales	Former customers	Previous enquiries	New business

Fig. 4.1 Response rates by category of customer

in the knowledge that they will be able to cultivate quite profitable relationships with the customers they recruit, over the full duration of their relationship with them.

As a consequence, more enlightened organizations develop very different approaches to the direct marketing employed to address new and existing customer groups. This reflects the difference in profitability between the two groups but also ensures that adequate resources are expended on encouraging existing customers to remain loyal for as long as possible. In such organizations the direct marketing planning process might therefore resemble the framework provided in Figure 4.2.

As the figure makes clear, a number of the elements of the plan will still be common to both categories of direct marketing activity, but equally a number of the later stages will warrant separate development. Thus, whilst an effective marketing audit and consideration of overall marketing objectives and strategy will be essential to ensure the integration of planned activities, a separate tactical plan for each category of customer would normally be constructed.

In terms of the balance of resources, it makes sense to target the majority of the marketing resource at those customers that will be worth the most to an organization and generate the highest levels of profitability. Typically, therefore, in the case of an established organization, customer retention activity normally accounts for between 70 and 80 per cent of a direct marketing budget, with a much smaller percentage being allocated

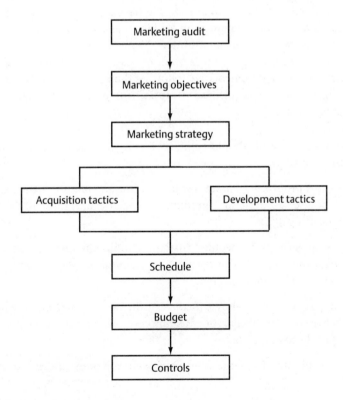

Fig. 4.2 Direct marketing planning process

to the more speculative customer acquisition side of the business. This balance will obviously vary depending on the direct marketing strategy adopted and will clearly, for example, be different in the case of organizations setting themselves aggressive market share targets, as the emphasis in this case would be on building numbers in the database.

This distinction between customer acquisition and customer retention activity, has been used as a structure for this text. In this chapter we will therefore consider how customer acquisition activities might be developed and implemented, and in subsequent chapters we will move on to a separate consideration of customer retention, loyalty, and development.

4.3 Customer acquisition

Every organization needs to consider ongoing customer acquisition. New customers will always be necessary to replace those that for one reason or another will stop doing business with an organization in a given year. Even if the service provided is excellent and levels of satisfaction are high, some customers will still terminate their relationship. In some markets, this may be because they have outgrown the need for the product, their interests have changed, they no longer have the necessary moneys, or they may have died or moved away. Customer acquisition activity is essential to preserve and if necessary enhance the overall number of customers on the database. It can also help inject 'freshness' into a house list, because it is often the case that customers will be at their most profitable in the period immediately following their recruitment (Holder, 1998).

In developing a customer acquisition campaign there are seven stages that should normally be considered.

Objectives—the organization should begin by identifying the objectives that must be achieved by the campaign.

Segmentation and profiling—market research and/or an analysis of the existing database can then be used to develop a profile of the individuals most likely to respond favourably to the campaign.

Targeting—having developed a detailed customer profile, the information can then be used to tailor the nature of the communication that will be received and the channel through which it will be communicated.

Media planning—allied to the above, media can then be selected which will reach the intended audience cost effectively. The integration of the various media to be employed must also be considered at this stage.

Communication of the offer—the offer may then be communicated to prospective customers.

Fulfilment—when the response from customers is received, the organization must then ensure that the order (or request for further information) is processed within the time-frame promised in the original communication.

Response analysis—it would also be usual to conduct a detailed analysis of the response achieved, to determine the efficiency/effectiveness of the activities employed.

The facets of this planning process that are unique to customer recruitment are outlined below. Media planning, the nature of the offer, and order fulfilment are dealt with in later chapters.

4.4 **Setting recruitment objectives**

The first step in developing a customer acquisition programme is to decide on the object-ives the organization wishes to achieve. Objectives are an important part of the plan as they are the only mechanism by which its success can be measured. If a plan achieves its stated objectives one might reasonably conclude that it has been a success. In the absence of objectives, the planner's original intentions and the effectiveness of the activities undertaken can only be speculated upon as there will be no benchmarks to make compar-isons. Valuable resources could be being wasted, but the organization would have no mechanism for identifying that was in fact the case.

Recruitment objectives would normally address issues such as

- the target response rate that will be achieved;
- the number of new customers that will be attracted over a given time period or cam-paign. This is not the same as (a), since it takes into account the conversion rate of new customers. Customers might respond to a press ad requesting a brochure, for example, but would be unlikely to make a purchase in every case;
- the desired Return On Investment (ROI), although it is important to note that many recruitment campaigns are expected to operate at a loss;
- the desired lifetime value of the customers recruited. Organizations with an established database will already know the profile of their high value customers. Newly recruited customers can be compared with this profile to assess their likely future potential. Objectives can therefore be couched in terms of the degree of 'match' obtained;
- the allowable cost per sale.

Recruitment objectives thus fit into the hierarchy of objectives as indicated in Figure 4.3. Whilst senior marketing management will undoubtedly be concerned with issues of prof-itability, volume, and efficiency, as one works down through the tree, these are developed into a number of more specific, perhaps campaign objectives, at the lower levels. The responsibility for the achievement of these latter objectives would normally rest with more junior direct marketing staff.

It is important to realize that the style in which the objectives are written is also a signifi-cant issue. Objectives are only of value if it is possible to use them as an aid to managing

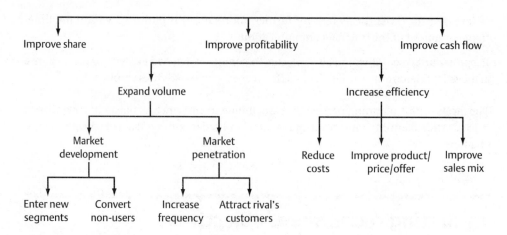

Fig. 4.3 Marketing objectives

the organization's resource and hence vague terms and needless ambiguity should be studiously avoided (MacDonald, 1984, p. 88):

'vague objectives, however emotionally appealing are counter-productive to sensible planning and are usually the result of the human propensity for wishful thinking which often smacks more of cheerleading than serious marketing leadership. What this means is that while it is arguable whether directional terms such as decrease, optimize, minimize, should be used as objectives, it seems logical that unless there is some measure, or yardstick, against which to measure a sense of locomotion towards achieving them, they do not serve any useful purpose.'

Hence, to be managerially useful good objectives should exhibit the following characteristics; they should be:

Specific—related to one particular aspect of marketing activity. Objectives that relate simultaneously to diverse aspects of marketing activity are difficult to assess since they may require the organization to use different techniques of measurement and to look across different planning horizons. Attempting to combine activities might therefore lead to confusion or, at best, a lack of focus.

Measurable—words such as 'maximize' or 'increase' are not particularly helpful, when it later becomes necessary to assess the effectiveness of marketing activity. To be useful objectives should avoid these terms and be capable of measurement. They should hence specify quantifiable values whenever possible, e.g. to achieve a 2 per cent response rate, or to achieve an ROI of 10 per cent.

Achievable—DM objectives should be derived from a thorough analysis of the content of the marketing audit and not creative thinking on the part of managers. Objectives that cannot be achieved will only serve to demoralize those responsible for their success and serve to deplete resources that could have had a greater potential impact elsewhere.

Relevant—direct marketing objectives should be consistent with the objectives of the organization as a whole. They should merely supply a greater level of detail—identifying specifically what the direct marketing function will have to achieve to move the organization in the desired direction.

Timescaled—good objectives should clearly specify the duration over which they are to be achieved. Not only does this help to plan the detail of how they will be accomplished, but it also assists in permitting the organization to set in place control procedures to ensure that the stated targets will be met.

A number of SMART objectives are provided as examples below:

Table 4.1 SMART objectives

Inappropriate objectives	SMART equivalent
To increase sales of product B	To achieve sales of 40,000 units of product B, by the end of February 2002.
To improve our response rates	To achieve a 3 per cent response rate to the January 2001 recruitment mailing
To build awareness	To build spontaneous awareness of the XYZ brand to 72 per cent amongst members of the target group by March 2002

4.5 **Market segmentation**

Having delineated recruitment objectives, the next stage is to determine which potential customers (or prospects) will be targeted. In essence, there are two approaches, the appropriateness of which will be determined by the extent to which an organization has a prior knowledge of its markets. These methods can be categorized as being either *a priori* or cluster based and *post hoc* (Green, 1977). An *a priori* approach is based on the notion that marketers decide in advance of any research which categories of customer they intend to target. Typically, this might involve categorizing customers according to their projected usage pattern (e.g. heavy, medium, or light user), demographic, and/or lifestyle characteristics. The marketer would then carry out research to identify the attractiveness of each segment and make a decision on the basis of the results as to which segment or segments to pursue. *Post hoc* segmentation, however, involves the marketer in carrying out an amount of initial research into the market place. The research might highlight attributes, attitudes, or benefits that relate to particular groups of customers. This information can often be obtained by profiling the individuals on the database that have purchased certain product categories in the past. If a certain type of individual emerges as 'typical', this information can be used to refine the criteria for list selection and other 'similar' individuals can be targeted.

4.5.1 What is market segmentation?

This process of identifying suitable groups of customers to target is known as 'market segmentation'. Kotler (1991, p. 66) defines it as 'the task of breaking the total market (which is typically too large to serve) into segments that share common properties'. In a similar vein, Wilson et al. (1994, p. 91) define it as 'the process of dividing a varied and differing group of buyers or potential buyers into smaller groups within which broadly similar patterns of buyer's needs exist'. Many examples of successful market segmentation abound. In consumer markets, for example, it would hardly be viable to produce a brand of breakfast cereal and expect to be able to market the product to every possible consumer in the market place. Rather, companies prefer to concentrate on targeting a particular sub-market or segment with a particular product and marketing mix. There are, therefore, cereals which appeal to the children's market, cereals which appeal to individuals who might be dieting, cereals which appeal to those who prefer a hot breakfast, and so on. Market segmentation is, therefore, an essential feature of the modern marketing mix as companies' struggle to cope with an increasing diversity of consumer needs and wants. It is for this reason that Wind (1978, p. 317) considers market segmentation as 'one of the most fundamental concepts in marketing'.

The development of the concept of segmentation is attributed to Wendell R. Smith in a paper first published in 1956. Smith (1956, p. 6) suggests that:

'segmentation is based upon developments on the demand side of the market and represents a rational and more precise adjustment of product and marketing effort to consumer or user requirements. In the language of the economist, segmentation is disaggregative in its effects and tends to bring about recognition of several demand schedules where only one was recognized before.'

Segmentation therefore allows the marketer to develop a specific marketing mix to service the needs of particularly attractive groups of customers. The fact that this adaptation has taken place makes it more attractive for these customers to purchase from the organization concerned and enhanced sales amongst members of the target group result.

As was noted earlier, the approach to segmenting a market may be either a *priori*, or *post hoc*. Irrespective of the approach adopted, there are a number of bases for segmentation that can be applied in both consumer and industrial markets. These are considered below.

4.5.2 Bases for segmentation in consumer markets

Wind (1978, p. 317) comments that 'over the years almost all variables have been used as bases for market segmentation'. Fortunately, however, the majority of these variables can be grouped as follows:

- demographic;
- geographic and geo-demographic;
- behavioural;
- psychological/psychographic.

(a) **Demographic variables**

It may be possible to segment a market on the basis of variables such as age, gender, socio-economic group, family size, family lifecycle, income, religion, race, nationality, occupation, or education. Collectively, these are referred to as demographic variables. Demographic segmentation is particularly popular in consumer markets since consumer wants, needs, and preferences are often highly correlated with such variables. The other reason for the popularity of demographic segmentation is a historical one. Such data has been collected over a great many years and hence much is known about the consumer behaviour of each specific group.

It should be noted though, that it is now rare for a company to use one demographic variable in isolation and organizations now tend to use some combination of the same (Stanton, 1978). Despite their popularity they are seen by many as offering only a low utility primarily because they are based on descriptive rather than causal factors and therefore cannot be relied upon as accurate predictors of future behaviour. Despite these reservations their use is still widespread and a number of demographic variables are described below.

(i) Age

Age has frequently been used as the basis for segmentation since purchasing patterns are often related to an individual's age. One interesting reason for this observation may have been revealed by a study carried out by Philips and Sternthal (1977) who concluded that age differences result in changes to the sources of information a particular individual will use. Age was also shown to affect the ability to learn and the susceptibility to social influence.

(ii) Gender

Kotler (1991) notes that an individual's gender has proven to be a good indicator of a propensity to buy a particular product or brand. In particular, he cites cosmetics, clothing, magazines, and toiletries. In these industries, manufacturers employ a variety of different marketing techniques, the exact mix of which will depend on the target gender. There is now considerable evidence that men and women respond differently, for example, to different forms of direct marketing appeal. Specifically, Meyrowitz et al. (1987) identify that the manner in which women respond to information is radically different from men. Among the feminine characteristics that must be accounted for when appealing to the women's market are:

- intuition over reason;
- concern with appearance;
- persuasion rather than aggression;
- the need to nurture;
- quality rather than quantity.

Whilst at first glance this might sound like something of a sexual stereotype, it is in fact common practice for agencies to develop 'male' or 'female' copy depending on the nature of the target market.

(iii) Family life cycle

The concept of a family lifecycle is certainly not new. It was first postulated by Rowntree at the beginning of the last century. However, the model now in most common usage is that developed by Wells and Gubar (1966). It is illustrated in Figure 4.4.

As a composite model (made up of age, number of years married, ages of children, and working status), the concept of the family life cycle has proved to be more useful than simple segmentation based on age alone (Lansing and Kish, 1957). It is, however, not without its critics since it is based on the conventional nuclear family. When one views the current pattern of family life within many countries the model is clearly no longer completely valid. In the UK, for example, it takes no account of the high divorce rate and subsequent increase in one person households and has a somewhat outdated view of women. Women are now able to work a much larger proportion of their lives and are able to continue working even during the early years of their child's development.

Stages in the family life cycle	Buying patterns
1. **Bachelor stage** – young single people living at home.	Few financial commitments – recreation and fashion oriented.
2. **Newly married couples** – young, no children.	High purchase rate of consumer durables – buy white goods, cars, furniture.
3. **Full nest 1** – youngest child under 6.	House buying is at a peak. Liquid assets are low – buy medicines, toys, baby food, white goods.
4. **Full nest 2** – youngest child 6 or over.	Financial position is improving – buy a wider variety of foods, bicycles, pianos.
5. **Full nest 3** – older married couples with dependent children.	Financial position is improving still further. Some children now have jobs and wives are working. Increasing purchase of desirables – buy furniture and luxury goods.
6. **Empty nest 1** – older married couples, no children at home, head of household still in workforce.	Home ownership is at a peak – savings have increased and financial position improved. Interested in travel, recreation and self education. Not interested in new products – buy luxuries and home improvements.
7. **Empty nest 2** – older married couples, no children living at home, head of household retired.	Substantial reduction in income – buy medical products and appliances that aid health, sleep, and digestion.
8. **Solitary survivor** – in the workforce.	Income still high but may sell home.
9. **Solitary survivor** – retired.	Same medical and product needs as group 7. Substantial cut in income. Need for attention and security.

Fig. 4.4 The family life cycle
Source: (Adapted from Wells and Gubar, 1966 and quoted in Wilson et al., 1944).

Despite the criticisms, however, the model is in wide usage and has been proved to be a good indicator of a propensity to buy a wide range of products and services.

(iv) Income/occupation

Income has also been proved to be a useful base for segmentation and despite difficulties in identifying a true picture of income for a particular group (i.e. taking account of the black economy and traditional reluctance to disclose such data) has been shown to be a good indicator of a propensity to purchase certain categories of products (see, e.g. Allt, 1975 or Slocum and Matthews, 1970).

A more common method of segmentation, however, is to be found by combining income and occupation into a single model. Since its conception in the UK, the NRS (National Readership Survey) has classified readers of press/magazines into one of six categories according to social grade. Buyers of magazine/press space may then select media that provide a high concentration of their target audience.This method of segmentation is also widely used by direct marketers. The classification is as shown in Figure 4.5.

It should be noted, however, that the system is almost 50 years old and therefore based on a time when society was considerably more stable than it is at present. As Chisnall (1992) notes, 'originally the grading system was intended to reflect the impact of life-style, income, and status; but society has been in a state of flux for years'. Social strata no longer exist in the way that they once did. Educational opportunities are now spread through all society levels and many wives are now providing a second income for their households. The system also takes no account of an individual's lifestyle, needs, or aspirations.

(b) Geographic segmentation

It has been argued that in terms of historic development, segmentation on the grounds of geography was the first system to develop (see, e.g. Haley, 1968, or Lunn, 1978). Until quite recently transportation systems would have limited the access that some firms may have had to certain geographical markets.They may, therefore, have had to set up their businesses in close proximity to a key concentration of their potential buyers, and would then have set about the task of satisfying the requirements of customers within that geographic area.

However, segmentation on the basis of geography represents a very broad-brush

Social grade	Example occupation
A	senior professional/managerial
B	middle professional/managerial
C1	supervisory management – clerical
C2	skilled manual labour – e.g. electrician
D	unskilled manual – e.g. labourer
E	unemployed, students, etc.

Fig. 4.5 Socio-economic groups

approach to segmentation and can supply little in the way of fine detail, particularly when one is investigating consumer markets. By contrast, geodemographics is an attempt to improve significantly on some of the limitations of the simple geographic model.

(c) Geodemographics

The study of geodemographics arose from work carried out by Webber in 1973. He was interested originally in studying urban deprivation in Liverpool and classifying neighbourhoods using techniques of cluster analysis to produce a system containing 25 separate neighbourhood types. Each exhibited different mixes of problems and required a different type of social policy. Each neighbourhood was also defined in terms of its population, housing, and socio-economic characteristics. With the collaboration of the census office he was later able to extend this analysis and derive 38 separate neighbourhood types with which he was able to classify the UK as a whole.

The next significant development came when the British Market Research Bureau was able to identify that Webber's system had considerable potential for controlling the activities of the TGI (target group index). They were able to identify that certain neighbourhood groups displayed a particular type of purchasing pattern. In short, similar neighbourhoods tended to buy similar types of products. The techniques of geodemographics have recently been refined and a number of commercial systems now exist. These include ACORN, MOSAIC, PINPOINT, and FINPIN.

The common point in all of these systems is their use of census data. In the UK, a detailed census of the population is conducted every ten years. The next is due in 2011. The census consists of a questionnaire sent to every household in the country, which gathers data on over 300 variables. The majority of households receive a standard census document, whilst a small percentage (15 per cent) receive a more detailed document for completion. In a typical census, over 96 per cent of the questionnaires will be completed.

Contrary to what many people believe, census information is not published at an individual level. Census information is available only at the level of the 'enumeration district', which typically contains ten postcodes (see Figure 4.6). For direct marketers this poses something of a problem, because the most useful unit of analysis for marketing purposes is undoubtedly the postcode. Geodemographic systems such as ACORN have, therefore, to match census data from the enumeration district to the relevant bundle of

Postal Unit	Example	Number in UK	Number of Households
Postal area	Reading (R)	121	200,000
Postal district	RG9	2900	8275
Postal sector	RG9 1	9000	2700
Enumeration district	Approx 10 postcodes	148,000	Circa 150
Postcode	RG9 1PD	1.6m	10–15

Fig. 4.6 Census information
Source: Royal Mail.

postcodes. They achieve this match by employing the relevant map references for enumeration districts and postcodes. In practice, this stage is the most common source of error in a geodemographic system because (Fairlie, 1992):

- The boundary for some enumeration districts can cut across a postcode. One postcode could thus include households in two different enumeration districts.
- The map references for postcodes are often imprecise.
- The only map references available outside London for Enumeration Districts (EDs) are those for the centroid of the ED. Since EDs do not have a regular shape, attempts to associate the relevant postcodes could introduce a substantial amount of error.

By this stage in the analysis, each postcode now has a mass of relevant census data associated with it. Geodemographic systems then employ a number of analytical processes that allow them to reduce the high number of census variables, down to a more manageable number that are capable of explaining key differences in consumer behaviour. Typically, some form of factor analysis, or principle components analysis might be employed for this purpose. To develop market segments, a technique such as cluster analysis, will then be utilized to identify groups of postcodes that appear to behave similarly in relation to this reduced number of variables. The aim is to group together postcodes with similar behaviours, whilst ensuring that the difference between these postcode groups is as large as possible.

All the major suppliers of geodemographic information employ slightly different sets of census data and employ differing statistical techniques to derive the final segments that will comprise their system. Typically, this might include information in respect of:

Age	Travel to work	Housing type
Marital status	Unemployment	Socio-economic group
Household composition	Car ownership	
Household size	Housing tenure	
Employment type	Amenities	

In the case of ACORN, the segments depicted in Figure 4.7 are derived from the analysis. Some suppliers of geodemographic systems will enhance the utility of their system, by conducting research with a representative sample of households from each segment. This allows the supplier to overlay information about the detailed purchasing behaviour of each group of customers. An example, drawn from the ACORN system is depicted in Figure 4.8.

The system has had a number of benefits for marketers, notably that when a particular company has some knowledge of its customer base, it may profile it and obtain a geodemographic 'picture' of the typical target segment (or segments) that it is addressing. This information may then be utilized to target other individuals who exhibit similar characteristics, perhaps with direct mail or doordrops. Wastage is minimized and response rates have been shown to be consistently higher than those achieved through the use of lists selected on the basis of geographical location alone.

Recently, there have been moves to create segmentation systems based on so called 'fuzzy geodemographics'. Instead of allocating households to one of a prescribed number

Acorn Groups	1991 % of population
Wealthy achievers, suburban areas	14.0
Affluent grays – rural communities	2.2
Prosperous pensioners, retirement areas	2.8
Affluent executives, family areas	3.4
Well-off workers, family areas	7.0
Affluent urbanites, town and city areas	2.5
Prosperous professionals, metropolitan areas	2.5
Better-off executives, inner city areas	4.0
Comfortable middle ages, mature home-owning areas	13.7
Skilled workers, home-owning areas	10.8
New home-owners, mature communities	9.9
White-collar workers, better-off multi-ethnic areas	4.0
Older people less prosperous areas	4.4
Council estate residents, better-off homes	10.9
Council estate residents, high unemployment	3.6
Council estate residents, great hardship	2.4
People in multi-ethnic areas, low income	2.8

Fig. 4.7 The ACORN classification system
Source: ACORN Information Services – CACI.

of segments on the basis of their response to a combination of census variables, these new systems will be capable of identifying the *key* census variables that drive behaviour in relation to *a given product category*. Using consumer responses to these variables, they will then identify an appropriate number of market segments and allocate postcodes to these segments accordingly. What results is, in essence, a separate geodemographic classification system for every corporate use of the system. Hence, for one manufacturer, the fuzzy system might group postcodes into 20 segments that behave differently in relation to their product. For another manufacturer, in a different sector, it might identify 63 distinct segments of customer behaviour. These new systems will allow direct marketers much more flexibility to relate geodemographic analysis, specifically to their own unique needs.

(d) Behavioural segmentation

Kotler (1991, p. 272) defines behavioural segmentation as dividing buyers 'on the basis of their knowledge, attitude, use, or response to a product'. Behavioural variables are often the best starting point for constructing market segments. There are many bases for segmentation under this general category, among them benefit segmentation, loyalty status, and usage rate (Tynan and Drayton, 1987).

These comfortable, mature neighbourhoods have very low levels of recent home movers. The largely middle-aged population contains very many people who own their homes outright. ACORN Type 26 is found all over Britain, but the highest concentrations are in Norfolk, the Isle of Wight and North Yorkshire. Cleethorpes is a typical town with many areas of this Type.

DEMOGRAPHICS
These neighbourhoods have a mature age profile. There are below average numbers of children, especially 0–4 year olds, and younger adults. The largest age group is the 45–64 year olds, of whom there are 35% more than average. The household structure is characterized by a high proportion of older couples, in the 55+ age group, with no dependent children. The proportion of adults who are married is 23% above average.

Fig. 4.8 Type 26 mature established home owning areas
Source: ACORN Information Services © CACI 2001.

(i) Benefit segmentation

Almost certainly the best known writer concerning benefit segmentation was Haley (1968). His research related to the toothpaste market and he identified four benefit segments: seeking economy, protection, cosmetic, and taste benefits. In Haley's view, the benefits identified in each case are the primary reason for the existence of true market segments. Interestingly, his analysis showed that each benefit group was associated with distinct sets of demographic, behavioural, and psychographic characteristics. For example, the category seeking decay prevention were found to have large families, consequently use large amounts of toothpaste, and were conservative in nature. All this information is clearly invaluable to toothpaste manufacturers who can use it to buy space in media channels which reach the target group cost effectively, and more importantly design promotional straplines (or unique selling propositions) that will appeal to the target group. A single product or brand may indeed be dedicated specifically to the needs of one target segment.

A further example of benefit segmentation was provided by Yankelovich (1964, p. 85) who applied the concept to the market for watches. He found that:

- approximately 23 per cent of buyers bought for the lowest price;
- another 46 per cent bought for durability and general product quality;

- and 32 per cent bought watches as symbols of some important occasion.

The results of his study were used to great effect since most companies at the time were competing for the business generated by the third of these market segments. Since one of the most important occasions in the year is Christmas the majority of competitors were understandably concentrating their advertising efforts at this time and pricing at a slight premium. Their analysis allowed Timex to enter the market with a lower priced watch that they advertised all year round. By so doing the company was able to pick up the business generated by the other two segments. This segmentation strategy led to Timex becoming one of the world leaders in the watch market.

(ii) Brand loyalty status
The second technique encompassed by behavioural segmentation is that of brand loyalty status. A popular typology for considering brand loyalty status is given below.

Hard Core Loyals—consumers who buy one brand all the time. Hence, a buying pattern of AAAAA may be used to represent the consistent purchasing pattern of brand A.

Soft Core Loyals—consumers who buy from a limited set of brands on a regular basis. Their purchasing pattern may be represented by AABABB.

Shifting Loyals—consumers who switch loyalty on a regular basis. Their purchasing pattern may be represented by AABBCC.

Switchers—consumers who show no loyalty to any one brand. This group may be considered especially susceptible to special offers or be attracted by regular variety. Their purchasing pattern may be represented by ABBCACB.

Even when various degrees of loyalty in the marketplace have been identified, however, it is not always a straightforward exercise to take advantage of this information. The utility of this information for recruitment will clearly be related to whether each segment exhibits a unique set of demographic, attitudinal or psychographic variables. Knowledge of these details may lead to the development of a strategy designed to influence traditional patterns of loyalty, specifically targeted at those groups of consumers most likely to respond. Soft-core loyals purchasing competing products may be a particularly worthwhile segment to address.

(iii) Product usage rate
A further popular method for segmenting the market is to utilize data relating to product/ service usage rate. Customers may be classified according to whether they are likely to be heavy, medium, or light users of the product and treated accordingly. This method may be particularly useful since it is often a relatively small percentage of the market that accounts for a large percentage of consumption. The Pareto rule states that 20 per cent of customers will often account for 80 per cent of an organization's turnover. In developing recruitment campaigns, it is therefore sensible to develop a profile of these higher value customers and to use the information to inform the targeting of the recruitment activity undertaken.

(e) **Psychological/psychographic segmentation**

There are a number of bases for segmentation that can be considered under the general heading of psychological/psychographic variables. A number of the most common are described briefly below.

(i) Personality

In attempting to go beyond the simple demographic approaches to segmentation, some researchers have advocated the use of personality as a suitable basis for segmentation. Unfortunately, there is no universally accepted definition of personality (Kassarjian, 1971) and this has historically made the application of such classifications somewhat difficult.

Despite the difficulties, Haire (1950) was among the first writers to moot the possibility of linking consumer behaviour to personality variables. To explore whether consumers perceived that certain products 'fitted' certain personalities he asked a number of respondents to speculate as to the personality of the owners of two anonymous shopping lists. The only difference between the two lists was the choice of coffee. One housewife has selected Nescafé Instant whilst the other had selected a brand of finely ground coffee bean (Maxwell House). The shopper who had listed Nescafé Instant was seen as being lazy and a poor household planner, whilst the buyer of Maxwell House was seen as being thrifty and a good housewife!

A number of other studies have established a correlation between personality variables and consumer buying behaviour, amongst the most notable that carried out by Tucker and Painter (1961). They found significant correlations between personality and the purchase of such products as mouthwash, alcoholic drinks, motor cars, chewing gum, and headache remedies.

Interestingly, however, the marketing literature remains divided over whether personality is an appropriate basis on which to segment a market. Some researchers argue in favour of its applicability, whilst a roughly even number argue against it. This is particularly interesting since studies in the former group often involved identical subject matter, personality tests, and experimental variables, to those in the latter. It may therefore be concluded that segmentation based on purely personality variables has met with mixed success. The only aspect of personality where a broad consensus has been reached appears to be the dimension of personality that relates to risk aversion.

Peter and Ryan (1976) were among the first to identify that the level of perceived risk a consumer experienced had the potential to inhibit a purchase decision. The riskier the decision, the less likely a consumer is to take it. Clearly, when a product or brand has satisfied a need successfully, consumers will experience a degree of risk in switching to another supplier. The greater the satisfaction with an existing supplier, the higher the perceived risk of switching. After all, a new product/brand may not satisfy the need to the same degree as the product/brand already experienced (Cunningham, 1967). Direct marketers targeting users of competing goods/services in a recruitment mailing, for example, must therefore ensure that they lower the perceived risk of switching, and reassure customers that the benefits of switching will outweigh the risks.

Interestingly, First Direct Bank developed a segmentation strategy based originally on seeking out non risk averse people. The reason for their choice of strategy was a simple one. Market research revealed that switching to a bank without branches was regarded by many as a high risk strategy. The Bank therefore decided to target risk takers with a highly focused direct mail campaign aimed at managers/directors in certain high risk industries. Interestingly, they also included in the list of those targeted, individuals known to be indulging in high risk leisure activities such as paragliding, skiing, etc.

(ii) Attitudes

Attitudes have been used as the basis for segmentation by a number of organizations but their use is probably more common in the not-for-profit sector where many marketing campaigns are aimed at changing societal attitudes to certain types of behaviour (e.g. smoking, drinking). To be of value in the for-profit sector one would need to establish a definite link between attitudes and actual purchase behaviour. Such a link has yet to be proved conclusively. Researchers are roughly evenly divided in the debate about whether such a link does in fact exist. See, for example, Crespi (1977) or Howitt and McCabe (1978) and, for an opposing view, either Ajzen and Fishbein (1973) or Pinson and Roberto (1973).

Milne and Gordon (1993) made an interesting use of attitudinal data to examine the targeting of direct mail. They note that the growing perception that direct marketing results in the invasion of consumer privacy has resulted in a series of proposals to limit marketing practices. The authors suggest that the solution to this problem may be for direct marketers to segment their markets based on consumer attitudes towards these direct marketing practices. Their study suggests that there is a substantial heterogeneity across groups of customers. Paying attention to consumers' attitudes toward direct mail can, they argue, reduce the possibility of government intervention in direct mail practices.

(iii) Values

Values and value systems have long been used as the basis for market segmentation (Kahle et al., 1986). One of the most common instruments used to assess individual values is the Rokeach Value Survey (Rokeach, 1973). Rokeach believed that values represent beliefs that certain goals in life (i.e terminal values) and modes of conduct (instrumental values) are preferable to others. These values are prioritized by individuals and used to guide their decision-making processes. Rokeach's original instrument consisted of 18 terminal and 18 instrumental values, each of which had to be separately ranked by respondents. Fortunately, Kahle (1983) suggested a shorter instrument—the so-called List of Values (LOV). This revised instrument was based closely on Maslow's (1954) heirarchy of needs. It consists of the following nine items, used to assess terminal values on nine point important/unimportant scales:

- sense of belonging
- excitement
- warm relationship with others
- self-fulfilment
- being well respected
- fun and enjoyment of life

- security

- self-respect

- sense of accomplishment.

Product offerings and associated communications can clearly be designed to appeal to individuals placing a high degree of emphasis on one or more of these terminal values. Information in respect of consumer values is now widely available and it is relatively easy to target individuals on this basis.

(f) **Psychographic/lifestyle segmentation**

Kotler (1991, p. 171) defines lifestyle as a 'person's pattern of living in the world as expressed in the person's activities, interests and opinions. Lifestyle (as a consequence) portrays the whole individual interacting with his/her environment.' It may therefore be considered as distinct from personality. Personality variables describe the pattern of psychological characteristics that an individual might posses, but say nothing of that individual's hobbies, interests, opinions, or activities. Lifestyle data, however, can supply these missing variables. Indeed, Lazer (1963), who first introduced the term lifestyle into marketing research, viewed it as consisting of three basic components: activities (work, hobbies, social events, entertainment, shopping, sports), interests (family, home job, community, recreation, media, achievments), and opinions (of oneself, social issues, politics, business, education, products, culture): (Plummer, 1974).

Boyd and Levy, 1967; p. 38) assessed the implications of the lifestyle concept and drew the following conclusions:

'Marketing is a process of providing customers with parts of a potential mosaic from which they, as artists of their own lifestyles, can pick and choose to develop the composition that for the time seems the best. The marketer who thinks about his products in this way will seek to understand their potential settings and relationships to other parts of consumer lifestyles and thereby to increase the number of ways they fit meaningfully into the pattern'.

A plethora of lifestyle information is now available commercially. Lifestyle databases differ from geodemographic databases since they collect data at an individual level. Organizations offering this service draw on the results from large consumer surveys, or product registration cards completed by individuals with a willingness to take part. Questionnaires are often very detailed with a typical lifestyle survey containing over 200 questions. To facilitate completion respondents are often lured by the prospect of a prize draw, or a promotional premium that ensures that they derive some direct benefit in exchange for the time necessary to complete the instrument. A number of typical lifestyle products are presented in Figure 4.9.

There are also systems available which effectively merge lifestyle and value data. VALS (Values and Lifestyle Segmentation), for example, explores the relationship between consumer values and their propensity to purchase certain categrories of product/service. Winters (1992) considers that a particular strength of the system is its international dimension. People in twelve different countries have now been categorized and the system can hence be used to inform a global marketing strategy.

Supplier	Product Name	Description	Size
CACI	Lifestyles UK	List and profiling tool, capable of tagging existing databases. Each individual may be selected by 300 different lifestyle attributes.	44 million individuals
NDL	The Lifestyle Selector	Data collected from product registration guarantees. Circa 4 million returned annually.	16 million
Claritas	Lifestyle Selector	Data collected from in-product questionnaires and satisfaction surveys.	12 million
ICD	Facts of Living Survey	Compiled by mailing members of the electoral roll.	8 million
Consumer Surveys Ltd	Lifestyle Focus	Compiled by mailing 14 million households. Typically 200 lifestyle questions posed.	4 million

Fig. 4.9 Lifestyle products

Developed in the US by Arnold Mitchell of the Stanford Research Institute the system categorizes people into one of nine lifestyle groups:

Survivors—who are generally disadvantaged and who tend to be depressed, withdrawn, and despairing.

Sustainers—who are disadvantaged but who are fighting hard to escape poverty.

Belongers—who tend to be conventional, nostalgic, conservative, and generally reluctant to experiment with new products or ideas.

Emulators—who are status conscious, ambitious, and upwardly mobile.

Achievers—who make things happen and enjoy life.

I-Am-Me—who are self engrossed, respond to whims, and are generally young.

Experientials—who want to experience a wide variety of what life can offer.

Socially conscious—people with a marked sense of social responsibility and who want to improve the conditions of society.

Integrateds—who are psychologically fully mature and who combine the best elements of inner and outer directedness.

The designers of VALS believe that individuals can be seen to pass through a number of development phases with the integrated stage being seen as the ultimate. In terms of marketing each segment can be seen to have very different needs and hence products/ services and their associated communications messages could be designed to focus specifically on a particular group of people.

There are many other systems available commercially most of which work on a similar principle although the variables tested in each case are slightly different. It would therefore be advantageous prior to utilizing one of these systems to have carried out some initial market research to identify specifically which lifestyle variables are significant in a given market. Other commercially available systems include Young and Rubicam's 4Cs and Taylor Nelson's Monitor.

4.5.3 **Segmenting business markets**

Many writers claim that it is possible to use the same criteria in industrial markets as the basis for segmentation as one might in consumer markets (see, e.g. Nicosia and Wind, 1977). Cardozo (1983, p. 264), however, suggests that there are a number of other criteria related to the additional complexity of the buying decision which could also be used as the basis for segmentation in this setting. The four dimensions he proposes are as follows:

- familiarity with the buying task and in particular whether it is a new task, modified rebuy or straight rebuy;
- the type of product and the degree of standardization;
- the significance of the purchase to the buying organization;
- the level of uncertainty in the purchase decision.

However, one of the most comprehensive works relating to the segmentation of industrial markets was developed by Bonoma and Shapiro (1983). Their taxonomy of segmentation variables is illustrated in Figure 4.10 on p. 140.

Of course, these criteria are not mutually exclusive and it would be quite usual for an organization to employ a number of these variables as the basis for segmentation in industrial markets. For their part, Bonoma and Shapiro argue that the variables towards the top of the table of are most importance since it is considerably easier to target organizations on the basis of demographic or operating variables, than it is by many of the other criteria listed.

4.5.4 **Criteria for evaluating the viability of market segments**

Having identified a number of suitable bases for market segmentation, an organization will then wish to appraise the suitability of each potential segment for its viability. In practice, segments should be evaluated against six criteria to assess their suitability for targeting. Only if a segment appears to perform well against each of the criteria listed below, should a separate marketing mix be developed to address it. Each segment should be:

Measurable—the market should be easily measurable and information should therefore either exist or be obtainable cost effectively about the segment and its characteristics.

Accessible—it should be possible to access the segment cost effectively. If, for example, appropriate channels of distribution do not exist, or it proves impossible to identify

Demographic

Industry type – which industries that buy the product should we focus on?
Company size – what size companies should we focus on?
Location – what geographical areas should we focus on?

Operating Variables

Technology – what customer technologies should we focus on?
User status (i.e. heavy, medium, light) – which type of user should be concentrated on?
Customer capabilities – should customers having many or few needs be concentrated on?

Purchasing Approaches

Buying criteria – should customers be targeted that are looking for price, quality, or service, etc.?
Buying policies – should customers requiring leasing facilities, for example, be targeted?
Current relationships – should the company focus only on those customers with whom a
   relationship already exists?

Situational Factors

Urgency – should customers requiring immediate delivery be targeted?
Size of order – should customers requiring large or small orders be targeted?
Applications – should customers requiring only a certain application of the product be targeted?

Personal Characteristics

Loyalty – should only companies exhibiting high degrees of loyalty to their suppliers be targeted?
Attitudes to risk – should risk taking or risk avoiding customers be targeted?
Buyer-seller similarity – should companies with similar characteristics to the seller be targeted?

Fig. 4.10 Criteria for segmentation of industrial markets

communications media capable of reaching the market without a high degree of wastage, attempts to access a segment could be costly and potentially unprofitable.

Substantial—it should be cost effective to market to the segment. Clearly, the segment should be large enough in terms of sales volume (or small, but with sufficiently high margins) to warrant separate exploitation.

Stable—the segment's behaviour should be relatively stable over time to ensure that its future development may be predicted with a high degree of accuracy for planning purposes.

Appropriate—it should be appropriate to exploit a particular segment given the organization's mission, resources, objectives, etc.

Unique—the segment should be unique in terms of its response (to marketing activity) so that it can be distinguished from other segments.

This final point warrants a little elaboration. There are occasions when two segments might differ greatly in terms, for example, of their demographic characteristics, but behave identically in terms of their response to marketing activity. In such circumstances it may make conceptual sense to distinguish between the two segments, but managerially it is not useful to do so. Thus, for example, a computer manufacturer may identify two segments of potential customers for its introductory, bottom of the range PCs. One segment might consist of young males/females purchasing a home computer for the first time to access the internet, run computer games, and manage their household finances. A second segment might consist of older, perhaps elderly, males wishing to use the internet for communication, home shopping, and information. Whilst these are two distinct demographic segments, it will only make sense for the computer manufacturer to develop a separate PC package and promotional approach if the two segments are likely to respond differently. If their response is likely to be similar, it would be preferable to consider these two segments as one group, perhaps 'PC Beginners' and treat them identically. This would save money on product development, print costs, advertising, etc. A separate marketing mix should, therefore, only be considered for a segment if its response to marketing activity is likely to differ from others.

4.6 **Customer profiling**

If an organization is entering a new market for the first time, two approaches to segmentation can be adopted. The organization may elect to select target groups on the basis of what managers feel to be appropriate, using many of the categories of variable alluded to above. Alternatively, it could also decide on some preliminary market research, an analysis of which might delineate a number of potentially attractive segments that could conceivably be targeted.

Where an organization already has considerable experience or a market, however, a third approach can be adopted. Even the most rudimentary of customer databases will often hold information in respect of customer contact details, some demographic information, a record of the communications customers have received, and some kind of purchase history. Where such information is forthcoming, an organization can develop a detailed profile of its customers and use this to inform customer acquisition activity.

At a simple level, the organization could profile the whole of its customer database. It could, for example, extract all its customers' postcodes and engage the services of a supplier of a system such as ACORN to determine whether one or more of the 38 categories predominates. If this proves to be the case, it would then be possible to buy lists of other consumers who might match these characteristics or to purchase other DM media to effectively target them in a recruitment campaign.

A more sophisticated approach would involve an organization profiling specific segments of its database. As an example, consider the database depicted in Figure 4.11. In this case customers on the database have been segmented by their value to the organization. As one would expect, there are fewer high value customers than low value

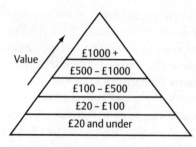

Fig. 4.11 Value segments

customers, hence the database has been depicted as a pyramid. Rather than using the profile of the whole database for recruitment purposes, an organization could elect to focus purely on the profile of its high value customers. Thus, recruitment campaigns could be targeted specifically at customers who match this profile, with the attraction of potentially high value new customers likely to result.

Many commercial databases now contain the necessary software tools to permit this form of analysis in house. Even where this is not possible, however, it is usually possible to have an amount of profiling done externally, perhaps by a supplier of a geodemographic of lifestyle database. Despite the initial expense of profiling activity, it can very quickly earn a respectable return on its investment, since the targeting of recruitment activity can be greatly honed. The RNID (Royal National Institute for the Deaf), for example, recently increased the response rate to its recruitment activity by over 50 per cent by recognizing that its existing supporters appeared to have a number of distinct lifestyle characteristics.

4.7 **Targeting key prospects**

Throughout this chapter we have made numerous references to the use of cold lists for recruitment purposes. Whilst these do typically represent a common source of new customers, they are by no means the only source that may be employed. Indeed, there are a number of sources of potential new customers. These are illustrated in Figure 4.12.

This diagram has also been arranged as a pyramid to reflect both the number of prospects likely to be generated and the likely response rates that will be achieved by an approach. The most high quality prospects any organization can hope to generate are those supplied by its own satisfied customers. So called, Member Get Member (MGM) schemes have become increasingly popular in recent times. In essence, current customers are invited to introduce a friend or acquaintance to a company in return for a small gift or premium. When the newly introduced customer makes their first purchase, the premium is shipped. Such schemes have a high conversion rate, since those newly introduced individuals are often expecting to receive their first mailing and have been recommended because they already possess an interest in the products/services available.

At the next level down are an organization's former customers. Companies often

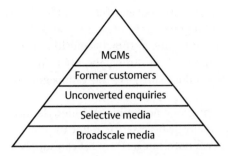

Fig. 4.12 Sources of new customers

neglect this group, feeling that perhaps they are no longer interested in the products/ services available. Whilst this may be true, organizations will still achieve a higher response rate from the members of this group than they will by targeting any of the remaining three groups in the pyramid. This is simply because an interest in the product category clearly exists. The problem lies in incentivizing former customers to make a further purchase and an organization may wish to test a combination of different offers and creatives, to identify the campaign with the greatest reactivation potential.

Unconverted Enquiries are also a good source of new customers. Again, such individuals must have had an interest in the broad product category available, but were unwilling or unable to make a purchase at the time the original enquiry was made. The enquirers' circumstances may change over time and a timely reminder may well pay dividends.

The remaining categories of selective and broadscale media are also available for recruitment purposes. Dell Computers, for example, could elect to advertise in either the selective media—e.g. *Personal Computer World*, or the broadscale media, e.g the *Daily Mail*. The response to an advert in the former is likely to be much stronger since all the readers of *Personal Computer World* have, by definition, an interest in personal computing. The same cannot be said of the readers of the *Daily Mail* and the relative levels of response will reflect this.

In attempting to meet recruitment objectives it would always be advisable to consider working down through the pyramid, progressing through each level, until such time as the recruitment objectives are met. Bearing in mind the likely response rates that will be obtained, it would be folly to progress immediately to broadscale media, without first exhausting the possibility to reactivate former customers or generate sales from unconverted enquiries.

4.8 List selection and management

Commercial lists are purchased for the purpose of customer recruitment. At the time of writing there are estimated to be over 4,000 such lists in existence in the UK alone. Navigating the range of alternatives can therefore be somewhat problematic, unless an organization has considerable past experience on which to draw. For this reason, many organizations engage the services of a highly specialized list broker, who can offer advice on the best lists to meet a specific set of recruitment requirements.

Targeting is the singularly most important concern in any customer acquisition campaign. No matter how strong the creative—no matter how strong the offer—if it is received by individuals with no interest in the product category, the campaign will undoubtedly fail.

Consumer lists fall broadly into the categories of geodemographic and lifestyle (discussed earlier) and an amount of profiling will normally be necessary to refine the criteria that are eventually used for list selection. Suppliers of both categories of list can supply a high level of detail and organizations failing to profile their customers in sufficient detail could miss opportunities to refine their targeting, wasting valuable marketing resource as a consequence.

Typically, 1,000 names and addresses may be purchased from a commercial list for between £80 and £150, a much lower cost than many people believe. In practice, the exact costs will be determined by:

- the level of detail that is to be employed in prospect selection (i.e some suppliers will charge less for a list of single males than they will for a list of single males owning their own homes, with a disposable income in excess of £30,000, and with an interest in rugby. In this latter example, it may take a supplier much longer to extract the required individuals from their system and costs will vary accordingly.

- whether it is intended to purchase the list or merely rent it. Most suppliers offer organizations a choice and lists can be purchased outright, or rented for a specified number of uses. Dummy addresses are often inserted to ensure that the list is used only on the number of occasions originally specified.

- whether the list can be bought 'off the shelf'. Organizations can elect either to employ an existing list, or to pay to have one constructed specifically to meet their requirements. This would be more normal in industrial markets where a very specific set of criteria may need to be met. This is an expensive option—due to the time required to conduct the necessary research, charges may reach as high as £30 per name.

Given the plethora of available lists, it is always essential to evaluate the alternatives available. A number of the criteria that can be employed to assess lists for their suitability are given below. They include:

- the level of detail that can be supplied. Lists vary considerably in terms of the sophistication they can offer marketers for targeting purposes.

- the level and nature of previous usage. It is important to clarify the extent to which prior use has been made of the list and, in particular, whether competitors have already employed the list to market their own goods and services. Lists can become 'tired' very quickly and assessing the extent to which they have been previously employed can therefore be a very significant issue.

- past results. Suppliers can often give an indication of the response rates achieved by previous clients. Accepting that these might tend to fall as the list ages, such information can nevertheless prove invaluable in assessing the desirability of using a particular list.

- rollout potential. Those lists which can deliver large quantities of names are preferable to those which will be quickly exhausted as a source of new recruits.

There are also a number of tests that can be conducted in house. Whilst most suppliers have a minimum order quantity, it should always be possible to obtain a small sample of the members of a list and to test response rates with a test mailing. Subsequent analysis of the response should allow an organization to predict with a high degree of accuracy the response it will achieve when the whole list is eventually mailed. If two competing lists are being evaluated, the pattern of response can be compared and the most appropriate option pursued.

4.9 **Managing the acquisition process**

Having identified the individuals it is intended to target, the recruitment campaign can then be instigated. As was noted above, the beauty of direct marketing is that opportunities for testing abound. It is usually possible to test the most critical dimensions of a campaign prior to launch and relax confident in the knowledge that a particular pattern of performance will be attained. This is certainly the case if the medium of direct mail is selected, since one can test the list, the creative, the offer, etc. If other media such as magazines, inserts, DRTV are to be employed, testing becomes a little more problematic, but certainly not impossible (see Chapter 12).

When testing is complete and the campaign is initiated, it is essential that the response is handled as efficiently and effectively as possible. Testing will have suggested the likely response rates that will be achieved and the organization can use this information to plan fulfilment resources accordingly. In many consumer markets, manufacturers will elect to outsource the fulfilment aspect of the campaign to ensure that an adequate level of service is provided. Fulfilment is a highly specialized operation and it will often be more economic for a manufacturer to rely on an external supplier than to have resources of their own standing idle between direct marketing campaigns.

4.10 **Key performance measures**

The final step in a recruitment campaign is perhaps the most critical. A detailed assessment of campaign performance can be invaluable in guiding future direct marketing strategy and tactics. Performance can be compared against the objectives that were originally set for the campaign and against other campaigns that have been run in the past. The profile of responding customers can also be compared with the profile that was originally envisaged and any refinements necessary can be made to the targeting of future campaigns.

The most common financial criteria that are employed to assess recruitment campaigns are given below:

Percentage response—the response rate received to the original communication.

Cost per response—total cost of campaign divided by the number of respondents.

Percentage conversion—if the purpose of the original communication was merely to solicit enquiries, it will also be necessary to examine the percentage of enquirers that were ultimately converted to a sale.

Cost per customer—total cost of campaign divided by number of customers recruited.

£ Revenue per customer—total value of sales divided by the number of customers attracted.

£ Profit per customer—total profit divided by the number of customers attracted.

£ Lifetime value per customer—mean projected lifetime value for each customer recruited by a given mailing.

Percentage return on investment—either calculated as an immediate return (i.e. an ROI for the recruitment campaign itself)—or a projected return given the forecast lifetime value of customers recruited.

4.11 Summary

In this chapter we have drawn a critical distinction between customer acquisition and customer development activities. In respect of the former a planning process was delineated, including the derivation of objectives, segmentation and profiling, targeting, media planning, communication of the offer, fulfilment, and response analysis. It is important to realize that this process does not occur in isolation and that in many ways it would be better regarded as a loop. Information about the performance of one recruitment campaign can be used to inform the development of those run subsequently and modifications to strategy can often result. In the next chapter we will use a similar framework to consider the application of marketing principles to the question of customer development and retention.

Discussion questions

1   Why is it important to draw a distinction between customer acquisition and customer development activities?

2   How might a catalogue company selling items of clothing segment the market for its products?

3 What are the advantages of using lifestyle variables as the basis for segmentation over traditional consumer demographics?

4 You work as a marketing communications executive with the magazine *PC World*. Your organization intends to achieve a 10 per cent increase in subscribers over the coming year. Develop a customer acquisition campaign to achieve this objective.

5 You are the marketing manager working with Virgin Financial Services, a direct selling financial services company. You are in the process of developing a new DRTV campaign designed to generate quality response and reinforce the brand. Summarize to your managing director how you would propose to measure and evaluate the campaign.

Further reading

Ajzen I. and Fishbein M. (1973) 'Attitudinal and Normative Variables As Predictors Of Specific Behaviour', *Journal of Personality and Social Psychology*, 27(1), 41–57.

Allt B. (1975) 'Money Or Class: New Light On Household Spending' *Advertising Quarterly*, 44, Summer, 6–9.

Bonoma T. V., and Shapiro B. P. (1983) *Segmenting The Industrial Market* (Lexington, MA: Lexington Books).

Boyd H. W. and Levy, S. J. (1967) *Promotion: A Behavioural View* (Englewood Cliffs, NJ: Prentice Hall).

CACI 'Acorn Information Systems', CACI Publicity Material 1993.

Cardozo R. N., (1980) 'Situational Segmentation Of Industrial Markets', *European Journal of Marketing*, 14, No. 5/6, 264–76.

Chisnall P. (1992) *Marketing Research* (London: McGraw Hill).

Crespi I. (1977) 'Attitude Measurement, Theory and Prediction', *Public Opinion Quarterly*, 41(3), 285–94.

Cunningham S.M. (1967) 'Perceived Risk and Brand Loyalty', in *Risk Taking and Information Handling in Consumer Behaviour*, (ed.) Cox D. F. Boston, MA: Harvard University Press, 522.

Fairlie R. (1992), 'Making The Most of Geodemographic and Psychographic Profiles', in *Practitioners Guide To Direct Marketing* (Teddington: IDM).

Green P. E. (1977) 'A New Approach To Market Segmentation', *Business Horizons* 20(1), 61–73.

Haire, M. (1950) 'Projective Techniques In Marketing Research', *Journal of Marketing* 14(5), 649–56.

Haley R. (1968) 'Benefit Segmentation: A Decision Oriented Research Tool', *Journal of Marketing*, 32(3), 30–5.

Holder D. (1998) *The Absolute Essentials*, Course Notes (Teddington: IDM).

Howitt D. and McCabe J. (1978) 'Attitudes Do Predict Behaviour—In Mails At Least', *British Journal of Social and Clinical Psychology*, 17(3), 285–6.

Kahle L. R. (1983) (ed.), *Social Values and Social Change: Adaptation to Life in America* (New York: Praeger).

Kahle L. R., Beatty S. E., and Holmer P. (1986) 'Alternative Measurement Approaches To Consumer Values: The list of Values (LOV) and Values and Life Style (VALS), *Journal of Consumer Research*, 13 (Dec.), 405–9.

Kamakura W. A., and Novak T. P. (1992) 'Value System Segmentation: Exploring The Meaning Of LOV', *Journal of Consumer Research*, 19(1), June, 119–32.

Kassarjian H. H. (1971) 'Personality and Consumer Behaviour' *Journal of Marketing Research*, 13(4), 409–18.

Kotler P. (1991) *Marketing Management* (Englewood Cliffs, NJ: Prentice Hall).

Lansing J. B. and Kish L. (1957) 'Family Life Cycle As An Independent Variable', *American Sociological Review*, 22(5), 512–19.

Lazer W. (1963) 'Lifestyle Concepts and Marketing', in *Toward Scientific Marketing*, Greyser S. (ed.) (Chicago, IL: AMA), 130.

Lunn T. (1978) 'Segmenting and Constructing Markets', in *Consumer Market Research Handbook* (2nd edn), (eds) Worcester, R. M. and Downham J. (London: Van Nostrand Reinhold (UK)), 343–76.

Maslow A. (1954) *Motivation and Personality* (New York: Harper Press).

MacDonald M. H. B. (1984) *Marketing Plans: How To Prepare Them, How To Use Them* (London: Heinemann).

Meyrowitz J., Ogilvy J., Settle R. B and Alreck P. L. (1987) 'The Female Mindset', *Marketing Communications* 12(9), 17–30.

Milne G. R. and Gordon M. E. (1993) 'Direct Mail Privacy Efficiency Trade-offs Within an Implied Social Contract Framework', *Journal of Public Policy and Marketing*, 12 (Fall), 206–15.

Nicosia F. and Wind, Y. (1977) 'Behavioural Models Of Organizational Buying Processes', in *Behavioural Models OF Market Analysis: Foundations For Marketing Action* (eds) Nicosia, F. and Wind, Y. (Hinsdale, IL: Dryden Press), 96–120.

Peter J. P. and Ryan M. J. (1976) 'An Investigation Of Perceived Risk At The Brand Level', *Journal of Marketing Research* 13(2), 184–8.

Philips L. W. and Sternthal B. (1977) 'Age differences in Information Processing: A Perspective On The Aged Consumer', *Journal of Marketing Research*, 14(4), 444–57.

Pinson C. and Roberto E. L. (1973) 'Do Attitude Changes Precede Behaviour Changes?' *Journal of Advertising Research*, 13(4), 33–8.

Plummer J. T. (1974) 'The Concept of Lifestyle Segmentation', *Journal of Marketing*, 38 (Jan), 33–7.

Rokeach M. (1973) *The Nature Of Human Values* (New York: Free Press).

Slocum J. W. and Matthews H. L. (1970) 'Social Class And Income As Indicators Of Consumer Credit Behaviour', *Journal Of Marketing*, 34(2), 69–74.

Smith W. R. (1956) 'Product Differentiation and Market Segmentation As Alternative Marketing Strategies', *Journal Of Marketing*, 21(3), 3–8.

Stanton W. J. (1978) *Fundamentals of Marketing* (5th edn.) (New York: McGraw Hill).

Tucker W. T. and Painter W. J. (1961) 'Personality and Product Use', *Journal Of Applied Psychology* 45(5), 325–9.

Tynan A. C. and Drayton J. (1987) 'Market Segmentation', *Journal Of Marketing Management* 2(3), 301–35.

Wells W. D. and Gubar G. (1966), 'Life Cycle Concept In Marketing Research', *Journal of Marketing Research* 3(4), 355–63.

Wilson R. M. S., Gilligan C. and Pearson D. J. (1994) *Strategic Marketing Management* (Oxford: Butterworth Heinemann).

Wind Y. (1978) 'Issues and advances in Segmentation Research', *Journal of Marketing Research* 15(3), 315–37.

Winters L. C. (1992) 'International Psychographics' *Marketing Research: A Magazine of Management and Applications*, 4(3) Sept, 49–59.

Yankelovich D. (1964) 'New Criteria For Market Segmentation', *Harvard Business Review* 42(2), 83–90.

Chapter 5

Building a Customer Database

Contents

5.1 **Objectives**

By the end of this chapter you should be able to:

(a) understand what a database is;

(b) describe the different types of database;

(c) identify appropriate information to hold on a database;

(d) describe the procedures necessary to maintain a database;

(e) describe how data mining can be used to inform marketing decisions;

(f) describe the legal framework which controls direct marketing activity.

5.2 **Introduction**

In Chapter 1 we illustrated how direct marketers use data for the purposes of improving the quality of customer interaction and refining the targeting of marketing activity to ensure a more timely and accurate delivery of communications. At that stage we noted that the information stored on a customer database is central to this process and guides how an organization strives to achieve these lofty goals. We said little, however, about the nature of a database, what information might be stored therein, or how that information might be managed over time. In this chapter it is our intention to correct that deficiency.

We intend to begin with an analysis of what a database actually is, the various types of database and what they look like in terms of content. We will then move on to examine the nature of the information that should be stored on a database and the potential sources of such information. A number of aspects of database management will then be considered, including the use of data mining tools and, in the case of larger databases, the utility offered by a data warehouse. The chapter will then conclude with a review of the legal framework in which direct marketers must operate and a summary of data protection principles in both the EU and beyond.

5.3 **What is a database?**

Ask any group of business people this question and probably pretty much everyone will claim to know what you're talking about. Unfortunately, the definitions you receive are likely to be confused and conflicting. This is simply because the term *database* can be used to mean many different things, depending on who you are talking to and what you are trying to accomplish.

The broadest definition of a database would be the sum total of all the information that an organization keeps. It could thus comprise information stored in various computers, files, tapes, and even handwritten data such as letters and memos. Although this can be a very powerful conceptualization it is certainly a lot broader than that which the majority of managers might employ. A more limited definition is offered by Mattison (1997, p. 19):

> A database is a collection of data, organized logically and managed by a unifying set of principles, procedures and functionalities, that helps guarantee the consistent application and interpretation of that data across the organization.

Courtheux (1992) narrows this definition still further in his now classic definition of a marketing database.

> A marketing database is a comprehensive collection of interrelated data serving multiple applications, allowing timely and accurate on-demand retrieval of relevant data, and having a data management system independent of applications.

Courtheux thus makes it clear that a database can draw on a variety of different data allowing the user instant access without interfering with any other applications that might be running within an organization's computer system (e.g. inventory control, account processing, etc). It would clearly be inappropriate for a database to tie up (or slow down) these important applications when users submit queries of their data.

Whilst Courtheux's definition is now widely cited, it could perhaps be criticized for not making clear what a database can be used for. Whilst it outlines in detail the characteristics, the reader is left with little idea of how these characteristics might benefit a business organization. Kotler (1994) corrects this deficiency:

> A marketing database is an organized collection of comprehensive data about individual customers, prospects or suspects that is current, accessible and actionable for such marketing purposes as lead generation, lead qualification, sale of a product or service, or maintenance of customer relationships.

5.4 A simple database

A marketing database consists ostensibly of two elements. A collection of customer data and a software programme designed to manage this data. Each of these aspects will now be considered in turn.

5.4.1 **Storing customer data**

At a minimum, a database consists of a series of building blocks or files. A file is essentially a set of information about a specific set of items, people, or events. Each file is constructed according to a specific set of rules. Unlike other files, a database file must usually be arranged in rows and columns. It thus appears very similar to a spreadsheet. A sample database file is provided in Figure 5.1.

In this very simple example we have provided a snapshot of part of a customer database taken from a credit card company. The database contains the name and address of card-holders, their contact telephone number, the credit limit arranged on their card, and details of their outstanding balance. The database also assigns each customer a URN or Unique Reference Number which as we shall see later assists in the efficient management of customer data.

As the example illustrates, every row of the database contains the details in respect of one individual customer. For this reason each row is therefore referred to as a 'record'.

Each of the columns in the database are known as fields. Database marketers would thus refer to the *name field*, not the name column. There are four fields for address data, although the system may permit the operator to omit a second line to the address if none exists (e.g. as in the case of Mr Cobbles). What can be entered in each field is usually strictly controlled. It would therefore not be unusual for the system to limit entries in the credit field to numerical digits only. More sophisticated applications can also be trained to recognize valid entries, so that invalid codes, for example, would be rejected. The aim here is to minimize the potential for operator error as new data is added to the file.

The following details are usually specified for each field:

Field name—each field must be given a name. Usually, each Database Management System (DBMS) will strictly control what are considered to be valid names. Each field name could thus be restricted to ten characters, with only the characters A-Z allowed in the name. By convention, it would be normal to use names that reflect the items—thus the field name for a telephone number might be PHONE.

Field type—users often want to treat different categories of data in different ways. For this reason database systems require users to specify the type of each field. A number of the more common types are depicted in Figure 5.2.

Name	Address Line (1)	Address Line (2)	City	Postcode	Tel	Credit
Mr D. Thomas	14 Belle Vue Drive	Hooe	Plymouth	PL9 9XP		
Mrs C. Jones	17 Western Terrace	Hilston	Warminster	WA3 4FT		
Miss A. Jones	23 Church Street	Bletchley	London	SW14 1DT		
Mr F. Cobbles	19 Seaview		Cookham	SL6 9TY		

Fig. 5.1 Sample database file

Field Type	Comments
Alphanumeric	Contains textual data. Allowable characters would include the majority of those found on keyboards
Numeric: integer decimal	Integer values do not contain decimal points whereas decimal values do. Many DMBSs do not distinguish between these two types. Allowable characters in the latter case are usually the ten digits, a decimal point and plus or minus signs
Date	Usually in a form such as MM/DD/YY
Logical or Boolean	Limited to values of true and false

Fig. 5.2 Field types

Figure 5.3 shows the detail of the fields for our Customer file. It should be noted that our field names have been selected to reflect the nature of the items and that field lengths have been selected so as to be large enough to accommodate the largest expected values. We have selected the fields *Credit* and *Balance* as numeric types because it is very likely that database users will wish to perform calculations on these items. Whilst phone numbers are also numeric in nature, by convention it would be normal to specify these fields as character, since they will never need to be manipulated for the purposes of calculation.

It should be noted that the terminology employed by a given database application will vary, but this very simple model is a useful starting point in beginning our exploration of what a database is and how it can be used to inform direct marketing practice.

Data Item	Field Name	Type	Length
Customer name	Name	C	25
Address	Street	C	25
	District	C	15
	City	C	15
	Postcode	C	8
Telephone number	Phone	C	13
Credit limit	Credit	N	8,2*
Outstanding balance	Balance	N	8,2*

*The first digit specifies the total field length and the second the number of decimal places permitted. (Adapted from Litton 1987)

Fig. 5.3 Details of fields

5.4.2 **Database software**

Since the late 1960s when commercial databases began to appear for the first time a plethora of database software products have appeared in the market. For our purposes a database product is:

> a computer software product (a program or collection of programs) that manages the storage and retrieval of a set of data, organizes it logically and provides the user with certain functionalities to guarantee that the data will be organized logically and applied consistently.

A typical database product should:

- allow users to build new databases and to specify their schema (or structure of the data they will contain). To achieve this a specialized programming language known as a data-definition language is often employed.

- allow the user to ask questions of, or 'query', the stored data. Users should also be able to modify the data as required, perhaps adding new information, or correcting existing information that is now out of date.

- facilitate the storage of very large amounts of data. Often large organizations have tera-bytes of data that they need to store for future use.[1] The DMBS must facilitate this and keep the data secure from unauthorized access, tampering or environmental problems such as long-term power failures.

- control access to the data from multiple users without allowing the actions of one user to affect others and without allowing multiple access to corrupt the stored information.

In practice, modern database software now provides managers with a range of additional and very practical benefits:

- Users should be able to generate selections of customers to be contacted. In our example quoted above, customers who have used only 10 per cent of their available credit might be targeted with a mailing designed to persuade them to transfer the credit balance from other cards they might hold. There would clearly be little point in sending such a communication to those who have already exhausted their available credit, but it would make sense in the case of those customers whose balances are currently low. Marketing databases should be able to generate a specific list of customers to be contacted.

- The database software should be flexible enough to liaise with other systems. Thus, in our example, it should be possible to feed the names and addresses of the customers to a printer that would then generate address labels for the mailing. Alternatively, it should be possible to merge the addresses directly into the text of the covering letter, thus personalizing the content.

---

[1] A terabyte is equivalent to 1000 gigabytes or 10^{12} bytes of data.

- Database software should also be capable of performing basic forms of analysis. Functions such as an ability to be able to calculate the response rate to each campaign, the average order value and the total value of each customer are now commonly found in marketing software.

- Allied to above, most database applications allow the user to print one of a number of standard reports. Thus reports might be generated which compare the performance of one campaign with another, one media with another, or one segment of customers with another. This can provide valuable information for future marketing planning, although the generation of reports for their own sake should be studiously avoided.

5.5 Categories of database

There are many different ways in which we can classify a database, the three most common being the platform on which they are designed to run, the functions they are designed to perform, or by their underlying architecture. In respect of the former, there are several products currently on the market, each designed to run on a different platform. There are PC-based products such as dBase, Access, and Paradxo. There are also client server systems such as Oracle and Sybase and minicomputer databases such as RDB and SQL400. In the case of organizations requiring a much greater storage capacity there are also mainframe database management systems such as DB2 and IDMS.

5.5.1 Database functions

In a typical business context there are five types of database that will normally be encountered:

Master customer file—this database stores essential customer information such as the name, address, and purchase history of a given individual or organization. In the past this could well have been a stand-alone database—in effect a repository for the most basic of information. In the modern era where firms have striven to integrate various systems it is unlikely to be stand-alone and is much more likely to be found integrated within another company database. In the case of organizations serving customers on a regular basis it will probably be found in the operational database or customer database.

Operational database—this database is concerned with the management of service transactions containing data such as order, shipping, and accounting records. It is likely to be widely accessed by individuals throughout the firm and is particularly essential to the management of the fulfilment and billing functions, since it often provides real-time information in respect of the state of a customer's order and account. The operational database usually contains details of all the transactions a customer might have with an organization independent of specific product categories.

Customer database—the customer database is often built from the operational database.

It contains a detailed profile of each individual customer and the transactions recorded from the operational database are carefully merged, cleaned and de-duped (see below) to ensure a high degree of accuracy. The customer database will also contain data in respect of the policies the organization adopts in dealing with each customer and in the case of a business to business database, the detail of any relationships that might exist between various company personnel and those working for the customer. It may also be a source of data in respect of a customer inventory in those cases where delivery and shipment are programmed to arrive *Just-In-Time* for manufacture.

Marketing database—The marketing database will also contain a detailed profile of each customer, but it may here be supplemented by SIC codes, or in the case of consumer databases with other pertinent variables such as geodemographic or lifestyle data. It will also contain details of each customer's response to promotional activity, lifetime value and indeed any additional data that might be necessary to manage a customer relationship over time. Aside from this additional marketing data, a marketing database differs from the operational database in the sense that not every piece of operational data will be helpful for marketing decisions. There is little point in storing information for its own sake and before designing their database marketers therefore need to ask the question 'what do I need this database to do?' The answer should guide the creation of relevant fields.

Data warehouse—While it is listed here as a separate category, a data warehouse is likely to be an amalgam of those listed above. It is built for the purpose of analysis or as a central resource that other applications might share. It could be a batch warehouse (i.e. constructed for a specific purpose) or an on-line warehouse designed to provide support for a range of on-line activities.

5.5.2 Database architecture

The term 'database architecture' is a simple way of saying 'how the database will be built'. In a sense, 'architecture' has a very similar meaning in this context to its more common application in the realm of construction. Anyone familiar with the architecture of the Renaissance period will appreciate that the architecture then differed quite considerably from that employed by the city planners of the 1960s! Yet despite this great disparity the two forms of architecture share some fundamental characteristics, it is only the manner in which these are implemented in terms of style, craftsmanship, and materials that differs. Instead of architectures such as Renaissance, database developers refer to flat-file, xBase, hierarchical, sequential, network, relational, star schema, OLAP, and object oriented. These describe the operational and logical organization that will be assumed in the execution of tasks. Fortunately, the majority of these, whilst of historical interest, have been superseded by the pace of technological change. The two architectures to be found most commonly in use today are sequential files and relational. We will examine both in turn.

(a) **Sequential files**

In the example we cited earlier of a credit card company's database the computer data has been stored in files. For customer data to be accessed and reported on it must be stored in a very specific format along the lines depicted in Figure 5.2. Each customer record must be created and data entered according to these particular specifications. A customer file is made up of a number of these individual records. If we wanted to find an individual customer in the file, it would seem sensible to search the NAME field for the individual we were interested in. Alternatively, if the URN were known we could simply search the URN field and identify the customer that way. You can probably imagine, however, that when a database starts to grow in size (in some cases to several million names), the speed with which the computer could complete this task decreases quite substantially.

Despite this drawback, many customer databases still work on the same basic principles. Various fields are selected as the basis on which a search might take place and the computer will grind through the file until it finds the actual individual sought. Companies tend not to rely just on any one criterion for a search to take place. Thus, if you call your gas company to raise a query about your account, not being able to remember your account number is not the end of the world. The company will probably be able to search by surname and/or postcode to pull up the details of your account.

Sequential file databases have the merit of being relatively low cost, particularly in terms of their initial development, and the technology is well proven having been used successfully for a number of years by both individual organizations and specialized computer bureaux (which provide a service to organizations wishing to locate their system externally).

The biggest problem with sequential file databases, however, is that the relationships that are likely to be of interest must be specified in advance. Thus, in our example, the gas company would have to decide in advance the fields that will be searchable. Other problems include the fact that since the outputs from this type of database are limited, so too are the opportunities for integration with other systems. There are also quite considerable costs associated with making changes to the structure or operation of this type of database at a later date. Specialist programming skills will inevitably be required. To get around these problems a new generation of database products have now emerged—relational databases.

(b) **Relational databases**

Relational databases first emerged in the early 1980s and products such as Oracle were welcomed by a direct marketing industry hungry for more powerful systems. A relational database should really be regarded as a series of groups of tables, rather than records per se. Data from these tables can be combined as and when required by the user. Table joins or *relations* (hence the term 'relational' do not have to be decided when the database is being constructed. Rather, the user employs specialist software to create the relations at a later date. For marketers this is a significant development, since they do not have to specify from the outset, perhaps when they are unfamiliar with the true power of the data, the relations that will be of interest.

To allow managers the optimal use of the database information modern relational databases have front-end software that is user friendly and menu driven. The most common of these packages is SQL (Structured Query Language) and it allows marketers to conduct analyses on their own without the need to involve specialist technicians.

When an SQL command is executed against a relational database a special program known as an *optimizer program* determines the best way to carry out the request. When the method for retrieving the relevant data is determined it is turned into a special program known as a 'plan'. As the plan is executed the tables are searched and the requested information returned.

To speed the processing of the request, relational databases have common working areas or *temp tables* which the database uses to conduct its analysis. The optimizer program decides from the outset what the best way of responding to a given request might be and the plan processes the request in the working area before reporting back to the user.

A relational database allows all types of relationships to be accessed at any time (Mattison, 1997). Indeed data can be added and relations changed without the need to change the application software. Relational databases can also offer enhanced security since access to both fields and specific relations can be barred for certain users. On-line access is also greatly enhanced—a feature of great importance to those organizations wishing to call up and modify customer information regularly.

(c) **Sequential versus relational**

Despite the flexibility offered by a relational database it would be a mistake to assume that it is right for every organization. Early systems tended to be slow and required considerable computing capacity thereby adding to the cost. In the case of organizations with very rigid data-reporting requirements, these additional costs are unwarranted

Marketing Requirements	Database Sequential	Favoured Relational
Your data requirements are clearly defined and unlikely to change	✓	
Your reporting requirements will change		✓
Your market structure is complex and likely to change		✓
You need to integrate with other systems		✓
The system is likely to be enhanced to include other applications in the future		✓
You need quick development	✓	
Initial cost is important to you	✓	
You require to add/modify/browse data on-line		✓
You want a user-friendly, flexible environment		✓
You know what queries you will be making and what sort of reports you require	✓	
You are happy for selections and queries to be carried out by specialists	✓	
You will be making long batch processing runs (often)	✓	
You need to make ad hoc queries		✓

Fig. 5.4 Choice of database

and the additional flexibility unnecessary. Woodcock (1999) therefore outlines the circumstances that can affect the optimal choice of a database (see Figure 5.4)

(d) **Object oriented**

Whilst the relational revolution has impacted very favourably on many different categories of business, it is unlikely to be the end of the story as far as database development goes. More recently, a new architecture has begun to appear on the software shelves—so called *object-oriented* databases. At this point there are still few applications available and their use has largely been restricted to low volume, lower transaction rate applications. Few catalogue companies will be found as yet that employ this particular technology! As a consequence, little is as yet understood about the utility that these systems will ultimately yield.

Object-oriented databases work on the principle of *polymorphism*. They bundle together operations (code) and objects (data) into one thing known as an *object*. To add a customer record to a table in a non-object oriented database, a program must collect all of the relevant information about that customer, validate all the spellings, classifications, and interdependencies between this record and others on the system and then finally proceed to insert it. With object-oriented programming, a customer 'object' is created which performs all of these routines and inserts the record into the database on behalf of the program.

In terms of practical impact the speed of operation should be greatly enhanced and it should ultimately be possible for objects, for example, to take decisions in respect of what would be best for individual customers on the database in terms of marketing communications, promotional offers, and even the availability of credit. It should be noted, however, that this technology has yet to prove its practical worth and until more applications of object-oriented databases are created a detailed comparison with other forms of database architecture remains impractical.

5.6 **What information should be stored?**

In the context of a marketing database there is a variety of information that organizations should consider storing in respect of their customers. The detail of exactly what is required will, as we noted earlier, depend on the tasks it is intended that the database should accomplish. The data stored will also vary by context, with perhaps the most marked difference occurring between consumer and business to business databases. The typical contents of the former are illustrated in Figure 5.5, and the latter in Figure 5.6.

It is interesting to note that the collection of a customer's telephone number has recently taken on a new significance as many new telephone systems are equipped with a facility known as caller recognition. This allows the system to recognize the person calling by their telephone number and to display the relevant customer file in front of an operator so that he/she can welcome the caller by name. Not only is this a more personal service, since the operator has immediate access to the customer record, the time taken to

Field	Example
Name	Donald Smith
Street address	14 Abbotsbury Crescent
Postal town	Small Hampton
County	Devon
Zipcode/postcode	EX16 6TY
Gender	Male
Date of birth	27/10/64
Age	36
Number of children	2
External data	
Geodemographic code[1]	34
Lifestyle indicators	Reads *Times*, investment oriented
Credit rating	Good
MPS membership[2]	N
TPS membership[3]	N
Communication history[4]	
Campaign code number[5]	01
Date of contact	20/02/01
Response	Y
Date of purchase	25/02/01
Number of items	2
Returns	0
Amount	78
Activity data	
Date of last purchase	25/02/01
Categories purchased	3,5
RFM value[6]	87
Method of payment	Visa
Loyalty points	321
Total historic value	1110
Forecast lifetime value	4320
Recruitment code[7]	3

Key
1 = ACORN code 34
2 = Mailing Preference Service—a public service consisting of records of individuals who have indicated they do not wish to receive unsolicited direct mail. Most reputable organizations would look to ensure that they do not mail these individuals and would check their database against this list prior to conducting cold campaigns.
3 = Telephone Preference Service—similar to the above the TPS is designed to ensure that listed individuals are not telephoned by companies.
4 = The marketing database would normally hold details of the communications each individual has received and the response that was generated. Thus, these four fields would be generated for each communication initiated.
5 = A code designed to identify a unique campaign, thus making it possible for the marketer to subsequently track its performance and compare it with other campaigns the company has run.
6 = A code unique to a particular recruitment campaign. This assists the direct marketer in identifying the media that perform particularly well in terms of the quality (and volume) of the customer so recruited.
7 = RFM scores indicate the quality of the customer. Often scored out of 100 points, this is a high rating suggesting that the customer is a good prospect for future contact.

Fig. 5.5 Contents of consumer database

Field	Example
Name of business	Pearson and Sons
Address line 1	17-24 Avenue Road
Address line 2	Sydenham
City	London
County	
Country	UK
Zipcode/postcode	SE16 7RS
General telephone number	020 8659 5961
Name of 1st contact	Alan Pearson
Job title	Managing Director
Job code	03
Telephone number	020 8659 5962
Fax number	020 8659 7000
e-mail	Apearson@psns.net
Responsibilities	
Notes	
SIC code	421
Turnover	£2 million
Number of employees	25
Categories of purchase	9,4,8
Channel of distribution	
Credit rating	Good
Communications and activity data would be structured as per Figure 5.5	

Fig. 5.6 Contents of business to business database

process an enquiry is considerably shortened—something of benefit to both parties to the transaction. Over the next ten years this facility is likely to become ever more powerful since a move is currently being made to allocate telephone users their own unique telephone number which they can then use for a lifetime, taking it with them when they move from house to house.

5.7 **Database applications**

Stone (1998) draws a useful distinction between customer and managerial applications for the marketing database. Each of these is described briefly below:

5.7.1 **Customer applications**

Direct marketing—the most obvious application of the marketing database is to inform direct marketing activity. A knowledge of a customer's past purchase pattern, for example, can be used to ensure that he/she receives only those communications most likely to elicit a response. Thus, a catalogue customer with a history of purchasing baby clothes, can be targeted with additional clothing, perhaps (with the passage of time) switching to clothing more suitable for toddlers. They could also be targeted with offers for children's toys and even life insurance as the birth of a child can often trigger a demand for this category of product. Direct marketers can also use database information to ensure that customers only receive communications at pre-determined intervals and are not deluged, for example, with mail promoting similar items shortly after a purchase has been made.

Identifying an organization's best customers—the transactional data stored on the database can be used to identify the organization's best customers, either by the volume of their purchases, or by the profitability that they generate. This is important because in a business to business context, for example, when customer value reaches a certain level, the companies involved might be separated from other direct mail customers and identified as being worthy of more personal contact, such as a visit from a salesperson. Identifying higher value customers can also be useful since an organization would typically want to ensure that attrition rates (i.e. the percentage of customers lapsing each year) were as low as possible amongst this high value segment. A higher quality of marketing strategy might therefore be employed for this purpose.

Identification of best prospects—this really operates at two levels. In the first, a company simply identifies the individuals who have purchased a given product category in the past and despatches a new offer designed to instigate a further purchase. Companies such as Time Life would therefore target customers with a known interest in Rhythm and Blues music with new CDs in this category as they become available. At the second level, the profile of a typical purchaser of a given product category can be generated. In the case of our example, it may transpire that a typical R and B customer would be male aged 30–50, living in ACORN categories 23, 24, and 25 and possessing an interest in gardening. This information could then be used to select the best prospects from lists. Rather than mail everyone on the list, only those with statistically more likelihood of responding would be contacted.

Targeting offers—specific offers can be targeted at specific categories of customer. In a business to business context, a supplier might wish to increase the volume of product certain categories of customer are purchasing. It may therefore offer them some incentive to buy in greater volume through promotional discounts and/or alterations to their credit terms. Similarly, in a consumer context an airline might decide to offer its frequent fliers access to their VIP lounges at a reduced rate.

Suggesting appropriate forms of contact—recording the media that was utilized for the purposes of recruitment and the ongoing customer response to communications will, over time, generate valuable data in respect of a customer's preferred mode of contact. At a simple level, some customers like to be contacted by telephone, others by mail, or increasingly e-mail. If a strong customer preference is in evidence it would seem foolish to ignore it in the generation of future campaigns.

Cross-selling—whilst a customer might first contact Dell to buy a PC, it is likely that they will also require a VDU, printer, and other accessories. Indeed, over time the customer is likely to have a need for upgrades, computer supplies, and maintenance. A good database should be capable of recognizing the purchases that have been made and suggesting other merchandise that the customer is also likely to find of interest.

Response handling and fulfilment—most organizations have a given capacity to respond to requests from customers for purchase. Begin to accept too many orders and an organization can quickly find itself in a back-order position where customers start to have to wait unusually long periods of time to receive their merchandise. Equipped with a knowledge of response rates and the typical orders generated from previous campaigns it should be possible for a direct marketer to ensure that their communications generate a steady flow of orders from the customer base, without swamping the order handling department with demand.

Telemarketing—the database can also be used to generate lists of customers who have not subscribed to the Telephone Preference Service and who, experience suggests, would be likely to respond to outbound telemarketing. Response rates can be particularly high to this medium although its increased cost means that it may not be appropriate to employ with every customer on the database. It can be a particularly good vehicle for upgrading customers or informing them of special offers that the company feels will be of interest. Such forms of 'warm' telemarketing can be very effective; particularly if the organization concerned records the response obtained and does not bother customers further if they indicate that they prefer not to be approached via this medium.

Channel support—it is also possible to use database information to support other marketing channels. Thus, whilst an automotive manufacturer might maintain a database of its customers for its own use, it might also share information with intermediaries such as dealerships. Thus when a new model of car is about to be introduced onto the market, promotional material outlining the features, performance, and benefits of purchase might be sent direct from the manufacturer. A more personalized invitation to view could also be despatched from the local dealer designed to entice the customer into the showroom.

Targeted branding—mention has already been made many times in this text of the need to treat higher value customers with an especially differentiated standard of care. The loyalty of this particular customer group is of particular significance and interest. To achieve this, it makes little sense to focus solely on promotional offers, since one is in effect training these customers to be sensitive to price. It makes more sense to try to inculcate a strong degree of loyalty to the brand. Such loyalty will likely insulate this group of customers from short-term price reductions offered by the competition. For those companies who, unlike the Coca-Colas of this world, cannot afford to invest millions in mass advertising, direct marketing can be a very effective means of engendering loyalty to the brand. The manufacturers of the liqueur Benedictine, for example, have recently built a database of customers (from on pack promotions) which they now use to communicate with on a quarterly basis. The aim of each pack is to generate involvement in the brand so that consumers feel part of the Benedictine Experience. The pack therefore offers recipes, lifestyle interest stories, and an occasional opportunity to buy a rare vintage of the Benedictine liqueur.

Data marketing—the data stored on a typical organization's database is a valuable commodity. In the past many organizations have traded in this data, selling lists of their customers to other organizations whose typical customer profile matches their own. They might also have shared data with nonprofits looking to fundraise from a particular organization's customer base. It should be noted that an organization's ability to trade in data in this way has now been severely curtailed in the UK by the Data Protection Act 1998 and customers must now give their permission for their data to be used in this way. For this reason, opt-out boxes which consumers can tick to preclude receiving mail from other organizations are now commonplace in direct mail customer acquisition programmes.

5.7.2 **Management applications**

Analysis and planning—direct marketers are continually looking to improve the quality and precision of what they do. Information stored on the database provides the key to how this might be best accomplished. Considerable time and effort is devoted to identifying how each campaign performed in terms of measures such as response rate, ROI, profitability, cost per sale, etc. This painstaking analysis can help shape the future communications an organization might plan. Do some messages work better than others? Are four mailings a year better than three? Is this method of segmentation more effective than that one? Which recruitment media are most cost effective? All these are questions database personnel are well placed to answer. The results of their analysis should be continually fed back into the planning cycle to ensure an optimal communication strategy is adopted.

Campaign monitoring—similarly, it may be possible for an organization to track the ongoing success of a campaign as it begins to be rolled out across the customer file. Are the desired levels of sales being achieved? Is the response rate as the pilot suggested? Are certain products/offers proving more attractive than others? Whilst any competent direct marketer will usually have conducted a pilot test with any new communication to ensure its efficacy, it would be unusual for a company not to track the success of the eventual full campaign. Whilst a pilot offers some security, campaigns have been known to go awry even after a successful pilot. Ongoing monitoring can therefore provide an organization with a useful early warning system of likely campaign failure.

Campaign co-ordination—recording data in respect of the communications a given customer has received can offer an organization the opportunity to maintain a dialogue with that customer. Rather than writing to them with a series of 'one-off' letters that assume no prior relationship exists (all too common a practice), smarter organizations design their communications to pick up where the last one left off. Each communication that the customer receives and their response thereto begins to build to a genuine dialogue between the two parties.

Project management—database information can be used by managers to assess the viability of potential new projects. Before decisions are taken to extend existing product lines, or to withdraw from a particular business, the pattern of recorded behaviour on the database can be used to assess the financial impact of each decision.

5.8 Sources of customer information

Of course, all the preceding applications assume that the organization has identified and gathered the information that it needs to manage customer relationships successfully. In this section it is our intention to look at where an organization might gather this data from.

There are really only two categories of information source, namely: internal and external. A good starting point in building a database is to exhaust all internal sources first. Internal data, such as accounting records, billing systems, and transaction records, will likely offer considerable utility. Companies may also have held details of enquiries, or requests for product information. This information can potentially be gathered and input to a marketing database.

Of course, all this assumes that an organization has some form of direct contact with the end user. This is frequently not the case—and in such instances Goldwag suggests the following sources of data:

- product registration documents, or warranty cards;
- credit card details;
- subscription details;
- questionnaire responses;
- in-store offer details;
- requests for product information;
- records from events or promotions requiring a response from the consumer.

There are also a variety of external sources of data which might be employed to build a database. Specialized research companies such as Neilsen, and lifestyle houses such as

Consumer Surveys, will happily supply the names and addresses of customers purchasing a particular company's products.

It is also possible for companies selling through intermediaries to establish a one-to-one dialogue by providing some incentive for customers to contact the company directly. The most common of these approaches involves the use of competitions or on-pack promotions, where the consumer is invited to write in to apply for a coupon or other form of promotional premium. The most basic of consumer information may thereby be captured and perhaps supplemented at a later date by having it profiled by either geodemographic code or various lifestyle categories.

In the extreme, it may also be desirable for a company to set up a new direct channel to begin gathering data about end users. In the past this has proved very expensive, typically involving the setting up of a direct mail or telemarketing operation to deal direct. With the advent of the internet it is now much easier to capture consumer data without the need to establish a completely new direct to end user operation. Visitors to a company's website can be asked to register in return for access to certain data, and simple contact details may easily be gained in this way. Once again, the resulting data can be supplemented as necessary to build up a more detailed understanding of the customer base.

5.9 Database maintenance

However, merely gathering data is not enough. There are several processes through which this data must pass before the decision is taken that it can reasonably be added to a database. Even after data entry has occurred companies wisely take steps to secure the data and ensure that it is subsequently updated as and when required. Indeed, there are a number of important database management issues and it is our intention to address the most critical of these below.

5.9.1 Managing data sources

One of the most difficult problems for marketers takes the form of tracking down the data they need in the first instance. A variety of sources for this information has already been suggested in the previous section and it would be usual for the marketing department to have to gather its data from other functions such as sales, operations, and accounting/finance. The problem is that this reliance on others means that the pertinent data may well not be available in the right format. Sales and order handling, for example, may prefer to store information by product category rather than customer per se—as this allows them to keep a better track of product sales and inventory levels respectively. Getting the data back to a format that can be linked to the record of an individual customer may therefore not be an easy task. There is a potential for errors to creep into the data and delays in transmission that ensure that the marketing department is never quite in possession of the most up-to-date data.

The process of identifying which data should be transferred, from which departments and at what frequency (if not on-line) should be carefully managed. The quality and, therefore, utility of the marketing database will only be as good as the quality of data that has been entered. The often necessary reliance on third parties can make this process problematic.

5.9.2 Verification/validation

In cases where data has to be input manually to the database, perhaps from product warranty cards, there is a potential that errors can be introduced as the data is scanned, or typed into the system. Verification is the process by which an organization checks that the data has been input correctly. One way of doing this is for the data to be keyed in twice and for the computer to compare the two versions. Unfortunately, this also doubles the time required and therefore the cost, so it would be normal to have a sample of data from each data entry operative checked for errors by a supervisor.

Of course, the fact that data has been input correctly, does not mean that the original data was in itself valid. Staying with the warranty card example, customers might have filled in the wrong product code, or have supplied an incomplete postcode for their address. A painstaking process of validation is therefore necessary to ensure that the resultant customer record is accurate. Tapp (1998) suggests four distinct means of checking for validity:

Checking product/source codes against an internal 'master' list of all valid codes—the validity of postal addresses can be checked (in the UK) by comparing with the Postal Address File (PAF), supplied and updated regularly by the Royal Mail.

Carrying out audits—the number of customers or sales of a given product, for example, can be compared from one internal database to another. Any discrepancies that are detected can then be thoroughly investigated.

Accuracy tests—the database (as noted above) can be programmed to allow only certain types of entry—thus preventing many typographical errors.

Doing a sanity check—periodically conducting a visual inspection of a random sample of records.

5.9.3 De-duplication

A significant amount of marketing resource can easily be wasted each year if the database is not checked regularly for duplicate customer records. These can occur for a number of reasons, but most commonly because new records can mistakenly be created every time a customer makes a purchase, or the system fails to recognize when an individual moves house and instead creates a new record. Duplicates can also occur when more than one member of a family initiates a purchase and because the name appears differently, a new record is created.

Aside from the waste in resources that such duplication can generate, it can also be a source of annoyance for customers who typically find themselves receiving two or three versions of the same communication. This is a particular problem where the nature of the message was intended to be personalized with an air of exclusivity. Even worse, such duplications can send two simple messages to the customer. First, this company doesn't recognize me as an individual—and second—they clearly don't know what they're doing!

'De-duplication' is the phrase for the most common process undertaken to remove these errors in the database. The process can either be undertaken in-house or undertaken by a specialist computer bureau with algorithms that can easily detect what appear to be duplications in customer data.

5.9.4 Merge-purge

Merge-purge is really only a variant of de-duplication. The difference between the two is simply that with merge-purge the aim is to combine two different sets of records, or contact lists and then purge the resultant merged list of duplicates. When the two data-sets are combined the resultant list is termed a gross list. When the de-duplication process has been completed the list is known as a net list. This can clearly be used as a master file or as the basis for some form of direct marketing.

Merge-purge can be used to combine a series of rented lists which the organization wishes to use for customer acquisition. It can also be used to remove any existing customers from the gross list before recruitment activity takes place. Clearly, mailing existing credit card holders with a pack encouraging them to take out an identical card would be crass. Merge-purge can prevent this from happening. Merge-purge can also take data from several different departments in an organization and unify them into a single marketing database.

Aside from eliminating duplicates merge-purge technology is capable of detecting faulty addresses and mis-spellings that could potentially be offensive to the recipient (see Figure 5.7) In addition, merge-purge can remove the names of individuals who have opted to use the Mail Preference Service and who therefore do not wish to receive unsolicited direct mail. However, merge-purge is a highly specialist activity and it would usually only be undertaken with the help of a specialist computer bureau.

5.9.5 Updating data

Even after data has been successfully entered in the database, this is not the end of the story. This is simply because client data degrades with the passage of time. In the consumer context, individuals die, they move house, or decide to avail themselves of the mailing preference service. Organizations need to take account of these changes and to update their files accordingly. Individuals moving can be a particular problem in the use of commercial lists and it is estimated that as many as 17 per cent of the contacts supplied on a commercial MPS or TPS list can be out of date within a year of compilation (Stone, 1996). The problem is heightened further in the case of business to business marketing, where not only do addresses change, but the contact individuals can move on to work for another employer or be promoted (or move sideways) to another job function. The percentage of outdated contacts on a business list can be as high as 25 per cent after only a year from compilation.

Mis-spellings that could be offensive:

Mr P. Hart	Mr Phart
4 Riding Street	4 Riding Street
Tiverton	Tiverton
Devon	Devon
EX16 5YU	EX16 5YU
Mr D. Hume	Mr D. Hume
9 Worthington Close	9 Worthington Close
Whitstable	Shitstable
GH15 6RF	GH15 6RF

Hoax entries (Which software can often identify and eliminate)

Tony Blair
Donald Duck
Monty Python,
etc.

Duplications: Which need to be identified and eliminated

Mr W. Smith	Mr Bill. Smith
Hunting Meadows	Hunting Meadows
Bootle	Bootle
Merseyside	Merseyside
LP13 5FR	LP13 5FR
Jane Cummings	Jane Cummings
45 Graves End Road	45 Graves End Road
Ipswich	Ipswich
IP5 6UP	IP5 6PU
Mrs J. Cummings	Jane Cummings
45 Graves End Road	Ipswich
Ipswich	IP5 6PU
IP5 6UP	

Fig. 5.7 Problems with names

A marketing database is, of course, a form of list and can easily decay at the same rate as a commercial list if steps are not taken to protect its integrity. Use can obviously be made of the Public Address File referred to earlier and/or the electoral roll for this purpose. Customers should also be given ample opportunity to self-advise the organization of a move and it is therefore not unusual to find many warm mailings containing a change of address form that the customer can complete to keep in touch.

5.9.6 **Archiving**

To prevent the marketing database from becoming too large and unwieldy, spurious or out-of-date information is periodically removed. In setting about this task organizations need to be clear how long it is appropriate to hold customer data. They need to decide how far back it is desirable to keep a record of the history of active customers and in the case of lapsed customers, just exactly what period of time will need to pass before they are considered genuinely lapsed. In each case the old data may be removed from the active portion of the organization's database and either deleted, or more likely archived for some future use. It is often helpful to maintain an archive of this data since it can be helpful when it comes to modelling certain aspects of customer behaviour.

5.9.7 **Access/security**

An issue of critical concern to many organizations is that of security. It is unlikely that every individual with access to a database will have equal rights of access to every level of information contained therein. More likely, they will be given access only to those fields that are necessary for completion of the task in hand. On other occasions, they may be allowed to view certain fields but are not given the ability to alter them. This ensures that the integrity of the database is maintained and that data cannot be altered or deleted without the proper authority. There was one notable case of a disgruntled bank employee who decided to change the salutation field in a letter designed to be targeted at the organization's highest value customers. Instead of 'Dear Sir/Madam', the salutation was changed to 'Dear Rich Bastard'.

Organizations also need to take reasonable steps to prevent unauthorized access to their database files. With the increasing integration of database technology with other on-line systems, the capacity for individuals to hack in to a database and download personal data is greatly enhanced. Security is becoming an increasingly hot topic for database professionals to address.

5.10 **Data warehousing**

At the beginning of the chapter we highlighted the fact that a data warehouse could legitimately be regarded as another form of database. It is of particular interest to the direct marketer because a data warehouse can provide considerable insight into the behaviour of a given organization's customers. Kelly (1997, p. 22) defines a data warehouse as:

> A single data store directed at the entire enterprise or a subject area of an enterprise. Here data can be integrated and cleansed in such a manner that it can be analysed, manipulated, transformed and combined to discover correlations, trends and patterns that add value to the data.

A data warehouse is therefore:

- separate from the operational systems of an enterprise;
- available solely for the task of being interrogated by business users;
- time stamped—to match business, accounting, or various reporting periods;
- subject oriented—and usually oriented to customers;
- non volatile—and thus not updated on an individual basis.

It is thus a powerful resource of data that can be queried to facilitate a wide range of direct marketing activities.

5.11 **Data mining**

Data mining is extraction of previously unknown yet comprehensible and actionable information from large repositories of data, used to make crucial business decisions and support their implementation, including formulating tactical and strategic marketing initiatives and measuring their success (Edelstein 1999, p. 15).

Data mining techniques are therefore ideally applied in the context of a data warehouse. They can certainly be applied to a live database, but the beauty of these techniques lies in the ability to be able to look across large quantities of data and/or variables and to discern relationships that would simply not be detectable by other means.

Data mining tools incorporate a variety of statistical tools—and most packages will find the optimum technique and models to provide the answers that marketers are looking for.

5.12 **Legal implications**

5.12.1 **Data protection**

The long awaited Data Protection Act 1988 was designed to bring the UK's regulatory framework into line with that now required by European regulations. It applies much more stringent controls over the use of personal data than was previously the case. Under the Act anyone the subject of data being held or processed about them, now has a number of specific rights:

- They may request of the data controller (i.e. the individual managing the data in an organization) a brief description of the personal data held, the purposes for which they are being—or are able to be—purchased, and the recipients to whom they are—or may be—disclosed.

- They may also request a copy of the personal data held and any information that might be available to the data controller in respect of how that data was acquired.

- Where the data is being processed to evaluate matters which relate to him/her directly, such as a credit check or an analysis of their performance at work, they also have the right to be informed of the logic involved in the decision-making process.

To control the potential for a spurious series of requests for information the Act provides that the data controller is not obliged to provide any of this information unless a request is made in writing and any fee demanded is paid. The Act controls the maximum that organizations are permitted to charge for this purpose.

The Act also provides an individual with the right to apply in writing to a data controller to prevent their information being processed for the purposes of direct marketing. This is a significant new right, and data controllers will need to ensure that subjects availing themselves do not have their data processed in the usual way.

The Act also creates a new category of personal data—namely sensitive personal data. This is information consisting of:

- the racial or ethnic origin of the data subject;
- his/her political opinions;
- their religious beliefs;
- whether he/she is a member of a trade union;
- his/her physical or mental condition;
- the subject's sexual life;
- the commission or alleged commission of any offence;
- the proceedings for any offence committed or alleged to have been committed by him, the disposal of such proceedings or the sentence of any court in such proceedings.

The same rules as for personal data apply, but in addition a number of other restrictions are imposed on organizations holding or planning to hold one of these categories of data.

5.12.2 Maintaining communications standards

There are two types of control currently in operation around the world. The first is statutory and controlled by a country's legislative framework, whilst the second is voluntary and self-regulatory. Some countries opt for the former approach, whilst some opt for the latter. In the UK, a series of voluntary controls have been in existence for over forty years. At the core of these voluntary controls is the British Code of Advertising Practice and a number of different bodies established to ensure that this code is upheld. The system is funded by a levy on advertising expenditures.

For non-broadcast media the ASA (Advertising Standards Authority) oversees the code, whilst for radio it is the Radio Authority (RA) and the ITC (Independent Television Commission) in the case of television. All three bodies work in very similar ways.

If a member of the public suspects that a piece of direct mail has contravened the code he/she may complain to the ASA who are then obligated to investigate the complaint and issue a ruling. If the ASA finds in favour of the complainant, it issues a media notice ordering the offending ad to be withdrawn or, in the case of a direct marketing programme, terminated. Given that most suppliers in the direct marketing industry are members of a trade association, this is usually enough to ensure compliance. In the handful of cases where unscrupulous operators continue with activities that contravene the code the government may now intervene under the Control of Misleading Advertisements Regulations (1988) and issue an injunction preventing the activity from continuing.

In addition to responding to public complaints the ASA also conducts an ongoing programme of monitoring and currently scrutinizes more than 15,000 advertisements per annum (Fill, 1996). Whilst the code contains a number of specific guidelines for product categories such as alcohol and tobacco, the general rule is that all advertising must be:

- legal;
- decent;
- honest; and
- truthful.

In the US, the FTC (Federal Trade Commission) is the primary body with responsibility for overseeing advertising activity. The FTC's goal is to protect consumers from false claims, deception, and misrepresentation. Where advertising claims are alleged to be unfair or deceptive the FTC examines the materials to determine whether they are deceptive, or likely to be deceptive in the way the public is likely to interpret them. It also considers the net impression of an ad and investigates the materiality of any claims that are alleged to be false. Finally, the FTC will attempt to distinguish between puff (or normal sales exaggerations) and genuinely deceptive ads. In recent years the FTC has had considerable clout. It can order cessation of offending advertising material, but it can also impose the tougher sanction of corrective advertising in cases where misleading claims have been shown to be made. In 1975, for example, the FTC compelled Warner Lambert, the makers of Listerine Mouth Wash to undertake corrective advertising. They had previously claimed that Listerine could prevent colds by killing the germs that were associated with them. This was found to be an unsubstantiated claim and the company was forced to place advertisements indicating that this was not, in fact, the case. Indeed, in subsequent years, offenders have had to devote as much as 25 per cent of the advertising budgets to putting right false claims in previous advertising.

5.12.3 **Direct Mail Services Standards Board (DMSSB)**

In the UK, the DMSSB offers an accreditation scheme for companies operating in the direct marketing arena. In essence it offers a guarantee that its members will abide by a certain code of conduct and adopt certain ethical and professional standards. Whilst the accreditation scheme carries no legal status, it is likely that a company losing its accreditation would lose business and ultimately (in the case of persistent offenders) be declined service by the Royal Mail.

To achieve accreditation, service suppliers must ensure that their activities conform to a given set of regulations. These are concentrated in the realm of direct mail and designed to control abuses such as misleading envelope messages, false claims for products, and failing to disclose the true costs of premium rate telephone numbers which might be used as a response device.

5.13 Summary

In this chapter we have defined the nature and role of a marketing database and identified the data that a typical application might hold. We have also examined how a database might be maintained and the information that can be drawn from a database to inform marketing activity. We have also examined a number of the legislative frameworks which govern how a database may or may not be used.

In the next chapter we turn our attention to a specific and critical application of the customer database, namely the realm of customer retention. Specifically, we will explore how a database can be used for the purposes of identifying and retaining high value customers and developing appropriate communication strategies for customers with differing needs, preferences, etc.

Further reading

Courtheux R. (1992) 'The Absolute Essentials of Direct Marketing', from the video series *The Database* (Teddington, Richmond-Upon-Thames, Institute of Direct Marketing: video 4).

Edelstein H. A. (1999) *Introduction to Data Mining and Knowledge Discovery* (Chicago: Two Crows Corporation).

Fill C. (1999) *Marketing Communications: Contexts, Contents, and Strategies* (Harlow: Pearson Publishing).

Kelly S. (1997) *Data Warehousing in Action* (New York: John Wiley).

Kotler P. (1994) *Marketing Management: Analysis, Strategy, Planning and Control*, 7th edn. (Upper Saddle River, NJ: Prentice Hall).

Mattison R. (1997) *Understanding Database Management Systems*, 2nd edn. (New York: McGraw Hill).

Stone B. (1996) *Successful Direct Marketing Methods*, 5th edn. (Chicago: NTC Business Books).

Stone B. (1998) 'Putting Your Database To Work', *The Direct Marketing Guide* (Teddington, Richmond-Upon-Thames: Institute of Direct Marketing).

Tapp A. (1998) *Principles of Direct and Database Marketing* (London: FT Pitman Publishing).

Wooodcock N. (1998) 'Choosing Your Database Software and Systems' *The Direct Marketing Guide* (Teddington, Richmond-Upon-Thames: Institute of Direct Marketing), 3. 4–2–3. 4–24.

Chapter 6

Customer Retention — Building Customer Loyalty

Contents

6.1 **Objectives**

By the end of this chapter you should be able to:

(a) define the concept of customer loyalty;

(b) identify why loyalty is important;

(c) describe the key determinants of customer loyalty;

(d) define and calculate customer lifetime value;

(e) develop a customer loyalty programme;

(f) measure, monitor, and benchmark the payback.

6.2 **What is customer loyalty?**

At its simplest level loyalty is:

> the desire on the part of a customer to continue to do business with a given supplier over time.

Loyal customers are therefore those that keep coming back, time after time. Of course, there are several different kinds of loyalty and in fact loyalty is best conceptualized as comprising four distinct levels (see Figure 6.1):

No loyalty—at the first level there is no loyalty at all. Consumers in a particular product category simply move around from one supplier to another, seemingly at random. The perception is that all the products in a category are alike and that there is no benefit in buying from one particular supplier. Under such circumstances manufacturers may well resort to sales promotion activities, possibly money off or discount packages, in the hope of giving consumers a reason for buying their particular version of a product. The danger with this form of activity, in a market where customer loyalty is absent, is that when the promotion ends, sales will return to their pre-promotion levels. Consumers no longer have a reason for purchasing a particular product. It is probably this kind of behaviour that famously provoked Jim Hodgkinson, the Director responsible for Kingfisher's B and Q group to remark 'if you want loyalty, buy a dog!'.

At the second level—consumers can often exhibit what is known as spurious loyalty. They still perceive little difference between the product or brands available, but see no reason to switch to suppliers. This kind of behaviour is driven not by feelings of genuine loyalty to the supplier concerned, but rather by inertia. In simple terms, the consumer can't be bothered to make a change and continues to buy the product they've always bought. Perhaps the best example of spurious loyalty is the 'loyalty' many customers exhibit to their bank. It is estimated that only 10 per cent of customers describe themselves as loyal to their bank, yet only a small percentage of customers actually switch banks each year. Most probably never quite get around to it, or feel the change would not be worth the effort necessary to affect it. The Henley Centre (1994) estimated that almost 90–95 per cent of all loyalty may be spurious or passive loyalty—unstable and apathetic.

Latent loyalty—this occurs in situations where the consumer does actually feel an element of loyalty to a supplier in a given product category, yet does not buy from that supplier on every occasion a purchase is made. Most of us, for example, could probably name our favourite restaurant and feel that we exhibit a degree of loyalty to the establishment concerned, yet we would never dream of eating there every time we went out for a meal. Loyalty in this context is driven by normative and situational constraints. Normative, in the sense that most people would expect to eat at a variety of different places, perhaps returning to their favourite on every fourth or fifth occasion. Situational, in the sense that one's choice of restaurant may be driven by other factors than a love for the establishment concerned. Most people, for example, would tend to choose a different restaurant for a business luncheon than for a romantic dinner for two.

True loyalty—at the top of our pyramid, customers exhibit a purchase pattern that is dominated by the use of only one supplier or brand. Customers could hence choose to fly United as their airline of first choice, or to buy Budweiser as their beer of first choice. They purchase competing products only when their first choice is not available. The important thing to note is that genuine loyalty is exhibited in the presence of competition. On the face of it most of us are probably quite loyal to our domestic water supplier, yet this could hardly be considered genuine loyalty. We don't have much choice but to purchase from this one company. Genuine customer loyalty exists where customers have a range of other choices available to them, are aware of these choices and yet still *choose* to continue to do business with only one supplier.

Fig. 6.1 The loyalty pyramid

Jenkinson (1996, p. 148), thus defines true loyalty as:

'the devoted and steadfast attachment of a customer to one supplier, even when attracted to one or more competitive alternatives.'

In assessing loyalty in any one context it is important to remember, however, that all things are relative. In consumer markets 95 per cent of motorists, for example, buy fuel from more than one supplier and about 85 per cent of us will buy food from more than one grocery retail outlet. The success of organizations competing in these sectors in building customer loyalty would therefore be measured against their sector 'norms' of behaviour. Loyalty is rarely absolute.

In fact, consumers tend to be loyal to multiple brands in a single category. The advertising agency Oglivy and Mather, when it conducted a survey of a representative cross-section of FMCG brands in the US, found that on average a company's highest value customers would only buy its brand 30 per cent of the time. Seven times out of ten they would purchase competitive brands! Consumers, especially high-value consumers distribute their purchases across many brands which are in their 'considered set' or 'brand repertoire'. The battle for loyalty thus becomes one of a battle for a greater 'share of a customer'.

6.3 Why is loyalty important?

Firms can build their business in one of three ways. They can:

- strive to obtain new customers;
- do more business with their existing customers;
- actively endeavour to lose fewer customers;

We noted in the previous chapter that firms have historically placed great emphasis on the former of these alternatives, at the expense of the latter. Indeed, Raphel (1991) criticizes organizations for the missionary zeal they apply to the attraction of ever larger numbers of new customers, at the expense of looking after those they already have (see also Ryans and Wittkink 1977).

Reichheld and Sasser (1990) in their now classic Harvard Business Review article describe the consequences of this omission. Based on an analysis of more than 100 companies in two dozen industries, the researchers found that firms could improve profits from 25 per cent to 85 per cent by reducing customer defections by just 5 per cent. An analysis of a credit card company showed that lowering the defection rate from 20 per cent to 10 per cent doubled the longevity of the average customer's relationship from five years to ten and more than doubled the cumulative profit streams for this customer from £135 to £300. If the defection rate declined another 5 per cent, the duration of the relationship was found to double again and profits increased 75 per cent from £300 to £525. Firms which lose customers are therefore spending more than they need to and are squandering a most valuable resource.

The answer to the question we posed at the beginning of this section is therefore that loyalty is important because even small increases in loyalty can have a dramatic impact on the financial health of an organization. Why should this be? Building loyalty pays because:

- It frequently costs many organizations more to recruit a customer than they can ever hope to make on the initial transaction. Much customer acquisition activity therefore operates at a loss. Response rates to mailings are low and customer expenditure tentative. Companies make their money by developing an ongoing relationship over time. As an organization learns more about its customers it can serve them better, tailor its communication strategy and develop the typical purchase value.

- Aside from the costs of acquisition, there are also switching costs a company has to incur when customers leave. In many cases it will take a while to recognize that they have lapsed and hence considerable moneys could be expended in communicating with individuals no longer interested in doing business with the company concerned. There are also costs associated with the setting up and maintenance of company records, all of which will have been wasted when customers decide to lapse.

- As we noted in the previous chapter, loyal customers are also those most likely to be warm to cross selling and up selling opportunities. Customers can be sold other product lines (cross selling), or persuaded to make higher value purchases over time (up selling).

- In a business to business context a fourth benefit accrues, namely the reduction of contract negotiation and order processing costs. It can take considerable organizational effort to win a new corporate client. Salespersons may be tied up negotiating the terms of the contract and the order processing team will need to spend time ascertaining the customer's delivery requirements and setting up systems to ensure that these are met. The longer that this category of customer can be kept, the longer the organization has to obtain a reasonable return on this investment.

- There are also human costs associated with failure. Organizations with high levels of customer loyalty tend to be those where levels of staff morale and pride in the organization are also high. The converse is also true and organizations with low customer loyalty are frequently those that will exhibit the highest levels of staff turnover.

- Finally, in both industrial and consumer contexts, loyal customers 'spread the word' about how they feel to their friends and peers. So, unfortunately, do customers that were not satisfied with their experience. Satisfied customers, on average, tell five other people about their good treatment, whilst dissatisfied customers share their experience with nine other people. Loyal satisfied customers can therefore provide a considerable amount of free 'advertising' to others who could potentially be interested in the products/services available.

6.4 **So what drives loyalty?**

To address this question it is probably best to begin by turning the issue on its head and asking why do customers defect? A number of studies have addressed the primary reasons why customers stop doing business with a particular organization. De Souza (1992), for example, identified six different types of defector:

Price—customers who defect because they identify a lower price elsewhere.

Product—customers who defect because they prefer the features or design of a product provided by another supplier.

Service—the overall quality of service provided may be better in the case of an alternative supplier.

Market—some customers may be lost to the market. They may die, move away, or cease to have a need for the product category in question.

Technological—some customers may be tempted away by alternative channels of distribution, making it easier for them to do business with the organization concerned. They may elect to purchase, for example, direct from an internet supplier.

Organizational—equally, some customers are lost to the organization. This occurs when an alternative supplier is successful in achieving a greater 'share of spend' than the original supplier. It may be appropriate in an industrial context, for example, for a customer to rationalize the number of suppliers with whom they do business, even if they are satisfied with the quality of service provided.

It should be noted, however, that underlying these six distinct categories from a service quality perspective, there are only two types of defector. The first of these is 'natural' (since customers often only have a finite lifetime of demand for a specific product category), whilst the second is 'unnatural' and caused by the manner in which the organization treats its customers. Indeed, the relationship between service quality and customer retention has been explored at length in the literature. It has now been well established that achieving a baseline of appropriate service quality is essential if the longevity of a customer relationship is to be assured.

This very simple idea has recently taken on a whole new significance because of the work of Jones and Sasser (1995). Consider the graph in Figure 6.2 on p 183.

The figure illustrates the satisfaction ratings recently obtained from a survey of customers to an internet bookstore. In common with many such surveys, customers have been asked to assess their satisfaction with their last purchase experience on a five point scale, from 1 (= very dissatisfied) to 5 (= very satisfied). At first glance, the graph appears to contain relatively good news, since a high proportion of customers were either satisfied or very satisfied with their experience. Indeed, 82 per cent of customers can be seen to fall in this general category.

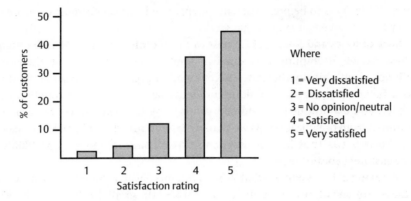

Fig. 6.2 Customer satisfaction chart

One might reasonably suppose that any effort to increase customer loyalty should be targeted at the remaining 18 per cent of customers who rated the service as either a 1, 2, or 3. Clearly, they are not satisfied and efforts should be made to improve the experience of these groups of customers.

At least that has always been the conventional wisdom. In a study that embraced a variety of different sectors, Jones and Sasser (1995) identified marked differences between each level of customer satisfaction in terms of the subsequent repurchase rate exhibited. Of most interest is their finding that customers rating the service a 5, were six times more likely to repurchase than customers rating it only a 4. To put it another way, even if *all* the customers who rated their satisfaction as a 5 repurchase, only 17 per cent of those who rated it as a 4 will do so. This revelation focuses the mind somewhat on the group of customers who should clearly be regarded as most important. If an organization can improve on the percentage of customers that rate their satisfaction as a 5, it can substantially improve on the levels of loyalty that will be exhibited as a result.

Before moving on, it is worth noting that the factor of six quoted above, is not static across all industries and sectors, it will clearly depend on the availability of substitute services and the nature of the competition. For some product categories this multiple will be higher and for some it is likely to be considerably lower, but even if it should prove to be as low as 2 or 3, a significant difference can still be ascertained between the loyalty patterns exhibited by the customers who consider themselves 'satisfied' and those who consider themselves 'very satisfied'.

The reason for elaborating on this research is a simple one. The key to moving customers from a 4 to a 5 is customer value. If you think back to some of your own experiences with service organizations and in particular those that you might have been asked to evaluate, you can probably very quickly recall why you failed to award a '5' yourself to a particular organization. The organization almost certainly met your basic requirements, but did not excel in one area that was of particular importance to you. As a result, organizations need to be particularly alert to those aspects of their service offering that customers perceive to be most important and ensure that they 'engineer in' value in these key areas. If loyalty is to be preserved and/or enhanced, customers must be made to feel that they have received an exceptional service.

The work of Jones and Sasser (1995) poses a further interesting problem for marketers to address, namely attempting to explain why some customers who do rate the service a 5 will still not exhibit loyalty thereafter. Recent work suggests that instead of viewing loyalty as a function of satisfaction alone, it should be conceived as a function of both satisfaction and commitment. Customers can be very satisfied and yet have almost no commitment to an organization. As we shall see later in this chapter, the key to successful loyalty schemes has thus lain in providing this missing ingredient and building up genuine customer commitment.

Before leaving a discussion of what drives customer loyalty, however, we need to consider the role of one more important factor. Consider the graph in Figure 6.3. In this case we are looking at a graph depicting the percentage of customers who will typically buy again from an organization after they have experienced some kind of problem with the quality of service provided. In each case a distinction has been made between minor problems and major problems.

Working from left to right, the first group of customers we encounter is a group who have experienced a problem and not taken the trouble to complain. In this case only 8 per cent of customers will repurchase if it was a major problem, 31 per cent if it were a minor problem. In the next category, we have a group of customers who have had a problem, complained, and the organization has taken no corrective action. In this case 18 per cent will buy again if it was a major problem, 46 per cent if it was a minor problem.

In the next category, we are looking at a group of customers who have had a problem, they've complained and the organization has taken some steps to resolve it. In this case 53 per cent will buy again if it were a major problem, 69 per cent if it were a minor problem.

Finally, we have a group of customers who have had a problem, they've complained and the organization has immediately taken steps to resolve the issue to their satisfaction. In this case 82 per cent will buy again if it was a major problem, 94 per cent if it were a minor problem.

The graph actually reveals two interesting facets of consumer behaviour. Consider the difference between the first two categories. Organizations will actually be better off encouraging customers to complain, even if they choose not to act on the information received. It is almost as though the act of complaining is in itself a kind of catharsis. Customers seem to feel better after they have been allowed to vent their frustration.

The second point worthy of note derives from the fact that in this sector the average repurchase rate for customers who did not experience a problem is only 78 per cent. This suggests that companies would actually be better off supplying a faulty service, waiting for the customer to complain and then immediately resolving the issue to everyone's satisfaction. The customer exposed to this practice would tend on average to be more loyal than if they had never had a problem in the first place!

Of course, we are not advocating that any organization should follow such a strategy, but it does serve to illustrate why many companies now refer to service problems as 'opportunities'. Opportunities in the sense that if they can be dealt with speedily and

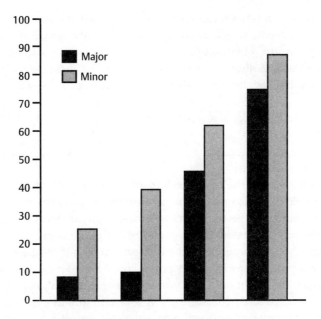

Fig.6.3 Will customers buy from you again?

effectively, the customer concerned will tend to be more loyal than if he/she had never had a problem in the first place.

It would therefore appear that loyalty is a function of satisfaction, commitment, and, where necessary, the effective handling of complaints.

6.5 **Lifetime value**

6.5.1 **An overview**

Having now examined what loyalty is and how organizations can strive to achieve it, it will now be instructive to consider whether fostering loyalty is always desirable. Customers come in many different shapes and sizes and their spending power can be equally diverse. We know, for example, that 25 per cent of households account for 74 per cent of coffee sales, 16 per cent of households account for 79 per cent of yoghurt sales, and 24 per cent of women account for 71 per cent of clothing purchases. In attempting to formulate a strategy to retain customers and develop loyalty, these figures suggest that perhaps we should be focusing our effort on certain very specific groups of people.

It would clearly be preferable for a coffee manufacturer, for example, to develop high levels of loyalty amongst those customers who account for a high proportion of overall coffee sales. Customers with the potential to spend greater sums should hence attract the proportion of loyalty marketing effort that reflects this greater value.

To be in a position to take decisions over the most desirable customers to target with loyalty/retention campaigns, one needs to understand just how much each customer might be worth to the organization over time. This leads us to one of the most fundamental concepts in direct marketing—the concept of customer lifetime value.

Bitran and Mondschein (1997, p. 109) define lifetime value (LTV) as:

> 'the total net contribution that a customer generates during his/her lifetime on a house-list.'

It is therefore a measure of the total worth to an organization of its relationship with a particular customer. To calculate it one has to estimate the costs and revenues that will be associated with managing the communication with that customer during each year of his/her relationship. If, for example, the relationship extends over a period of four years, one can subtract the costs of servicing the relationship with that customer (e.g. product costs, newsletters, product brochures, telephone contact, etc.) from the revenue so generated. In essence, the contribution each year to the organization's overheads and profitability can be calculated. Of course, there is a certain amount of crystal ball gazing involved since it becomes increasingly more difficult to predict costs and revenues the further one looks into the future. To take account of this uncertainty and to reflect the fact that a £20 purchase in four years' time will be worth in real terms much less than it would today, it is also important to discount the value of the future revenue streams that will be generated. After all, instead of investing the money in customer retention the organization could simply elect to place the money concerned in an interest bearing account. Unless the return from the marketing activity can be expected to match, or hopefully exceed, what could be generated by an interest bearing account, it will clearly not be worthwhile. If this analysis is conducted right across the database a key advantage accrues. Organizations can employ an LTV analysis to increase their overall profitability by getting rid of customers who will never be profitable and concentrating resources on recruiting and retaining those that will.

6.5.2 **A conceptual framework**

There are a variety of different ways in which lifetime value might be examined. These are presented in Figure 6.4. Organizations can elect to focus on historic or projected future value. They can also calculate value on an individual basis, or, more usually on a segment by segment basis, examining specific groups of customers on their database. Sargeant (1998) identified that the majority of companies continue to equate lifetime value with 'total historic value' and thus to calculate lifetime value by conducting a simple historic analysis of their database. The question marketers are asking by conducting their analysis in this way is simply 'how much has this particular individual, or segment, been worth to my organization in the past?'. This they regard as lifetime value. However, lifetime value as a direct marketer would define it is actually a projective measure, offering the marketer information in respect of how much a given customer or segment will likely be worth to them in the future. Thus whilst all four approaches to the calculation of

Fig. 6.4 Perspectives on value

customer value will undoubtedly yield valuable information, only quadrants 3 and 4 represent an analysis of true 'customer lifetime value'.

6.5.3 **Calculating the LTV of individual customers**

The formula for calculating LTV in the case of an individual customer (i.e. quadrant 3) is as follows:

$$LTV = \sum_{i=1}^{n} C i (1 + d)^{-i}$$

Where:

c = net contribution from each year's marketing activities
d = discount rate
i = the expected duration of the relationship (in years).

This somewhat complex looking equation merely indicates that it is necessary to calculate the likely future contribution by a customer to each year's marketing activities, discount these future contributions and then add them all together. The grand total is the LTV of a given customer.

Table 6.1 shows a case where the lifetime value of a customer subscribing to a fishing magazine for an estimated five-year period has been calculated. The subscription currently costs $25.00 per annum and there are no plans to increase this in the foreseeable future. The first row of the table therefore indicates that the company can expect to generate $25 a year from this customer in direct income. However, there are also plans to cross-sell the consumer with other items relating to their interest. An analysis of historic data suggests that this consumer would be likely to spend the amounts shown in the second row of the table on other items during each year of the relationship.

In the next two rows the likely costs of providing the magazine have been plotted (direct costs), together with the costs associated with generating the indirect income referred to earlier (indirect costs). In the next row the net contribution made by this subscriber each year has been calculated.

Table 6.1 Example LTV calculation

	Year 1	Year 2	Year 3	Year 4	Year 5
Direct income	25.00	25.00	25.00	25.00	25.00
Indirect income	3.00	15.00	20.00	30.00	35.00
Direct cost	10.00	10.00	10.00	10.00	10.00
Indirect costs	1.00	2.00	3.00	4.00	5.00
Net contribution	17.00	28.00	32.00	41.00	45.00
NPV per annum	17.00	24.35	24.20	26.96	25.73
NPV total	101.24				

As you will appreciate the example in Table 6.1 is peppered with assumptions; assumptions that the customer will remain loyal for five years and assumptions about future revenues and costs. To take account of this variation and the fact that the future revenue streams are not going to be worth as much as they would be today, the value of these future contributions has been discounted. In this case, a discount rate of 15 per cent has been applied. The resultant NPVs can then be summed to arrive at a 'lifetime value' of $101.24 for this particular customer.

6.5.4 The benefits of LTV analysis

At this stage, it may not be immediately obvious why we might want to perform a calculation such as the one alluded to above. In fact, lifetime value can be used to drive five key management decisions:

- assigning acquisition allowances;
- choosing media for initial customer acquisition;
- setting selection criteria for customer marketing;
- investing in the reactivation of lapsed customers;
- assigning an asset value to the marketing database.

Each of these will now be considered in turn.

(a) Assigning acquisition allowances

An understanding of the lifetime value of an organization's customers can guide the determination of how much a particular organization may be willing to spend to recruit each new customer. Many organizations strive conscientiously to achieve a break-even position at the end of each of their recruitment campaigns. Whilst commendable, this is not at all necessary, so long as the future income stream from the customers being recruited is a healthy one. Organizations employing the lifetime value concept would therefore tend to assign somewhat higher acquisition allowances than those who do not.

To take an example, Domino Pizzas calculated originally the amount they could afford to spend on customer acquisition on the basis of the expected $6–7 sale. They soon realized that over the duration of a 'lifetime' of business a typical customer would actually be worth of the order of $5,000. This had a dramatic impact on thinking within the organization and it became much more relaxed about customer acquisition costs. It knew that provided it could keep customers loyal, a more than satisfactory return on their recruitment investment would accrue over time.

(b) Refining the targeting for customer acquisition campaigns

Marketers engaged in the perennial problem of customer recruitment are well versed in the necessity of asking questions such as:

'Which media should I be using for my recruitment activity?'

'What balance should I adopt between the media options that are available?'

'On what basis should I select potential customers for target?'

The traditional approach to answering these questions would have been to calculate the immediate ROI for each media and consider the response rates typically received from each media in the past. Some marketers may have gone further and calculated the cost per new customer attracted (i.e. cost of campaign ÷ number of customers attracted), the level of the average purchase, etc.

Such analyses suggest sub-optimal allocations of marketing resource, because they ignore certain known customer behaviours. Customers recruited from one medium may never buy again, whilst customers recruited by another medium might exhibit much greater degrees of loyalty. To take an example, a company marketing jewellery items might find that it generates a better immediate return on acquisition expenditure by using DRTV in preference to Direct Mail. By looking only at this immediate return it might therefore decide to invest heavily in DRTV. Looking at the lifetime value of customers recruited by each medium might, however, paint a different picture. Suppose only 10 per cent of customers recruited by DRTV ever buy again and the organization loses about 30 per cent of those that remain each year thereafter. Further suppose that 40 per cent of customers recruited by direct mail will buy again and only a 20 per cent attrition rate will be experienced each year thereafter. In this case, a consideration of lifetime value (assuming average purchase levels were similar) might lead the organization to favour direct mail over DRTV.

(c) Setting selection criteria for customer marketing

Lifetime value calculations can prove instructive, for more than just recruitment planning. The information can also be utilized to guide contact strategies for ongoing customer development.

For example, organizations could calculate the projected LTV for all the individuals on the database and assign them to one of, say, ten segments of value as a result. Such an analysis is presented in Figure 6.5 on p. 190.

When most companies perform this analysis for the first time they often obtain a result typical to that depicted in the figure. It is not at all unusual for a company to be doing business with a percentage of customers who will never be profitable. In some cases this figure can be as high as 30 per cent of the total customer base. Clearly, this is an

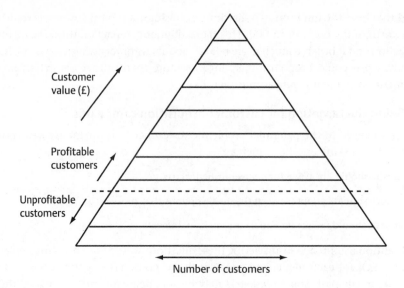

Fig. 6.5 Decile analysis of database by value

unsatisfactory state of affairs and, in practice, there are four alternative strategies for handling this group of customers:

- Attempts could be made to upgrade the lifetime value of the individuals concerned, perhaps by employing up selling or cross selling techniques.
- The individuals could be offered a new channel of distribution—perhaps instead of including them in the standard mailing programme, or contacting them by using a salesforce, they could be managed more cost effectively through the internet.
- The individuals could simply be deleted from the database and ongoing business contact could be refused.
- The organization could follow a strategy of 'benign neglect' and terminate all outgoing communication with the individuals concerned. This differs from (c) in that incoming requests for purchase would continue to be processed, but repeat business would not actively be encouraged.

The analysis depicted in Figure 6.5 could also be used to assign individuals who do have satisfactory LTVs to particular standards of care. It makes good sense for the airlines, for example, to develop frequent flier programmes to reflect the value of individuals who fly frequently. In essence, the airlines are recognizing that the balance of their marketing effort should follow the balance of their revenue. Losing a customer who flies only once every five years might be sad, but ultimately it is of little significance. Losing a customer who flies transatlantic three times a month is quite another matter. The balance of organizational effort should reflect the value of different categories of customers and hence LTV analysis can help guide an organization's retention expenditure to the customers who warrant it.

(d) **Investing in the reactivation of lapsed customers**

Without exception, all organizations now recognize the value of their database. Few would question the established wisdom that existing customers will always be the most cost-effective source of additional business. Few would also disagree with the notion that reactivating lapsed customers can be profitable. Having been sufficiently motivated to make a purchase at least once in the past, with the proper encouragement it is eminently possible that some lapsed customers will do so again, The problem, however, for many organizations lies in deciding which lapsed customers should be selected for contact. Whilst one could do this easily on the basis of the total amount they spent in the past, the average purchase level, or the length of time since the last purchase, it can be instructive to use projected lifetime value to inform the decision. With the right persuasion to respond, targeting those with a higher forecast LTV is likely to prove a most efficient use of resources. A 'reactivation allowance' can be built into the budget. A knowledge of how much an organization is prepared to commit to reactivating one customer, would inform the nature and quality of the contact strategy employed.

(e) **Assigning an asset value to the marketing database**

There are many competing demands upon the income of a typical organization. Quite reasonably, expenditure on marketing is often perceived as a cost to be minimized. Whilst it is certainly true that marketing can be regarded as a cost, it could also be seen as an investment. Using LTV analyses, organizations can explore the future behaviour of their database; this information can be used to place an overall value on customers as intangible assets. In the authors' experience, this can have a remarkably sobering impact on those responsible for the organization's financial management. The justification for customer recruitment activity suddenly becomes clearer, and the rationale for doing more for customers than simply writing to them with 'sales offers' is suddenly illuminated.

6.5.5 **Some common mistakes**

In section 6.5.3 we introduced a simple formula that could be used to calculate lifetime value in the case of an individual customer. Clearly, lifetime value is not difficult to calculate, yet there remains much confusion over which costs and revenues should be included in the calculation. In particular, many organizations continue to make two key mistakes in its application:

(a) **Mis-allocation of recruitment costs**

Initial acquisition costs should only be included in an LTV analysis, if an organization is looking either to decide on an appropriate allocation of recruitment expenditure (between the different media options available), or to predict the returns that will ultimately be generated by a given recruitment campaign. These are the only circumstances where recruitment costs have relevance. Generally speaking, therefore, lifetime value calculations should NOT include of the costs of acquisition. There is no justification for this, since this cost reflects merely the quality of an organization's fundraising, not the giving behaviour of a customer per se. To take a simple example, suppose the net contribution generated by a customer recruited from door to door activity is £250. He/she may well have been recruited from a campaign that was poorly targeted with a creative strategy that did not really complement the nature of the product. As a result, comparatively few customers may have been recruited and the cost of acquiring each new customer could have been as high as £270. Subtracting this value from the projected future contribution of that customer would leave an LTV of –£20. This would place the customer in a negative value segment making them a good candidate for deletion and yet they are actually, in relative terms, a high value customer! Recruitment costs are a past measure of the efficiency of an organization's marketing strategy—nothing more. They should not be used in any way to determine the standard of care a given customer will receive.

(b) Mis-allocation of overhead

The second key mistake organizations make in calculating lifetime value is to include indirect costs in the equation. Many organizations set off a percentage of future marketing overheads against customer revenues—fixed costs like database, administration costs, or even (in one case the authors' have encountered) brand advertising, on the grounds that by contributing to the overall image of the organization, it facilitates selling. A simple example will again serve to illustrate the folly of this strategy.

It has already been suggested that LTV calculations can be employed to deselect those customers who will never be profitable so as to concentrate resources on those that will. Many organizations simply delete, or deliberately neglect, those customers with a negative LTV. If overhead costs are included in LTV calculations this can result in a somewhat unfortunate cycle of events.

For example, imagine a very small organization with a customer base of only 100 individuals. Each customer has an LTV varying between £50 and £500 when only the direct costs/revenues in equation (1) above, are taken into consideration. By adding in a proportion of marketing overhead to the costs, LTV figures are reduced to a range from –£50 to £450. Suddenly, it appears to be unprofitable to deal with a number of customers—i.e. those with a negative LTV value. Assuming that there were ten such individuals, the prevailing logic would be to delete them from the active portion of the database. So far, so good.

What many organizations fail to understand is the marginal contribution each customer makes. If they now run a second LTV analysis, they find (probably to their surprise) that they still have customers in the negative range—perhaps this time from –£30 to £400. This is simply because the organization's overhead costs have not changed, but they now have only 90 customers to allocate these costs to. Each customer therefore bears a larger percentage of the overhead and some previously profitable customers now appear unprofitable. We might then decide to delete these leaving us with only 80 customers. Following this to its logical conclusion, an organization could continue to delete negative customers until it actually looks sensible to abandon its marketing activities altogether!

It is for this reason that LTV was earlier defined as the total net *contribution* from a customer. As long as a given customer generates more revenue than it costs an organization in direct costs to service them, they will make some form of contribution towards general organizational overhead. Whilst, therefore, in an accounting sense they might be unprofitable, it would be folly to stop contacting them. It is only when the direct costs of marketing look likely to exceed the revenues generated, that a customer should be deleted from the 'live' portion of the database.

6.5.6 **Calculating the LTV of discrete customer segments**

In section 6.5.3 we were concerned only with calculating the LTV for individual customers. More usually, organizations want to understand whether specific segments of their database exhibit higher lifetime values than others. This calls for a more sophisticated degree of analysis. In attempting to measure lifetime value the following process is recommended.

The first stage is to decide what the purpose of the analysis will be. Although this sounds rather obvious, many organizations are not clear from the outset exactly what they are hoping to gain from it. In many sectors, the technique is typically employed to determine whether specific segments of the database have a higher or lower value than others. Thus, if female customers appear to be worth more than male customers, or customers recruited by direct mail have a higher lifetime value than those recruited by press advertising, marketing resources can be allocated accordingly. Not only can recruitment resources be more appropriately targeted, but contact strategies employing appropriate degrees of care can be developed to ensure the highest possible degrees of loyalty amongst those segments with the strongest lifetime values. Lifetime value analysis is therefore commonly employed to determine the LTV of customers who have specific characteristics. The nature of these characteristics needs to be determined from the outset.

The next stage is to decide the period of analysis to use. It is not essential here that the chosen time period selected is based on the longest standing customers. Since predicting behaviour becomes progressively more difficult the further one looks into the future, and since contributions arising in the medium to long term will be heavily discounted, it is only important that the time period selected captures the majority of the contribution for a given segment of customers. As Dwyer (1989, p. 11) notes:

'We could forecast forever. Practically, however, because the retained account base typically is shrinking and the net benefits are so heavily discounted, the preponderance of LTV accrues in the first four or five years.'

As a consequence, most organizations adopt a time frame of five years for LTV analysis. The value of future contributions that occur beyond this period will be increasingly difficult to predict, as will the rates of customer attrition. In a sense, therefore, the term 'lifetime' value is something of a misnomer. It is entirely up to the organization concerned to set a suitable time frame for the analysis and to look at the lifetime value of its customers over this very specific horizon.

The next step should be to divide, or segment, the database into a manageable but distinct group of cells on the basis of the primary variable to be explored. Suppose we wish to explore the LTV of customers recruited by different media. To investigate this issue the database should be divided into groups of customers recruited by mail, DRTV, door-to-door, etc.

It is then necessary to establish the purchase behaviour of each of the cells identified above. A historical analysis of customer behaviour for medium should yield valuable information in respect of:

Attrition rate—this will almost certainly vary from year to year. For example, a large percentage of customers may make only one purchase. Those that do make two or more purchases tend to be more loyal and a much smaller percentage of this group will be lost from one year to another thereafter. Forecast attrition rates for the customers recruited by each medium should reflect this annual variation.

Purchase history—it should be possible to calculate typical response rates for members of each value cell according to the type of customer development activity employed. It should also be possible to track any trends in the actual amount spent in response to each campaign.

The final stage is to outline the intended development strategy, including, for example, the number of mailings, telephone calls, and the projected costs thereof.

The preceding information can then gainfully be employed to predict the likely future behaviour of new customers recruited into a particular cell. Armed with information about likely attrition rates, the future costs of servicing those customers, the predicted revenue streams, and an appropriate discount rate, one can then proceed to make predictions about the projected lifetime value of each cell, or category of purchaser.

Analytically, there are, of course, a whole range of alternative ways to explore the lifetime value of customers; for example, by, gender, age, geodemographic coding, or indeed any other categorizing variable stored in the database. LTV can even be used to help organizations in appropriate list selection based on past experience with a given supplier. In this case, it would be advisable to compute the gain from using a list, i.e. G, where:

$$G = (P \times N \times L) - (R - N/1000) - (C \times N) - F$$

Where

P = estimated response rate
N = number of names on the rental list
L = lifetime value (given that the customer enters the house list)
R = rental costs per 1000 names of the list
C = in the mail cost per piece mailed
F = fixed cost associated with renting the list

If $G > 0$, lifetime revenues will exceed costs and the list should be rented. In comparing one list with another, clearly the list with the highest value of G should be favoured.

Indeed, one could even turn this whole analysis on its head and begin by calculating the historical contribution made by each customer recruited in a given base year. Customers could then be allocated to a cell on the basis of their actual 'historic' value and the relationship between cell membership and other variables such as the amount of the first purchase, product categories purchased, gender, list of origin, etc. could then subsequently be explored. In this way, organizations can identify those variables that offer the greatest utility in terms of *predicting* the lifetime value of their customers and can, in essence, build up a profile of those individuals who are worth the most to their organization. This analysis is rather more elaborate, typically involving the use of a regression model.

6.5.7 **Why the reticence?**

Given the utility of the LTV, one could legitimately ask why greater use is currently not being made of the valuable information that such an analysis can yield. Dwyer (1989) suggests three reasons why LTV analysis has been slow to filter into direct marketing practice:

- Failure to disseminate the technology—neither professional nor academic writers have disseminated the technology effectively. The concept of lifetime value remains somewhat nebulous and ill-defined. Numerous magazine and trade-press articles make reference to LTV, but few authors are genuinely prepared to share their proprietary models and knowledge.

- Many computerized databases, particularly those more than five years old, are simply not capable of capturing the details of transactional data necessary to develop good predictive models. This has been a particular problem in the nonprofit sector, where databases are comparatively small and where, as a consequence, a significant number of low cost, yet from a data capture perspective, sub-optimal packages, have been available.

- The third 'problem' has already been alluded to earlier, as a potential opportunity. A key part of the utility of the LTV analysis is undoubtedly the ability to decide on the appropriate marketing strategies to follow. However, as Battberg (1987, p. 13) notes, 'clearly, the greater the mailing frequency, the higher the chances of buying again'. LTV is therefore a very fluid variable directly dependent on the contact strategy it was employed to select. This leads to an interesting paradox and creates a genuine problem for marketers in the selection of an appropriate method for combining response probabilities into each of the customer segments under analysis.

Writers such as Lewis (1995) have identified other more practical reasons why an LTV analysis has yet to become common practice:

- A disproportionate amount of effort expended on creative execution as the most tangible element of marketing. Experience suggests that the most cost effective form of customer recruitment activity will outperform the least by an average multiple of between three and four times. The best recruitment lists will also perform five or six times better than the worst. The best creative, however, will perform no more than 50 per cent better than the worst. It is difficult to see, therefore, why a disproportionate focus on direct marketing creative can be justified.

- Successful data driven marketing requires a synthesis of skills. To employ LTV successfully marketers need a combination of marketing, statistical analysis, and data processing skills. Whilst the sector has no difficulty recruiting and retaining bright, able individuals, the sophistication of tailored training programmes to develop their specific analytical skills is sometimes sadly lacking.

- Financial myopia—the majority of marketing targets continue to be short term in nature. For LTV data to gain the status within an organization that it warrants, the criteria against which individuals will be assessed must be radically reviewed. Until marketers are rewarded for positive changes in the forecast LTV of their database, the concept will always be subordinated to other less effective short-term measures of performance.

These problems are, however, not insurmountable and as the benefits that LTV analysis can offer become more fully understood, it seems inevitable that they will be overcome.

6.5.8 **FRAC analysis**

An alternative to lifetime value analysis, now commonly available on many database systems is FRAC. This is simply a mnemonic standing for:

Frequency—the time elapsing between purchases

Recency—the date of the last purchase

Amount—the average value of a customer's purchases

Category—the categories of product a consumer has purchased.

FRAC data can be helpful in determining an appropriate development strategy and, in particular, for deciding which segments of customers will receive a particular campaign. Over time, customers can be developed by their frequency of purchase, the amount of their average purchase, or the range of product categories they elect to buy. Recency data can also be used to prevent customers from lapsing. Communications and, if necessary, promotional offers can be targeted at customers who have not made a recent purchase to encourage further interest in the products a given company has to offer.

FRAC data can also be used to develop a score for each customer on a database. In this case, the score indicates the desirability of communicating with a given customer. It works on the following principles:

- Higher value customers are more attractive than lower value customers.
- Customers who buy frequently are statistically more likely to respond to a communication than those that don't.
- Customers who have bought from you in the past six months are more likely to buy from you than someone who hasn't made a purchase in over two years.

FRAC scoring can reflect these differences in individual customer behaviour and give the direct marketer considerable insight into who to target with a particular campaign.

Stone (1996) reports a common FRAC scoring method, showing how points might be derived in a particular case:

Recency

24 points = purchase in current quarter
12 points = purchase in the last six months
6 points = purchase in last nine months
3 points = purchase in last 12 months

Frequency Points

Number of points = number of purchases × 4

Amount Points

Number of points = 10 per cent of purchase value with a ceiling of 9 points.

The FRAC score then becomes F + R + A and customers with a high FRAC score in a given product category can then be selected to receive a campaign.

It should be noted that non-profit organizations also use this technique. In this case, many fundraising systems refer to RFV (Recency, Frequency, Value) and RFV scores are calculated on exactly the same principle.

6.6 **Loyalty programmes**

Having identified their higher value customers, many organizations set about designing marketing programmes designed to keep them loyal. United Airlines, for example, offers its frequent fliers a series of escalating benefits, the quality and range of which is dependent on the value and behaviour of the customer concerned (see Exhibit 1). Other companies interested in fostering loyalty elect to cast their net a little wider, making their scheme accessible to a wide proportion of the customer base. Exhibit 2 contains an example of this latter approach, detailing how Paramount were able to use a loyalty programme both to reward higher value purchasers and to attract new fans who might have enjoyed an occasional film, but who were not currently buying Star Trek products.

The essential feature of both these programmes is that the customer collects a certain number of points for each purchase they make and as they accumulate certain levels of points, they become eligible for a number of different premiums or rewards. All loyalty programmes work on essentially the same principle. However, the experience of over 30 years of various forms of customer loyalty initiative suggests that to be successful, loyalty programmes should:

Begin with a good base product that performs well in the market and is in some way differentiated—there will be little point in attempting to build loyalty to a product or brand that the consumer knows is defective, or frequently fails to live up to expectations. In such circumstances, consumers will be unlikely to suffer sufficient levels of the mediocre service to even begin to qualify for rewards. Indeed, if the base product is poor, attempts to induce repeat purchase are likely to be futile. The base product needs to be good and, in an ideal world, it should also be differentiated. In other words, there should be a clear reason why this particular product should be favoured. As will become clear later, it is this feature that can help shape the nature of the rewards available, to ensure that loyalty is fostered to the product/brand not to the loyalty programme. This is more than just a play on words. Loyalty programmes that generate loyalty to the scheme alone will be ineffective in fostering long-term changes in behaviour. As soon as the scheme is suspended, so too is the customer 'loyalty' exhibited. Indeed, there is now a considerable body of research that suggests this will be the case. A recent experiment, for example, studied the behaviour of children rewarded for drinking a flavoured fruit drink. The children were divided into three groups; those who were simply given the drink; those who were praised for drinking it; and those who were given a free cinema ticket if they finished the glass. Perhaps, not surprisingly, those who were rewarded with the free cinema ticket were most likely to drink and finish the product. But a week later they were the least likely to drink it.

Focus on intrinsic rather than extrinsic rewards—in the example quoted above, the offering of cinema tickets would be classified as an extrinsic reward. The reward of a cinema ticket has no link whatsoever to the product category. Indeed, extrinsic rewards by definition do not have a high affinity with the core product and will only lead to the desired behaviour whilst the reward is sustained. Intrinsic rewards, by contrast, are those that are inherently linked to the nature of the core product. In the case of the Latinuum Perspective, for example, (see Exhibit 2), the loyal Star Trek purchaser can expect to receive merchandise embedded in the Star Trek brand and not available elsewhere for sale. By participating in the scheme they are therefore buying into the brand and being rewarded with items that are unique.

The reward is genuinely valued and perceived as taking some effort on the part of the company to deliver—the consumer of 2001 is becoming ever more sophisticated. Consumers are alert to attempts to deceive or manipulate and have become ever more discerning in their choice of schemes in which to participate. Those that will ultimately be successful are those that add value to the core experience the consumer is buying anyway. The scheme offered by the upmarket High Street retailer 'Liberty' provides one such example. Like many high street stores, Liberty has its own storecard scheme. Every £1 spent generates one reward point that may be redeemed in the store. The interesting facet of the Liberty strategy, however, is that the rewards provide the consumer with benefits that their money can't buy. Consumers have therefore been offered books signed by the author, or, if the highest level of reward is attained, even a Xmas tree delivered in December by store designers and decorated to the consumer's own specification.

Offer a strong personalization factor—superior loyalty schemes offer the consumer considerable choice in respect of how their reward may be redeemed. Virgin Atlantic, for example, offers fliers accumulating over 250,000 miles in its frequent flier programme the opportunity to request tailor made rewards, which could include such diverse activities as parachuting over the desert or sailing in the Caribbean. The choice is up to the consumer and the more loyalty they exhibit to the airline, the greater that choice becomes. Of course, one might argue that in offering this kind of premium, the airline is tending towards the provision of extrinsic rewards. Whilst one could argue this case, it should be remembered that rewards such as those described are still in keeping with the character of the 'adventurous' Virgin brand and there is therefore still a clear rationale for their inclusion in the programme.

Be maintained at a profit—there are a number of examples where companies have failed to do the maths on their loyalty programmes and been caught off-guard by the resultant hyper-demand. Hoover famously failed to set the qualification level for awards at an appropriate level. It became possible under their scheme to qualify for a free transatlantic flight through the purchase of only one low-value household appliance. Whilst the company was, fortunately, able to honour its commitments, it became the target for ridicule and abuse from consumers who found that their first choice of flight was not available. In the US, the Old Kent Financial Corp. encountered similar difficulties. It had to stop offering frequent flier awards through its CardMiles programme after a fall in air fares and the programme's generous redemption policy made the scheme so popular it was no longer profitable. Cardholders could obtain a $100 discount for every 500 miles earned, four certificates being enough to qualify for a free domestic US flight.

Distance itself from price discounts—all too many loyalty programmes are little more than discount schemes designed on the principle of the more you buy the more you get. In this case, it is not brand loyalty that is being built up, but transactional loyalty. The danger with this approach is that whenever the competition comes up with a better scheme, consumers will defect in their thousands. There is also a danger here that firms engaging in such practices could actually serve to undermine the dynamics of their industry. Consider Figure 6.6. Typically, brand loyalty programmes are delivered in 2–4 mail contacts each year. High and low value customers therefore tend to get a somewhat even exposure to this activity. Figure 6.6 also shows the exposure that the same customer might have to transactional loyalty activity centred on price. By virtue of their higher frequency of purchase it is actually the high value customers who have the greatest

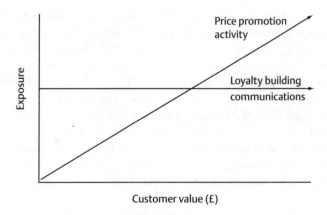

Fig. 6.6 Customer exposure to marketing promotions

exposure to this category of activity. In effect, many firms are conditioning their highest value customers to become price sensitive! An effective loyalty programme should have the opposite effect and actually decrease consumer sensitivity to price as a genuine affinity with the brand is engendered.

6.7 **Card based programmes**

A brief look through the average wallet should be enough to convince most of us of the utility of card based loyalty programmes. Such schemes became particularly fashionable in the 1990s. High street stores, DIY outlets, and petrol retailers seem to have been particularly prolific in their development and use of this loyalty device.

Cards generally fall into one of two categories: magnetic stripe and smart cards. The former are very cheap, typically costing only a few pence to produce. The customer data is stored on a database and each time the card is swiped, data in respect of the purchase made is captured and centrally stored. Smart cards, by contrast, are considerably more expensive, currently about a £1 each to produce. The reason for the expense is that customer data is actually stored on the card. The customer thus takes this data with them from one transaction to another, a useful feature, particularly if the loyalty programme is being shared by a number of different suppliers.

Card based schemes are certainly not cheap. Recent experience in the UK suggests that a company with over a million customers could expect to spend £5–10 million in set up costs and around 70p per year thereafter communicating with each customer on the database. When the costs of the rewards are factored in as well, the organization needs to be sure that the additional revenue accruing will be worth what amounts to a substantial investment.

The loyalty scheme developed by the food retailer Tesco is a good example of a card based programme. Every time the customer visits a store to make a purchase, they are invited to use their loyalty card. The card is swiped at the check-out terminal and details and value of the purchases are stored on a central computer. Vouchers are then generated by the scheme at regular intervals throughout the year and posted to customers participating in the scheme. These 'rewards' fall into one of two categories. Firstly, the customer receives money off coupons that allow him/her to save money on their next visit to the store buying whatever products they wish. The value of these vouchers is directly proportional to the amount spent during the period. The second category of voucher is designed to generate interest in specific products or product categories. The consumer could thus be offered 50p off a particular brand of coffee or 40p off their next purchase of fruit and vegetables. The power of the database is such that these vouchers should be of direct relevance to the consumer. Thus, for example, those consumers known to have purchased baby food, could be targeted in the future with a promotional offer for a specific brand.

At the time of writing, some retailers have taken this a step further and now print vouchers directly at the point of sale for use on the next visit to a store. This works on the same principle as Tesco's scheme, in that a knowledge of past purchases is used to guide the vouchers that are printed in any one case. Thus, a customer buying a pack of disposable razors in week one, could be printed a voucher enticing them to try a different brand in week three, which the system knows is about a week before they would be due to make their next purchase of this product category.

6.8 Cross-category programmes

So far in this discussion of loyalty programmes we have confined our discussion to schemes that are unique to one supplier. This isn't always the case and there are now a number of successful examples of cross-category promotions. One of the most well known of these is undoubtedly the Air Miles Scheme. It was founded by Air Miles Travel Promotions Ltd in 1988, to help organizations such as banks and petrol suppliers differentiate themselves in the market, whilst at the same time helping the participating airline to fill empty seats on its aircraft. The Air Miles organization therefore signed up a series of clients in different industries who stood to benefit from the excitement and high profile that participation in the scheme would engender. Customers of these organizations were rewarded for their loyalty by an award of air miles, the size of which would be proportional to their value to the organization. Air Miles Travel Promotions Ltd charged their clients for this service and used the funds to buy 'empty' seats on flights from BA. Its revenue stream therefore comprised the difference between the fees paid by the corporate clients and the payments to BA. From the customer's perspective, the scheme was unique as it offered the opportunity to collect air miles at a variety of different categories of outlet, making it possible to accrue the necessary points to exchange for rewards much faster. Indeed, an average family was able to earn enough miles to exchange for a free return flight from London to Paris in only a few months.

6.9 Measuring and benchmarking the payback

As was noted above, effective customer loyalty programmes should enhance profitability not detract from it. It is therefore essential that adequate planning and monitoring/control mechanisms are set in place to ensure this proves to be the case.

In approaching programme monitoring it is essential to begin with a prediction of baseline sales (i.e. the sales that would have been achieved anyway in the absence of the programme) over the duration of the planning cycle. From this, the marketer should attempt to forecast the uplift in sales each month (or planning period) that will result from the loyalty marketing activity. The additional revenue accruing can then be compared with the costs of the programme and a programme ROI calculated. If this ROI is acceptable the programme can be initiated. If not, the programme can be modified in some way until a satisfactory projected ROI is achieved. Revenue and cost targets for each month can then be derived and as the programme is implemented, forecast revenues and costs can be compared with actual revenues and costs. Any significant deviation from the projected figures can be flagged and corrective action initiated to ensure that future targets are met.

Of course, following our discussion of customer lifetime value, you could be forgiven for thinking this approach is a little simplistic. Whilst the initial returns accruing to loyalty marketing activity will be of interest, it is hoped that the effects of the programme will be particularly long term in nature. It may, therefore, make more sense to measure the impact of loyalty marketing on projected customer lifetime values and quantify success accordingly. As Peppers and Rogers (1995, p. 49) note:

'Instead of measuring the effectiveness of a marketing programme by how many sales transactions occur across an entire market during a particular period, the new marketer will gauge success by the projected increase or decrease in a customer's expected future value to the company.'

6.10 **Summary**

In this chapter we have examined the issue of customer loyalty which we defined as the desire on the part of a customer to continue to do business with a given supplier over time. We looked at why loyalty is important and the fact that even small increases in customer loyalty can have a marked impact on overall profitability. We also examined how loyalty could be fostered, building up baseline service quality and commitment to the product or brand. We have also established that not all customers are created equal and that in building loyalty it is particularly important for an organization to concentrate on its higher value customers. We concluded the chapter by looking at the characteristics of successful loyalty marketing programmes, offering a number of concrete examples for the purpose of illustration.

Discussion questions

1 With the proliferation of customer loyalty programmes, to what extent do you think organizations can really build genuine customer loyalty?

2 You work as the customer retention manager for a catalogue company that currently loses 40 per cent of its active customers each year. Outline to your Managing Director the steps you would take to verify the cause of this high rate of attrition and how you suspect you might subsequently engender higher levels of loyalty.

3 Faith Popcorn famously remarked that marketers should strive to 'wrap the product in the soul of the company'? What point do you think she was trying to make? What are the implications for loyalty marketing?

4   How might an understanding of customer lifetime value impact on the design of direct marketing strategy?

5   What advice would you offer an internet bookseller looking to develop a customer loyalty programme for the first time? What form might such a programme take — and what pitfalls should they look to avoid?

Further reading

Battberg R. C. (1987) 'Research Opportunities in Direct Marketing', *Journal of Direct Marketing* 1(1), 7–14.

Bitran G. and Mondschein S. (1997) 'A Comparative Analysis of Decision Making Procedures in the Catalogu Sales Industry', *European Management Journal* 15(2), 105–16.

De Souza G. (1992) 'Designing A Customer Retention Plan', *Journal of Business Strategy*, March-April, 24–8.

Dwyer F. R., Schurr P. H. and Oh S. (1989) 'Developing Buyer-Seller Relationships', *Journal of Marketing*, 51(2), 11–27.

Henley Centre (1994) *The Loyalty Report* (London: Henley Centre).

Jenkinson A. (1996) *Valuing Your Customers: From Quality Relations to Quality Relationships Through Database Marketing* (Maidenhead: McGraw-Hill).

Jones T. and Sasser W. E. Jr (1995) 'Why Satisfied Customers Defect', *Harvard Business Review*, Nov./Dec., 88–99.

Lewis T. (1995) 'Using Data-Driven Marketing To Enhance Acquisition Performance', *Journal of Database Marketing*, 3(1), 13–23.

Peppers D. and Rogers M. (1995), 'A New Marketing Paradigm: Share of Customer NotMarket Share', Managing Service Quality, 5(3), 48–51.

Raphel M. (1991), 'Stop Mailing To Everyone . . . ', *Direct Marketing* (Feb.), 53–4.

Reichheld F. and Sasser W. E. Jr (1990) 'Zero Defections: Quality Comes To Services', *Harvard Business Review*, Sept./Oct., 105–11.

Ryans A. B. and Wittnk D. R. (1977) 'The Marketing of Services: Categorization with Implications for Strategy', *Contemporary Marketing Thought*, Greenberg B. and Bellenger D. (eds.) (Chicago, IL: American Marketing Association), 312–14.

Sargeant A. (1998) *A Lifetime of Giving* (West Malling, Kent: Charities Aid Foundation).

Stone B. (1996) *Successful Direct Marketing Methods*, 5th edn. (Chicago: NTC Business Books).

Exhibit 1: United Airlines

The United Airlines Frequent Flier Programme has been designed in partnership with the airline's star alliance partners, namely Air Canada, Air New Zealand, Air Nippon Airways, Ansett Australia, Lufthansa, SAS, THAI, and VARIG. Passengers flying on any one of these airlines can earn mileage points for every mile they fly. Miles can also be earned with associated Car Hire firms, Hotels, and Cruise Lines. Miles can also be earned by travel on Amtrak, Eurostar, and by using a range of financial service products. Miles can even be earned by purchasing flowers at 1800Flowers.Com

Participants in the programme can acquire one of three classes of membership. Participants acquiring at least 25,000 miles in a calendar year attain Premier Status. Participants earning over 50,000 or more miles reach Premier Executive Status and those acquiring 100,000 miles attain the highest level of membership—Premier Executive 1K. Each grade of membership is entitled to a different pattern of benefits, the details of which are reported in Table 6.2. There is, therefore, an incentive for individuals to remain loyal to the airline, for not only will they attract awards such as free upgrades, they can also achieve a higher grade of membership and qualify for an enhanced series of benefits.

Exhibit 2: It's mail Jim but not as we know it!!

For over 30 years Star Trek fans have been avidly following the adventures of their heroes as they boldly went where no man has gone before. Recent years, though, have seen something of a revolution in the Star Trek genre. The original television series has been succeeded by a New Generation crew and two new series, Star Trek Voyager and Star Trek Deep Space Nine. During 1998 and 1999 26 new videos a year were released onto the UK market and Paramount Home Entertainment, the UK distributors of Star Trek, were looking for new ways to keep the fans interested.

The Paramount team decided on the development of a loyalty programme known as the Latinum Perspective. The name 'Latinum' was suggested as it was the currency used in the Deep Space Nine television series. Customers are invited to save up the strips of Latinum they receive with their video purchases and exchange them for unique Star Trek merchandise. By early 1999, 25,000 Star Trek fans had joined the scheme.

In the first year of its operation, the programme did not encourage a dialogue and the emphasis was firmly on in-pack communication and the subsequent fulfilment of merchandise orders. In the second year of its operation, however, the programme became interactive. A welcome pack was generated at the beginning of 1999 and customers were asked to specify the nature of the gifts they would like to receive. There was also a Member-Get-Member scheme where fans were invited to suggest other fans who would benefit from membership. The result was a dramatic growth in numbers to around 40,000 by the end of the year.

The programme yielded valuable information about the average Star Trek fan, who appears to be predominantly male and aged between 14 and 40. The fans have a high internet usage and a large proportion still live with their parents, reflecting the number of teenagers that buy into the genre.

Case Study Table 1 Frequent flier benefits by membership grade

Premier benefits include:	Premier	Premier executive	1K
Mileage qualification	25,000	50,000	100,000
Mileage bonus	25%	100%	100%
Priority check-in on United	X	X	X
Priority boarding	(where available)	X	X
Dedicated reservations phone line in many locations	X	X	X
Premier Seating in United Economy	X	X	X
Complimentary North American Upgrade Certificates	X	X	X
Use of Upgrade Certificates with purchase of any published fare	X	X	X
Upgrade priority (hours prior to flight departure that upgrades are processed)	24 hrs. on any published fare*	72 hrs. on any published fare	100 hrs. on any published fare
Priority reservation waitlist on all Star Alliance airlines	X	X	X
Priority airport standby for flights on all Star Alliance airlines	X	X	X
Rebooking assistance		X	X
Extra baggage allowance		X	X
Priority check-in on Star Alliance airlines, where indicated by Star Alliance Gold sign		X	X
Access to select Star Alliance member lounges when travelling on Star Alliance members (international travel only)		X	X
Top waitlist priority			X
Outcalls during irregular operations			X
Saver Award blackout dates waived			X
Special 1K Service Centers at selected U.S. airports			X

* 72 hrs. with full-fare ticket.
Please Note: The requirements for achieving these Premier membership levels and their benefits are subject to change from year to year. Some classes of service may not qualify.

The initial welcome mailing was followed up by regular newsletters which detailed new video releases, kept fans up to date with Star Trek trivia, encouraged participation in Star Trek competitions, and invited feedback from subscribers. The mailings are initiated by the fictional Starfleet Captain Rundoc Zill who provides what the creative agency regard as the personal touch giving fans a reference point within the Paramount organization.

Paramount also tried during 1999 to strengthen the relationship with the fans by running a series of Star Trek events with key retailers such as HMV and MVC. These events were invitation-only evenings for Latinum Perspective members and designed to allow the fans to meet other local 'Trekkies' and discuss their favourite episodes.

Case Study Fig. 1 Latinum Perspective
Case materials kindly supplied by Paramount Home Entertainment (UK) and the Haygarth Group (a full-service marketing agency).

Case study: County Insurance Services

Robin Hammond gazed transfixed, from the window of his tenth floor office, watching a seemingly endless stream of cars enter the car-park below. It wasn't the first time his mind had wandered since taking on his new role at the end of January 1997. In the four months that had passed since his appointment as the new Marketing Director of County Insurance Services, he seemed to have been deluged with a mountain of paperwork, none of which appeared, on the face of it, to be particularly illuminating.

It wasn't going to be as easy to meet the requirements of his new role as he had at first thought. To begin with, this was his first financial service appointment as he came from a background in a very different industry. Having spent the last five years as a marketing manager for a UK subsiduary of Ford, he had had considerable marketing planning experience, particularly in the realm of relationships. Indeed, that had been one of the key reasons for his appointment as County were keen to draw on his successful experience of relationship management in the automotive sector. He remembered the conversation that had taken place with the CEO directly after his appointment:

'Ah Robin, good to meet with you again. We're expecting great things of you. County has been struggling for some months now to achieve a new identity in the market. I'm afraid we've lost a lot of ground to our competitors just recently, and to be honest we're not entirely clear why our portfolio has suddenly lost its attractiveness. We've been historically one of the most aggressive companies in the marketplace, successfully recruiting customers from each of our major competitors. The problem is we just can't seem to keep them'.

At his first formal briefing two days later, it became apparent that one of his first responsibilities would be to propose to the board a strategy for remedying this problem. The turnover rate amongst policyholders was 5 per cent higher than the industry-wide average despite the fact that premiums compared very favourably with each of the other major players. To salvage this situation, he remembered thinking at the time that he could well be able to instigate many of the changes he had recommended to Ford, but as time went on, the possibility of simply borrowing ideas from one sector and successfully applying them to another was getting ever more remote.

To complicate matters still further, he had also received a number of suggestions in respect of possible ways forward from members of staff across the organization who clearly felt threatened by current developments. Whilst these were obviously intended to be helpful, the diversity of views being expressed were only serving to heighten the sense of confusion he was already experiencing.

A selection of this material is provided in the portfolio which follows:

Memorandum

To: Robin Hammond
From: Peter Clarke (Director — Car Insurance Services)
Date: 10/01/98

I know you've only just taken over Robin, but I need your support for a major new customer acquisition programme. With our current attrition rate of 25 per cent per annum I need to continue to recruit new customers to make up the shortfall, otherwise this division is going to be far short of its financial targets for both 1999 and 2000.

We were able to get a good response to the cold recruitment mailings we did last year, but I think we can do even better. I thought about offering an extra incentive for people to transfer their existing policy to us. Possibilities include, a reduced rate of premium for the first twelve months, flexible payment methods, or perhaps some form of promotional voucher.

I'd be grateful for any suggestions you could offer.

To: Robin Hammond
Marketing Director

From: Sally Clark
Information Services

In response to your request for information I write to confirm that we do currently segment the databases we hold in each division by 'customer value'. Taking the premium paid over the previous year we allocate each user to one of three value bands and profile each segment using the demographic information we gathered when they first joined us. The information we gain doesn't really tell us much though. Our best customers for each insurance product tend to be either A or B type individuals.

We obviously use this information to target new customers, but we don't yet use it for any other purpose. What did you have in mind? I know Jack is not in favour of segmented mailings, since this would obviously triple our costs.

Hope this is helpful.

To: All Staff

From: Jack Mayhew
Chairman

Re: Satisfaction Ratings

I am pleased to report it has been another good year for County. The changes we have made in customer service appear to have paid off. Over 76 per cent of customers are either satisfied or very satisfied with the level of service provided. Our research agency report that our current levels of satisfaction are 3 per cent up on last year. They have helpfully provided a graph of overall satisfaction levels using the usual 5 point scale. I've attached a copy below for your reference.

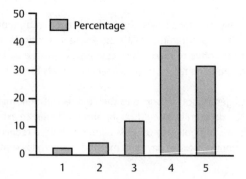

We also have this by value segment

Value segment	Rating (%)				
	1	2	3	4	5
High	0	0	15	65	20
Average	3	5	14	55	23
Low	4	7	15	45	29

There are no appreciable differences in performance across each division. Hence the results are reported here in aggregate terms only.

To: **Robin Hammond**
From: **Jack Mayhew**
Date: **07/01/97**

Re: **Organization Structure**

I am attaching a copy of County's organization structure. This version is greatly simplified, because each of our Directors have their own team, (i.e Marketing, Risk, Human Resources, Finance, Information Services) and these would obviously provide input into the various divisions as and when necessary. I've found over the years that it pays to allow the divisions as much autonomy as possible. It allows their respective Directors the flexibility they need to respond effectively to the needs of their customers.

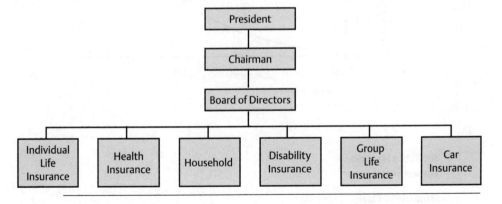

To **Robin Hammond**
From: **Susan James**
Director: Healthcare Division
Date: **24/02/97**

Re: **Defection Curve**

I have been calculating some statistics that I thought you might be interested in. I have been trying to calculate the real worth of our customers. If one of our customers leaves after only the first year we currently take a £30 loss on the relationship (the costs of acquisition in this sector are high). In the graph below I have tried to look beyond this first year to look at the lifetime value of a typical customer assuming County were to have a variety of different defection rates. If we can keep a customer for four years we generate a profit stream the net present value of which would be around £100. This is pretty much the level of loyalty we're hitting at the moment. Customers stay on average for around 4.5 years.

What bothers me though is what happens to the defection curve beyond year five. If we were able to cut our defection rate from 20 per cent to 10 per cent, the average life span of our relationship would double from five years to ten years, but the value of each customer would more than double from £134 to £300. As the defection rate drops another 5 per cent, the average lifespan of a customer doubles again and profits rise 75 per cent — from £300 to £525. I feel sure we should be using this information.

Defection Curve

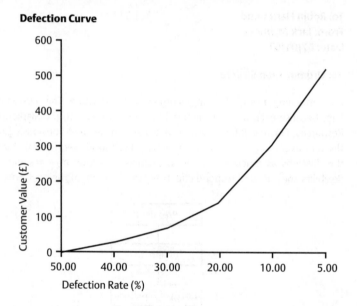

To: Robin Hammond
Marketing Director

From: Sally Clark
Information Services

You were asking at the meeting the other day about what priorities the customer places on what elements of the decision making process. I promised to look out the research we did 18 months ago.

In fact the priority they give things changes depending on whether they are buying for the first time or renewing after having had some experience of us (this can involve any form of contact — including making a claim). The following are the priorities the research suggested.

New Business	Those with experience of us
Price (cheapest)	Service issues
Reputable	Price (value for money)
Service issues	People
People	Reputable
Product	Product

It is interesting to note that product issues are the lowest in terms of priority to the customer.

The research also showed that customers want a company that:

1. Offers service (with a capital S)
2. Pays claims quickly
3. Treats the customer fairly
4. Has a good reputation or is the one that they already deal with

To: Robin Hammond
From Rob Davies, First Choice Research
Date: 13th March 1997

I now have the information you requested about County's key competitors

County Compared To The Main Direct Writers (Number of Policies and Growth Rates Achieved)

Year	County policies	Annual growth	Direct line	Annual growth	Norwich Union	Annual growth
1990	480,000		120,000			
1991	499,000	4.0%	190,000	58.3%		
1992	510,000	2.2%	245,000	28.9%	30,000	
1993	519,000	1.8%	290,000	14.3%	85,000	183.3%
1994	533,000	2.6%	400,000	37.9%	150,000	76.5%
1995	566,000	6.2%	700,000	75.0%	260,000	73.3%
1996	589,000	4.1%	1,200,000	71.4%	325,000	25.0%

I must admit I found these figures disappointing particularly as a number of your divisions opened their own telemarketing service in 1993. I can't see why your performance is not catching up with Direct Line.

I was able to find a secondary study conducted in 1996 though, which might shed some light on this. It indicates the levels of awareness amongst the general public of a number of major insurance companies.

Comparative Spontaneous Awareness

Company	General public
Direct Line	67%
Norwich Union	55%
AA	45%
Lloyds	37%
County	27%

To: Robin Hammond
Marketing Director

From: Sally Clark
Information Services

John Brake mentioned that you were looking for information on what customers think of us. We conducted research some three ago which might be helpful. It was part of some research we did into County's image—unfortunately it was only conducted among existing or recently lapsed insurance customers

Positive association	Negative association
Reliable	Only motor insurance
Easy to deal with	Remote
Good reputation	Old fashioned
You can trust them	Boring
Understanding	Just average
Competitive	Sometimes slow

We all felt rather pleased at the time. The positives are how we want to be seen and the first point on the negative side is not surprising—especially as we only asked people with motor insurance! 'Old fashioned' and 'Boring' were the ones we really worried about.

To: Robin Hammond

From: Mike Richards
Finance Director

Re: Lapse Rates

You recently asked for details on lapse rates. Our lapse rate of 20 per cent conceals some considerable variation by sector. In the motor and household sectors it is around 25 per cent, whilst in the life insurance sector it is somewhat lower at only 12 per cent. These are all slightly above the sector norms, of 15 per cent and 10 per cent respectively. At present we have no real understanding of why this might be so. When we ask customers about their satisfaction they always rate us highly.

To: Robin Hammond
From: Peter Clarke
Date: 23/03/97

Re: Memo

I have just received a memo from Finance which I am copying to you. How do they expect me to do my job! I need the recruitment budget if I'm going to make my future targets. They're so short sighted — Any chance you could have a chat with them on my behalf?

To: Peter Clarke
From: Leslie Jones
Finance Director

Re: Customer Acquisition Programme

I am not prepared to authorize your latest budget request unless you do something about your cost structure. The figures just don't add up. You want to spend £200K on a major new direct mail recruitment campaign, but given our usual response rate to your mailings, this will likely only attract 1,200 new customers. It is thus costing us £167 to recruit each new customer, even when you make no allowance for admin costs! At present there just isn't enough margin on these policies to make this worthwhile. I just can't justify this to our Chairman.

Can't you do something about our lapse rates instead?

Discussion questions

1   In your role as Robin Hammond, identify the weaknesses with County's current marketing operations.

2   Develop specific acquisition and retention plans to resolve these problems.

Chapter 7

Testing and Research

Contents

7.1 Objectives

By the end of this chapter you should understand:

(a) how the research industry is structured;

(b) the role of instinct in testing and research;

(c) the different types and purposes of market research;

(d) how knowledge management fits in;

(e) the scope and content of a test and research plan.

7.2 **Introduction**

Testing and research plays a pivotal role in the development of successful direct marketing strategies. The direct marketing environment is an increasingly complicated one with a myriad of choices facing decision makers where testing and research may be utilized to reduce risk. Is the voice-over for a DRTV offer of a rowing machine pitched correctly? Is the use of emotion appropriate for a direct mail campaign for a charity? Would local radio be more effective than the local press for a promotion by a car dealer?

The aim is to provide information to assist managers in making better direct marketing decisions. This chapter will review the key concepts and practices when it comes to testing and research in direct marketing. As a process, direct testing and research identifies a management problem or opportunity and translates it to a research problem for which data are collected, analysed and reported. As such the direct market researcher should set out to (1) gather, (2) analyse, and (3) interpret data in a cost effective and professional manner.

7.3 **Market research industry**

There are five strands to the market research industry: custom research, field services, data analysis, syndicated services, and branded research products. **Custom research** is conducted by a variety of organizations from small one-person consultancies to major companies who undertake bespoke marketing projects. For example, a company may wish to learn, in depth, what motivates people when choosing a new credit card and, in particular, how they would view a cash-back offer. A series of focus groups might be undertaken. The aim would be to use the information to model a direct marketing campaign at a later stage. While it may be possible to find out a great deal of information from secondary (existing published information) sources about credit cards and their use, the use of empirical (specifically collected information) sources via focus groups may be seen as necessary to gain extra insight into the market.

To undertake empirical research there is a veritable army of **field services** available.

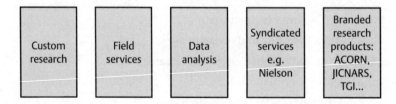

Fig. 7.1 Market research industry

These are small consultancies to large organizations whose staff go out and conduct research, often using surveys or observation techniques directly or indirectly through CCTV. From here, the information may be sent to **data analysis** consultancies or larger organizations which undertake the data analyses. They deal with all kinds of data from consumer surveys and purchasing bar-code information to business to business relational information and/or internally generated material using sophisticated software.

Syndicated services are as they sound—research services offered to a syndicate of companies. For example, Nielson offers panel surveys to companies. For a particular audience or a cross-section, you pay a set price per question. This is more cost-effective than setting up your own panel but is generally more useful to companies that have specific and limited information needs rather than more complex and wider, in which case custom research might be more appropriate. Finally, **branded research products** such as ACORN residential neighbourhood types based on the 10 yearly national census, JICNARS newspaper and magazine readership surveys, or TGI panels which combine purchasing, attitudinal, and media behaviour are available. Such branded research is regularly updated and published and available by subscription and provides valuable overall market planning data for direct marketers.

7.4 **Instinct**

It is often the case that direct marketers attach magical qualities to the results of research: 'aha—the numbers show we should . . .'. In reality, testing and research helps eliminate options, but the results might not be conclusive or definitive. Direct marketers often feel that market testing will provide the complete solution to any direct research question. Unfortunately, this is rarely the case as the marketing environment is dynamic and isolating one or two research variables in a test is unlikely, in itself, to provide all the answers. At some point or other, direct marketers, like everyone else in marketing, have to make decisions. Certainly, market tests may help narrow the options, but nevertheless, there is rarely any 100 per cent certain direct marketing decision.

For example, several different direct mailings may be made by a garden design company with each one at a slightly varied price to see which one works best. At this point intuition, experience, and instinct come into play along with the research findings. For a start, you might find that the mailing did not vary the price sufficiently to make a difference in response. Furthermore, if there was a difference in response, you can never be entirely sure that the price change was the key. People interested in garden design are few and far between and the mailing might have just hit some prospects for whom price was not the issue—despite this being your test criterion. Indeed, other research techniques than a direct mail test might have been faster, cheaper, and more effective. Whatever the results, intuition and experience will play a role in the final decision.

Why test and do research? If you do not test or do some research, then nothing is eliminated, all choices are viable and there are lots of options. Solid testing and research can eliminate some of the options and narrow the field of decision-making.

7.5 **Types of direct marketing research**

There are three types of direct marketing research: applied, basic, and methodological. Each one will now be examined in turn.

7.5.1 **Applied direct testing and research**

The vast majority of direct marketing testing and research is applied—that is it is designed to be used in the decision-making process directly. Applied research can range from research into the nature of the development of competitive strategies or how consumers are changing in their buying patterns, to specific research into varied creative approaches or the use of different direct media. Because of its nature, applied research is usually bespoke, i.e. specifically designed for the company or organization concerned, and, therefore, proprietary—owned by the company or organization doing the research. Basic research is done to give an edge to direct marketing and is rarely shared with other organizations until the owners of the data no longer feel it has any market value.

7.5.2 **Basic direct testing and research**

Basic testing and research is quite different to applied. Whereas applied research is specific to the needs of a specific company or organization, basic research is more generally applicable. This is because basic research deals in the realms of general principles and theories that can be used in direct marketing. An applied piece of research might examine the effect of differently worded headlines in a press ad eliciting a direct response for a fire alarm company. The equivalent basic research might identify the best headline approaches and kinds of layouts for direct response advertisements in the press as a whole. Therefore, the findings of basic research can be used by any company or organization. Such research is often sponsored by direct marketing associations and conducted by practitioners and/or academics and published in trade or academic journals or texts for widespread consumption.

7.5.3 **Methodological testing and research**

Methodological testing and research provides a completely separate function to applied and basic. The point of methodological testing and research is to find new and better ways to conduct direct research and add value for practitioners as a whole. For example, as consumers increasingly adapt and use direct mail, methodological researchers need to monitor techniques constantly to maintain response rates and interest. Researchers have examined such issues as the role of incentives in response rates and whether it helps or not to include postage stamps on reply envelopes or to use business postal reply codes, as well as the impact of follow-up letters. Such research is made widely available to enhance the practices within the direct marketing business as a whole rather than for the benefit of a specific company or organization.

7.6 **Purposes of direct testing and research**

There are three purposes for direct testing and research: descriptive, exploratory, and explanatory (Churchill, 1999). Each one or a combination can be applied to applied, basic, and methodological research types.

7.6.1 **Descriptive**

Given its name, it is easy to see that descriptive research is done to provide a report or depiction of a problem or issue. Researchers normally do not start off with any sense of how to explain anything, the aim is simply to describe the position. Thus, direct marketers might examine the size of the industry in the UK by number of firms or expenditure and audiences to different direct media. The results of the research would be valuable for the industry, but would not be linked to any hypotheses about the industry.

7.6.2 **Exploratory**

Exploratory research differs from descriptive in that it sets out to answer a specific question with an explanation of some kind. It is deemed exploratory because it is normally the first stage in a programme of research. Such an approach is suitable if direct marketers want to attempt to discover the relationship between some variables like the use of colour in a mailing. This might be a forerunner to a more elaborate and expensive study that will use the findings of the exploratory work to inform the research plan. Normally, exploratory research studies use small sample sizes and are often conducted using focus groups. For example, a company might test several different propositions for a credit card company on 10–20 people from the target market before going into production and direct testing.

7.6.3 **Explanatory**

You can guess by now that explanatory research is undertaken to try to explain likely responses to direct marketing approaches and relationships between variables. It goes well beyond description as the intent is to provide an explanation of what will happen and why. In order to do such research you need to control as many variables as possible. So, for example, you might do some exploratory research which identifies two main target markets for a new power tool for the DIY market. Having narrowed the field to two targets (house owners: 25–34 year old men and women/35–44 year old men), the explanatory research can be used to undertake a controlled study involving both the identified targets with a neutral control group (house owners: 18–65 year old men and women). Any differences in response from either target group could be compared to the control group.

7.7 **A note on knowledge management**

Direct marketers have sold themselves as being smart people who solve clients' problems. The 'smart direct people' proposition will have to be replaced by one based upon the benefits of broad experience and access to knowledge. MISs (management information systems) have been around for the past 20 years. These are systems based on internal records, decision support systems and marketing intelligence and research that provide a steady stream of information for managers as well as being able to respond to specific questions; for example, sales, market share, and competitive conditions. However, relatively recent software and computer developments have enabled firms to codify, store, and share knowledge more easily and cheaper than ever before. 'Knowledge management' (KM) concerns any direct marketing organization depending on smart people and a flow of ideas (Hansen et al., 1999; Sarvary, 1999; Zack, 1999). It is no longer enough for direct marketers to show clients that they are working for many clients on different problems and synthesizing the experience—direct marketers have to demonstrate that they can use their collective knowledge base. KM represents a quantum leap in the direct research process.

Defined formally, knowledge management is the process of creating value from an organization's intangible assets. It is the amalgamation of concepts from the applied artificial intelligence, software engineering, business process re-engineering, organizational behaviour, and information technology fields. Knowledge management deals with creating, securing, combining, retrieving, and distributing knowledge in an organization, both internally and externally. Web-based and intranet technologies now provide the 'connectivity' between these knowledge bases to form the necessary bridges and facilitate the sharing of knowledge. For many firms, implementing knowledge management requires a fairly advanced IT infrastructure of databases, computer networks, and software.

Testing and research often takes on less significance in a knowledge-based organization as there is a plethora of 'other' information which could provide direct marketers with those 'missing ingredients' to enable them to solve problems more effectively. The kinds of 'other' information might be production schedules, forecasts, sales force reports, product information, engineering reports, customer feedback, and the like. All might play a role in the success or otherwise of a direct campaign. Such information is often reviewed on a routine basis along with standard market reports or bespoke investigations, but KM occurs when it is linked to previous experience. Two knowledge management paradigms have emerged as models to mine such data systematically: 'codification' and 'personalization'.

In codification, explicit knowledge (totally transferable knowledge, such as a book on chemistry or the blueprint of a robot design) is carefully classified and stored in databases ready to be accessed by anyone in the company. For example, management consultants Ernst and Young will remove client sensitive information from a project and then develop knowledge objects, such as market segmentation and benchmarking data that are stored electronically. This enables lots of people within the firm to retrieve data without contacting the originators. An alternative approach is the 'personalization strategy' based upon tacit knowledge (requires learning by doing and trial and error leading to the build-up of skills) as used by consultants Bain and McKinsey. Tacit knowledge is tied to the person who developed it and is shared by direct person-to-person contacts. A personalization strategy concentrates on the belief that the most valuable knowledge is tacit knowledge existing in people's heads, augmented or shared via interpersonal interaction or social relationships. In this approach, computers are used to help people get 'up-to-speed' on topics and to communicate, rather than to store knowledge. The focus is on dialogue rather than knowledge objects. Building networks is, therefore, more important as knowledge is transferred by meetings and one-to-one conversations.

Different strategies suit particular direct markets. If the market is standardized, then a codified strategy is most appropriate, but if it is customized, a personalization strategy should be used. Codification provides a 're-use' knowledge model that enables a company to complete more projects quickly and cheaply: a perfect strategy for direct marketers dealing with similar problems. Personalization is suited to one-off client problems requiring deep tacit agency knowledge that cannot be systematized efficiently. The key to the viable use of KM is to know when to enter or exit from the marketplace so that you do not have to change your systems. Direct marketers using codification predominantly will need to be able to recognize when a market is reaching commodity status and quickly be able to move their expertise into those markets to reap the benefits of scale and reuse. On the other hand, those following a personalization model need to get out of markets as they mature.

In direct marketing the economies of scale generally associated with 'learning organizations' is enormous. In the normal course of day-to-day operations, direct marketers generate vast amounts of specific knowledge: for example about markets, response rates, product categories, media and client-situational. For the most part, this knowledge is tacit and highly personalized. There are examples to the contrary, but knowledge generally rests with relatively few individuals directly involved with particular direct campaigns. Whether the direct campaign is successful or not, few other members of the direct marketing organization benefit from the experience.

7.8 Testing and research plan

Any direct testing and research plan should follow four distinct phases: (1) define the problem, (2) select the data collection method, (3) select the sample, and (4) select the measurement technique. We shall now consider each in turn.

7.8.1 Define the problem

As a starting point, the problem needs to be defined. For example, is the issue how to position the product in the market, or the most effective headline, or whether a personalized

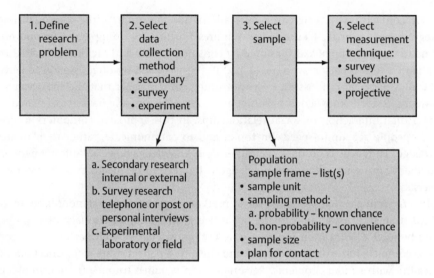

Fig. 7.2 Testing and research process

letter should be included. So, the first stage to any direct testing and research plan is to establish the criteria to be used. Three questions should be asked:

- What information do I want?
- How will I use this information?
- Will the information be new?

The next stage is to establish what is required to obtain the information. There are four issues to consider:

- Specify direct marketing objectives.
- Establish a research plan.
- Allocate sufficient funds and time.
- Whenever possible use a control.

7.8.2 **Select the data collection method**

The next stage is to select the data collection method. Will it be secondary, survey, or experiment? Secondary research is information that is already available and includes internal data (existing reports and studies) and external (the information found in books, journals, directories, and pubished reports). The internet is proving very useful in this respect. The internet has some useful tools for the market researcher. There are hundreds of search engines available to internet users. The user simply types in one or more key words for documents worldwide to be scanned. The most 'relevant' documents are displayed within seconds. Alta Vista is one of the best known search engines. The internet is likely to revolutionize the reporting phase of market research. Already, the web carries results from numerous government studies. It offers a fast, cheap, and efficient method to deliver information. Increasingly, multi-national companies and market research institutes are using the medium to deliver results.

There are a variety of research methods that might typically be used. A number of the most common are briefly described below.

7.8.3 Internet questionnaires

To date, primary research conducted on the internet has been to evaluate web-sites, to examine employee satisfaction, and to survey specific target groups. Despite the challenging sampling tasks, internet-questionnaire writing is becoming a study in its own right. Questionnaires can be interactive or static; in colour or not; with/out edit checks; with/out filters; closed or open; with radio buttons or check boxes; questions can be rotated; script can be single page scroll or multiple page. The following sites show a selection of questionnaires that illustrate these different facilities.

What is your VALS type? It is another black and white survey showing how the single-scroll page works (*http://future.sri.com/vals/valsindex.shtml*). Quantime Demonstrations, on the other hand, show full colour capability and the benefits of single questions per page (*http://www.quantime.com/web_bureau/demos/demos.htm*). Similarly, a publisher has posted a popular game of Test Your Marketing IQ!, which shows the power of interactive interviewing (*http://www.copernicusmarketing.com/*). Finally, a choice of MR Panels is presented at the Volition site. Here, anyone can sign up to be a respondent (*http://www.volition.com/opinions.html*).

The internet offers the researcher a rich store of resources which can assist each stage of the market research process. For some, the major barrier to using such resources is not knowing how to find them.

7.8.4 Select the sample

There are a number of elements to consider with the selection of a sample. The first consideration is the selection of a **sampling frame**, that is the list of names to be used. A sample has to be contacted in some way. A direct marketer might, for example, buy a list or use a list of current customers. Next is the **sampling unit**, which is about the level of your sample, for example you might sample individuals, households, or companies. Following from this, the question of **sampling method** has to be reviewed as to whether the choice will be for a **probability** or **nonprobability** sample. A 'probability' sample means that there is a known chance of each element of the sample being included, whereas with a 'nonprobability' sample there is no way of estimating the probability of inclusion of any unit, thus the extent to which the sample is representative of the population is unknown.

(a) Nonprobability samples

Nonprobability samples come in three forms: convenience, judgement, and quota;

Convenience samples—are chosen because they just happen to be the easiest to pick. A direct marketer might ask friends or colleagues which colour they like best in a proposed direct response brochure. Whether or not the people concerned will be representative of the target population might be doubtful, but they were easy to contact.

Judgement samples—are picked on purpose. In doing a radical new piece of direct creative work for a computer company, a direct marketing agency might be tracking the opinions of a panel selected from the primary target audience. They can work extremely well if you do not need to have representative views.

Quota samples—attempt to ensure that the sample is representative. For example, an airline might wish to test out a new offer aimed at female business executives in amongst 25–34, 35–44, 45–54, and 55–64 year old age groups. They find that the sales in their market are as follows: 25–34—10 per cent; 35–44—20 per cent; 45–54—60 per cent; and 55+—10 per cent. This means if they chose to interview 50 female executives that the following numbers would be chosen:

> 25–34: 5 people   > 45–54: 30 people

> 35–44: 10 people   > 55+: 5 people

Fig. 7.3 Quota

The key point is that the sample is chosen by judgement, rather than randomly. While the age groups of the people chosen reflect the general breakdown required, the researchers have used their judgement to select them.

(b) Probability samples

Probability samples are so-called because you can calculate the likelihood of any given element in their population. This is because the sample has been collected objectively using a set process rather than by the ideas of the researcher. However, it does not mean that a probability sample will be more representative than a nonprobability. A nonprobability sample can often be more representative than a probability, the point is that probability samples allow for the calculation of sample error—the extent to which error occurs because a sample was used rather than a census. You cannot do this with a nonprobability sample because no objective method is used in the fist place to gather the sample. **Random** samples are probably the most well-known types to gather probability samples. With a random sample each member of the population has an equal chance of being chosen and every combination of members has as much chance of joining the sample as every other combination. For example, a direct marketing company might test a new product concept by contacting every 99th listed person in a local census.

(c) **Sample size**

The question of how big a sample to use for a direct marketing test is not easy to answer as it depends on a number of factors (Ehrenberg, 1982). Much depends on the type of the sample, the statistics that you want to find out, the homogeneity of the population, and the resources (time, people, and money) available. It is impossible in this chapter to give justice to all the aspects of the decision of sample size. Sample size estimation and significance testing has traditionally been a tedious task made easier by such devices as tables, nomograms, and programmed calculators. The reader may wish to consult statistical reference texts for more details and there are several web-sites that have 'sponsored' on-line tools to help. Furthermore, there are several marketing discussion groups on the internet.

There are several 'basics' to consider with sample size. One key aspect is the sampling distribution, as this will indicate the error that can be associated with any estimate. Consider that the error associated with the estimation of a population mean is given by the standard error of that mean. Similarly, the standard error of the estimate obtained from a sampling distribution statistic is important. Another issue is the precision you want. If you want to test the likely response interval to a direct marketing offer within 0.5 per cent it will require a different sample size than if you allow a 1.0 per cent interval. The final factor is the desired degree of confidence required traded against the degree of precision. If you have a fixed sample size, you cannot specify both confidence and precision at the same time—you need to allow the sample size to vary to be able to do this and even then you have to balance the two. For example, say you randomly sample 50 people with an offer of a clock-CD-radio as a test, and get a 25 per cent response rate. Experience suggests that the 25 per cent response rate is not right (it is far too high) so you have no confidence in it. However, we can have complete confidence in the statement that the average response is somewhere between 0 and 25 per cent! This is not exactly helpful to us in taking our plans forward as the statement is too imprecise.

An often surprising point to consider when calculating the sample size is that it has nothing to do with the size of the population. The reason for this is quite straightforward. Rather than the size of the population being the key, it is the extent to which all the members of the population have the same value or response. If you had 20,000 people in a sample who all responded in exactly the same way to an offer, then obviously you would only need to sample one of them to find out the response rate. Not very likely! But the basic point holds true for any size of population, of course. So, the thing that affects the size of the sample is the variability of the members of the population. Obviously, the more variable, the greater sample size required to estimate with any precision. Thus, population size only has an indirect effect on sample size. This occurs through the likely impact on population variability. All things being equal, bigger populations are more likely to be varied than smaller ones.

For many direct marketers the key question is how big should the test be? Precision is the key dimension here, so let us explore sample size using precision. Say a direct marketing company contacts 50 members of a tennis club with an offer of tennis training/recreation weekend and gets two firm enquiries. This represents a response rate of 4 per cent. Another two tests of 50 members each of the tennis club yield responses of 7.7 and

The formula for calcualtion is:

Limits of error, L = k $\sqrt{\dfrac{R\,(100-R)}{n}}$

Where

k = constant dependent on confidence level chosen (k = 1.96 for 95% confidence level)
R = response percentage obtained for the test
n = sample size

In this case we have:

k = 1.96
R = 3.9
n = 150

$$L = 1.96 \times \sqrt{\frac{3.9\,(100-3.9)}{150}}$$

$$L = 1.96 \times \sqrt{\frac{3.9 \times 96.1}{150}}$$

$$L = 1.96 \times \sqrt{2.4986}$$

$$L = 1.96 \times 1.58$$

$$L = 3.09$$

Fig. 7.4 Limits of error

4.1 per cent. This gives us a range of 0.4 and an average of 7.9. It looks like a national roll-out of the offer will yield limits of error between 7.7 and 4.1 per cent. However, the direct marketing company cannot be 100 per cent sure that these limits of error will transpire. When it goes national it might be that the average response is outside 7.7–4.1 per cent. Let us assume that the company is 95 per cent confident in its results rather than 100 per cent, i.e. in 95 out of 100 times the response would be within 7.7–4.1 per cent.

Thus, it is 95 per cent certain that the national offer will be 7.9: ± 7.1. In essence, there is a 95 per cent chance that the response rate will be between 0.8 to 7.0 per cent! This is not too much help, so our direct marketers need to test again and raise the sample 150+ to gain a prediction with a smaller limit of error. Assuming they gained the same average of 7.9 responses for a sample size of 2,000 would reduce the error from ± 7.1 to ± .37 and a sample of 4,000 to ± 0.18 (see Figure 7.4).

(d) **Select the measurement technique**

(i) **Strategic and tactical**

Testing is the most prevalent research technique in direct marketing. The ability of direct marketers to test is one of the many features that distinguish direct marketers from classic marketers. The decision of which measurement technique to use is not a matter of identifying the single correct approach but of avoiding misfits between the technique and the requirements for any given piece of research (Davis, 1997). Furthermore, no matter how appropriate a particular approach may be, if the researcher does not have the appropriate skills then that particular technique should not be pursued.

In testing you have to make the distinction between strategic and tactical issues. **Strategic** issues are generally called the 'big things' by direct marketers and five main areas addressed:

(a) Have you set achievable objectives?

(b) Have you selected the right target market?

(c) Is the direct campaign using the right positioning (creative, motivation, and overall package format) platform?

(d) Have the best media been chosen?

(e) Is it the best time of year to make the offer?

Such strategic issues are central to campaign success or failure. No amount of production values will save an offer that is fundamentally unattractive or poorly targeted.

Tactical issues are operational. Here, you might test a whole range of aspects of the direct campaign such as specific prices, words, headlines, images, and use of colours. There is only value in devoting resources to testing tactical issues when it is clear that the campaign strategy is right. For example, there is not much point in spending time on testing different headlines if the overall offer is being directed at the wrong target market.

(ii) **Pre-testing**

Testing can be applied in the pre and post-testing phases. Pre-testing is the process of showing a direct marketing idea or concept to a sample who are representative of the potential audience and gauging their response before running a full-blown version of the plan. Pre-testing can test a B2B (business-to-business) or B2C (business-to-consumer) strategy and its comprehension as well as test an execution and its comprehension. There are three kinds of direct pre-testing methods: verbal/written responses, projective, and behavioural.

Verbal/written—involves just that, tests where a sample of respondents express their thoughts on the campaign idea verbally or in writing. The issues might be big, e.g. does the overall proposition of the direct campaign appeal to them? Or it might be tactical, do they find the headlines memorable? Respondents might be shown a variety of different campaigns and tracked in terms of their attention, noting, or awareness of different copy points. Other issues might be do they comprehend the offer, like it, or have any interest in it? What are their attitudes, how much can they recall when the different kinds of materials are used, and how involved do they feel?

Researchers often begin verbal/written research methods with the use of **focus groups** because it enables the key elements of the research to be explored before a major commitment is made to a quantitative survey. Focus groups typically last between one and one-and-a-half to two hours with a moderator moving the discussion between the given topic area. Around eight to twelve participants are involved in the discussion at the same time. Such groups are highly flexible and can meet a number of needs for research in direct marketing. They are especially useful in the areas of positioning, creative evaluations, new product idea generation, product and package screening, and for explorations into awareness, beliefs, and attitudes.

The key advantages are that they enable respondents to expand on and refine their ideas and that they are often more stimulating and interesting for participants than personal interviews. They can also be more spontaneous than personal interviews and quicker to conduct and analyse and often cheaper per respondent to conduct. Of course, focus groups are not without problems. The moderator has to be alert to the likelihood of one person dominating the discussion or influencing the general tone. Sometimes, the moderator falls into the same trap and dominates the group to the detriment of the participants' views. It is also important to enable more reserved or shy members to feel that they can express their views. A final issue to be clear about is that a focus group is just that—a group discussion. As such, they cannot provide the rich detail given by personal interviews.

Sometimes, personal interviews will be chosen instead of focus groups or surveys. Surveys, and to a lesser extent, focus groups, have the ability to efficiently collect large amounts of information but suitability has to be considered as well. Personal interviews might be preferred when:

- answers need to be explored or clarified;
- non-verbal information is needed;
- responses are sufficiently complex that respondents would be unwilling or unable to communicate them otherwise;
- respondents may be unwilling to communicate in other formats due to commercial or personal sensitivity of the information;

- the complexity or variability of the information required is not easily addressed in step-by-step questions.

When it comes to surveys there are a number of common pitfalls to avoid. In particular, presenting two questions as one and having questions which contain a lot of meaningful words (possibly quite simple ones) in a short space and where each contributes an element of meaning necessary to the question. Other problems are questions which conclude qualifying clauses or phrases, multiple ideas or subjects and difficult or unfamiliar words. Never start with words meant to soften the question's impact or its seeming harshness or directness. Be aware of difficult phrases in questions and ones that contain conditional or hypothetical clauses. Another difficulty is when questions which have the term 'if any', or 'if at all' are used and when the present and past tense are used and/or both the singular and plural. Finally, one simple piece of advice with surveys is to watch out for questions which are simply too long.

The choice of 'open' or 'closed' questions in surveys is an important issue to consider. Open questions allow the respondent to answer as they wish, i.e. 'how satisfied are you with your bank?'; whereas closed questions shut-down the options, i.e. 'how satisfied are you with your bank?—choose from: highly unsatisfactory, unsatisfactory, neutral, satisfactory, highly satisfactory, and don't know'.

Respondent results for open questions may differ substantially from closed questions, even when the closed questions present all the major categories. If a major category is omitted from a closed question, respondents will often not consider the category in their response, even if provided with the opportunity through an 'other category' alternative. Open questions face a similar problem in that the failure to prompt the respondent with possible responses may result in the respondent failing inadvertently to consider valid alternatives. Thus, the results of open questions and closed questions can be very different.

Since open questions can yield different results than closed questions, a decision on which format to be used is required. Closed questions are preferable to open questions for surveys because of problems associated with open questions: vague responses, inadequate probing by interviewers, and incorrect classification by coders. However, open question interviews should be used to first identify the categories to be used in the closed questions, determining the respondent's frame of reference and wording alternatives appropriately. As both formats have their strengths and weaknesses, closed questions are generally used to collect data on known topics and categories with open questions included at the end to catch any remaining unexplored issues.

A related topic is the consideration of how 'open' an open question is. For example, the question: 'How satisfied are you with your bank?' appears to be open ended, but is not fully open as it restricts the respondent to answering along one dimension. A more open-ended question would be: 'how do you feel about your bank?' or 'what do you think about your bank?'. Even here, it could be argued that the first alternative is focused on feelings and the second is focused on cognitive opinion. However, the example illustrates the concept that there are various levels of openness and an apparently open question can inadvertently restrict the range of likely responses.

Wording in surveys is, consequently, of considerable importance. The best advice is to use simple words, avoid ambiguous words or questions, avoid words with multiple meanings (e.g., about, all, always, and, any, bad, could, ever, go, heard, less, like, you). If such words (i.e. words that do not have the same meaning for all respondents) are required, then definitions should be provided to all respondents.

Another issue is the underlying assumptions in questions, for example: 'how do banks deal with your problems?'. This assumes that you have more than one problem with your bank. Such a question is perfectly valid if a respondent has just stated that they have problems with their bank, but not otherwise. Related to this is the issue of asking questions beyond the respondents' capabilities. Questions about causality of actions or events, e.g. 'why is your bank failing to deal with your problems?', are unlikely to produce credible or useful data. Requests for solutions to complex problems are also unlikely to be handled well, e.g. 'how should your bank re-organize its customer care services to deal with your problems more effectively?'. Respondents are also limited in terms of the number of categories or alternatives they can handle. Five to seven categories is probably as many categories as most respondents can handle meaningfully for most rating tasks. Even this number may be suspect as respondents have a bias towards the first or last alternative when a number of alternatives are read out to them.

The issues discussed above are largely concerned with the ability of respondents to understand and answer the questions. There are a separate set of issues based around whether they deliberately bias their responses due to self-interest or due to reactions to the interviewer or the survey instrument. These effects may be exacerbated or reduced as a result of question wording. It is the researchers' responsibility to be sensitive to how the interviewee may be affected by different questions and various question formats. For example, the question: 'how do banks rip you off?' is somewhat threatening and aggressive. It might be reworded to: 'suppose someone you trusted asked you how fairly your bank set it service charges, what would you tell them?'.

The overall structure of a survey also needs to be considered. A normative effect has been found in questionnaires where respondents often feel a need to make responses to later questions consistent with earlier responses. This effect is increased if the wording of the questions highlights the fact that they deal with similar topics or issues. Thus, the way in which later questions are interpreted is affected by earlier questions and as this occurs the consciousness of or feelings towards a general topic are affected by raising awareness with each specific question. Bear in mind that 'fatigue effects' can reduce the response rate and reduce the use of extreme categories, e.g. end points of a Likert-type (1–5 or 1–7 or 1–9) scales towards the end of surveys. Also, a series of choices increasingly provides a frame of reference, so early questions may have extreme responses while responses to latter questions may be more moderate as they are affected by consideration of the range of choices presented earlier. This is fine if the research is searching for facts rather than opinions as raising respondent subject awareness and encouraging respondents to consider inconsistencies of response may be of great value. Consequently, the grouping of contextually similar questions is not in itself something to either support or avoid. Rather, the potential consequences of such groupings need to be considered within the framework of the research.

One last issue to consider is that the order in which possible alternatives are sequenced in a survey can significantly affect response rates for the different alternatives. There is no definitive answer. In some cases, the last alternative to be read tends to be chosen, especially if the last alternative is seen as a middle rather than an extreme response. However, there is also some evidence of the opposite, i.e. where the first alternative is most likely to be chosen. So, it is not clear. There is an effect to sequencing, but it is not consistent. A number of researchers recommend that surveys or interviews begin with generalities that will put respondents at ease and that they will find interesting, placing difficult or sensitive questions towards the end, but again there is little empirical support that beginning an interview with questions that the respondent would find uncomfortable affected the responses.

Projective techniques—allow for respondents to express their ideas in less prescriptive ways by relating to analogous objects. Popular examples are to ask respondents to say if a company was a well-known person, who would it be? What kind of car might it be or what kind of animal? Such research is invaluable in framing the strategic issues in a direct campaign. Another technique is the use of psychographic drawing. This is where a respondent is invited to draw, on a blank page, how they see a particular company or organization if that company or organization was a person or object. For example, in one famous case IBM was found to be commonly drawn as a man in dark suit, clean-cut with a briefcase. By comparison, Apple was drawn as man wearing jeans and a T-shirt with long hair and a beard. Such drawings can provide insight as to whether the strategy is being interpreted correctly or not. One central drawback with projective techniques is that a great deal is left open to interpretation by the researcher, especially with psychographic drawing. A respondent's intention with his/her drawing might be quite different to how it is viewed and interpreted by the researcher.

Behavioural research techniques—are often used in direct marketing. This is where different market tests are run and the responses to each analysed, normally against a control market where everything was kept constant. What this means is that the key measure is how people behave in the market rather by evaluating their views. Aside from telemarketing, it is more expensive to test in this way because you need a professional and finished piece of direct marketing. If you tried to conduct a test in a different market with a crude and badly finished piece of direct marketing, it would be hard to make any sense of the results! Even with telemarketing you may need a professionally finished direct package to send out to prospects who show an interest. Overall, 'best practice' for testing would be to start off with some verbal/written and/or projective techniques to narrow your choices and then use behavioural market tests to finalize the strategy. For example, after eliminating and incorporating the key elements from verbal and/or written tests, two direct mail packages might be compared in terms of envelope size, letter, and order form as to which ones gives the best response against a control.

An alternative approach would be to skip the verbal/written and/or projective techniques and go in with 'both feet' by testing two completely different packages straight away. Having found which package works best, you could then use verbal/written and/or projective techniques, or simply more mailings, to refine the offer. It would be difficult to undertake this approach without having some existing insight, experience, and/or understanding of the how the market will behave. There are a myriad of variables that could affect response that would be difficult, if not impossible, to isolate without other research techniques. Thus, it would be a potentially blundering and expensive series of tests where 'whatever seems to work' directs the process.

Other direct media can be used for pre-tests. In telemarketing, pre-tests might involve such aspects as different timings and characteristics of audience types. Telemarketing is extremely cheap to conduct tests with, but the packages sent after a successful telemarketing call will be more expensive and akin to direct marketing in costs. The internet can also be used for pre-testing when no publicity is made for a test site and the address is not obvious. For example, Procter & Gamble established a direct marketing internet site for testing purposes that was not widely publicized to the public. Such sites can be evaluated by staff or used in pre-tests with a selected and screened sample and the final launch site developed interactively. Measures include clicks, links between pages, and time hovered. With DRTV and direct radio you can evaluate different creative, timings and audiences. Similar tests can be made with the press. For example, a clothing company might test five regional weekly magazines and ten different advertisements prior to a national launch over a three month period. The idea would be to phone an 0800 number or send off a coupon to receive a catalogue. Response rates could be compared for:

- different weeks;
- pulling power of different creative approaches;
- pulling power of different magazines by target audience;
- the cost efficiency of the magazines per 1,000 of their audience;
- miscellaneous issues such as the position in the publication, the weather, the content of the issues, and so on.

'Split runs' offer a similar opportunity. Here, a newspaper or magazine is able to place alternative versions of a direct advertisement in alternate copies of the publication as the copies come off the press. Thus, every other copy of a newspaper would have version A of an advertisement and the alternate version B. Half the readers would see version A and half B. Given that each version is distributed randomly, groups A and B are assumed to be matched samples in all characteristics (buying behaviour, geodemographics, pyschographics, and benefits). This means you can prepare two versions of the advertisement, ideally being identical save for one variable—the one being tested. For example, you might change an image or a headline, but not both. Readers need to be able to respond by coupon, internet, reply card, or telephone. Different codes identify the different advertisements, such as different telephone numbers to call or different dating codes (e.g. 18DEXA printed on cut-out coupons = 18 December, journal X, advertisement A).

Not all journals are capable of offering split runs. The most attractive feature of a split run is that you can assume that the extraneous variables, such as age or income, have been controlled because both groups are matched. Any differences in response to the advertisement can be attributed to the test variable, e.g. the headline.

A different or complimentary approach might be to use 'regional runs'. Here, different regional editions of the same advertisement or inserts are run in the same journal, such as the *Radio Times*. The assumption is that the medium attracts broadly similar readers nationally, so that responses to different creative approaches in other regional editions can be compared.

Overall, behavioural pre-tests are much more powerful than verbal/written and projective techniques as they more closely mirror what is likely to happen when a full launch is made. The drawback is that they cost a lot more (save for telemarketing), so a balance between the two might be desirable.

(iii) Post-testing

Post-testing is the process of gauging the response to a direct marketing plan either during and/or after running the full-blown plan. A variety of measures may be employed:

- response rate;
- exposure—what percentage of the target market had an opportunity to see and/or hear the communications?;
- attention factor—what percentage of the target market paid attention to the communication (generally a much smaller number than those exposed to it)?;
- communication achieved (medium, advertisement content/theme, specific 'copy points', product/brand/service);
- attitudes (product, firm/institution, aspects of advertising, buying the brand).

In direct marketing behavioural post-testing is what it is all about. The response rate is the key measure, e.g. 2 per cent of the target market making enquiries as opposed to 2.5 per cent.

7.9 **Conclusion**

Direct testing and research is designed to reduce the risk in direct marketing decision-making. Similar tools can be used to classic marketing, but the overall emphasis is upon testing. It is important to separate the testing of strategy and tactics. Strategic testing is key to successful direct marketing because no amount of product values or creativity can save a direct campaign that has the wrong strategy.

Discussion questions

1   Identify the five strands of the market research industry and explain what each one does.

2   What is the role of testing and research? In what way does instinct fit?

3   How does exploratory research differ from descriptive and explanatory?

4   An advertiser of soft drinks is considering doing some research on adding new flavours. What kinds of issues need to be considered in selecting the sample?

5   What is the difference between the codification and personalization of knowledge?

6   A business software company is considering testing a new communications package for groups. What factors should be considered in selecting sample size?

7   What is it about testing that gives direct marketers such a competitive edge over traditional marketers?

8   An IT department within a large government organization has decided to undertake a questionnaire to measure customer satisfaction. The aim is to use the results to develop internal direct marketing. What generic advice would you offer for wording and layout?

Further reading

Churchill G. A. (1999) *Marketing Research: Methodological Foundations* (Orlando, FL: Dryden).

Davis J. J. (1997) *Advertising Research: Theory and Practice* (Engelwood Cliffs, NJ: Prentice Hall).

Ehrenberg A. S. C. (1982) *A Primer in Data Reduction: An Introductory Statistics Textbook* (London: John Wiley).

Hansen M. T., Nohria N., and Tierney T. (1999) 'What's Your Strategy for Managing Knowledge?', *Harvard Business Review*, March–April, 106–16.

Sarvary M. (1999) 'Knowledge management and competition in the consulting industry', *California Management Review*, 41(2), 95–107.

Zack, M. H. (1999) 'Developing a knowledge strategy', *California Management Review*, 41(3), 125–45.

Chapter 8

Analytical Procedures

Contents

8.1 **Objectives**

By the end of this chapter you should be able to:

(a) appreciate the role of statistical analysis in informing direct marketing decisions;

(b) calculate and present simple descriptive statistics;

(c) appreciate the role of hypothesis testing in direct marketing research;

(d) appreciate the range of bivariate and multivariate procedures of relevance to direct marketing.

8.2 **Introduction**

It is our intention in this chapter to introduce a number of the fundamental principles of statistical analysis. Our aim is not to provide a detailed or technical account of all the techniques that are listed. Rather, we aim to provide an overview of the forms of analysis that are available in the hope that a direct marketer will then recognize those techniques that might yield the most utility given both the categories of data and the research questions set. For an account of the mechanics of exactly how to use each of these techniques the reader would subsequently be advised to consult a detailed statistical text such as Hair et al. (1995) or Davidson (1996).

Many students faced with the idea of some form of statistical analysis for the first time break into a cold sweat at the prospect. Hopefully, over the course of the next few pages we can assuage some of the more common fears and illustrate just how insightful statistical analysis can be, when the proper tools are applied. Direct marketing, as was noted earlier, is the art of losing money in small amounts. The secret to keeping these amounts as small as possible lies in amassing more than a passing knowledge of statistics. Armed with this knowledge, the direct marketer can test and re-test the results obtained from the various forms of communication attempted and interpret the results to decide on the optimal strategy or strategies to pursue.

In essence, we are concerned here with the interpretation of evidence. Evidence that our customers will behave in a particular way, that certain forms of communication will work better than others, etc. Of course, it is necessary to have some idea of what might be expected from the analysis from the outset to avoid being swamped by the volume of statistics that might result. In this chapter we will therefore consider how research hypotheses are formulated, how errors can be made in attempting to prove or disprove these hypotheses and finally the range of techniques that may be applied for this purpose.

8.3 **The fundamentals**

In examining behaviour the researcher is often interested in determining the likelihood that a given behaviour might be influenced by a particular variable. In other words, for example, a direct marketer might be interested in determining whether a mailing with a message printed on an envelope would typically outperform a mailing enclosed in a plain envelope—and thus warrant the extra expense entailed. A sensible way to proceed might be to conduct a test of this feature with a small sample of the database. Suppose that each version of the mailing was sent to 500 individuals and 100 individuals responded to the mailing with an envelope message and 90 to that with the blank envelope. The task then becomes one of deciding which of the packs performed the best. On the face of it, it would seem that the mailing with the envelope message works the better of the two versions, yet is there a genuine difference here? After all, it would be unlikely that an identical number of customers would respond to each mailing in any event. How do we decide whether the difference in response is genuinely due to a difference in pack performance and not due to a fluctuation in response simply due to the operation of random chance in our choice of people to mail?

To be in a position to answer questions like this it is important to begin with the theory on which all of modern statistics is built—namely the theory of probability. What is the probability that certain outcomes will be obtained from an experiment such as the one alluded to above? To begin an exploration of probability let us consider a simpler example. Suppose that we spin a coin and ask 'what is the probability of the coin landing heads rather than tails?' Ask this of most people and they would likely say 50–50 or 1 in 2. But what exactly does this mean and are there other ways of explaining the outcomes we might expect each time we spin a coin in this way?

The simple answer to this question is yes—and there are in fact three ways of looking at probability:

- One could take the *a priori* approach alluded to above—we could assume that a thing called probability exists and derive laws/theorems to outline how it works. We could then attempt to match predictions with experiments. Thus, in our experiment we could assume that the result is just as likely to be heads as tails and there is thus a 50 per cent chance of obtaining a head.

- A second approach would be to look at long run frequencies. Indeed, many people intuitively think about probability in this way. If we spin the coin a thousand times we would expect to observe about 50 per cent heads and 50 per cent tails. So if we conducted such an experiment and obtained 506 heads and 494 tails would this result be close enough to 500–500 for us to say that both results are equally likely? As we shall see later, it is fortunately possible to test whether this is, or is not, the case

- The third approach might best be referred to as the casino approach and will be of more than passing interest to gamblers. Later in his life the English philosopher John Stuart Mill rejected the two earlier approaches and gave the following definition of probability in his text 'Logic'.

'We must remember that the probability of an event is not a quality of the event itself, but a mere name for the degree of ground which we have for expecting it. Every event is in itself certain, not probable: if we knew all, we should either know positively that it will happen, or positively that it will not. But its probability means to us the degree of expectation of its occurrence, which we are warranted in entertaining by our present evidence'. (Bulmer 1979:6)

In this view, probability is thus a measurement of how confident we might that a particular outcome will be achieved.

In conducting any form of social research it is always advisable to adopt the approach that best suits your needs.

Adopting the first approach the researcher could define *a priori* an unbiased coin as one where the probability of a head is 0.5. The laws of probability can then be invoked to decide whether achieving 506 heads in 1,000 throws is a reasonable outcome given the hypothesis of an unbiased coin. It is a common approach in the physical and life sciences to begin by stating a hypothesis and then conducting an experiment to see whether the results obtained are in reasonable agreement with our expectations. If this is not the case the hypothesis may need to be re-evaluated and possibly the evidence as well.

On other occasions, perhaps when frequencies or probabilities cannot be assigned from the outset, the second approach might prove the most useful. This can also be of value when researchers wish to identify the important factors to include in an experiment. In this case the question to ask is 'what would we expect to happen if this experiment were repeated many times?'.

The third approach can, in addition, be helpful as it reminds us of the provisional nature of much of scientific knowledge. In much of social research the apparent random nature of observations arises (at least in part) from our lack of understanding of all the factors that could potentially affect the outcome of an experiment. Whilst we might reasonably formulate predictions on the basis of the evidence we have to hand today— more information provided in the future may lead us to refine these predictions.

8.4 Presentation of data

Before going on to consider how we might use our knowledge of probability to test various hypothesis, it is worth taking time out to look at how the various outcomes from statistical analysis might be presented. The most common forms of summary that are used to represent data include data tables, bar charts, histograms, and simple numerical summaries such as the mean and standard deviation.

8.4.1 Charts

Bar charts or frequency histograms are probably the most common forms of graphical representation of statistical data. They consists of a series of bars, the height of which is either proportional to the frequency with which a particular outcome occurs, or to the probability that this outcome will occur.

A simple bar chart is presented in Figure 8.1. In this example the total sales of Smart-Co's six product lines during 1999 are shown. Whilst the same information could be provided in tabular form, the reader will appreciate the greater degree of impact that can be achieved with a graphic presentation. It is immediately obvious to the eye, which of the products has sold the best.

A second type of chart commonly employed for the presentation of data is the histogram. In this case it is not only the height of the bars that is significant, but also the dimensions of the base. In the example in Figure 8.2, SmartCo has plotted the response rates that it has historically received to one of its most popular recruitment mailings. It seems clear that a common outcome for this particular mailing would be to achieve a response rate of circa 1–1.5 per cent. Not at all bad for a recruitment mailing!!

If a histogram is 'well behaved' with a peak in the middle and tailing off at the sides, further observations can be tested to see whether they fall within the expected distribution or whether they are outliers warranting further investigation. This is an idea we shall return to later.

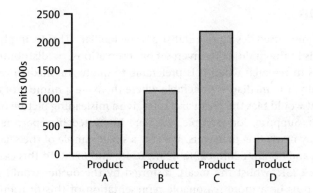

Fig. 8.1 SmartCo sales (1999)

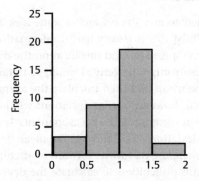

Fig. 8.2 Response rates to SmartCo mailings

8.4.2 **Mean**

One of the most commonly encountered descriptive statistics is the mean (denoted by $\bar{x}$. It is also one of the simplest to calculate. You simply add up the results of a given set of measurements and then divide by the number of measurements. This is shown in mathematical notation below:

$$\bar{x} = \frac{\sum_{i=1}^{n} x_i}{n}$$

It may seem a little obtuse to use such a complex looking formula to explain such a simple idea. Whilst this may be true in this case, lengthy word descriptions can soon develop as more complex ideas in statistics are espoused. Mathematical notation can, therefore, save a lot of needless description and define an idea very clearly. In this case the formula simply indicates that to calculate the mean, one has to calculate the sum of the values of x from the first observation to the last and then divide by the number of observations (denoted by n).

8.4.3 **Median**

A second commonly used descriptive statistic is the median. This is simply the measurement which falls in the middle of a given set of observations, or 'distribution'. There are many occasions in research when it is preferable to quote the median rather than the mean. Specifically, the median is preferable where there are a number of outliers in the distribution that would bias the mean and thus give a misleading picture of the nature of the distribution. Suppose, for example, we were interested in reporting the 'average' salaries earned by marketing managers. We take a small sample of the salaries earned by five individuals and obtain £20K, £22K, £23K, £24K, and £70K. In this case, the median value would be £23K, whilst the mean, distorted by the outlier would be £31.8. The median would thus be a more reasonable representation of this distribution than the mean.

8.4.4 **Standard deviation**

Both the mean and the median give the researcher some idea of where the centre of the distribution is located. Whilst this is clearly useful information researchers are usually also interested to know how spread around this location the distribution might be. One possible way that this measure might be derived would be to take the difference between each measurement and the mean and then calculate the average of this deviation. The problem with this approach, however, is that deviations will be both positive and negative. Consider a distribution containing the measurements 1, 2, and 3. In this case the mean would be 2 and the deviation – 1, 0, and + 1. The mean deviation in this case would hence be zero and we are therefore no further forward in attempting to find a measure of spread! The way around this difficulty is to calculate the deviations from the mean (as previously), then to square these numbers (which removes any negative signs), add these squared numbers together, divide by the number of measurements and then take the square root of the answer. In our previous example the squared deviations would be 1, 0, 1, and their sum would be two. If we then divide this by three to get the mean of the squared deviations and take the square root of the answer we obtain a result of circa 0.8. This somewhat wordy description is represented in mathematical notation below.

$$s = \sqrt{\frac{\sum_{i=1}^{N} (X - \bar{X})^2}{N}}$$

The more spread out a given distribution might be, the greater will be its standard deviation.

8.4.5 Standard error

Researchers have particular reason to be interested in the mean. It is often the best estimate that they have of the 'true' value. Managers, in a catalogue company, for example, might wish to ascertain the average height of its customers to ensure that its clothing products will adequately meet the needs of its market. To establish the mean it would clearly not be possible to measure the height of every individual in the target market, but a sample of heights could be taken and the mean height calculated from the sample. Of course, given that we have used a sample, our mean height may be very far away from the actual population mean and we need some kind of measure of how accurate our estimate actually is. We can use the standard error for this purpose. It is simply the standard deviation of the mean. Its formula reflects the fact that the more measurements of height we were able to take, the more accurate we will be in estimating the true population mean. The standard error is therefore calculated thus:

$$s.e. = s/\sqrt{n}$$

In other words, to halve the error, we would need to take four times as many measurements. We are then in a position to decide whether this is feasible and/or desirable.

8.4.6 Range

In cases where the median has been used to describe the 'average' point on a distribution a good measure of spread to use to accompany this value is the range. The range is simply the highest value observed, minus the lowest value. Whilst this is a useful figure it is helpful to recognize that this too can be strongly influenced by outliers. For this reason some researchers prefer to quote the inter-quartile range. This is simply the difference between two points. The lower of these corresponds to a point below which one quarter of the observations lie (the lower quartile) and the second to the point above which one quarter of the points lie (the upper quartile).

8.5 **Distributions**

In the preceding sections we have been talking about the representation of various distributions (i.e. a central measure and measure of spread). It is important to recognize that there are a number of distributions that commonly occur in statistics. These include the Binomial, Poisson, F, T, and normal distributions.

Of all these distributions, however, it is the normal distribution that has the most significance for statisticians. It follows the familiar bell shaped curve shown in Figure 8.3. Very many continuous variables such as weights, speed, sales, values, costs, etc. have distributions that approximate very closely to the normal distribution. The most important feature of the normal distribution is that the probability associated with any value can be worked out, provided we know how many standard deviations there are between that value and the mean.

The entire value under the curve represents 100 per cent probability. Since the curve is symmetrical 50 per cent of frequencies must lie on either side of the mean.

About 68 per cent of frequencies have a value within plus or minus 1 standard deviation from the mean. Thus, if a normally shaped frequency distribution has a mean of 80 and a standard deviation of 3, 68 per cent of the total frequencies would occur within the range +/– one standard deviation from the mean (i.e. within the range 77–83.) This is represented in Figure 8.4.

Since the curve is symmetrical 34 per cent of frequencies must fall in the range 77–80 and 34 per cent in the range 80–83. We can express the above statements in terms of probabilities. Suppose the values being investigated are weights, with an average of 80 kg and a standard deviation of 3 kg. The probability that a randomly selected item weighs between 77 kg and 80 kg is 0.34.

Similarly, about 95 per cent of the frequencies in a normal distribution occur in the range +/– 1.96 standard deviations from the mean. In our example, 95 per cent of items will have weights lying between 80 – (1.96 × 3) and 80 + (1.96 × 3) (i.e. between 74.12 kg and 85.88 kg). A randomly selected item would have a 0.95 probability of falling into this range.

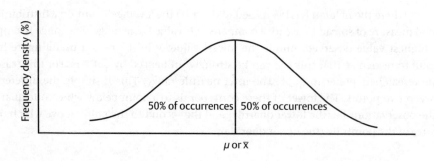

Fig. 8.3 Normal distribution

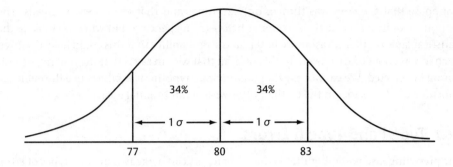

Fig. 8.4 Normal distribution (an example)

As we shall see later, the properties of a normal distribution can be used to great effect in testing various research hypotheses.

8.6 Hypothesis testing

Before we can move to examine the various statistical tools that are available it is useful to begin by considering exactly what is being asked of the evidence. Returning to our coin example, we might wish to determine whether our coin is biased, thus more likely when spun to land heads than tails.

Clearly, such an experiment would not be conducted if the researchers did not have some reason *a priori* to consider that there was indeed a biased coin. They are therefore motivated to believe the hypothesis that the coin is biased. For the sake of balance, though, researchers also establish what is known as the 'null hypothesis', which in this case would be that the coin were not biased.

Having generated the hypothesis, the researcher is then in a position to gather the experimental data. In our case this is gathered by spinning the coin 100 times. This produces a result of 65 heads and 35 tails. On the face of it this would seem to confirm the original hypothesis, but of course such a result might have been obtained purely through the operation of random chance. Since there are only two possible outcomes in the case of the coin the distribution of heads and tails will follow a binomial distribution. Using a statistical package, we could now ask 'what is the probability that there could have been 65 heads or more in 100 throws if the null hypothesis is true?'. In this example, the package would tell us that the chances of getting 65 or more heads in 100 throws is about 1 in 500. We can therefore safely conclude that the outcome is very unlikely to have arisen by chance and that, therefore, it is likely the coin is biased.

Thus, having made a decision about whether or not the result could have been achieved by chance, we are in a position to accept or reject the null hypothesis. It should be stressed that these results do not prove the original hypothesis, they merely indicate that the result was unlikely to have occurred by chance.

Suppose that the coin was thrown only 20 times and that there were 13 heads. The proportion of heads is exactly the same as before (ie. 65 per cent) but when we look up the statistical table on this occasion we find that the probability that this could have occurred by chance is about one in seven. In this case, all that we can say is that the null hypothesis cannot be rejected. We cannot say that our original hypothesis is false, since the evidence is insufficient to decide on the truth or otherwise of our original idea.

8.6.1 **Type I and Type II Errors**

The preceding discussion highlights that researchers can make two distinct types of error.

Type I—where the null hypothesis is rejected when it is true.

Type II—where the null hypothesis is accepted when it is false.

In conducting research it is important to ensure when testing that the probability of a Type I error is as small as possible. This is referred to as the significance level of the test. If the probability of making a Type I error is less than 1 per cent it is described as having a 1 per cent significance level. Given that most researchers wish to reject the null hypothesis, the smaller the significance level the better. By convention, if the significance level is greater than 5 per cent then it is generally accepted that the results are not significant.

8.7 **Comparisons**

The direct marketer is often interested in testing two sets of measurements to identify whether their mean values differ. For example, a direct marketer might want to determine whether a series of direct response ads on two different television channels perform any differently in terms of the number of sales they are able to generate. In this case, it is possible to verify whether the mean sales generated differ significantly from one another. For example if the mean and standard errors of the means for the first set of measurements are m1 and s1, and for the second set are m2 and s2, then the difference in the means is d = m1 – m2 and the standard error of the difference is:

$$e = \sqrt{\frac{s^2_1}{n_1} + \frac{s^2_2}{n_2}}$$

In our example, the researchers would be interested to see whether d differs from zero and thus the null hypothesis is that the true value of d is equal to zero. Making the assumption that d is normally distributed, the absolute value of d should exceed ($1.96 \times e$) with less than 5 per cent probability. This is the same as saying that if d/e is greater than 1.96, the null hypothesis at the chosen 5 per cent significance level can be rejected. We therefore proceed by calculating the difference to test, divide it by the standard error of the difference and determine the empirical significance level from a table of a standard normal distribution.

Let's consider the direct marketing question posed earlier. Suppose that we are interested in determining whether a series of ads on two different television channels perform any differently on the criterion average order level. We monitor sales over a twelve month period attributable to each channel and record the number of sales each month accordingly. The results of such an investigation are recorded in Table 8.1

In the case of large sample, the procedure outlined above works well, but in the case of small samples, the standard error tends to be significantly understated. The way around this problem is to use a test known as a t-test developed by a mathematician called William Gossett. Gossett illustrated how it was possible still to test the ratio of d/e using his t-distribution instead of the normal distribution. In the case of the t-test it is necessary to know the number of degrees of freedom which is given by the number of observations minus the number of parameters estimated from the evidence (in this case two since 2 means have been used).

The evidence in Table 8.1 shows that a t-test with 22 degrees of freedom (24 points minus 2 means) should be employed for which the critical values are 2.07 and 2.82. These values are a little higher than calculated earlier for the normal distribution, but this simply reflects the more conservative nature of the t-test. The results of the test are still significant at the 5 per cent level and we may therefore reject the null hypothesis. It would appear that there is a significant difference between the two television channels in terms of their respective sales performance.

Table 8.1 Monthly sales by channel

Month	Sales Channel A	Sales Channel B	Difference
Jan	594	641	−47
Feb	576	623	−47
March	645	652	−7
April	653	668	−15
May	590	614	−24
June	512	550	−38
July	611	640	−29
Aug	598	610	−12
Sept	587	593	−6
Oct	567	630	−63
Nov	603	628	−25
Dec	614	650	−32
Mean	595.8	624.9	−29
Std Dev	36.5	31.2	
Mean Diff	−29.1		
Std Error Diff	13.9		
Test-Statistic	−2.09		

8.8 Tests of association

On other occasions the direct marketer needs to determine whether there is an association between specific factors of interest. Perhaps he/she needs to determine whether men or women spend different sums of money with the company each year. Clearly, if women spend more than men, then this would have important implications for their customer recruitment strategy. Illustratory results of just such an analysis (for a company with a very small database!) are reported in Table 8.2.

A cursory inspection of the table reveals that the company is doing business with marginally more females than males. Whether or not there are any real differences between the two groups in terms of their expenditure pattern remains to be determined.

As previously, we begin by formulating a null hypothesis. In this case, the no difference hypothesis takes the form of an assumption which states that the figures are consistent with patterns of expenditure that are the same for both genders. More succinctly, we would say that there was no association between gender and expenditure.

If this hypothesis were true we would expect that the same proportion of males as females could be found in each expenditure category. To test this we begin by finding the totals of individuals in each of the various categories. This is shown in Table 8.3.

Thus, out of a total of 350 customers we find that 164 are males. This equates to 47 per cent of the total customer base. Thus, if the null hypothesis were true we would expect to find 47 per cent of the customers spending less than £100 to be male, 47 per cent of the customers spending between £101 and £200 to be male, etc. We can therefore insert the expected numbers of males and females in each category. This has been done in Table 8.4.

Table 8.2 Expenditure category by customer gender

Expenditure category	Males	Females
Less than £100	34	31
£101–200	45	35
£201–299	56	60
£300 and over	29	60
Total	164	186

Table 8.3 Total individuals in each category

Expenditure category	Males	Females	Total
Less than £100	34	31	65
£101–200	45	35	80
£201–299	56	60	116
£300 and over	29	60	89
Total	164	186	350

Table 8.4 Observed and expected customer numbers

Expenditure category	Males	Females	Total
Less than £100	34 (30.5)	31 (34.5)	65
£101–200	45 (37.5)	35 (42.5)	80
£201–299	56 (54.3)	60 (61.7)	116
£300 and over	29 (41.7)	60 (47.3)	89
Total	164	186	350

It is now clear that more females spend over £300 per annum than would be expected as the null hypothesis would suggest. Yet is this difference significant? What is required is some way of measuring the disagreement between what actually happened (the observed values) and what the null hypothesis suggested should happen. If we take O to denote the observed values and E to denote the expected values, then the obvious way to examine the difference between them is to look at O – E for each category in the table. These figures are shown in the third column of Table 8.5. The most obvious thing to do at this stage is probably to sum all these differences, but as can be seen from the table these unfortunately total zero. Recalling our earlier discussion of standard deviation, the reader will appreciate that a more appropriate option is to square these differences thereby removing the negative values. The sum of $(O - E)^2$ should then give us a measure of the absolute disagreement between O and E. Unfortunately, this is not quite the end of the story since it is not so much the size of the disagreement that researchers are interested in, as the size of that disagreement relative to the figure expected. After all, a total figure for disagreement of 10 would constitute a major departure from the expected value if that expected value was only circa 5, but a minor departure if that expected value were 1005.

What is needed, therefore is a final column in the table giving the value of $(O - E)^2/E$— the size of the squared disagreement relative to the corresponding expected figure. The sum of this final column gives us an appropriate measure of disagreement. This is known as the Chi Squared statistic (pronounced 'ki-squared' and denoted by the Greek letter χ^2). Using mathematical notation to explain our calculation in Table 8.5 we get

$$x^2 = \sum_i \frac{(O_i - E_i)^2}{E_i}$$

We thus have a Chi Square value of 10.98, which, whilst interesting, tells us nothing in itself about the null hypothesis. We need some way to determine whether this value is large, indicating a lot of disagreement, or not. Fortunately these values follow a distribution known as the χ^2 distribution with $(R - 1) \times (C - 1)$ degrees of freedom, where R and C denote the number of rows and columns respectively. In this case we therefore have three degrees of freedom and the critical values of χ^2 are 7.815 and 11.345. The association between gender and expenditure is therefore significant at the 5 per cent level which means the null hypothesis may be rejected and we can conclude there is an association between gender and expenditure. It should be noted that χ^2 in itself does not tell us the direction of an association. We have to look back over the data and apply a little common

Table 8.5 Calculating the Chi Square statistic

O	E	(O–E)	(O–E)^2	(O–E)^2/E
34	30.5	3.5	12.25	0.40
45	37.5	7.5	56.25	1.50
56	54.4	1.6	2.56	0.05
29	41.7	−12.7	161.29	3.87
31	34.5	−3.5	12.25	0.38
35	42.5	−7.5	56.25	1.33
60	61.6	−1.6	2.56	0.04
60	47.3	12.7	161.29	3.41
			Total	10.98

sense to determine that it is females who spend more than males. Thinking back to the context of our example, we might therefore decide to alter the balance of our customer recruitment activities and target a greater proportion of females, who it would seem, would tend to spend larger sums with our organization.

8.9 Regression

So far in this chapter we have looked at comparisons or associations between different categories of data. Direct marketers may also be interested, however, in cases where the variables are continuous in nature and where the aim is to identify some kind of under-lying trend. Probably the most obvious example of this in a business context lies in an attempt to track sales, or profitability, over time. There may be considerable variation in these figures from month to month, but over time it could be possible to find a trend in this data. Despite the considerable variation in monthly sales, for example, the graph in Figure 8.5 shows quite clearly an upward trend in sales for the company concerned. In effect, a line of best fit has been drawn through the monthly sales points to derive the trend indicated. One might, of course draw this line by hand, but if a higher degree of accuracy is called for the technique of regression can be used to determine the optimal position of this line.

Aside from generating the line of best fit, regression also allows the researcher to deter-mine the error in the slope of the line to see whether the slope differs significantly from zero. Consider the dataset provided in Table 8.6:

In this case, the null hypothesis would be that the amount of sales generated does not depend on the amount spent on advertising. If the slope of the regression line does not differ significantly from zero it is not possible to establish a linear association.

To calculate the line of best fit we could begin by assuming that the line being fitted is a straight line. The equation of that line then becomes:

$y = a + bx$

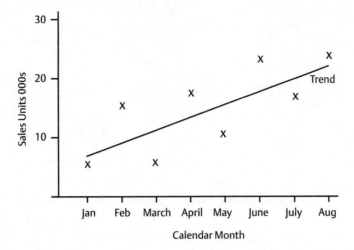

Fig. 8.5 Monthly sales figures

Table 8.6 Advertising expenditure and sales revenue

Year	Advertising expenditure (£000s)	Sales revenue (£000s)
1994	2	60
1995	4	90
1996	5	100
1997	3	70
1998	6	110

Where a is the intercept on the y axis and b is the slope of the line. A standard software package would then proceed to calculate values for a and b where the root mean square of the deviations from the line is at a minimum. For the data in Table 8.1 the line shown in Figure 8.6 is the line of best fit. Table 8.7 shows the details of this line, giving both the value of the intercept and the slope. The slope of the line is 13 which we can see is significant at the 1 per cent level (the P value or empirical significance level is less than 0.01). The figure for slope tells us that sales will increase by 13 (thousand) pounds for every additional £1 (thousand) of advertising expenditure.

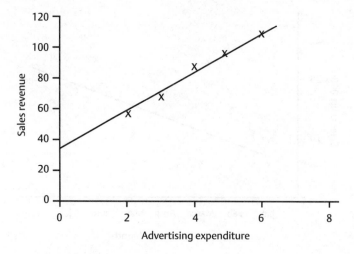

Fig. 8.6 Advertising expenditure/sales

Table 8.7 Regression analysis

	Coefficient	Std error	t-stat	p value
Intercept	34	4.243	8.014	0.004
Slope	13	1.000	13.000	0.001

8.10 Correlation

An alternative way of analysing the data in Table 8.6 would be to calculate the correlation between the two variables. In essence, one is asking does the value of sales increase or decrease as the level of advertising expenditure goes up. Calculating the correlation co-efficient furnishes us with this information. It is calculated as:

$$r = \frac{\sum_i (x_i - \bar{x})(y_i - \bar{y})}{n s_x s_y}$$

If there is a perfect correlation between x and y, then $r = 1$; if there is a perfect negative correlation then $r = -1$; and if there is no correlation then $r = 0$. Calculating the correlation coefficient for the data in Table 8.7 yields a value of 0.99 a very high degree of positive correlation indeed.

8.11 **Analysis of variance**

In cases where the researcher is interested in exploring a series of categorical variables, for each of which a continuous dependent variable can be measured, the technique of analysis of variance will be instructive.

Using a software package such as Minitab or SPSS (Statistical Package for the Social Sciences), the program calculates the mean value for each category and then tests are performed to see whether a particular factor influences the outcome. The program works by calculating the mean of all the evidence. It then calculates the sum of the squares of the differences from the means for each factor (sums of squares (ss). Each sum of squares is divided by the number of degrees of freedom for that factor to get a mean square. The ratio of two mean squares follows an F distribution and the table gives the significance level for each factor.

This is a somewhat complex sounding explanation, but it should be remembered that in practice, direct marketers need only understand how and when to apply the technique and how to interpret the output thereof. To illustrate this, consider the following example.

Suppose that a direct marketer wishes to assess the performance of each customer recruitment medium by the average purchase level of each customer so recruited. In other words, do some recruitment media generate higher value customers than others. This would clearly have implications for the future choice of media, since those under-performing could be deleted from the recruitment strategy. In conducting this analysis we therefore have a number of categories (the recruitment media) and a continuous dependent variable—average purchase level. The application of ANOVA would thus seem appropriate and the results of such an analysis are reported in Table 8.8.

The first column reports the names of the various recruitment media. The second indicates the number of individuals recruited by each method input to the analysis—a total of 767 individuals in all. The mean purchase level for each channel is reported in the third column and a visual inspection shows quite clearly that some differences do appear

Table 8.8 Descriptive statistics

	N	Mean	Std. deviation	Std. error	95% Confidence interval for mean Lower bound	Upper bound
DRTV	78	63.6667	25.8676	2.9289	57.8344	69.4989
Door drops	143	41.7273	26.8457	2.2450	37.2894	46.1651
Direct mail	351	50.9630	32.7751	1.7494	47.5223	54.4036
Press inserts	195	24.4000	16.6230	1.1904	22.0522	26.7478
Total	767	43.7797	30.3642	1.0964	41.6274	45.9319

to exist between the respective recruitment media. Of course, whether these differences are significant or not—we are not yet in a position to say. To answer this question we must look at F and its associated significance level. The details of the ANOVA are reported in Table 8.9, which shows quite clearly that the value of F is significant at the 1 per cent level—and we may therefore conclude that there are significant differences between customers recruited by each media in terms of their average purchase rate. On the basis of the descriptive information supplied in Table 8.8 it would therefore seem sensible to consider dropping the use of press inserts from our recruitment media strategy, perhaps using the money saved to invest in additional mail or DRTV. Further formal testing beyond the scope of this test would be necessary to confirm whether this was indeed an appropriate course of action.

8.12 Multivariate analysis

In the preceding section we have tended to focus on the relationship between no more than two variables, yet in so much of direct marketing activity, there are many more than two variables that are potentially of interest. The reader will therefore not be surprised to learn that there are in fact a number of techniques that can be used to 'throw the net' somewhat wider and to investigate the impact of a larger quantity of variables.

   In the section that follows, it is not our intention to explain the underlying maths of the techniques listed, but merely to provide an overview of when and how each technique might be used and to describe the utility it might offer the researcher. Specifically, three of the most commonly used techniques in direct marketing research will be examined, namely factor analysis, multiple regression, and cluster analysis.

8.13 Exploratory factor analysis

In the preceding sections we have been concerned with variables and ideas that are relatively easy to measure. Most organizations could easily calculate their average response rates to mailings, profitability, sales revenue, etc. Regrettably, research involving

Table 8.9 ANOVA

	Sum of squares	df	Mean square	F	Sig.
Between groups	122,798.747	3	10,932.916	53.530	0.00
Within groups	583,441.015	763	764.667		
Total	706,239.763	766			

customers is usually much less straightforward, particularly where the researcher might be looking to measure attitudes, beliefs, or perceptions of an organization and its products.

Typically, researchers are interested in constructs rather than simple items or variables per se. To take an example, suppose an organization were about to measure the quality of the service it provides to its customers, how might it do this? It would be possible to adopt a somewhat puerile approach and simply ask customers to rate the quality of service, yet this would fail to take account of just what a complex animal service quality actually is. After all, service quality is not directly observable and is probably a function of a whole series of different components of a typical customer-supplier relationship.

A more sophisticated approach might therefore entail asking a series of questions each designed to elicit a customer opinion in respect of what are felt to be the key components of service quality. Consider the questionnaire in Figure 8.7.

In this case we are looking at a questionnaire designed by a telemarketing company

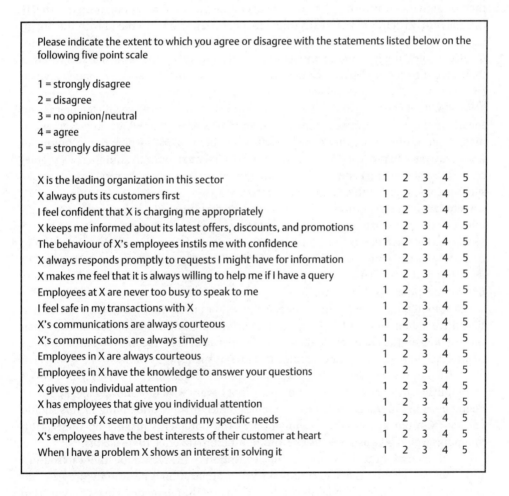

Fig. 8.7 Service quality questionnaire

looking to assess customer perceptions of the service quality it provides. The organization needed to assess current customer perceptions of service quality and to decide whether there might be a link between certain aspects of service quality and how much a given customer might elect to spend with the organization each year. Such knowledge would then be used to guide future investment in those areas found to be of most relevance to high value customers.

After some preliminary research with staff and customers the organization decided that these 18 statements seem to address what are viewed as the primary aspects of the service quality the organization provides. It could now conduct research with a representative sample of the customers on its database by despatching each a copy of the questionnaire and asking the individual to indicate the extent to which they agreed or disagreed with each of the statements listed.

On receipt of the responses the company could look at the individual responses to each question and it could even calculate the mean customer response to all 18 statements and thereby derive a measure of 'perception of overall service quality'. It might then correlate this measure with the amount each individual has been known to spend with the organization over the past 12 months. This would give it some idea of the importance of service quality to sales, but it wouldn't answer the question we originally set which was whether there might be a link between certain aspects of service quality and how much a given customer might elect to spend with the organization each year.

We could, of course, explore the relationship between each of the 18 statements and the amount spent by each customer. This could be somewhat tedious, however, and it might well be difficult to interpret the results we obtain. This is where the technique of factor analysis can prove useful. It allows the researcher to reduce the number of variables (in this case statements) down to a set of underlying dimensions or factors. This can make subsequent analysis of the dataset much easier.

Factor analysis serves three main purposes. The first is to assist the researcher in determining how many 'latent' variables underlie a set of items. Thus, in the case of our 18 service quality statements, it may be possible to group statements together that seem to be getting at the same underlying component of service quality. If this is the case we could adequately model customer perceptions of service quality by looking solely at these underlying dimensions or 'factors'.

The second purpose of factor analysis really follows from the first. Having ascertained that there are a number of underlying dimensions present in our dataset we can then proceed to see what relationship there might be between these factors and other variables of interest—in the case of our example, the amount spent per annum.

A third purpose is to define the substantive content or meaning of these factors. This is accomplished by identifying groups of items that covary with one another and appear to define meaningful underlying latent variables. Thus, if three underlying factors should emerge from our analysis, an examination of the statements making up these factor groupings would give us some insight into how best to describe these factors.

As with many statistical techniques the description of the technique itself can sound a little daunting when it is first encountered, yet its application is beautifully simple. Consider the results of a factor analysis conducted on our 18 statements. This is presented in Table 8.10.

Table 8.10 Factor analysis–perceived service quality provided

Statement	F1	F2	F3
X is the leading organization in this sector			0.55
X always puts its customers first			0.57
I feel confident that X is charging me appropriately			0.61
X keeps me informed about its latest offers, discounts, and promotions		0 .69	
The behaviour of X's employees instils me with confidence			0.59
X always responds promptly to requests I might have for information . . .	0.65		
X makes me feel that it is always willing to help me if I have a query	0.74		
Employees at X are never too busy to speak to me	0.82		
I feel safe in my transactions with X		0.60	
X's communications are always courteous		0.67	
X's communications are always timely		0.65	
Employees in X are always courteous	0.72		
Employees in X have the knowledge to answer your questions	0.77		
X gives you individual attention	0.85		
X has employees that give you individual attention	0.85		
Employees of X seem to understand my specific needs	0.81		
Xs employees have the best interests of their customers at heart			0.65
When I have a problem X shows an interest in solving it	0.70		
Eigenvalue	6.59	3.88	2.40
Variance explained	31.36	18.48	11.44

The first step in factor analysis is to determine the number of factors to extract from the dataset. Since we are in the business of data reduction it would seem sensible to select factors from the analysis that put us in a better position after the analysis than we were in before we started. We are therefore looking for factors which explain more variation in response than would our original statements. Fortunately statistical software furnishes us with this information as part of its output, in the form of eigenvalues. Those factors with an eigenvalue of less than one explain less variation than would one of our original statements, so it would seem sensible to select only those factors with an eigenvalue of larger than 1.0 (see, for example, Hair et al., 1995). The three eigenvalues that meet this criterion are displayed in the penultimate row of Table 8.10. The last row of Table 8.10 shows the percentage of variance in the full set of 18 attitudinal variables that can be attributed to the three factors. The cumulative value is 61.3 per cent. In simple terms we can explain over 60 per cent of the variation in response to our original statements by reference to only three factors. This would seem a satisfactory conclusion to our goal of data reduction. It is far easier to handle three items in subsequent analysis than our original 18.

The significant correlations between factors and statement variables are also shown in Table 8.10. Note that a positive correlation implies that customers scoring high on this factor tend to agree with the corresponding statement.

Of course, realizing that there are three factors is itself not the end of the story. It is often helpful to develop an understanding of what these factors represent. This is a little subjective, but the process involves looking at the correlations provided in Table 8.10 and deciding what the bundle of statements correlated with each factor might represent. This has been done for our example, below.

8.13.1 **Factor 1: responsiveness**

Individuals scoring highly on this factor would tend to agree that they received personal attention from the organization in question. They also believe that the organization responded to their specific needs, that staff had the ability to answer questions, and that staff were willing to respond quickly should a query arise. Since many of these statements relate to the nature of the organization's response to customers, the factor has been labelled 'responsiveness'.

8.13.2 **Factor 2: communication**

Individuals scoring highly on this factor are likely to view the communications they received from the organization in question as timely, relevant, and courteous. Since the majority of statements deal with communications issues, it seems appropriate to label this factor 'communication'.

8.13.3 **Factor 3: confidence**

The statements correlating with this factor seem to relate to the image of the organization, trust that the organization is charging appropriately, and a feeling of confidence in the organization's employees. On balance, it would therefore seem appropriate to label this factor 'confidence'.

At this point you can probably begin to appreciate why the labelling of these factors is a subjective process. Nevertheless, the three labels we have chosen would seem to be a fair representation of the underlying dimensions of service quality present in this case. In our subsequent work we could now look to see what link there might be between perceptions of responsiveness, communications, and confidence, and actual buying behaviour.

8.14 **Multiple regression**

Multiple regression is a technique that can be used to analyse the relationship between a single (criterion) dependent variable and a number of independent (predictor) variables. In essence, the researcher is aiming to use his/her knowledge of a number of independent variables to predict a single dependent variable of interest. Each dependent variable is weighted by the procedure to ensure that the best possible prediction of the dependent variable is obtained. These weights indicate to the researcher the relative contribution made by each of the independent variables to the prediction and also yield some insight in respect of the nature of that influence.

Earlier in this chapter we examined how to utilize the technique of regression when only one independent variable was involved. This is known as simple (univariate) regression in statistical parlance. When we have to deal with two or more independent variables the technique is known as multiple regression.

Consider an example. Suppose that a retailer is interested in predicting how much an individual might spend on books each year in its store. The retailer believes that this expenditure might depend on a number of variables including the income of the individual, the size of their family, the number of credit cards they hold, and the distance the individual lives from the store. If it can identify those variables that have most impact on buying behaviour it would then be in a position to use this information to develop and target a direct mail campaign designed to tease new and potentially higher value customers into the store.

As an initial step, the organization conducts some exploratory research with a number of its existing customers. The research dataset the organization assembles is provided in Table 8.11.

Table 8.12 contains the details of a multiple regression analysis run on this dataset with annual 'expenditure' as the dependent variable.

The output from a multiple regression analysis is very similar in format to the simple regression encountered earlier although the prediction equation it allows us to generate is necessarily somewhat longer. The regression model in the case of our example is of the form:

$$Expenditure = b_0 + b_1v_1 + b_2v_2 + b_3v_3 + b_4v_4 + e$$

Where

b_0 = constant expenditure independent of other variables
b_1 = change in expenditure associated with unit change in income
b_2 = change in expenditure associated with unit change in family size
b_3 = change in expenditure associated with unit change in credit card usage
b_4 = change in expenditure associated with unit change in distance from store
v_1 = income
v_2 = family size
v_3 = credit card usage
v_4 = distance from store
e = error

Fortunately, our ultimate regression equation is a little simpler to construct than this because the influence of some of the independent variables (i.e. credit card usage and distance from store) is not statistically significant. We may, therefore, drop them from our analysis, re-run the regression analysis and begin to substitute the pertinent figures from our analysis in the equation. We then obtain:

Table 8.11 Retailer research dataset

Shopper ID	Expenditure	Income	Family size	Credit cards held	Distance
1	20	13	1	1	20
2	30	15	1	2	25
3	40	17	1	3	15
4	60	14	1	4	14
5	70	20	1	3	16
6	120	16	1	2	17
7	120	22	2	3	16
8	150	19	1	4	15
9	170	27	2	3	14
10	180	18	1	4	3
11	190	19	1	4	22
12	220	26	2	6	26
13	240	28	2	6	28
14	240	16	2	7	29
15	250	25	3	8	32
16	250	30	3	7	33
17	260	34	4	8	23
18	270	22	3	3	24
19	280	16	4	2	25
20	290	18	4	5	21
21	300	25	4	6	22
22	320	24	4	4	32
23	340	26	4	4	34
24	350	29	4	3	33
25	360	30	5	4	2
26	370	31	3	5	54
27	430	32	3	6	45
28	440	34	4	4	65
29	450	43	2	3	45
30	560	50	2	4	32

Table 8.12 Regression analysis–annual expenditure

Variable	Coefficient	Significance
Constant	−121.4	0.004
Income	9.3	0.000
Family size	39.4	0.000
Credit cards	2.4	0.715
Distance	1.9	0.059
$R^2 = 0.837$	$F = 32.18$	$a = 0.000$

Expenditure $= 9.3V_1 + 39.4 V_2 - 121.4$

Where

$v_1 =$ Income
$v_2 =$ Family Size

A customer earning \$30K per annum with 3 members comprising his/her family would thus be expected to spend

$9.3(30) + 39.4(3) - 121.4$

$=$

$279 + 118.2 - 121.4$

$=$

\$275.80 per annum in the store

Aside from being able to use the equation to predict customer expenditures the analysis also tells us that higher value customers tend to have higher household incomes and larger families than would lower value customers. This information could be used to great effect in targeting a customer recruitment campaign at potentially higher value customers.

But what of the other information in Table 8.12? The F-Test in this case is designed to test the null hypothesis that none of the independent variables has an effect on expenditure. We can see that our F-Test rejects this null hypothesis with an empirical significance level of less than 1 per cent. Some of the independent variables do indeed have an impact on expenditure, although to determine which ones it is necessary to look at the significance levels associated with each co-efficient.

The R^2 measure is known as the Coefficient of Determination. It is a measure of the proportion of the variance in the dependent variable about its mean that can be explained by the independent variables. This co-efficient can vary between 0 and 1. The higher the value of R^2, the greater the explanatory power of the regression equation and therefore the better the prediction of the dependent variable. In the case of our model the prediction of the dependent variable is likely to be highly accurate.

8.15 Cluster analysis

The final technique we shall consider in this chapter is quite different from those discussed to date. Its primary utility for direct marketers lies in its ability to be able to determine whether or not distinct clusters or segments of customers might exist in a given market for goods and services.

Consider the example of a theatre that wishes to find out more about its customer base. At present, it has no real idea of the kinds of people that attend its events and has therefore used only advertising to attract clients to its events to date. The theatre hopes that by developing a more detailed understanding of its target audience it could begin a more highly targeted direct marketing campaign, both to recruit new customers and to build loyalty amongst its existing customer base.

A sensible approach might be to conduct a survey of its existing customers and to see whether indeed discrete segments of customers do exist. Suppose for the sake of argument that the questionnaire in Figure 8.8 is administered. Armed with the resulting dataset, the researcher is then in a position to utilize the technique of cluster analysis. The algorithm begins by searching the dataset for those two individuals whose questionnaire responses (to the variables selected) were most alike, and pairs these two individuals off. It then looks for the next two most similarly answered questionnaires and pairs these two individuals off. As the programme works through the dataset it continues to look for the next closest match in terms of the pattern of the responses. This may involve grouping two or more individuals, matching one individual to one of the newly created pairings, or even creating groups of 4, 8, 16, etc. as appropriate. This matching-up process continues until all the respondents are finally united in one large mass. Consider the example shown in Fig 8.9. In this case, there are only eight respondents to the questionnaire that we wish to analyse. The analysis proceeds as described from stage 1 where only individual responses exist, to stage 8 where they are all combined as one group. Whilst in itself this might appear a rather fruitless task, the algorithm helpfully records the level of difference that is being combined at each stage. Between stages 1 and 2 it is comparatively easy to find respondents who have given almost identical responses to the questionnaire. Between stages 5 and 6 it remains comparatively easy, but within each group of individuals there is almost certainly now an element of variation in the pattern of responses (a difference of opinion). Between stage 7 and 8 this variation will undoubtedly be more pronounced as individuals with ever differing responses are combined into the same group.

The trick in using this technique is to examine the measures of difference at each stage in the process and, when the amount of difference between the individuals within a group jumps sharply, to recognize that the pattern of responses within a new pairing is no longer similar. In plain English, one has to recognize when oranges begin to be combined with bananas. If, for example, the amount of difference measured in the response within each group is seen to jump sharply between stages 6 and 7, the researcher would recognize that there would appear to be three distinct segments of respondents amongst the eight individuals analysed. Any attempt to further reduce the number of segments to two would be inappropriate, since the software then begins to combine into the same group individuals who are not alike at all. Ideally the amount of difference in response within a segment should be as small as possible, and the amount of difference between the segments as large as possible. In our example a three cluster solution is recommended. Segment 1 containing respondents 1, 2, 3, 4, and 5. Segment 2 containing only respondent 6 and segment 3 containing respondents 7 and 8. Of course, in reality the number of respondents would have to be much greater for the analysis to be meaningful and a segment containing only a few respondents would normally be discounted, but the example does serve to illustrate how the clustering algorithm works.

In an effort to make this clearer, examine for a moment Table 8.13. The table contains the results of a cluster analysis performed on a sample of 300 respondents to the

Questionnaire

1. Are you
☐ Male   ☐ Female

2. Year of birth _____

3. Are you presently
☐ In full-time employment
☐ In part-time employment
☐ Retired
☐ Housewife
☐ Other

4. Are you
☐ Single
☐ Married
☐ Other

5. How many people are there in your household? _____

6. Do you have any children living with you at home?
☐ Yes ☐ No
If yes, how many? _____
What are their ages _____   _____   _____   _____   _____   _____

7. What are your hobbies and interests?
_____
_____
_____
_____

8. What is/was your main occupation?
_____

9. At what age did you complete your full-time education?
☐ Aged 16 or younger
☐ Aged 17/18
☐ Aged 18/20
☐ Aged 21+

10. How likely are you to attend any of the following categories of performance at the XYZ theatre? Please indicate your level of interest using the following scale.

1 = Not at all likely
2 = Not very likely
3 = No opinion/neutral
4 = Somewhat likely
5 = Very likely

Category of performance	Likelihood of attendance				
	1	2	3	4	5
Classic plays					
New plays					
Comedies					
Musical comedies					
Dance					
Ballet					
Other (please specify) _____					

11. When you attend the theatre, how important are each of the following factors in influencing your selection of which theatre to attend? Please use the following scale to select your response.

1 = Not at all important
2 = Not very important
3 = No opinion/neutral
4 = Important
5 = Very important

Factor	Importance				
	1	2	3	4	5
Category/type of performance					
Reputation of performers					
Presence of a 'big name'					
Cost of tickets					
Ease of booking					
Presence of a bar					
Cleanliness of the theatre					
Comfort of the seating					

12. On how many occasions would you attend the theatre in a typical year? _____

13. For what reason do you normally attend the theatre? Please tick any boxes that apply.

☐ To socialize with friends and relatives
☐ To celebrate a special occasion
☐ To learn something
☐ To enjoy a night out
☐ I enjoy attending arts events
☐ Other (please specify) _____

14. To what extent would each of the following factors be likely to encourage you to attend the theatre more often?

Factor	Would encourage more regular attendance	Would not encourage more regular attendance	No opinion/ unsure
Lower prices			
Easier booking facilities			
Availability of a season ticket			
Early booking facility			
Availability of discounts			
Better range of performances			
Other (please specify) _____			

15. How likely are you to attend any of the arts venues listed below during the next 12 months? Please use the following scale for your reply

1 = Not at all likely
2 = Not very likely
3 = No opinion/neutral
4 = Somewhat likely
5 = Very likely

Venue	Likelihood of attendance				
	1	2	3	4	5
Museums					
Concerts					
Art gallery					
Cinema					
Arts centre					

Fig. 8.8 Theatre questionnaire

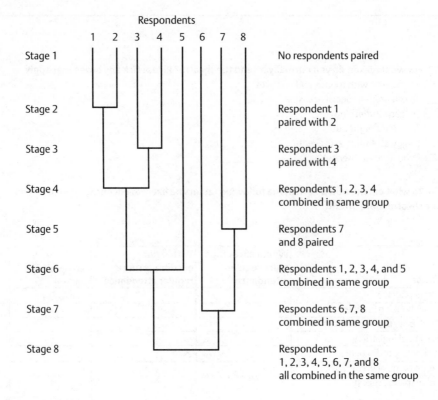

Fig. 8.9 The process of cluster analysis

questionnaire in Figure 8.8. Having performed the cluster analysis it appeared that three distinct groups of customers existed. The table presents the typical answer for each segment to each of the questions contained in the original questionnaire. Importantly, the motivations for attending the theatre were also found to vary quite considerably between the segments identified. They are shown in Table 8.14. Armed with this information it is then possible to proceed to naming each segment. In this case, the categories of Nouveaux Sophisticats, Blue Mooners, and Ageing Socialites suggested themselves. A brief profile of each segment is given below.

(a) Nouveaux Sophisticats (27 per cent of the population)

This is the youngest of the three segments and is comprised ostensibly of young adults many of whom may still be in full-time education. Of the three segments they are the most likely to be single and committed to attendance at a wide range of different arts events. They have an interest in most forms of art and would potentially consider viewing any type of performance at their local theatre.

They require few additional facilities from the theatre but expect that the accommodation will be clean and comfortable. Given that this segment appear committed to the arts in general they are less susceptible to price than other groups and are more likely to

Table 8.13 Cluster analysis

	Cluster 1	Cluster 2	Cluster 3
Demographics			
Education	16–18	16	21+
Age of children at home	Even distribution	Parents-younger children	Even distribution
Age	Predominantly younger (35 and under)	Predominantly middle aged (36–45)	Older (46+)
Marital status	Single	Married	Even distribution
Gender	Even distribution	Even distribution	Even distribution
Preferred performance type			
Dance	Very likely	Neutral	Somewhat likely
New play	Somewhat likely	Somewhat likely	Very likely
Drama	Somewhat likely	Neutral	Very likely
Ballet	Somewhat likely	Not at all likely	Not very likely
Classic plays	Somewhat likely	Neutral	Very likely
Musical comedy	Even distribution	Very likely	Not at all likely
Comedies	Neutral	Neutral	Neutral
Other arts venues attended			
Art gallery	Very likely	Not very likely	Likely
Cinema	Very likely	Unlikely	Neutral
Concerts	Somewhat likely	Neutral	Very likely
Museums	Neutral	Neutral	Neutral
Facilities required			
Bar	Neutral	Neutral	Very important
Ease of booking	Neutral	Neutral	Important
Cleanliness of theatre	Important	Important	Neutral
Comfort of seating	Important	Important	Fairly important
Factors capable of encouraging attendance			
Lower price	No	Neutral	Yes
Ease of ordering	Yes	No	Yes
Purchase of a season ticket	Yes	No	No
Ticket availability guaranteed	Neutral	No	No
Early booking	Neutral	No	Neutral
Availability of discounts	Neutral	Neutral	Yes
Better range of performances	Neutral	Neutral	Neutral
Attendance pattern			
Frequency of attendance	Medium	Low	High
Segment size			
Percentage of total	27%	24%	49%

Table 8.14 Reasons for theatre attendance

Reason	Segment 1	Segment 2	Segment 3
To socialize with friends and relatives	28%	63%	56%
Celebrating a special occasion	38%	75%	48%
To learn something	45%	27%	43%
A night out	43%	50%	26%
Enjoy arts events	52%	20%	25%

Please note that the column totals do not add up to 100% since respondents were asked to tick any reasons that they felt applied.

consider the purchase of a season ticket as a positive means of encouraging them to attend on a regular basis. It may also be the case that this segment is less susceptible to price than other segments because they already attract substantial discounts. Many theatres, for example, are willing to offer a discount on performances for those still in full-time education.

(b) Blue Mooners (24 per cent of the total population)

The least well educated segment. Blue Mooners are so named because they are only infrequent attenders (that is they attend only once in a blue moon). They are likely to be married couples, possibly with teenage children who view a trip to the theatre as a special occasion. They do not appear to be committed to a wide range of art forms and prefer to see only a limited number of types of performance at their local theatre. In particular, they are likely to attend musical comedies, and modern plays. They share with Nouveaux Sophisticats a need for few additional features in the theatre itself, but do require clean and comfortable surroundings. Blue Mooners are less susceptible than other groups to any promotional method that might be aimed at encouraging them to attend on a more frequent basis. Clearly, there is little demand in this segment for the theatrical product except for a special occasion and this is reflected in the fact that this segment exhibits the lowest attendance rate.

(c) Ageing Socialites (49 per cent of the population)

The oldest segment (predominantly over 45). Ageing Socialites have a particular interest in all types of play and would also consider viewing other related art forms such as concerts, ballet, and dance. The primary motivation for this group is to share in a social occasion and hence the presence of a bar is particularly important to share a drink during the performance. Theatre attendance clearly forms an integral part of their social life and this is reflected in the fact that they exhibit a higher rate of attendance than members of the other two segments. The exact nature of the performance seems less important to this group who instead cite price, discounts, and ease of ordering as being amongst the important factors that might influence their decision to attend.

As this example illustrates, cluster analysis can provide a very rich picture of the categories of customer doing business with a particular organization. It is important to realize that the term cluster analysis actually applies to a range of techniques each of which operates in a slightly different way. The whole family of techniques is quite versatile in so far as a technique can be found to handle most classes of data (binary, ordinal, metric).

Case study: The Game Conservancy Trust

Introduction

Tim Jenkins gazed out the window towards the parkland overlooked by his office. It was certainly a beautiful view. A few trees, open moorland and a small river gently snaking its way out of sight. Yesterday, he had counted ten species of bird in the trees outside the window and with fine weather in prospect he wondered whether he would be as lucky today.

It was a far cry from the view from his last office window. Clouds of acrid smoke from the chemical works at Salford couldn't really compare with the natural beauty of the Game Conservancy Trust's headquarters. Tim had changed career direction in 1997 and given up a good salary in industrial marketing to 'facilitate a change in lifestyle'. It wasn't only the opportunity to work in conservation that appealed, it was also the people he had to work with. As the Game Conservancy Trust's (GCT's) Head of Fundraising he was constantly on the move talking to farmers, gamekeepers and activity groups relating to the sports of hunting, shooting and fishing. That combined with the beauty of the organization's headquarters had made the opportunity just too good to pass up.

By early 1998, however, he was finding himself a little frustrated at not being in a position to apply all the marketing skills he had learned whilst in industry. The Trust's approach to marketing was very generic with every individual on the database receiving a very similar pattern of communication. Tim felt there had to be more opportunities to segment the database and to use the profile of the resultant segments to inform the creation of both donor recruitment and donor development activities. The primary problem was a lack of information, making it difficult to identify exactly what these opportunities might be.

Background

The Game Conservancy Trust was a unique organization. For over 60 years it had championed the conservation of game species, their habitats, and the wildlife that shared them. As a registered charity it derived the majority of its income from members and donors and attracted only a minority of income from the government.

Central to the work of the Trust was its programme of research. This was not research in a pure academic sense, but rather practical projects each of which designed to have a direct impact on the manner in which the countryside within the UK was managed. The research was communicated on a regular basis to farmers who needed advice on an annual basis to deal with the Common Agricultural Policy and who required advice in respect of land use, hedgerow conservation, long term effects of chemicals, etc. In addition, the Trust had an associated company, Game Conservancy Limited, a wholly owned subsidiary that provided practical advice on game management to farms throughout the UK as well as overseas. Profits made by Game Conservancy Ltd were covenanted to the Game Conservancy Trust.

As an example of their work the Trust had recently completed the following projects:

- designing practical techniques to make reared pheasants perform more like their wild cousins;
- planning for the unique and effective deployment of set-aside land to positively help partridges and wildlife;
- making practical suggestions in respect of the conservation of rare game species such as black grouse, capercaillie, woodcock and snipe;
- defining the influence of predators on maintaining the eco-balance.

The aspect that set the Trust aside from mainstream wildlife charities, however, was the support that it gained from the shooting and hunting fraternity. Clearly, such groups had a vested interest in conservation, since without it, species of pheasant and grouse would soon disappear and with them their sport. This did, however, create something of a marketing problem for the Trust. The message that the Game Conservancy Trust (GCT) wanted to get across was that of the importance of conservation—one of the most popular charitable causes in the UK. The market for the message in the GCT's case was severely limited, however, since traditional supporters of environmental causes would be horrified to learn that their money was being used to support the killing of animals whatever the justification might purport to be. The positioning of the Trust was therefore something of a sensitive issue and, therefore, in 1998 the Trust was concentrating solely on raising funds from those that either enjoyed hunting, or who regarded hunting as a necessary facet of country life.

As a consequence, the Trust had been positioned in the charity market as a specialist organization in the front line of importance to the future of game, requiring the support of everyone concerned with game and the countryside. This positioning did not preclude the possibility of raising funds from donors interested in wider conservation issues, whilst at the same time encouraging support from the traditional donor base.

By early 1998, the Trust employed over 40 scientists and spent well over £1.3 million per annum on research. The Trust had over 25,000 members within the UK and subscription fees were used in part to help fund its research. The membership of the Trust was very well defined with a range of different grades of membership being open to various classes of individuals. The classes of membership were as follows;

Full Member—i.e. entitled to receive journal and full details of the research.

Life Member—as above through payment of a one-off sum.

Young Member—individuals under 21.

Keeper Member—i.e. a unique grade of membership for gamekeepers.

Trade Member—for corporate organizations wishing to gain access to Trust members.

Corporate Member—i.e. major sponsors of the Trust (e.g. Agricultural Chemical Producers).

There were also a further 5,000 registered donors to the Trust who had decided not to join, but who nevertheless supported the Trust on an ongoing basis.

Every individual on the Trust's database, in addition to any membership communications that they might receive, also received approximately three fundraising appeals per annum. Efforts were made to target these to the known interests of the individual and thus those interested in fishing would be targeted with the financial needs of any related research project that might be planned for the future.

Aside from this very simple approach, however, the Trust undertook very little market segmentation and understood very little about why individuals might elect to support the organization, particularly with additional donations. By 1998, the Trust had therefore identified a number of information needs.

The research project

It was against this backdrop that Tim Jenkins had begun to map out a major new donor research project. He wished to be able to profile the fundraising database and determine whether the GCT's donors were very similar to those of other charities, or whether they had any unique characteristics, which would make it possible to target other similar individuals, cost effectively.

The second objective for the research related to understanding why people chose to give to the Trust as opposed to any other charity and perhaps more importantly understanding what the determinants were of the specific amount a person might choose to give. Tim felt that a greater effort should be expended on attracting and cultivating high net worth donors and deriving a profile of such a group was hence an immediate priority.

Tim had therefore approached a research agency to conduct a postal survey of his supporter base. A sample of 1,000 of the Trust's donors was taken and a postal questionnaire duly dispatched. In total 179 replies were received of which 13 were incomplete or unusable and hence the analysis the agency provided was based on a response rate of 16.6 per cent.

Who gives to the GCT?

The results indicated to Tim that the GCT had a donor profile quite distinct from that of other charitable organizations. They were similar in demographic respects, but certainly not in terms of lifestyle. Only one demographic variable appeared to define GCT donors as a distinct group—namely gender. Interestingly 91.6 per cent of GCT donors were found to be male. Since data from the Charities Aid Foundation suggested that for the sector as a whole a greater percentage of females will give than males, this was a significant result. Of particular interest, however, were the results of the lifestyle profile. The hobbies/interests that predominate neatly defined the current supporter base of the Trust.

Tables 1–9 provide a summary of the donor profile obtained.

Case Study Table 1 Donor gender

Gender	%
Male	91.6
Female	8.4

Case Study Table 2 Age of donors

Age group	%	Cumulative %
21–30	8.4	8.4
31–40	26.5	34.9
41–50	31.4	66.3
51–60	15.6	81.9
61–70	10.5	92.2
71+	7.8	100.0
Total	100.0	

Case Study Table 3 Donor marital status

Status	%
Single	15.1
Married	77.1
Other	7.8

Case Study Table 4 Donor socio-economic group

Socio-economic group	%
A	12.7
B	66.9
C1	7.8
C2	11.4
D	0.6
E	0.6

Case Study Table 5 Age completed full-time education

Age	%
16 or under	23.2
17–18	39.0
19–20	6.7
21–22	20.1
23+	11.0

Case Study Table 6 Existence of children in the household

Children	%
Yes	47
No	53

Case Study Table 7 Hobbies/interests

Activity	%
Angling	34.9
Art appreciation	15.7
Coarse angling	9.0
Attending concerts	16.9
Creative activities	21.1
Deer stalking	20.5
Eating out	44.6
Foxhunting	24.1
Gardening	47.6
Holidays abroad	49.4
Holidays in UK	41.6
Lotteries/competitions	18.7
Marine sports	22.3
Reading	47.6
Relaxing at home	48.8
Shooting (game)	81.9
Socializing	55.4
Social sports	29.5
Team sports	16.9
Theatre	20.5
Volunteering	8.4

To ascertain the primary motives for supporting the GCT, the questionnaire also contained a number of attitudinal statements which the respondents were asked to indicate the extent to which they agreed or disagreed with. The following five point scale was employed:

1 = strongly disagree
2 = disagree
3 = no opinion/neutral
4 = agree
5 = strongly agree

The responses in each case are given in Table 10.

Case Study Table 8 Sporting publications taken regularly

Publication	%
Angler's Mail	1.2
Angling Times	2.4
Crops	8.4
Farming and Conservation	6.0
Farmers News	12.0
Farmers Weekly	22.9
Shooting Gazette	9.0
Shooting Times	40.4
Sporting Gun	10.8
The Field	32.5
Trout and Salmon	13.9

Case Study Table 9 Newspapers taken regularly

Title	%
Financial Times	16.9
Mail on Sunday	18.7
News of the World	12.6
The Sun	11.4
Sunday Express	11.4
Sunday Telegraph	22.9
Sunday Times	27.1
Daily Telegraph	39.8
The Times	27.7

In the final section of the questionnaire, respondents were asked a series of questions relating to their giving behaviour and perceptions of how their moneys were actually used by the GCT for research and/or charity administration.

On receipt of each questionnaire the agency had been able to append data relating to actual giving behaviour and thus to identify the worth of each respondent to the organization each year. In common with many charities the GCT chose to use the composite measure RFM (Recency, Frequency, Monetary Value) giving the organization an idea of how much a given individual might be worth to the organization over the coming year. The mean RFM value for the sample was found to be £147.7 and approximately 80 per cent of the RFMs were between £130 and £160, while the minimum was found to be £50 and the maximum £225.

In an attempt to relate motives for support to forecast RFM, the research team decided to apply the technique of factor analysis to the attitudinal statements. They hoped that by reducing the number of statements they might get a clearer view of the influences on support and in particular those motives that appeared most strongly linked to RFM.

Case Study Table 10 Frequency table of response to attitudinal statements

	Frequencies					
Statement	1	2	3	4	5	Mean
I like to help people who are less fortunate than I am.	4	12	35	82	29	3.7
I like to be generous with my friends.	3	6	19	79	55	4.1
I can give without requiring the other person to appreciate what I give.	5	8	29	70	50	4.0
I find it difficult to get interested in what is happening to other people.	22	55	47	33	5	2.7
I enjoy helping people even when I don't know them very well.	10	20	55	64	13	3.3
I would avoid a job in which I had to help other people with their problems.	37	44	45	25	11	2.6
I am willing to share with others less fortunate.	4	19	61	66	12	3.4
I think I am a very sympathetic person.	4	7	58	62	21	3.5
I regularly invite guests home for meals.	5	29	29	66	33	3.6
I feel that animals in need are more deserving than humans.	51	41	32	24	14	2.4
People in 3rd world countries are less important to me than people living in the UK.	21	37	30	40	33	3.2
I feel charities use their money more wisely.	26	28	76	26	5	2.6
I need to get something back in exchange for my gift.	25	50	53	25	9	2.6
I only give to causes people I know can benefit from.	26	64	23	31	18	2.7
I need my gift to be recognized.	6	12	21	72	51	4.0
I prefer to give to local charities.	13	30	34	54	31	3.4
Charities spend too much of their money on administration.	8	5	43	48	59	3.9
Poor people could improve their situation through hard work.	11	22	52	52	25	3.4
There are too many charity appeals.	3	11	37	60	51	3.9

Case Study Table 11 Perception of percentage of gift actually applied to the cause

Amount	Frequency	%	Cum %
Up to 20%	32	19.3	19.3
21–40%	44	18.7	38.0
41–60%	58	34.9	72.9
61–80%	30	18.1	91.0
81–100%	15	9.0	100.0
Total	166	100.0	
Mean 48.3	Median 50.0	Mode 50.0	Std Dev 24.8

The results of the factor analysis are provided in Table 13. The first step in factor analysis is to determine the number of factors to extract from the dataset. It was decided in this case to follow the convention of selecting those factors which have an eigenvalue of larger than 1.0. The eigenvalues are displayed in the penultimate row of the table. The

Case Study Table 12 Preferred mode of giving

Mode of giving	1	2	3	4	5	Mean
TV appeals	95	32	22	10	3	1.7
Buying charity goods	41	46	15	49	11	2.7
Attending an event	26	26	9	75	24	3.0
Appeal advertising	94	35	24	8	0	1.5
Appeal letter	83	40	22	16	1	1.8
Purchasing raffle tickets	10	27	4	84	37	3.7
Church collection	39	10	12	36	64	3.4
Credit card	92	27	19	20	4	1.9
Street collection	24	46	16	60	16	3.0
Shop counter collection	70	44	13	30	4	2.0
Telephone appeal	113	24	23	2	0	1.5
Door-to-door collection	27	14	10	71	40	3.5
Pub collection	60	28	21	43	10	2.5

eigenvalue criterion suggest a seven factor solution although it is worth noting that two factors have eigenvalues that are only marginally larger than 1.0.

The significant correlations between factors and statement variables are also shown in the table. Taking into account both practical and statistical significance, the sample size suggested the selection of a cut-off value of 0.5 for correlation coefficients to be considered as significant. Note that a positive correlation implies that donors scoring high on this factor tended to agree with the corresponding statement. Similarly, a negative correlation indicates that a high factor score is associated with disagreement with the statement.

The next and most subjective step in the analysis required the labeling of factors. The following suggestions were made in the light of the loadings in Table 13.

Factor 1: Compassion

The variables that had a high correlation with this factor were statements 6, 18 and 19. The negative nature of the correlation co-efficient indicates that individuals scoring highly on this factor tended to disagree with these statements. They would thus feel comfortable with the number of charitable appeals, not try to avoid helping others and have compassion for the poor. On balance, it therefore seemed appropriate to label this factor 'Compassion'.

Factor 2: Sympathy

Statements 1, 2, 5, 7, 8 and 9 are highly correlated with this factor. A high score on this factor thus implied that an individual would be willing to share with others less fortunate, and derive some pleasure therefrom. They are also likely to regard themselves as sympathetic individuals. The factor has hence been labelled 'Sympathy'.

Case Study Table 13 Factor analysis of attitudinal statements

Statement	F1	F2	F3	F4	F5	F6	F7
1. I like to help people who are less fortunate than I am.		.64					
2. I like to be generous with my friends.		.57					
3. I can give without requiring the other person to appreciate what I give.				-0.68			
4. I find it difficult to get interested in what is happening to other people.						.62	
5. I enjoy helping people even when I don't know them very well.		.60					
6. I would avoid a job in which I had to help other people with their problems.	-0.63						
7. I am willing to share with others less fortunate.		.70					
8. I think I am a very sympathetic person.		.67					
9. I regularly invite guests home for meals.		.50					
10. I feel that animals in need are more deserving than humans.						.80	
11. People in 3rd world countries are less important to me than people living in the UK.							.80
12. I feel charities use their money wisely.			.69				
13. I need to get something back in exchange for my gift.					.52		
14. I only give to causes people I know can benefit from.					.83		
15. I need my gift to be recognized.				.65			
16. I prefer to give to local charities.							.67
17. Charities spend too much of their money on administration.			-0.61				
18. Poor people could improve their situation through hard work.	-0.58						
19. There are too many charity appeals.	-0.57						

Factor 3: Efficiency

Individuals scoring highly on this factor tended to agree that charities use their money wisely and disagreed that too much money is spent on administration. The factor was therefore been labelled 'Efficiency'.

Factor 4: Need for recognition

This factor correlates highly with two statements. Individuals scoring highly feel a need for their gift to be recognized and do not feel able to give should that gift be unappreciated. The factor has thus been labelled 'Need For Recognition'.

Factor 5: Direct benefit

Individuals scoring highly on this factor felt the need to obtain something in return for their gift and would tend only to give to causes that people they knew might benefit from. The factor would thus seem appropriately labelled as 'Direct Benefit'.

Factor 6: Animal lovers

The two statements correlated with this factor suggest that individuals scoring highly would tend to be more concerned with animal welfare than with the welfare of other human beings. The factor has thus been labelled 'Animal Lovers'.

Factor 7: Proximity

Individuals scoring highly on this factor believe that people in the third world are less important than those in the UK, and would tend only to support local causes. The factor has hence been labelled 'Proximity'.

Having completed the factor analysis, it was then possible for the researchers to return to the question of whether or not attitudinal variables are able to explain the size of donations as measured by RFM. The seven factors were entered into a regression analysis to determine their explanatory power. The results are shown in Table 14.
It would thus appear that:

$$RFM = 131.03 + 8.95C + 7.95E + 6.80AL$$

Where

C = Compassion
E = Efficiency
AL = Animal Lover

The data collected in the survey were also subjected to a further series of analyses in an attempt to determine whether distinct sub-groups or segments of donors might exist in the dataset.

The application of cluster analysis was therefore warranted. A three cluster solution was found to be appropriate. The population was well balanced at this point and had a good descriptive appeal.

A selection of the characteristics of each cluster is outlined in Table 15
Clearly, the most subjective step in cluster analysis lies in interpreting the results and

Case Study Table 14 Regression analysis: RFM(£)

Factor	Coefficient	Significance
Compassion	8.95	0.011
Sympathy	1.50	0.600
Efficiency	7.95	0.014
Recognition	5.44	0.097
Direct benefit	−5.36	0.073
Animal lover	6.80	0.045
Proximity	1.25	0.680
Constant	131.03	0.000
$R^2 = 0.35$	$F = 2.13$	$a = 0.025$

hence naming the segments. An analysis of the data suggested that the three segments could be named committed philanthropists, mild benefactors, and blinkered. A detailed description of each segment is given below.

1. Committed Philanthropists (20 per cent of the population)

The members of this group are the highest value donors to the Game Conservancy Trust. They regularly give at least twice the sums committed by the other two segments. They appear to have the least association with game sports and rank animal charities as amongst the most important to support. They have the least need for a direct benefit to accrue to them from making a charity donation and appear to give out of a genuine concern for the cause. Despite the fact that members of this group are more likely to be B class individuals and hence not on the highest income levels of all three groups, their level of support appears to have been consistently high.

2. Mild Benefactors (47 per cent of the population)

Primarily 'A' class individuals, the members of this group give out of a sense of compassion for the environment and for others. They believe that ostensibly charities are spending their money wisely and although they are likely to enjoy sport and game sports, they are unlikely to read the publications associated with their interest, such as the *Sporting Gun* or the *Shooting Times*.

Case Study Table 15 Cluster analysis of GCT donors

Variable	Cluster 1	Cluster 2	Cluster 3
Demographic			
Occupation	B	A	C
Behavioural			
Amount given per annum	High	Medium	Low
Lifestyle variables			
Read the *Sporting Gun*	No	No	Yes
Read the *Sporting Times*	Neutral	No	Yes
Enjoy angling	No	N o	Yes
Enjoy social sports	Yes	No	No
Factors			
Direct benefit	Neutral	Neutral	Need direct benefit
Compassion	Neutral	Compassionate	Neutral
Attitudes			
Charities spend too much on administration	Neutral	Neutral	Agree
Animals are more deserving than humans	Agree	Disagree	Neutral
There are too many charity appeals	Agree	Neutral	Agree

3. Blinkered (33 per cent of the population)

Members of this group appear to be motivated to give primarily out of enlightened self interest and are more likely to come from a lower socio-economic group (primarily C). They are generally unsupportive of charities and dislike giving by many of the traditional means. This may in part be due to a perception that charities are wasteful of their funds. They have a clear need to perceive some form of direct benefit from their charitable donation and would appear to rank this as their most important motivation for giving.

The decision

Tim Jenkins reviewed the analysis presented to him by the agency. There was a lot of information contained in the tables and it looked as though he would have his work cut out over the next few days to make some sense of it. He had four goals:

(a) to design a new and highly targeted donor acquisition strategy. Recruiting more donors who would not necessarily take up the membership option, but who could be approached for donations for specific research projects;

(b) to develop a donor retention strategy, to retain and develop particularly the higher value donors in the database;

(c) to convert a larger percentage of existing members to donors (At present only 20 per cent of members volunteered additional donations);

(d) to decide on an appropriate positioning strategy for the organization that all classes of supporter might feel comfortable with.

Task

In your role as Tim Jenkins, prepare a presentation to the board of the GCT outlining the nature of your proposals.

Further reading

Davidson F. (1996) *Principles of Statistical Data Handling* (San Francisco, CA: Sage Publications).

Chapter 9

Agencies and Direct Marketing Specialists

Contents

9.1 Objectives

By the end of this chapter you should understand:

(a) The types of agencies and direct marketing specialists;

(b) The kinds of personnel working employed in agencies and direct marketing specialists;

(c) Criteria used in selecting agencies and direct marketing specialists;

(d) The importance of solid direct marketing agency briefing and the role of presentations;

(e) Payment options;

(f) The nature of the direct marketing agency–client relationship.

9.2 **Introduction**

In conducting direct marketing it is likely at one stage or another that an organization will need to call on the specific expertise of a number or specialist agencies (Belch and Belch, 1995). A number of the most common that may be encountered are described below.

9.2.1 **Full service agency**

This type of agency, as the name suggests, is capable of providing a full range of services to the client. These would typically include creative advice and development, purchase of media space, printing/design/layout, mailing and fulfilment. Whilst it is fashionable for a number of agencies to claim that they are full service, the number that can competently provide each of the services listed is comparatively low. Generally speaking, unless an activity is considered central to the business of the agency it is unlikely it will have attracted much development resource and/or adequately experienced or qualified staff.

9.2.2 **Creative shops**

Creative shops, or boutiques, as they are sometimes known, specialize solely in the generation of ideas. Many organizations use these if they have adequate media buying expertise available in house, or if they are simply not satisfied with the creative work of the agencies that support other aspects of their direct marketing work.

9.2.3 **Media independents**

This agency specializes in media buying. It does not attempt to assist the client with more than the most mundane of design issues and instead focuses on obtaining the best possible deal that it can on media. The specialist nature of this activity makes this an attractive form of agency to use. It can also be helpful in circumstances where the client is likely to be able to handle their own creative better than would an agency. The most common example of this is undoubtedly the fashion industry where many companies already have considerable skill and expertise to offer in making their products look good. They need only advice in respect of the best media to suit their needs.

9.2.4 **New media agencies**

The fast developing nature of digital technology and, in particular, the internet has led to a plethora of new agency start-ups. Many organizations now offer specific design expertise in the realm of web site design, banner advertising or icons/screen displays for the new interactive generation of television. Often, the requisite skills are as much about technical expertise as they are about a flair for design and clients may therefore prefer to use a specialist agency for this purpose.

9.2.5 **Database strategy/analysis**

This category really embraces two distinct forms of agency. On the one hand, there are organizations which will offer specific advice about the management of a database, the manner in which it might be integrated with other computerized systems, and the reports that might be generated. Advice may also be given in respect of how to manage various categories of data or segments and how to grow the customer base, revenues, and profitability. On the other hand, there are also agencies which specialize purely in analysis. Organizations without specialist staff may derive value from having analyses undertaken of the behaviour and/or profile of the customers on the database. Sophisticated techniques such as cluster analysis, multiple regression, and CHAID can often yield considerable insight when applied to a dataset. Those companies not employing their own statisticians can therefore find this type of agency invaluable.

9.2.6 **List brokers**

Mention has already been made in earlier chapters of this category of agency. In buying lists for the first time it can often be helpful to employ the services of a specialist broker who will sift through many thousands of potential lists to find the best ones to meet a particular client's needs. They often have a better understanding of the performance and history of specific lists than would a client and make it their business to be appraised of new or refined lists as developments take place.

9.2.7 **Mailing/fulfilment houses**

Companies engaged in direct mail will often elect to employ an agency to handle the putting together of a mailing. This might typically include: printing materials, folding and insertion of material into envelopes, and despatch at the appropriate postal rate into the postal system. Often, these agencies will also deal with the fulfilment side of the operation in that they will collate responses and ensure that information and/or products requested are safely and timely despatched.

9.2.8 **Consultants**

For the sake of completeness it is also worth mentioning that there are now a plethora of consulting organizations that specialize in each aspect of direct marketing planning.

There are consultants that specialize in strategy, database technology, statistical analysis, etc. They may be part of a large organization, or they may be freelance individuals attracting business by virtue of their own standing and reputation.

9.3 **The direct marketing 'product'**

Direct marketing is just one of many services that companies buy, but it is a significant one. Conventional wisdom allows agencies and direct marketing specialists to use resources to purchase goods and services on the client's behalf without too much control or supervision. The available evidence suggests that the key decisions on the hiring, firing, and monitoring of agencies and direct marketing specialists largely rests upon top management and marketing/direct marketing departments. Collaborative direct marketing agency-client relationships continue to be the norm for medium and larger advertisers. Trade evidence suggests that the average lifetime of agency-client relationships is about seven years. Some have lasted for much longer, such as in the case of Unilever and J. Walter Thompson which has lasted for nearly 90 years and AT&T and N. W. Ayer for over 80.

A common assumption is that agency services are *intangible*. They are performances and cannot be seen, felt, tasted, inspected, or touched in the same manner as goods (e.g. legal representation). Another assumption is that of the *inseparability* of production and consumption as buyers often have direct contact with the production process of the service provider and production and consumption occur simultaneously (e.g. the repair of a computer network). *Heterogeneity* is another issue: quality may vary on a day-to-day, customer-by-customer basis (e.g. contractors may service trucks to varying standards). *Perishability* relates to the issue that services cannot be saved and stored.

From the purchasing perspective, another important service consideration is the ease of evaluation. It is generally agreed that there is a continuum of product evaluation from 'easy' to 'difficult':

Easy to evaluate products—e.g. computer monitors and office furniture that are high in search qualities (mainly goods).

Intermediate to evaluate products—e.g., conference locations and interior design/decoration that are high in experience qualities (part goods and services).

Difficult to evaluate products—e.g., auto fleet repair and software development that are high in credence values and difficult to evaluate (mainly services)

To compensate for the higher perceived risk of professional services, corporate buyers often seek the endorsements of peers and seek positive word-of-mouth (WOM). WOM is one of the key ways in which buyers of services exchange information. Related to WOM is the theory of perceived risk. Risk plays a greater role in the purchasing of services because of intangibility. Losses arising from risks include financial, time, physical, and pschycosocial (embarrassment or loss of self-esteem). Intangibility makes services difficult and sometimes impossible to measure pre-purchase, and even post-purchase and reference groups and WOM are important to reduce such risks.

A more recent development in the agency-client relationship is the trend towards the establishment of service level agreements. Whilst the agency service is largely intangible there are a multitude of ways in which the quality of the relationship might be measured. Service level agreements generally include reference to the specific outputs that will be achieved (sales, enquiries, etc.) together with the degree of contact that will be maintained. The latter will usually specify how often contact will take place and the frequency, length, and content of the reports that will be generated.

Direct marketing and communications agencies and the variety of associated companies (creative, media, public relations) generate communication *ideas* and *plans*, and *implement* them. The starting point in examining the selection and development of the direct marketing agency-client relationship is the two prevalent kinds of direct marketing agency-client relationship: the short-term 'project' and the long-term 'collaborative'.

Short-term project-based relationships rarely last much longer than the specific problem at hand and the clients concerned generally have relatively small direct marketing budgets. Once the direct marketing agency has offered and implemented a solution, the relationship is dissolved. It is impossible to say whether or not such short-term commitments between direct marketers and advertisers are increasing, but the general perception amongst the direct marketing business is that they are, and spreading to middle and some large advertisers. By placing direct marketing on a project-by-project basis, clients gain new ideas each time as well as learn what different agencies can offer. The trade-off is that there may be a lack of commitment from either side and there is a need for greater co-ordination. The project-based direct marketing agency-client relationship would be classified as 'arm's length' and adversarial, but appropriate in certain circumstances. It equates to the traditional purchasing paradigm of putting a specific job out to tender and choosing the best bid. Purchasing could provide the commercial framework required for short-term projects.

Collaborative direct marketing agency-client relationships continue to be the norm for medium and larger advertisers. To obtain an understanding of the dimensions of direct marketing agency-client collaborative relationships, the IMP Group offers one of the best equipped models to deal with the various aspects involved (IMP, 1982; Wilson, 1986). Apart from money, the IMP group have identified three elements that are exchanged by buyer and seller in their Interaction Model:

Products—the characteristics of the product will have a significant effect on the process of the interaction.

Information—some relationships require extensive exchanges of information, e.g., joint product development or JIT, whereas others do not.

Sociality—interpersonal relationships are the cornerstone of long-term relationships between buyers and sellers.

Exchange of these three elements may become routine over time and lead to a clear set of roles for the direct marketing agency and client. Key *product* characteristics for direct marketing are the degree of standardization, complexity, and novelty of the campaign, the importance of the direct marketing objectives and frequency of the transactions. For example, contracts may need to be re-drawn more frequently when campaigns are novel even with long-standing relationships. Similarly, the complexity of the direct marketing campaign will have a profound effect on the *information* exchange requirement. Finally, the *sociality* is often high between client and direct marketing agency and reflects the need for trust between both parties. Sociality is a well-known phenomenon in the direct marketing agency-client relationship as mutual trust serves as a risk reduction mechanism.

According to the IMP model, the primary result of these exchanges over time is *co-operation*. This refers to the extent to which the work of the buyer and seller is co-ordinated with the sharing of common goals. In turn, the cooperation between members leads to the process of *adaptation*, when buyers and sellers make substantial investments in the relationship. Adaptations may be made by either partner with regard to basic business procedures, such as a direct marketing agency opening an office near a major client or changing its work practices to accommodate a client. One or both parties might even adapt their attitudes, values and/or goals in order to enhance the relationship. Buyers or sellers may initiate adaptation and they can be mutual or one-sided. Generally, adaptations represent a commitment to the maintenance of the relationship.

9.4 Personnel in agencies and direct marketing specialists

One of the key issues to consider regarding staff in a direct marketing agency is their general 'professionalism'. Clearly a subjective construct, professionalism relates to the extent of persons' skills and knowledge of direct marketing and degree of belief in the principle of payment in order to work, rather than working for pay, and in the superiority of the motive of the service to the client. A broadly related issue is how they see direct marketing 'working'.

9.4.1 Account executives

Account executives are involved in account management. They represent the direct marketing agency to the client in terms of what the agency's capabilities are and what it can deliver. On the other hand, they represent the client back to the agency. It is the job of the account executive to fully interpret the aims of the client and translate these requirements into specific tasks within the agency. As part of their routine they normally fill-in 'contact reports' that detail their meetings with clients so that the agency has a documented record of what the client wanted. Overall, account executives need a comprehensive understanding of direct marketing and to have the ability to co-ordinate such activities as research and print production.

Account Management:

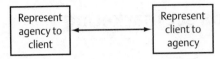

- Comprehensive understanding
- Coordinate strategy/research

Fig. 9.1 Account executives

9.4.2 **Creatives**

On the creative side, copywriters are concerned with both the development of strategy and execution. Strategy is about the client's 'game plan'. Where is the client now? Where does the client want to go to? These are the two key questions in creative strategy. Execution then relates to the question of how the client will get there. For example, strategically a client may wish to develop greater loyalty. In terms of execution, this may involve direct marketing promotions which aim at 'switchers' or disloyal customers. Copywriters in agencies and direct marketing specialists often work with art directors who visualize creative ideas for the agency, clients, or research as well as contribute towards their development. They normally work in teams of two, and advances in desktop publishing over the past ten years have enabled agencies to finish a great deal of artwork in house. Nevertheless, some finished artwork/and most TV, radio, cinema commercials, and posters are normally produced by separate production houses or studios. It is important to focus on an agency's past and immediate creative work rather than be swayed by the number or prestige of their awards.

9.4.3 **Media**

Media planners utilize quantitative and qualitative criteria to plan where direct marketing executions should be placed. They also plan where spaces should be booked if above-the-line media are to be used. Media buyers negotiate media prices for spaces with above-the-line media reps (e.g. newspapers and TV) or with below-the-line reps (e.g. direct mail and telephone) to get the best deals for their clients. In the largest agencies and direct marketing specialists these functions are extremely specialized, e.g. TV buyers and press planners. However, in smaller agencies it is less specialized and planning/buying is performed by the same people. Specialist agencies often book and plan outdoor, radio, and business to business press.

9.4.4 **Database management and research**

Database management and research is becoming an increasingly important part of the work for direct marketing agencies. Most companies use database marketing to pinpoint new customers and to build loyalty and, therefore, require specialist staff to operate databases. Researchers are also employed to examine and identify customer behaviour to inform strategy and execution and to assess the effectiveness pre- and post-direct marketing.

9.5 Selecting agencies and direct marketing specialists

The 1980s and early 1990s saw the development of an interesting, diverse, and relevant body of literature on the client-agency relationship which offers considerable insight for agencies and direct marketing specialists (Beltramini et al., 1991). One of the key issues focused upon in the client-agency literature has been the key attributes valued by clients (Doyle et al., 1980). An interesting finding has been that advertisers and agencies generally agree on the importance of the majority of attributes in agency selection (Cagley, 1986). When it comes to winning business it has been found the main factors are positive recommendations by satisfied clients, personal contacts with top management, and presentations. Compatibility has also been found to be an issue. Larger firms have been found to prefer associations with agencies similar in size and capability to themselves. It has also been found that larger advertisers, and those in frequently purchased packaged goods industries, change their agencies less frequently than others.

Another area of interest has been how the relationship has changed over time. The research indicates that relationship factors become increasingly important over time compared to more tangible performance measures. Internal and external variables and their effect on client dissatisfaction has been another area of interest. Four key factors have been found to lead to trouble in the client-agency relationship: (1) agency personnel changes, (2) the amount of assistance given by the client to the agency, (3) the effectiveness of the client organizations in dealing with direct marketing, and (4) the agreement between both parties over the agency's role.

Difficulties between agencies and clients are not usually the result of poor agency work, but from unsystematic performance appraisal. When it comes to termination, dissatisfaction with agency performance has been found to be the main factor followed by changes in direct marketing management. Unfortunately, the evidence suggests that agencies tend to be insensitive to signals of client dissatisfaction and failed to anticipate emerging crises in relationships with clients. Often, agencies lack a developed marketing orientation towards clients and fail to recognize impending client dissatisfaction.

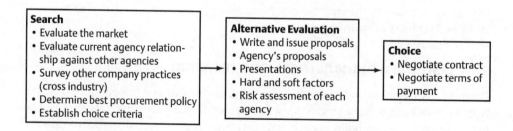

Search
- Evaluate the market
- Evaluate current agency relationship against other agencies
- Survey other company practices (cross industry)
- Determine best procurement policy
- Establish choice criteria

Alternative Evaluation
- Write and issue proposals
- Agency's proposals
- Presentations
- Hard and soft factors
- Risk assessment of each agency

Choice
- Negotiate contract
- Negotiate terms of payment

Fig. 9.2 Process in purchasing an advertising or direct marketing agency

9.6 **Agency briefing and presentations**

The general norm in the direct marketing business is for the client to brief four to six agencies on the problem and invite 'speculative schemes', i.e. solutions. The practice is commonplace. Agencies and direct marketing specialists then 'pitch' for the business. Agencies normally receive the brief a minimum of three weeks before presenting. The pitches normally last for about two to three hours and are generally given in the direct marketing agency's boardroom. Clients need to be aware that they might be billed for the work involved in the pitch if the direct marketing agency fails to win the account because a considerable amount of time and effort can be devoted. From the client perspective, it is generally best to judge pitches by their professionalism, creativity, and above all, planning and research (creative ideas can always be changed, but a well-planned and researched direct marketing campaign lays the foundation for good direct marketing). Unfortunately, 'showbiz' has often proved useful and speculative schemes are often criticized for being shallow. Many agencies argue good direct marketing is the product of a long-term relationship, not a hastily prepared pitch from a written brief. Creative briefing will be dealt with at length in the next chapter.

9.7 **Payment**

9.7.1 **History**

Before assessing the current role of fees and payment by results (PBR), it is worth while to consider the historic role of the commission system, which has its roots in the advertising business. Payment of the advertising agent by commission had arisen historically from the early nineteenth century newspaper space-broker, who, on securing advertising space for a particular newspaper, would be paid commission. However, a legal case in 1917, the case of *Tranton v. Astor*, established that an advertising agent purchased space as a *principal* rather than a client. The claim has since been repeated in the courts and remains undisputed.

Thus, the term 'advertising agent' is something of a misnomer. The agency does not operate as a neutral broker between advertiser and medium owner, but takes full legal responsibility in its negotiations with the media. From the point of view of the media, therefore, the financial standing of the agency is of the utmost importance. Not surprisingly, the media quickly developed a preference for conducting business with those advertising agencies considered to have adequate resources to guarantee payment for advertising space.

Following negotiations between representatives of the national press and the Institute of Practitioners in Advertising in 1921, an agreement was reached whereby the rate of commission paid to advertising agencies by the press was standardized, and the number of agencies entitled to commission restricted to a 'recognized' group. The qualifications for recognition were that the agent should have 'sufficient financial standing to enable him to justify his having a credit account with the newspapers in the country'. In other words, the Institute minimized price competition among its members by standardizing the rate of commission; while in return the press won (easily recognizable) assurances as to the status of the agencies. The press linked sufficient financial standing to turnover. Obviously, the size of the required turnover varied over the period and between different press organizations, but one example will illustrate the principle: in 1961, for instance, the Newspaper Proprietors Association required that an agent should have a minimum of three advertising accounts and that these accounts should spend £50,000 in the press as a whole or £20,000 in the papers of the Newspaper Proprietors Association.

Prior to the agreement advertisers had been able to obtain rebates in commission from agents. This acted as a form of price competition. For example, one agent would offer to rebate 5 per cent while another might offer only 2 per cent. The Incorporated Society of British Advertisers (ISBA), the representatives of advertisers in general, were therefore against the agreement. In 1921, when the agreement was first published, the General Secretary of the ISBA complained that 'the position, as put to our members, is that a group of advertising agents tried to protect their monopoly by securing from the publishers an undertaking not to recognise or grant commission to any agents other than "recognised agents" . . . the obvious aim is to abolish competition for agency accounts'. The ISBA only acquiesced to the terms of agreement after certain minor concessions were made, such that accounts receiving a rebate from an agent at the time of the agreement were allowed to continue until the account was transferred to another agent, and after it became clear that agents outside the membership of the Institute of Practitioners in Advertising were able to sign the agreement.

Other similar agreements were negotiated with other media including commercial television. The new TV companies were particularly keen to negotiate a commission system. After all, television companies transacted with large-scale advertisers, who, if they failed to pay for advertising time, might leave significant debts. The recognized commission system was a policy established and encouraged throughout the period by agencies and national media owners. This is where the term 'above' and 'below-the-line' media developed whereby agency accountants drew a line between those media granting commission (press, TV, radio, cinema, and posters) and the rest who did not. Thus, if an agency undertook a direct marketing campaign there was no medium as such to grant commission on the spaces taken and so a fee had to be charged instead. Commission

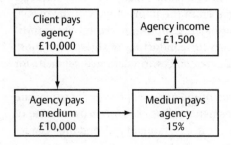

Fig. 9.3 Traditional commission system

remained the most important mode of payment for as late as the mid-1960s less than a quarter of agencies' income was provided by fees.

9.7.2 Implications of commission

On the face of it, two important repercussions followed the system of recognized commission, affecting the growth and development of the business. First, it would have hindered new entrants into the industry, and secondly, price competition would have been restricted. The extent of the validity of these propositions requires further investigation.

Essentially, the point is this. Few advertisers would have chosen an unrecognized agency as this would have necessitated the payment of fees at the going rate, whereas on the other hand, a recognized agent would have received commission from the media owner where the advertisement was placed, at no additional cost to the advertiser. For example, on an advertising expenditure of £100,000 a newspaper owner would give an agent a commission of 10 per cent, and the advertiser's costs would be nil. However, an advertising expenditure of £100,000 through an unrecognized agency would require that the advertiser pay a fee to the agency as it would not be eligible for commission. Such a situation would have made for a static membership of the industry: new agencies could obtain recognition only if they *already* had a high turnover, but they could not acquire a high turnover without recognition.

But other methods of entry were possible. A new agency might first establish itself in the field of B2B (Business to business) advertising. B2B advertising was one of the sectors of the press represented by the Periodical Proprietors Association, which required a relatively lower turnover of advertising accounts than the national press. Eventually, the successful agency would develop a sufficiently high turnover to become recognized by the national press. Another method of entry was to purchase a recognized agency (or an unrecognized one with the potential of gaining recognition). Obviously, such a purchase would have required capital.

However, the system of recognition may not have been such a significant deterrent to potential new entrants. For it was common practice for employees within an agency (normally those dealing directly with clients) to break away from their agency and form a new agency with clients taken with them. New advertising agencies have therefore developed in a rather amoeba-like manner. In the absence of contractual obligations between either the client, the agency, or the agency's employees, prominent members of agencies have been able to establish new agencies with clients taken from their previous agency. Thus, the problem of recognized commission was surmounted.

Nevertheless, the system of recognized commission did successfully reduce price competition between agencies. The system of commission, *ipso facto*, mitigates against price cutting, which inevitably leads to inefficiency, and encourages competition between its members rather on the basis of the amount and quality of the services they have to offer. While economic theory has emphasized the importance of competitive strategies other than price, competition based on the different quality of service offered by agencies would only have been effective given the condition that advertisers possessed full knowledge of those differences.

Overall, the commission system was well established and simple. Commission paid for the overall running of accounts and was generally topped-up when non-media related services were provided (e.g. research and production). Furthermore, there was an inherent logic involved. Agencies were rewarded for the scale of media activity undertaken. Successful advertising would lead to greater media activity and so there was an in-built incentive to perform well. It also shifted the focus on competition through quality rather than price.

9.7.3 Current payment methods

Methods of payment began to change in the 1970s and 1980s and particularly in the 1990s through to today. Fees now dominate payments in the business and PBR (Payment By Results) is growing significantly. Observers have pointed to several reasons for the demise of the commission system. For a start, the standard rate of 15 per cent was relatively high compared to most other service industries. As competition for business has accelerated, and especially during slumps in the economy, many agencies have been prepared to rebate part of their media commission back to clients and in effect offer price discounts. Media independents have accelerated this trend as most work on the basis of a 3 per cent commission. Clients increasingly questioned whether non-media services were worth the remaining 12 per cent. Of course, the over-arching issue of how unbiased media choices are when agencies are paid by the degree of above-the-line activity remains a thorny and controversial issue.

It is also worth remembering that the commission system was not entirely in the interest of agencies either. Commission payments were made well after completion of the work, so they presented agencies with constant cash-flow problems. Moreover, in times of recession, they exaggerated difficulties as advertisers commonly reduced above-the-line expenditures but agencies often had the same amount of work to perform.

9.7.4 Fees and PBR

Fees now dominate the advertising and marketing business amongst the various agencies and direct marketing specialists. The system is straightforward. All commissions are fully rebated and a fixed fee is charged instead based on agreed work with the client. Alternatively, a combined fee-commission system might be agreed whereby if the fee is below the commission income the difference is rebated or if it is above, the client tops-up. Of course, direct marketing media activities have been weighted towards below-the-line media which have never provided commission for many years, such as direct mail, telemarketing, and the internet. So, direct marketing specialists have been used to charging fees for the work performed rather than media activity. Fees enable agencies sometimes to advise spending less without jeopardizing income and to be media-neutral. There is greater adaptability. Furthermore, fees enable even cash flow and budgeted expenditures to ensure provision for costs and profits.

No payment system is without its problems. There are two main difficulties about fees: (1) they can be cumbersome and time-consuming to estimate (e.g. staff may need to log all their hours working on particular accounts), (2) they do not provide any performance incentive as with commission.

PBR has developed in response to the lack of performance incentive with fees. It takes the form of a contract based on the outcome of the campaign. For example, DDB Needham famously announced its guaranteed results programme in 1990, whereby, in addition to a base rate of compensation, remuneration would be increased or decreased inline with changes in sales. This had the advantage of transferring the alignment directly to the goals of the client. Risk arises in such an agreement based on sales because the sales outcome of any campaign will be a function of a multitude of uncontrollable variables so the client may end up paying more or less to its agency for unrelated factors (e.g. a direct marketing campaign to sell new houses will be more or less successful depending upon mainly uncontrollable demand factors). Generally, PBR schemes relate to:

- *Client business performance*: e.g. sales, volume growth, and market share.
- *Advertising performance*: e.g. awareness, interest, comprehension, and brand image.
- *Agency performance*: e.g. competency, service quality, and timeliness.

9.7.5 **The nature of fees**

Full-service direct marketing agencies working in partnership with a client to meet strategic objectives will tend to be paid a monthly retainer fee. This will cover the basic allocation of staff and agency resource to the client, and signals a commitment on both sides to a long-term relationship. In addition to any retainer fee, agencies may make a charge for:

- *Creative*: i.e. for creative concepts and ideas. This charge will usually cover all copywriting and design required to complete a project.
- *Artwork*: i.e. pre-production preparation of the creative work. This may include charges for illustration or photography where the agency may have employed specialist freelancers.
- *Production*: i.e. costs for printing, folding, enclosing, etc.
- *Distribution/delivery* i.e. of printed items.
- *Media*: i.e. the costs for the purchase of media space/lists, plus costs for media planning.
- *Planning*: i.e. strategic support.
- *Database*: i.e. database analysis or development.

Many clients will perform some of these functions in-house, or will prefer to employ a series of specialist suppliers rather than committing all the work to a single 'one stop shop'. Clients may prefer to use one agency for all tasks if the client staff levels are low, as it is easier to retain control when you have a central point of contact. The disadvantages of this arrangement are that it is usually more expensive and that many so-called 'full service' agencies are in reality little more than a loosely linked collection of separate business centres.

Clients using a full service agency on a more tactical basis will be charged a project fee in place of a retainer. In this instance, the agency will keep a record of the staff time spent on a client/project, and will charge this out to the client at an agreed hourly rate. Other costs such as creative and production will be charged on top.

Specialist suppliers in each area of direct marketing will traditionally be paid for their services in different ways. List brokers are paid on commission by list owners—the client will tend to pay a cost per thousand names rented to the broker, who will, in turn, pay the list owner for the supply of names, minus an agreed commission. Database services tend to be charged as a project/set up fee, though list selections, database cleaning, and deduplication services will also incur a cost per thousand records processed as a reflection of the machine time involved in the data processing.

Planning services will be charged as a fee—often, like charges for creative work, this sort of consultancy service is the hardest to cost out, as the output is new ideas and recommendations rather than a measurable, visible product.

There are a number of different ways to charge media. Commonly, the media buyer will receive a commission for the media owner of a standard percentage (e.g. press space usually attracts a commission of 15 per cent for the buyer). Some agencies will charge an additional fee for media planning services, or for buyer time.

9.8 Agency and direct marketing specialist client relationship

There have been several studies applying organizational theory frameworks to the agency-client relationship. The overall result of this has been a rather fragmented platform of literature applying organizational theory concepts to the direct marketing agency-client relationship. Traditionally, the organizational buying behaviour literature has focused on the buying decision and examined different buyphases along a time continuum. These have ranged from problem recognition and diagnosis through the selection stages, to a commitment to one supplier and then to the post-decision stage of monitoring, evaluation, and cognitive dissonance. What has changed, as the literature has developed, has been the degree of perceived complexity. There has been a shift away from the decision of the buyer, who is supposed to exist in a state of perfect awareness of suppliers and their innovative offerings, to a more integrated holistic view of the decision process examining the inputs of the key actors involved (in this case—the client and the agency). Essentially, this has been characterized by an organizational focus on the roles of 'buying' to the 'black box' of individual perceptual distortions based on expectations and outcomes. These influence each individual's approach to the buying task, to the point where non-purchasing personnel have become recognized as a part of the buying decision. This relates to the informal decision making unit composed of users, influencers, deciders, and gatekeepers as well as the professional buyers, and the concept of a buying centre with multi-person influences. The industrial buying decision does not take place at one discrete point in time but is the culmination of a number of activities spanning a considerable period of time.

Thus, it is necessary to have an appreciation of interpersonal influences across buying and supplying organizations. Two separate halves of the equation have now been fused together, that of the buyer and that of the supplier. Where attention had previously focused on a decision or transaction, now it is on a complex relationship. Levitt argued prophetically in *The Marketing Imagination* (1983) of a need to recognize the coming importance of the relationship over the transaction. The difference was reflected in the longevity of the supplier. His work foreshadowed the acceleration of global competition in the 1980s and early 90s with the trend towards industrial concentration and spiralling research and development costs that have led to the need for a critical mass for production efficiency. As costs increase, risks increase almost in unison. Thus, the need for interaction and information sharing at the customer level to diminish risk, both real and perceived, is another measure against which a service provider may be evaluated.

What influences the decision process has also come under scrutiny. This makes it possible to identify not just who is involved in the buying situation, but how and why they buy. Most importantly, empirical research undertaken in Europe by the so-called IMP Group, a group of British and Nordic academics, has revealed the nature of the exchange between the buyer and seller to be composed of a number of different elements in which information exchange may be only one part. Alongside exchange are other factors such as the mutual benefits to be drawn from a relationship, the commitments made, technological interdependence, inter-organizational personal contacts, and adaptive behaviour of the organization over time. This creates a distinction between the formal and the informal organization as portrayed by inter-company contacts. Customers form attitudes based upon their experiences of different suppliers and this helps them assess attributes. These attributes have been found to include: customer orientation, general reputation, technical competence, commercial competence, supply performance capability, price competitiveness, and the quality of the relationship. The ability to compete could, therefore, be gauged according to performance on these measures. Clearly, 'bonding' is crucial in any relationship. When two partners are satisfied, they often choose to invest in the relationship further, which leads, in turn, to a commitment and bonding. 'Structural bonding' has been identified to occur when an increasing number of transactions have taken place and switching costs (moving to another supplier) rise concurrently. Alternative relationships at this stage are, thus, rarely considered.

Another aspect of the buying and selling relationship that has been explored by the IMP Group is the *interaction approach*. The interaction approach states that each relationship forms its own 'atmosphere' resulting from the interaction and characteristics of the parties to that relationship. Five atmosphere dimensions have been identified, namely: closeness/distance, co-operation/conflict, power/dependence, trustworthiness, and expectations. Atmosphere plays a key role in business relationships. Relationships are initiated, developed, and strengthened through interaction between parties who invest resources, which cannot be put to use elsewhere, and require to be managed. Social exchange then builds up trust by demonstrating a capacity to keep promises and show commitment. When people move towards greater involvement with each other, certain ties or bonds develop, linking them together strongly economically and/or socially. Using the interaction approach encourages the idea of companies being viewed within the context of their network of interactions. It is through such interactions that resources are mobilized, strategies implemented, and the nature of the company defined.

The extent to which the direct marketing business has followed these overall trends has yet to be tested. At an indirect and formal level, the breadth of involvement may have widened in response to the re-structuring since the late 1980s. It has become increasingly common practice to use broadly based company committees to select or terminate direct agencies—despite the problem that very few of the committee members may have been directly involved in the running of the account on a regular basis.

From an organizational-buying perspective, the three key areas to consider in the client-direct marketing agency relationship are the task, the buying centre, and the process. Direct marketing agency tasks may be classified as follows:

New task—completely new direct marketing.

Modified task—familiar direct marketing task, but there is a need to modify.

Straight re-buy—repetitive placement of direct marketing.

The nature of the direct marketing task may be an important factor in the client–direct marketing agency relationship. Clients involved in new tasks are likely to enjoy a close relationship with their direct marketing agency as the need to reduce perceived risk will be paramount. This is particularly the case when the client is launching a new product and/or entering a new market. For example, Microsoft Corporation and the Wieden & Kennedy direct marketing agency worked extremely closely together on direct marketing for the introduction of the Windows 95 operating system.

Modifying familiar campaigns to provide something innovative, but not necessarily 'new to the world', is the mainstay of many agencies' work. While trade journals tend to focus on account changes, the predominant routine of most agencies is to modify previous work. After the initial campaign idea, the agencies and direct marketing specialists' role at the modified stage will still be important, but more moderate than at the new task stage. The client is likely to have a greater say over the direction of the campaign and nature of the client-direct marketing agency relationship because of the experience gained over the effect of the previous creative work. Having made these points, the direct marketing agency may be stronger at the modifying stage than with the straight re-buy.

With the **straight re-buy**, perceived client risk is minimal because the task is characterized by the repetitive replacement of direct marketing. Here, the direct marketing agency's role is largely one of a media shop, placing the direct marketing in the media without the development of new creative work.

Of course, from the buying perspective, some services are often bought as 'generics', like secretarial services and cleaning. Others are 'professional', like application software development, telecommunications, and direct marketing. Generics are low cost and normally low risk. Professional services have far higher risks and profit opportunities associated with them. Sustaining a longer-term client-direct marketing agency relationship requires developing a close personal bond between both parties and, thus, the nature of the buying centre is another key organizational buying issue. Developing a bond is easier to achieve with a small client than a corporate one, given the number of parties and influences involved. Agencies tend to liaise regularly with a distinct and small group of senior managers and/or marketers whatever the size of the company. However, the decision to select, continue, or terminate the client-direct marketing agency relationship at larger corporations has long been known often to be the product of joint-decision making processes, involving a large number of decision makers and influencers. Furthermore, with Total Quality Management (TQM) and increasingly decentralized management structures amongst clients in recent years, many agencies and direct marketing specialists find that they are increasingly isolated from key decision makers. They may be too closely associated with the 'old' management structure when such changes are made. From the perspective of the marketing literature the buying centre incorporates the five roles of 'user', 'buyer', 'influencer', 'decider', and 'gatekeeper'.

Users—people who use the services of a direct marketing agency on a regular basis.

Buyers—people who are authorized to negotiate with the direct marketing agency.

Influencers—people who influence the selection (for example, define selection criteria).

Deciders—people who determine and approve the final selection of the direct marketing agency.

Gatekeepers—people who guide the flow of information regarding the selection of the direct marketing agency.

Individuals within the client company may assume one or more of these roles and have direct or indirect influence on the client-direct marketing agency relationship (Beltramini and Pitta, 1991). **Users** are the most easily identified by a direct marketing agency, and likely to be marketers or in PR. They may wish to have greater involvement with the development of the creative strategy than agencies and direct marketing specialists often appreciate. **Buyers**, senior managers, may be easily identified, but can often be more conspicuous than their 'real' importance to direct marketing decisions. **Influencers** may cover a wide group of people such as finance directors, production managers, and lawyers who may help establish relationship criteria and direction. The **Decider** may be the 'buyer', but in many organizations may involve someone removed from day-to-day direct marketing activities—top management. Their criteria are likely to be less well informed and far more subjective than those of the marketing personnel. Additionally, they may involve issues of prestige or making judgements based on an direct marketing agency's client roster: exhibiting dissonance reducing behaviour of seeking 'reassurance' or 'safety'. **Gatekeepers**, who control the access of information through to the buying centre (either positively or negatively), may include marketers, PR, sales, PAs/secretaries and receptionists. Senior and top managers may also channel information on direct marketing agencies that they have gathered.

The consequences of organizational processes are also important. It is well recognized that organizational processes have a significant impact on marketing. For example, it has been found that organizational process can have a significant effect on budgeting, creativity, and risk as shown with studies of top-down and bottom-up processes. Similarly, it can be argued that the process of developing a direct marketing campaign will have a major impact on the client-direct marketing agency relationship. For example, it has been found that indecisiveness and too many approval levels within the client organization can lead to ineffective direct marketing campaign planning, indecisive goals, compromise on key decisions, and watered-down creative ideas. In general, it is likely that top-down approaches lead to more focused campaign planning than bottom up, given that in top-down there is just a small group of managers dealing directly with the direct marketing agency. Additionally, the direct marketing agency will have considerable power over decision-making, given its expertise and closeness to this small group of managers. In the bottom-up model, the number of parties involved is likely to be far greater, relationships more distant and the implementation of more stringent direct marketing agency performance measures more probable. This will shift the balance of influence towards the client. In light of this, here are the main processes in direct marketing planning:

Bottom-up—manager(s) in sub-units (primarily marketing) are responsible for establishing the direct marketing campaign.

Bottom-up/top down—manager(s) in sub-units are responsible for establishing the direct marketing campaign. Top management adjusts the campaign to conform with overall goals.

Top-down—top management establishes the direct marketing campaign independently of sub-units.

Top-down/bottom-up—top management establishes the promotion campaign. Sub-units adjust the campaign to conform with their goals. A final campaign is co-ordinated by top-management.

Essentially, there are two processes here: bottom-up and bottom-up/top-down;, and top-down and top-down/bottom-up. This is because bottom-up campaign planning inevitably requires management sanction, and top-down/bottom-up is a predominantly top-down process.

Top-down approaches tend to have more focused campaigns, given that this relatively small group of managers can deal directly with the direct marketing agency and have greater autonomy to act. Recent trends in team working and knowledge management have begun to empower more people and reduce the influence of bureaucratic and hierarchical organizations, as has the move to integrated marketing communications (IMC). When organizations move towards IMC it is often necessary to bring more individuals into the decision-making process in a consensus-type arrangement and so the concentration of power is diluted.

9.9 **Future of agencies and direct marketing specialists**

Consumer information is, of course, at the centre of direct marketing. Several observers have pointed to the signs of an emerging multi-£million industry that will handle the bargaining process of information between consumers and companies and may well affect the way agencies and direct marketing specialists do business. What will be the impact on agencies and direct marketing specialists? This new industry will be a business devoted to capturing consumer information and developing detailed profiles of individual customers for use by selected third-party vendors. Vendor-orientated 'infomediaries' will use information for targeting. This side of the industry will consist of 'audience brokers' (e.g. DoubleClick currently evaluates potential customers on the web for companies) and 'lead generators' (e.g. Auto-By-Tel currently provides car dealers with prospects). On the other side of the industry will be customer-orientated infomediaries such as 'agents' who will match customers to the best vendors (e.g. Independent Financial Advisors). 'Proxy' infomediaries will negotiate on behalf of customers with vendors who seek information on them, (such as the Firefly Network, which recommends CDs to members). 'Filterers' will screen irrelevant commercial messages from vendors (such as CUC International, which offers members pre-chosen products at just above cost, in exchange for membership fees). It has been predicted that vendor-orientated infomediaries will predominate in the short run, but as new technologies develop to provide consumers with total anonymity in their transactions, customer-orientated infomediaries will dominate. Customers will build-up their own integrated profile of activities on their PCs which they will sell to vendors. Initially, infomediaries will be restricted to the online world, but will soon spread to physical transactions, using smart cards to capture all goods and services spending. Agencies and direct marketing specialists with a combination of brand presence and database skills are likely to do well. However, the basic message to direct marketers is 'don't be too complacent about customer information'. The world of infomediaries may be many years ahead, but it is coming, and consumer information will be less accessible and more expensive.

9.10 **Summary**

In this chapter, we have reviewed the plethora of different categories of agency that a direct marketing organization might wish to use at one stage or another in the planning and implementation of their communications mix. In the modern era there is an increasingly diverse range of agencies specializing in ever more fragmented aspects of the industry. We have also reviewed the nature of remuneration in this context, noting the switch from commission to fee based or PBR approaches. It should be remembered that many forms of direct marketing were always below the line and thus always attracted a fee rather than commission per se. Direct response advertising, by contrast, has historically attracted commission rather than a fee. The nature of remuneration has changed quite dramatically over the past 20 years with fees increasingly dominating standard practice. In this chapter, we have thus detailed the form that such a fee may take and the implications for the agency-client relationship.

Discussion questions

1   What information should a typical creative brief for a direct marketing campaign contain?

2   What are the implications of PBR for the agency–client relationship?

3   How might a creative brief for a press advertisement differ from that of a direct mailshot?

4   As the marketing director of an internet start-up organization, explain the criteria that you might use to select an agency to handle a direct marketing campaign to promote your organization both on the web and through the medium of DRTV. What type(s) of agency might you employ?

Further reading

Belch G. E. and Belch M. A. (1995) *Introduction to Advertising and Promotion: An Integrated Marketing Communications Perspective* (3rd edn., Chicago: Irwin).

Beltramini R. F., and Pitta D. A. (1991) 'Underlying Dimensions and Communications Strategies of the Advertising Agency-Client Relationship', *International Journal of Advertising* 10, 151–9.

Cagley J. W. (1986) 'A Comparison of Advertising Agency Selection Factors: Advertiser and Agency Perceptions' *Journal of Advertising Research*, 26(3), 39–44.

Doyle P., Corstjens M. and Michell P. (1980) 'Signals of Vulnerability in Agency-Client Relations', *Journal of Marketing*, 44, 18–23

IMP Group (1982) *International Marketing and Purchasing of Industrial Goods*, ed. Hakannsson H. (New York: John Wiley and Sons).

Levitt T. (1983) *The Marketing Imagination* (New York: Free Press).

Michell P. C. N., Cataquet H. and Hague S. (1982) 'Establishing the Causes of Disaffection in Agency-Client Relations', *Journal of Advertising Research*, 32(2), 41–8.

Morgan R. M. and Hunt S. D. (1994) 'The Commitment-Trust Theory of Relationship Marketing', *Journal of Marketing*, 58, 20–38.

Wilson D. T. and Mummalaneni V. (1986) 'Bonding and Commitment in Buyer-Seller Relationships: A Preliminary Conceptualization', *Industrial Marketing and Purchasing* 1(3), 44–58.

Chapter 10

Creative Briefing

Contents

10.1 Objectives

By the end of this chapter you should be able to:

(a) understand what a creative brief is;

(b) identify the information required in undertaking effective creative briefing;

(c) understand how the creative process is managed in a direct marketing agency;

(d) describe the main theories of creative motivation and personality;

(e) describe some of the key creative philosophies;

(f) summarize the ethical debates around direct marketing creativity.

10.2 **Introduction**

Communications strategy relates to the stream of decisions made over time which reflect the marketing goals and marketing resources of the organization applied to direct communications. This chapter looks at how the chosen strategy may be applied. There are two stages to direct marketing communications development: *what* message will be communicated—the strategy; and *how* that message will be communicated—the execution. The creative brief is the vehicle that translates the business problem into a creative context. The result is business creativity. Such creativity is based upon combining expertise, creative thinking skills (particularly the ability to put existing ideas together in new combinations) extrinsic motivation (mainly money), and intrinsic (passion and interest in the task). Of all the aspects of creativity, intrinsic motivation is the best one to ignite, because then creatives will engage in their work for the sheer challenge and enjoyment of it. Business creativity is aligned with artistic creativity—a direct marketing creative idea should be original, appropriate, useful, and actionable.

10.3 **Writing the creative brief**

The 'Reason-Why' format is one of the most popular ways of writing the creative brief for a direct marketing campaign. The three main elements of the brief are:

- proposition
- supporting evidence
- tone.

10.3.1 **Issues**

One thing to bear in mind when reviewing creative briefs is that formats of any kind can be a trap (Corstjens, 1990). Formats help clarify issues, but they need not be so slavishly followed as to dampen down or restrict good creative ideas. Another point is that jargon is almost a 'disease' in direct marketing and should be avoided when designing or filling out a brief. The key point is that the brief represents a process more than a document. Customers should never read the brief, they simply see the direct marketing coming out of the brief and so the process of writing it is much more salient than the document per se. What do you need it to do for you? That is the key issue as the goal is breakthrough direct marketing ideas.

10.3.2 **Should you use a creative brief?**

(a) **Against**

- Some successful agencies don't use them.
- Creatives often don't respect them.
- They take a lot of time.
- They can cause pain and confusion.

(b) **In favour**

- Because the brief is going to be there anyway.
- Most great direct marketing communications are based on great briefs.
- The right kind of brief is a great help to creatives.
- Briefs help creatives to 'sell' their ideas.
- Briefs organize the facts and help manage client expectations.

10.3.3 **Problems**

Having made these points, the reality is that briefs inevitably describe the facts. Nothing more. They are not pieces of creativity in themselves. In addition, there are several 'deadly sins' in writing creative briefs. One is to re-state the strategy as the brief. Another is to confuse the client's problem with the customer's and not be able to disentangle the two. One serious one is to lose any sense of a meaningful target audience with a particular position. Perhaps the most common is simply a lack of focus and clarity. Another problem is that there are often two views of the creative brief in a direct marketing agency. The one sets expectations by being:

- disciplined;
- logical;
- differentiating.

On the other hand, there is often an unwritten and more flexible 'creative' strategy that exists for the creative team. This has no 'excess fat'. It might be a line, a thought, or a word. It is based on the public strategy, but is a creative leap from it.

10.4 **What should be included in a creative brief?**

Creative briefs are short (ideally one-page) documents that are about direct marketing intent. They should be focused, sustainable, measurable, and able to inspire. At the lowest level, the aim is to communicate to the creatives the objectives of the direct marketing campaign—both in terms of directly measurable results, e.g. number of enquiry responses to be generated, target return on investment; and in less measurable performance terms, e.g. what image is to be communicated to the prospect, what product values should the communication promote? Taken at a slightly higher level, the campaign may aim to provide an image of performance superiority, perhaps based on solving a problem or better fulfilling a customer desire. Beyond this, the intention might be emotional, perhaps by helping the brand to matter to the consumer or even some kind of cultural identification by making the brand part of the consumer's world. One of the most difficult intents is something like a paradigm shift where the aim is to alter the consumer's definition of category by the use of direct marketing.

'Big ideas' are the holy grail of direct marketing creatives. These are truly innovative and inspirational communications. They often require a great deal of collaboration and hard work and choices, judgements, and exclusion of product facts. Normally, they have to be sold and defended and may change a lot in execution, but they are central to the strategy. Here is a run-down of the typical format of a creative brief:

10.4.1 **Campaign requirements**

- identify the direct marketing objectives;
- quantify these objectives;
- relate to sales or market share;
- isolate, in a simple statement, the relevant trends in the market place (avoid jargon and statistics, etc.).

10.4.2 **Target audience**

Overall, try and avoid generalizations. Give a succinct description of prospects as people. Try and go 'beyond numbers':

- Who are we trying to reach and change?
- A person, not a 'target'.
- Beyond reports—talk to customers. Get a sense of what motivates them.
- Paint a personal picture, e.g. where would they live? What would they drive?
- What's really important to them?

10.4.3 **Purpose of direct marketing**

- What is it that you hope to achieve with direct marketing?
- Should be measurable and achievable.
- How do we hope to do this?
- Focus on awareness, attitudes, and propensity to act as these are the main roles of direct marketing.
- Review the key issues: why are we doing this direct marketing?
- What change do we want to make with this person?

10.4.4 **Single-minded proposition**

- The specific core benefit that the brand delivers.
- The key emotion or reason or blend of both.

Some questions to ask are: is it relevant to the prospect?; what exactly do we want the prospect to take from this communication?; what do we want the prospect to do?; how does it relate to their problems or desires?; how is it competitively different?; can it be expressed as a single, simple idea?

10.4.5 **Substantiation**

- The key points or facts that justify the promise.
- They need not appear in the advertising, e.g. Volvo owns the safety position and rarely needs to provide evidence for it.

10.4.6 **Mandatory inclusions**

These are the things that the client insists must appear in the direct marketing. It might be:

- Logo, phone number, web site, colour, factory, etc.
- Legal constraints, etc.
- Client's house rules (e.g. 'I don't want you to mention my competitors by name').

10.4.7 **Mood and tone**

- How brand should be positioned.
- For example: funny, serious, established, sad, shocking—what is the communication's 'tone of voice'?

10.4.8 **Media selected**

- Classes (e.g. direct TV or direct mail).
- Vehicles, if known (e.g. Carlton TV).

10.4.9 **Budget**

- Total available budget.
- For media (i.e. mailing lists, press or TV space).
- For production (i.e. print,artwork, TV production).
- For creative (i.e. illustration, photography).

Sometimes, clients will want to tailor the specific headings that they will use to suit the nature of the product/service and context. To illustrate this, two very different briefs are included in Figures 10.2 and 10.3. The first is a creative brief for a series of television ads promoting an Australian lager, whilst the second was the creative brief drawn up by Cadbury's for a recent Cadbury's Roses promotional mailing. Figure 10.4 illustrates the pack that was ultimately developed.

10.5 **Working on a communications brief**

Direct marketing creative staff are employed, permanently or on a freelance basis, to produce communications from the creative brief. In contrast to artistic work, which is normally exhibited, sold, or performed to the public, direct marketing sets out with the intention of modifying consumer or business behaviour in some way. Be it to stay loyal to a particular brand or respect the environment or vote for New Labour, the product of direct marketing creatives is developed for and owned by the client. The same forms of communication as art can be used, such as photography, film, drawing, and music, but it is business.

The management of the creative process in direct marketing is the responsibility of the Creative Director (CD). In large direct marketing agencies the CD generally heads the creative department and plays an important role in pointing the campaign strategy of many of the campaigns. Such direct agencies usually have several junior Creative Directors who oversee campaigns and report back to the CD, who may also have an agency-wide administrative role. In medium-sized to small direct marketing agencies the CD may solely direct every campaign strategy.

All direct marketing agencies have copywriters and art directors who are responsible for the development of the creative execution. They frequently work in teams of two and are often hired and fired as a team, and may successfully work together for a number of years. Copywriters come from a variety of backgrounds, but are often literature graduates. Art directors are typically trained artists. Their roles are loosely defined—each may offer advice on the words, layout, and pictures. They develop executional ideas for the client

Creative Brief	Client/Brand
Campaign requirement	
Target audience	
Purpose of direct marketing	
Single-minded proposition	
Substantiation of the proposition	
Mandatory inclusions	
Mood and tone of advertising	
Media	
Budget	

Fig. 10.1 Typical creative brief format

Fosters Creative Brief

1. Brand personality

The Fosters brand personality is rich and multifaceted, but largely derived from Paul Hogan. Through Hogan a positive combination of personality and product quality dimensions were established, the main features of which are: -

– Warm and sociable.
– Honesty/unpretentious.
– Individual and personal.
– Australian.
– Fun and mature.
– Relaxed/casual/ and dynamic/confident.
– Life in perspective.
– The best standard lager available.
– The choice of discerning lager drinkers.

In summary: The epitome and the pinnacle of the positive core values of lager drinking.

2. Creative requirement

1. Create a new, original and unique advertising idea which can grow and develop the brand personality.
2. Set the standard for advertising within the lager market.
3. Clearly differentiate Fosters advertising from its main competitors i.e. Carling Black Label, Heineken, Castlemaine XXXX.
4. Communicate Fosters as the 'Gold Standard' of session lager in terms of product quality.

3. Campaign elements

3.1 Consumer take out

Primary : A positive emotional response characterized by personal/intuitive/instinctive feelings rather than unthinking entertainment.

Secondary: Great advertising for a great brand.

– Entertain through sardonic wit (not jokes).
– Insight into the human condition.
– Refer to the Australian heritage (not Castlemaine Australia).
– Simplicity of idea – (can be sophisticated but not complicated).

Fig. 10.2 Fosters creative brief

within the context of the defined direct marketing strategy as agreed with the CD. The relationship between the CD and their copywriter/art director teams is managerial, but there is an important mentor relationship as well. Building creative teams requires the formation of mutually supportive groups with a diversity of perspectives and backgrounds in order for ideas to combine and combust in new and useful ways. Suggested codes of conduct for groups include sharing 'excitement' in the goal, being willing to help team-mates, and recognizing the talents of others.

Creative Brief

Client:	Cadbury
Job title:	Roses Pack
Job number:	32225
Group Account Director:	Simon Clarke
Account Handlers:	Karen Williams, Andrew Tucker
Project Manager:	Phil Hall
Planners:	Paul Becque; Kerry Torrens
Creative Budget:	£12,000
Quantity:	200,000 (tbc)

Approvals:

GAD: Simon Clarke ....

Planner: Paul Becque ....

Creative Director: Jon Dytor/Bob Crampton ....

Client: Sarah Mobsby ....
                      Guy Cunningham ....

Introduction/background

Cadbury's Roses is number one in the twistwrap market. In order to protect and maintain its position, it is vital that Roses maximizes gifting opportunities by seeking out new occasions and reasons for saying 'thank you' more often. For this reason, a key objective for Roses in 2000 is to explore the school end of term occasion and investigate its potential ownership. This mailing in June/July 2000 will go to Mums with children aged 5–11, and will follow with a Yowie communication in April 2000.

Requirement

Develop a mailpack for Cadbury's Roses.

Product

- Cadbury's Roses.
- Cadbury's Roses is the No. 1 assortment brand and the second largest Cadbury brand behind CDM. It competes directly with Quality Street within token gifting, and indirectly with Mars Celebrations within everyday sharing. It also competes with other gifting products such as flowers.
- Pack sizes: 300g   £2.59
                     500g   £4.09

Objectives

- Own end of term as a gifting occasion for Roses.
- Build end of term as incremental opportunity for the Roses brand.
- Build younger consumers into token gifting and the Roses brand.
- Reinforce 'thank you' ownership.
- Encourage consumers to redeem coupons/take up offers.

Fig. 10.3 Cadbury's brief

Consumer

We will be mailing 200,000 consumers, who are mothers with children aged 5–11 who buy a lot of chocolate, including a variety of Cadbury products. They will be aware of the Roses brand and 'thank you' positioning but may be buying competing products or gifts.

Mums are key, as they are the gatekeepers for household purchases. As a typical 'broad brush' portrait . . . .

Alison Thomas lives in a 3 bedroom semi-detached house on a modern estate on the outskirts of Reading. Her husband, Dave, works in a factory nearby and their two kids, a girl and a boy aged 6 and 7, attend local schools. Alison works part time as a school dinner lady and in her spare time likes reading women's magazines such as Chat, and doing puzzles, quizzes, competitions etc. She always does the lottery. The family eats a lot of chocolate – Alison always buys chocolate when she does her weekly shop at Asda and often buys chocolate for the kids as a treat.

N.B. We will also be mailing consumers who buy a lot of assortment products (Roses, Quality Street, Celebrations) who will receive an adapted version i.e. a smaller value coupon.

Roses profile

- Core market 25–44 female
- Mothers with children
- They buy Roses cartons as gifts, as thank yous and for sharing through the year, and also buy Roses tins for sharing at Christmas, Easter etc.
- Family orientated, sociable and contemporary in their tastes.

Proposition

'For saying "Thank you, Teacher", only Cadbury's Roses will do.'

Brand properties

- Informal, sociable, easy 'thank you'.
- Uncomplicated, safe gesture gift.
- The 'thank you' gift which 'brings you closer'.
- Accessible, reliable, family brand.

Point of difference

- Only roses are covered in thick Cadbury's chocolate.
- Roses own unique 'thank you' positioning – the gift without embarrassment.

Tone

- Warm and genuine, reliable and friendly, loved by everyone.

Mandatory inclusions

- Cadbury masterbrand branding.
- Cadbury chocolate.
- Roses, logo, typeface and branding.
- 'Thank You'.
- Incentive to purchase.
- Cost per pack – approx 80p (incl creative and redemption).

Other activity

- Coronation Street sponsorship.
- Advertorial in June edition of *Voila* (consortium magazine).
- PR, adshells.

Timing

Scamps to client	4th February
Full concepts	18th February
To print	22nd May
Mailing commence	12th June

Exact timing tbc.

Management encouragement is necessary to sustain the passion of creativity—most people need to feel their work matters to the organization or to some important group of people. Direct marketers who fail to develop creativity either fail to acknowledge innovation or greet new ideas with scepticism. Research also indicates that people appear smarter to their bosses if they are more critical. Careers are often enhanced if you are critical of new ideas.

10.6 **Cross-national communications**

Comparisons of the output of advertisements of different countries are notoriously controversial and subjective in nature (Nevett, 1992). Nevertheless, many professional observers of the North American communications industry have argued that creative standards declined after the recession of the early 1970s (Reid, Whitehill King, and DeLorme, 1998). During these years and afterwards, many advertisers, often in leading positions, opted for less risky hard-sell approaches (for example, in the case of television commercials, an emphasis on the product and its packaging and loud-talking salespeople). This occurred just as UK advertising creatives were learning from some of America's finest creatives of the 1960s such as Bill Bernbach (best known for the 'Think Small' Volkswagen Beetle advertising of the early 1960s). The so-called 'new wave' UK agencies of the late 1970s and 1980s won and dominated numerous international advertising award ceremonies over this period. Since then there have been numerous articles in the trade press and academic studies comparing the irreverent, humorous, and 'soft' UK approach to advertising to the hard-sell and aggressiveness which characterizes so much of North American advertising. Cultural factors play an important role here, and differences in the respective advertising industries and approaches to advertising (Unwin, 1974; Andrews, et al., 1991).

Fig. 10.4 Cadbury's mailing pack

10.7 **Creative work practices**

10.7.1 **Work patterns and activities**

There is considerable, if anecdotal, evidence that many creatives find certain work patterns and activities important to their work. For example, Alex Osborn, a leading American advertising executive of the 1950s and 60s, suggested that creatives needed to keep an open mind (Osborn, 1963). He recommended them to work in hotels or inns, or wherever, to escape the office routine. He also advocated sleeping, walking, and/or lying down as ways of gaining creative insights. Certainly, there is some evidence in favour of lying down. Einstein formed his time and space theory while sick in bed and James Brindley, a leading engineer, would take to his bed for days in order to solve a problem. Similarly, on the artistic side, there are numerous examples of the importance of other kinds of work patterns and activities to creative thought. Emile Zola pulled the curtains at midday in order to simulate the night; Ralph Waldo Emerson left his family and rented a hotel to gain solitary conditions to write; Hemingway wrote in the mornings and spent the nights carousing; Debussy and Beethoven needed nature to work, whereas Schubert had a regimented schedule from 9.00am to 2.00pm, Haydn rose at 6.30am to work and Berlioz and Beethoven worked all day and night if needed. Such work patterns and activities may seem trivial, but to the individual concerned they often are an integral part of the creative process (West, 1994).

10.7.2 **Experience**

There is general support for the proposition that wide experience is a pre-requisite to creativity. For example, master chess players largely play from experience. They use their knowledge to determine the possible moves and how they should respond. It has been found that many experts, too, solved creative problems from knowledge. A great deal of creative problem solving normally involves combining disparate thoughts and has become known as 'bisociation', where previously unrelated ideas are combined (Marra, 1990). To combine in such ways, creative thinkers needed to draw upon wide experience. It has been demonstrated by several researchers that knowledge and experience are potent factors in creative problem solving (Reid and Rotfeld, 1976). Direct marketing communications commonly uses bisociation in order to produce innovative ideas. To do so, direct marketing creatives need to keep up-to-date with a wide range of trends and tastes in society, particularly in the arts.

10.7.3 **Motivation**

Several principal motivations have been identified amongst creatives in the literature, namely: competitive teams, awards, and deadlines (Van den Bergh et al., 1983; Fletcher, 1990; West, 1993). Competitive teams are an important motivational issue. Research on student-based advertising ideas has generally supported the assumption that increased numbers of creative alternatives enhanced the chance of finding the 'best' creative idea. However, the best idea could be the first or 300th idea. Direct marketers can increase the number of ideas by pitting creative teams against each other to work competitively on a client's account. The issue is a controversial one in the business because the CD has to adjudicate which idea 'wins' and will be offered to the client. Having said that, assigning more than one team to the same account is a widespread policy. Assigning more than one team to the same account is believed to be a positive and realistic way to work as it is argued that competition was a good creative motivation. The main reason for doing so is safety. As the client only takes the account to the problem-solving stage, many agencies feel they need to explore different routes to get to what the client 'really' wants. Those CDs opposed to the practice feel that accounts need individual responsibility and assigning more than one team to a problem dilutes ownership and is not constructive. Many CDs say that they use it only when the time frame is short, the problem is particularly acute, or the client is very important. The primary problem is that too much time can be spent adjudicating between teams and the losing team will always be severely disappointed, even if the difference in the quality of ideas was marginal. Furthermore, one team might believe that the other team would win the brief early on in the process and lose confidence in their own abilities to win. Thus, the apparent competition for the best idea would become a sham.

Awards and deadlines are another powerful motivation. Creatives, like artists, are often identified with their work either by peer recognition or industry-standard awards . This often puts pressure on creatives to do their best. The effects of awards on advertising work has largely been seen as positive. Many CDs believe that awards make communications more original and competitive. Nevertheless, campaigns are never conceived in order to win awards—no particular style is 'award prone', so it is not a direct motivation. However, awards provide a powerful motivational force in other ways. Creative awards help direct marketing agencies to win new clients and can boost a creative's salary and support the creative ego.

Deadlines may also play a role. For example, Rossini was known to leave all his composing to the last minute. His advice was to leave work 'until the evening before the opening night'. The 'tyranny' of the deadline is an everyday occurrence for direct marketing creatives as all creative briefs are given a set time limit. Deadlines are seen to be generally positive to creative work. They can be negative if the deadline is too short. For example, a whole campaign idea should be given several weeks, but a spin-off idea might be completed satisfactorily in a few days. The personalities concerned also need to be considered. Some teams need the pressure of a deadline to get the work done, but others get 'deadline phobia'. Consequently, the length of the deadline effects the choice of a team for a particular problem. Overall, the general opinion is that realistic deadlines focus teams and have a good effect in most cases, but short ones in bad circumstances rarely work well.

10.7.4 Creative leadership

Direct marketing agencies have unique organizational characteristics that do not always follow the more traditional management techniques used by industry in general. How should the mix of work patterns and activities, experience, and motivation be led ? David Ogilvy argued that a good agency executive should be a 'father figure' offering understanding, consideration, and affection and should hire subordinates good enough to succeed by themselves (Ogilvy, 1963/1983). He further argued that no creative organization of any kind had produced a great body of work without being led by a formidable individual. Alex Osborn (1963) commented that ideal creative directors would be both creative 'pace-setters' and creative coaches, ideally cultivating the creativity of those around them and making it bloom. Above all else, he contended that CDs should feel a regard for the power of ideas. However, it has been argued that creative managers should not lead by example, but instead should concentrate on 'igniting' the creativity in others. According to Fletcher(1990), too many CDs divide their time uncomfortably between producing their own creative work and running their department, 'trying to do two jobs at once, they rarely do either consummately well'. Many CDs see their roles as cultivating and igniting the talent around them, rather than leading by the example of their own work. Bringing out the best in their teams is the byword. You cannot just be a 'talker', you need to gain respect to manage. Of course, there will always be cases of the 'brilliant' practitioner who is hopeless at managing others.

In terms of work patterns, many CDs have commented that it depends on the individuals and whatever 'worked' for them. Having lunch or going to a pub is often seen as a good way of finalizing a creative idea. Not being interrupted is a standard theme. Going for a walk, changing desks, and physically moving is often cited as well. One leading advertising agency, McCanns, advocates keeping the mornings free of all meetings and appointments to allow its creative teams to work without interruption. Keeping a notebook on hand at all times was a common suggestion because creative ideas could 'pop up' at any time.

10.8 Creative personality and process

Studies of the creative personality per se are numerous (West, 1993). It has been found that creative people are spontaneous, expressive, uninhibited, not frightened by the unknown, bold, and courageous. Freud simply argued that they were frustrated, neurotic failures. Others have pointed out that there is no correlation between creativity and IQ beyond a low minimum level. Independence of mind has been emphasized and it has also been found that creative people tend to be socially aloof, introspective, self-sufficient, radical, experimental, and non conformist. They have also been found to be open to experience, with an internal locus of evaluation and an ability to toy with concepts, play spontaneously, and juggle elements. It has been suggested that experience of problem solving over time and the ability to edit creative solutions are key components of the creative personality. Overall, creatives have been found to break rules, but at the same time, have an internal discipline.

Overall, it appears that creatives in 'creative industries' (e.g. advertising, architecture, and film) tend to be insecure, egotistical, stubborn, rebellious, poor timekeepers, perfectionists, fame seekers, and not possessing out-of-the-ordinary intelligence (Fletcher, 1988) . The available empirical evidence and conventional wisdom suggests that creative people are 'different', but that the nature of this difference cannot be easily categorized. Creative personalities of people working in creative departments in the US, Canada, and the UK have been found to be very much alike: originality and intelligence are the most sought after qualities (West, 1993). Senior creatives in all three countries are mainly artistic in nature.

When it comes to the creative process, it has been noted that creative ideas often appear mysteriously, even to the person responsible. Nevertheless, in most businesses these ideas are the result of organizational processes (Kover and Goldberg, 1995). The key organizational issue in the creative process is how to balance and optimize the degree of freedom or control. Early work on the management of creativity found that managers should shift between involvement and detachment throughout the process. Control and freedom should be alternated strategically throughout. However, it has been suggested that in the early idea-generation stage there should be complete freedom, whereas during execution control is necessary. Creative people have an innate rebelliousness which inevitably leads them to dislike taking orders and they are awkward to 'control'.

Nevertheless, it is imperative for managers to show understanding of creative people and their ideas, but they must retain overall control and make few concessions.

The form of management of the creative process is likely to vary across firms within different countries. What little evidence there is suggests that the North American management style is based on a more liberal model compared to Europe. Some significant differences in the nature of the creative involvement with strategy development and execution, and the perceived degree of freedom afforded copywriters and art directors, has been found in the UK compared to North America. Senior UK creatives regard themselves as more involved and more independent than their North American counterparts in these processes. This is particularly important in relation to clients and in the selection of ideas. However, the monitoring and control of the final advertising production process have been found to be extremely similar. North American creatives have a closer and more strategic relationship with their clients than their UK counterparts, who operate with greater autonomy and control.

10.9 **Philosophies**

The earliest agency philosophies (approaches to the way advertising 'works') were developed in the interwar years by prominent advertisers, such as Procter & Gamble, and then adopted by various agencies (Channon, 1981; Moriarty, 1996; West, 1988). Unlike creative strategies, they occupy a relatively narrow band of approaches and greatly affect the nature of the communication brief. A proof of their usefulness is that many philosophies have survived to today. In the interwar years Lord & Thomas used the philosophy of its founder, Albert Lasker, that advertising is 'salesmanship in print'— the argument approach. Agencies who believe in such argument advertising strongly appeal to classical marketing clients because the task is often the communication of performance benefits over the competition, e.g. Colgate. This is not to suggest that an argument-based agency sees all communications in that way—all agencies depart from their key beliefs in certain circumstances. Similarly, problem-solution (advertising that presents a problem that is then solved by the brand—for example, headaches and aspirins) was another popular inter-war approach that has continued to be employed today.

Since the Second World War the two most influential philosophies have been Rosser Reeves' (1961) 'unique selling proposition' (USP) and David Ogilvy's (1963) 'brand image'. Reeves, of Ted Bates, stated that 'each advertisement must say to each reader: "buy this product, and you will get this specific benefit".' The USP school argued that advertisers must offer strong, unique, and relevant benefits to consumers to be successful and has been used by, for example, Saatchi and Saatchi, to good effect.

Ogilvy made an important contribution to advertising with his philosophy of brand image. Rather than telling consumers about the product's singular benefits, moods and images were evoked, such as 'stylish and sophisticated'. Music, colours, scenery, and so on, became more significant in such advertising than the words heard or read (for example, Levi's). Increasingly, more recent philosophies have built on Ogilvy's feeling-oriented assumptions of consumer motivation, of which brand identity, associating the brand with pleasurable social norms, was the best example. A good illustration was McCann-Erickson's advertising for Coca-Cola which associated youth with fun.

The strong use of emotion, using communications to modify consumers' feelings about brands without focusing on brand benefits or images, for example, 'Welcome to Miller Time' has evolved during the 70s and 80s (Frazer, 1983). Schwartz (1973) called this the 'resonance strategy' of presenting circumstances, situations, or emotions which find counterparts in the realm of imagined experiences in some consumers' minds.

Philosophies are not mutually exclusive either. Agencies 'mix and match' dominant philosophies to produce their own hybrids. Moreover, it must be emphasized that it is only an orientation. Nevertheless, advertising practitioners and researchers agree that accounts and consumers may be won or lost by the nature of the agency philosophy. Empirical evidence suggests that just under two thirds of agencies in the UK employ formal agency philosophies of one kind or another. The most popular types of philosophies are problem-solution and the USP, followed by emotion.

However, many agencies, small and large, had, and have, no philosophies. The personalities and views of their owners and/or managers were and are the main criteria affecting the styles of advertising produced or the ways agency personnel work. Furthermore, some agencies have used the absence of a philosophy as a selling point and argued that it enables a flexible response to a client's needs.

10.10 How does direct marketing work?

Direct marketing's raison d'être is a call to action, be it to buy a good or service, make a donation to a charity, or join a group. In the purest sense, methodological problems make it extremely difficult to connect, beyond doubt, the creativity of direct marketing to the action (e.g. the effect of regions, seasons, competitors, unemployment, government policy, price, product, place). However, testing can be used to help select the most effective, in terms of achieving objectives, creative work. Put simply, a variety of creative work can be tried out and the most effective selected. Nevertheless, this does not help identify why certain appeals and approaches are more successful than others. The key issue here is *how* direct communications work. There is a well developed literature on how communications work that can be applied to direct marketing (Lannon, 1983; Vakratsas and Ambler, 1999).

10.10.1 Linear-sequential models

Linear-sequential models take a logical and rational view of how communications work. The premiss is that the following step-by-step process occurs:

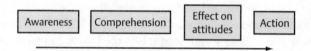

Fig. 10.5 Hierarchy models

(a) **Well-known examples**

Daniel Starch, a New York advertising practitioner, suggested, in 1925, that advertising works by taking people through the following stages:

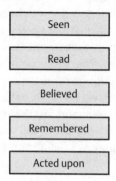

Fig. 10.6 Starch, 1925

Bear in mind that it was suggested before mass broadcast media's impact had been felt. Today, he would undoubtedly include viewing and listening as well as reading. At the same time, E. K. Strong, a US psychologist, published the influential AIDA model which suggested that communications work in four-step process:

Fig. 10.7 AIDA (E. K. Strong, 1925)

Colley's DAGMAR model has also received widespread support. DAGMAR stands for 'defined advertising goals for measured advertising results'. Colley's aim was to propose a model that would enable advertisers to measure the success of their communications at each stage of what he viewed as the following process:

Rosser Reeves has been attributed with the USP model from 1961. In reality, it pre-dates Reeves, and was first suggested by John E. Kennedy, a Canadian copywriter working at a then famous US advertising agency, Lord & Thomas, back in the 1930s. Working on a brewery account, Kennedy, as all good copywriters should do, examined every stage of the process. The key thing that interested him was that the brewery sterilized each bottle

'Defined advertising goals for
measured advertising results'

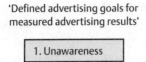

1. Unawareness

2. Awareness

3. Comprehension

4. Conviction

5. Action

Fig. 10.8 DAGMAR (Colley, 1961)

with steam just before the beer was placed. He went back to his office and drew-up a campaign highlighting the cleanliness of the beer. When the brewery pointed out that all the breweries used the same equipment and process he argued that it was of no concern. No other brewery was making a similar claim, therefore, they could own the cleanliness claim even if rivals later made a similar claim. The idea was to say something unique in terms of communication rather than uniquely related to the product. Reeves coined the phrase Unique Selling Proposition to describe this approach and suggested that to gain a purchase an advertiser must persuade the potential buyer that there is a unique benefit from the product. The USP is a different kind of linear-sequential model to Starch or AIDA, as it relates to the nature of the appeal rather than process that people go through with communications.

Lavidge and Steiner's 1961 model is also worth mentioning. It provides a series of stages in the process from awareness to purchase that have provided researchers with a number of items to measure:

1. Awareness

2. Knowledge

3. Liking

4. Preference

5. Conviction

6. Purchase   **Fig. 10.9** Lavidge and Steiner (1961)

(b) Problems of hierarchy models?

There are several problems with hierarchy models. For a start, it is clear that consumers do not store knowledge in quite the way being suggested. Consumers' minds are not uncluttered repositories for direct marketing communications. People rarely remember all the points being made in direct marketing and form preferences that they act upon. Of course, another straightforward point is that consumers are not always rational. Furthermore, none of these models take account of consumers' participation or experience. If you already know about Barclaycard, a direct mailing is hardly moving you from unawareness to comprehension. Moreover, if you have decided that you do not want a

Barclaycard it is unlikely that a direct marketing communication will move you to conviction. Finally, no allowance is made for competing or previous direct marketing communications. None of these models explain how a consumer might respond to a direct mailing from both Barclaycard and the Egg card. The assumption is that the communication will simply be seen in isolation. However, while it is true that linear-sequential models have problems, they correctly point out that in some way communications are perceived and they can motivate people to action. Consequently, it is worthwhile to consider what factors affect perception and motivation to get a better sense of how direct marketing communications work.

10.10.2 Factors affecting perception

Examining what factors affect perception is fairly straightforward. The evidence suggests that relevance and novelty are key elements. For example, if you have a cat and a local pet shop sends you a brochure highlighting a range of foodstuffs and products for cats, you are more likely to consider the offers than if you do not have a cat. People are generally known to scan widely and be extremely adept at perceiving communications that have relevance. Novelty goes hand-in-hand with relevance. For example, a radio commercial for an exclusive book on gardening is far more likely to be perceived if a well-known gardening personality does the voice-over than someone unknown. Novelty is, of course, closely allied to 'creativity', but in this context represents any means by which a direct communication can 'stand-out' and be noticed.

Size is another factor. An A4 letter size direct mailing will certainly grab someone's attention more than an ordinary letter size. All things being equal, a double page spread with a call to action for a charity is likely to be read more than a ½ page—a 60 second direct TV commercial has more chance of being viewed than a ten second one. Despite this, the effect of size on perception is not a linear one. Thus, a double page spread is not four times as likely to be read than a ½ page. It is more likely to be read, but not as much as by a factor of four (and the cost may well be more than four times higher) Smaller spaces give 'bigger bangs for the buck'. The trade-off is that as you reduce size, you reduce the impact.

Colour and repetition are also worthy of mention when it comes to perception. There are significant differences in the perception of communications between the use of black and white and colour. When it comes to full-page advertisements, the evidence suggests that colour enhances perception by about 50 per cent. Complications in the impact of colour arise when it comes to juxtapositioning because placing a black and white advertisement into a predominant colour medium is extremely noticeable. Repetition also has an important impact on perception. The conventional wisdom used to suggest that a frequency of three to four advertisements was required to 'cut through' and be perceived. However, the current prevailing paradigm is that the greatest impact is had with the first impression and that subsequent impressions add less rather than more. The type of medium needs to be considered as well, as some media set the time allowed, whereas others allow the recipient to decide. Thus, linear broadcast media like direct response TV and radio often need more frequency than print media like direct mail or the press. With direct mail or the press, people can quickly scan the offer, decide if it interests them or not, and, accordingly, they can decide to spend more or less time on the offer.

10.10.3 **Factors affecting motivation**

There are numerous theories as to what affects motivation in communications. This section will review several important ones related to direct marketing.

(a) **Appeals to fear**

Janis and Feshbach's (1953) work on 'appeals to fear' is an interesting theory to start with. These two researchers hypothesized that communications can motivate people by raising anxieties and fears. The sequence suggested is as follows:

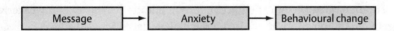

Fig. 10.10 Appeals to fear

While Janis and Feshbach concluded that communications raising fears have a weak effect, other researchers have examined the topic and concluded that it does. Just ask yourself whether a direct mailing for electric toothbrush manufacturer would be likely to have more success with you if it raised anxieties about tooth decay, showing a tooth being painfully extracted, or if it just explained how the product worked. It is undoubtedly the case that people change their behaviour when they feel anxious. For example, people who have a fear of flying will not 'be themselves' when flying or if they have to walk across high bridges. They will be more anxious and concerned. The question is whether raising such anxieties and fears with communications can affect purchasing behaviour.

Of course, there are also ethical questions to consider. Should a life insurance company communicate the features of the product or raise anxiety amongst the target market of leaving their families without provision? The issue is particularly pertinent for social communicators as with government anti-smoking campaigns or not-for-profit organizations. For example, should a government anti-smoking campaign show people having their legs being amputated? Clearly, this would be gross, but it raises an important issue about the strength of the anxiety raised. It has been found that high-level fear appeals of this kind do not have the hoped-for effects as people often switch off and discount the appeal. People say: 'yes, I could have my legs amputated—but equally I might get knocked down by a bus'. It simply is not a fear that people can easily relate to. Consequently, anti-smoking campaigns aimed at younger age groups often focus on low-level fears like not finding a partner because of bad breath from smoking.

(b) **Ehrenberg**

Andrew Ehrenberg (1974) has suggested a significantly different perspective on the impact of communications. Advertising reinforces initial brand purchases and helps repeat purchases of the same brand. His model looks like this:

Advertising reinforces the initial brand
purchase and helps repeat purchase of the brand:

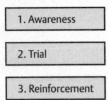

Fig. 10.11 Ehrenberg

For example, Ehrenberg would argue that you might see a new Cadbury's chocolate bar in a supermarket. You have no opinion about it and cannot remember any communications about it. It isn't hugely expensive, so you buy it and like it. Having tried and liked it you now see the advertisements because you can relate to the product. Thus, the advertising works post-purchase not to affect choice, but to re-enforce it. This is a far weaker view of the effect of communications than the hierarchial models discussed above.

(c) **Elaboration likelihood model**

Petty and Cacioppo's Elaboration Likelihood Model (1983) is an attempt to explain process by which communications influences attitudes. Their argument is that attitude formation depends on elaboration or processing of information. High to low elaboration (making inferences from cues) are possible. However, the deegree of elaboration will vary:

High elaboration—is the central route to persuasion and is enduring. It may lead to positive or negative attitudes.

Low elaboration—is the peripheral route to persuasion and depends on how the receiver decodes cues. Positive or negative attitudes may be formed by response to such cues as who is in the ad or predominant colours. Such cues may be liked or disliked.

The implication is that ELM is a function of the motivation to process (involvement, relevance, needs) and the ability (intellect, knowledge) to process. Distractions such as humour can affect elaboration. Key implications for direct marketing are that strong arguments are relevant for high elaborators, but peripheral cues may be more important for the rest. High elaborators do not care about celebrities in ads, for example, they care about the central message. However, low elaborators may well take more notice of the celebrity and attach their understanding of the communication correspondingly. The ELM is useful because it takes the consumer perspective and takes account of how consumers use communications.

The message for direct marketers is that all communications need to operate comfortably at both levels. On the one hand, direct marketing needs to make its point and be persuasive and on the other all the peripheral cues need to be appealing to people who just are not that interested to pay attention to the message. For example, a high elaborator will read the copy and so the points are important for them. Whereas the low elaborator is likely just to scan, so the layout and typeface are more important to the overall image created for them.

10.10.4 **What makes effective direct marketing?**

- Performance 'edges' are often short lived.
- Many edges are not important to the consumer.
- Many edges address category issues but not consumer problems.
- Leads to problems when performance image does not match up to reality (e.g. typical airline ads).

(a) **Emotion**

- Takes position beyond logic.
- Adds value to performance claims.
- Builds relevance and brand personality.
- Puts performance edges into a context for consumers.

(b) **However . . .**

- Purely performance is 'cold'.
- Purely emotional direct marketing tends to be 'empty'.

(c) **You need a combination**

- 'I understand it'.
- 'I like the "feel" of it'.

(d) **Strategic development**

- Determine the best product image.
- Determine the best emotional image.
- Integrate the two seamlessly.

(e) **Find prime prospect's problems**

- Benefit approach (e.g. owners want nutrition and good taste in dog food).
- Problem-solving approach (e.g. owners hate dog's bad breath and food odour).
- The benefit is for the category—the second solves a personal problem.

(f) **Example: Pepsi**

- Rational stance is 'tastes best'.
- Emotional stance is 'contemporary' and 'in'.
- Resultant combination:

'Pepsi. The Choice of a New Generation'

(g) **Overall**

- Understand the emotional needs of consumers, or business to business customers, to differentiate the traditional performance-based appeals.

- Marry the performance image with the emotional image of the product.
- Aim to accommodate both high and low elaborators.

10.10.5 What has been the advice of top creatives over the years?

(a) Claude Hopkins

- Use standards of salespeople.
- Don't be brief.
- Don't use loud type or big headlines.
- People are used to 8 point type.
- 'The more you tell the more you sell.'
- Accumulate a list of claims and always use them.

(b) Rosser Reeves

- 'The consumer tends to remember just one thing from an advertisement—one strong claim or concept.'
- 'I do not mean that the campaign should not say a dozen things about the product. These can add depth, colour, dimension, and persuasiveness.'
- Need a unifying concept.

(c) David Ogilvy

- Promise is the soul of the ad.
- Need a good idea.
- Give the facts.
- You cannot bore people into buying.
- Use charm.
- Committees cannot write ads.
- Repeat your winners.
- Always consider the image of the brand.
- Always tell the truth.

(d) Some Ogilvy specifics

- Headlines should appeal to self-interest.
- Arouse curiosity and use words like 'suddenly', and 'now'.
- When writing copy put yourself in the frame of mind of someone giving advice or recommendations.

- Use everyday language.
- Don't boast.

(e) **Bill Bernbach**

- Be original and fresh.
- Everything you write or show should further your message.
- Break the rules when you want to, but know the rules.

(f) **Key themes**

- Both long and short copy can be OK. (Creatives often prefer long copy.)
- Appeal to self interest.
- Be direct and relevant.
- Arouse curiosity and interest.
- Be original.

(g) **Drayton Bird**

- Tell people what it does for them, not what it is.
- Talk about the prospect—not yourself.
- Give news of a benefit with the incentive, if any, quickly seen.
- Get to the point.
- Make it simple—most people are not clever.
- Be surprising but relevant.
- Ask for action forcefully.

10.11 **Ethical Considerations**

Ethics is a branch of philosophy concerned with human character and conduct. It is the science of morals, e.g. not being criminal, not cheating, etc. Applied to direct marketing, the ethical debate focuses on two aspects of the business: 'direct marketing' and 'direct marketing advertisements'. In general, direct marketing, as an activity, is well accepted the world over in all economic systems. Concerns over certain direct marketing advertisements or groups of direct marketed products are more widespread.

10.11.1 **Direct marketing**

The primary criticism of direct marketing as an activity is that direct marketing advertisements work within the general advertising system to promote materialism. The argument is that people buy products that they do not otherwise want in part owing to direct marketing. This, in turn, drives a materialistic society:

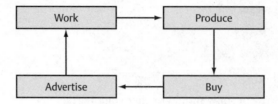

Fig. 10.12 Materialism

There are many difficulties with the creation of needs approach. What is a 'need'? The concept is clearly relative, for example is a carpet a need? There is also considerable evidence that direct marketing cannot force people to buy what they do not 'need' (80 per cent of new products are rejected by consumers). Perhaps the most written about case of this kind was Ford's Edsel in 1957. Rather than create needs, direct marketing arouses latent needs and focuses on brand preferences.

When people place too much emphasis on material goods rather than non-material values such as love and friendship, we say that they are materialistic. The problem is seen to be particularly acute for less affluent consumers.

Overall, it is difficult to be objective. Is the problem that people buy products critics do not think they should buy? Even if consumers could be completely isolated from direct marketing they would see expensive products on TV, the street, in stores, and homes.

On the other hand, some sociologists have argued that direct marketing has been a catalyst for social change. Less affluent people have seen another way of life with advertising and direct marketing and this has led them to struggle to improve their status. Certainly, direct marketing may contribute to discontent from less affluent people, but it is not the only source of the problem. A more logical place for the criticism would be the economic system of which direct marketing is a part. Direct marketing is one institution of the economic system, and it is therefore misleading to attack direct marketing in isolation.

Social critics of direct marketing have argued that direct marketing is manipulative through its use of motivational research and subliminal direct marketing. People buy products that they do not need as a result. Motivational research got underway with the work of Dichter (1964) in the 1950s and 60s. The aim was to invent the motives for purchasing or not purchasing in the mind's 'subconscious'. For example, Dichter argued people did not buy prunes because they reminded them of growing old and that the true motive for a man buying a convertible was 'to have a mistress'. Packard (1957) gave wide publicity to these ideas. Few if any direct marketing agencies attempt to design direct marketing according to the entreaties of psychologists today. For a start, it is debateable whether or not the sub-conscious even exists. By definition, the sub-conscious cannot be reached because there is no way of reaching it other than by conscious or semi-conscious methods (hypnosis), so how do we know it is there? Moreover, the whole nub of the technique is the interpretation of the results by the psychologist concerned. You are not dealing with subjective data that can easily be assessed. Another major limitation has been the need for successful translation of the so-called sub-conscious motive into an effective direct marketing campaign. If you discover, as Dichter argued, that men smoke cigars as a substitute for sucking their thumbs, how do you use that in an direct marketing campaign?!

Subliminal direct marketing occurs when the direct marketing messages are not consciously visible or audible. For example, a frame inserted into a direct TV commercial or a sound at a high or low frequency, or where the 'meaning' is buried deep into the advertisement (structuralism).

It is difficult to say much about subliminal direct marketing with any certainty. Research is unproven and often contradictory and the most clearly documented effects obtained only in highly contrived and artificial situations. The problem of the subconscious presents itself again. If I 'sub-consciously' see or hear a direct marketing advertisement, how can you find out if I did 'see' or 'hear' it and with what effect? The answer is we do not know, and for obvious reasons subliminal direct marketing is banned the world over.

Structuralist critics of direct marketing have argued that advertising and direct marketing is 'symbolism'. Direct marketing symbols are structures of meaning manipulating social images to create a 'message'. Sociologists have examined advertisements in a way which suggests they are a complex of hierarchical meanings. Basically, structuralists add order to the interpretation of the meaning of an advertisement. Thus, an apparent tangle of elements in a magazine advertisement is dissected by a series of complex layers to 'decode' its true meaning (Buttle, 1991).

Here is an example of the different layers of meaning in a series of butter and margarine advertisements analysed by Leymore (1975). The argument is that images presented in an advertisement represent positive ideas. Even if negatives are not mentioned they must be there as all positives have negatives associated with them. The advertisements Leymore chose did not mention the other product, but the argument is that the meaning was there. In the case of butter marketing the layers of 'meaning' uncovered were as follows:

Butter		**Margarine**
expensive	–	cheap
concord	–	protest
content	–	discontent
care	–	negligence
love	–	hate

Fig. 10.13 Butter marketing

The next stage of her analysis was to reduce the set of contrasts to a single opposition which was:

$$\text{peace} \quad — \quad \text{war!}$$

The problem here is that Leymore instructs us to interpret buy butter ads in this way, the meaning is not obvious. Certainly there is a 'marketing war' between butter and margarine, but do consumers see the same meaning as above?

Williamson (1978) has argued advertisements have 'latent' insidious messages. Her work has focused on brand differentiation where no 'real' differences exist (this is often so, of course). In particular, she has focused on perfume advertising because it is difficult to convey the smell (scratch and sniff is still too crude a device). Thus, in a Chanel No. 5 advertisement using Catherine Deneuve's face juxtaposed with the bottle the following is argued:

Deneuve	=	Glamour & Beauty
Chanel No. 5	=	Glamour & Beauty
Buying No. 5	=	Catherine Deneuve

Fig. 10.14 Deneuve and Chanel No. 5

In this case, it is difficult to believe this connection is not obvious to consumers. The essence of the problem of the structuralist approach is that whilst direct marketing advertisements are often technical constructions, they are meant to be interpreted easily and without too much effort. Structuralists focus too heavily on the 'signals' and not enough on the 'encoders'. Sociologist argue that because consumers fail to understand so much of the complexity of an advertisement, it is ideological. The trouble is, few people pay that much attention and so structuralists impose their own interpretation of meaning on the advertisement which the rest of us might disagree with or that are obvious. Sociological insight is to be welcomed, unfortunately structuralists have tried to turn the mundane into the momentous.

10.11.2 Specific issues

(a) Exploitation

Emotional exploitation of commendable and pleasurable emotions such as love, affection, friendship, and maternal feelings: 'Happy families buy . . . ', 'good mothers serve . . . ', 'attractive women like men who drink . . . ' is common. In the same way people recognize these ploys and discount them accordingly. Fear is also present. It has been argued that advertisers do not appeal to reasoned arguments, but raise anxieties and fears, e.g. use a particular soap and avoid BO or buy a certain hamburger and have a happy family, or watch out for stains on glasses if friends are coming over. Packard and Galbraith have argued that advertisements raise a great deal of anxiety in society, such as fear of losing one's job, social inferiority, marriage, parenthood, and science (who is that man in the white coat?).

Children and direct marketing is a particularly serious topic. The argument that direct marketing can potentially persuade children to desire products that parents either cannot afford or do not wish to give to their children is powerful. This became a special concern with the introduction of direct response TV campaigns, which can have a strong influence on the young.

At the same time, much research has demonstrated that children can develop scepticism towards advertising and direct marketing at the early age of around seven to eight years old, depending on the child. Evidence also suggests that once a child detects the persuasive intent they begin to guard against it. Direct marketing's impact then diminishes as the child loses confidence in its 'impartiality'. Age is the main factor with the development of scepticism.

Other interesting results from studies are that children who know they can get the products they want are most affected. Also, children, just like adults, suffer from direct marketing saturation effects. Some researchers have argued that adolescents should be exposed to direct marketing otherwise they will not have learnt to cope with it for adulthood.

Evidence on the exertion of pressure by children on adults indicates that attempts to exert pressure decrease as children age, but that instances when parents give in to their children's demands increase with age. This is probably because older children are more certain of what they want and parents acknowledge this. Stereotyping is another major topic. Direct marketing may be charged with stereotyping minorities and women in society. A stereotype is a rigid image. Such stereotyping acts as a drag on female emancipation and more equal roles for men, women, and ethnic minorities. There have been numerous studies. Studies have also shown significant improvements in the portrayal of women but that now men are often stereotyped in many ways as either hunks or slobs.

(b) **Aesthetics**

Aesthetically, direct marketing is criticized for being intrusive and repetitive. Many argue that direct marketing advertisements are in bad taste as well. What is considered bad taste is, of course, 'in the eyes of the beholder'. Unfortunately, it is true that many direct marketing advertisements are produced to sell at any cost with no concern for aesthetic values. Sometimes, the culprits are amateurs, local companies producing their own ads with little idea of what they are doing. Sometimes, large professional agencies are to blame. The latter case is less common and is often the result of a client imposing its will on the creative team. Imperfect segmentation is another factor where owing to targeting of a message to diluted media audiences, people see or hear messages not intended for them.

Both very enjoyable and very unpleasant direct marketing advertisements are more effective than the neutral kind. Direct marketers have to reconcile their marketing objectives with the artistic side of direct marketing. This should be seen as a duty because it is impossible to enact legislation to enforce it.

(c) **Dishonesty**

Dishonest direct marketing advertisements attempting to tell lies are thankfully rare today. All professional agencies and advertisers condemn such practices and it is also against UK and EU legislation. However, the half-truth remains. Brand comparisons are made on one criterion, or specific uses, or with some brands, but not others. Use of 'its better', 'amazing', 'wonderful', and 'perfect', are cases in point. These half truths are subjective offerings of information. Advertisers would argue that consumers do not want copious technical information about products and, therefore, they minimize the message to cut through all the clutter. Fortunately, advertisers compete with each other and consumers do not have to depend on the messages of a single advertiser. The reality is that most consumers weigh up competing claims, discount the puffery, and hopefully buy the best product for their needs. However, the naive, the trusting, and those of low intelligence need protection.

It has also been argued that direct marketing has raised the level and access to information in society. Consumers are less likely to be swayed by sharp salesmen, but can make more informed decisions.

(d) Products

Products society considers to be special or dangerous (e.g. alcohol, medicine, and food) have led automatically to direct marketing concerns. All these areas and more are subject to legislation and codes of practice.

10.11.3 Ethics overall

It is important to recognize three things in the whole debate: Criticism of direct marketing is not new—it has a long history back to the eighteenth century.

Some of the issues often have deeper ideological roots. At its core, the debate concerns different views over how society should function. Direct marketing cannot be viewed in isolation. Direct marketing is only one of the available marketing tools.

10.12 International direct marketing

The principles of international direct marketing follow the same process of:

SOURCE—COMMUNICATION—MEDIUM—RECEIVER

However, the international marketplace makes application less controllable. The source may be well respected in the home country, for example, but in the foreign country may be seen negatively owing to its foreign ownership. A source may have to de-emphasize its origins. The interpretation of the communication may be different owing to the nature of the receivers' cultural environment. Finally, foreign direct media may operate in a different way and context. There may be restrictions and a simple lack of availability compared to the domestic choices.

Direct marketing can offer a company the ability to do business in another country without establishing a presence in that country (but recognize that cross-national trade will inevitably involve the delays of the receiving country's customs system).

Telemarketing/internet is another growth area of direct marketing. Its growth has been spectacular in Britain, Canada, Denmark, France, Norway, Sweden, United States, and Germany in particular. Selling by telephone to consumers and businesses can be considerably cheaper than personal selling. Its effectiveness depends on the relevance of lists and the sensitivity of the operation. International telemarketing would only be viable with business to business prospects and if the numbers were relatively small (given the costs of international calls). In these circumstances, it would be more cost effective to phone rather than incur overseas travel costs.

10.12.1 **Issues**

(a) **Translation errors**

The issue of translation errors has received more attention by international marketers than almost any other topic. The most oft quoted blunder is probably General Motors, strapline: 'Body by Fisher'. The Flemish translation became 'Corpse by Fisher.'

However, most of the quoted blunders occurred over 20 years ago. It is rare in today's sophisticated international direct marketing environment for companies to make translation errors. Direct marketing executives are simply too aware of the dangers. The practice of backtranslating and seeking the advice of local agencies and/or distributors has made translation errors uncommon. But this is not to say that language is no longer a potential problem. *Meaning* rather than translation has become more of an area of concern.

(b) **Meaning**

International advertisers have sometimes encountered problems when their appeals have been counter to local culture. Take the case of the Gulda beer campaign in Nigeria. Nigerians failed to respond to the campaign because the general preference is for beer in green bottles. Additionally, the person in the advertisement always drank alone, whereas Nigerians see drinking as a social activity.

Assessment of meaning in advertising appeals is obviously more difficult than dealing with direct translations. The best advice is to check with locals such as distributors and agencies and if possible, local professionals such as market research consultants.

(c) **Global versus regional versus local**

Theodore Levitt's 1983 article on the 'Globalization of Markets' has sparked a lively, if irrelevant, debate on the role of global advertising in the 1980s. Levitt's thesis is simply that local markets are converging. A 'world market' is emerging, requiring a global approach to all aspects of marketing to produce economies of scale for 'world products' (Levitt joined the Board of Saatchi & Saatchi. Saatchi's is one of the leading advertising agency proponents of global advertising and its main global account is Procter & Gamble's pampers).

Why is the globalization debate irrelevant? The problem arises in providing truly global examples. Apart from Pampers and Martini, there are few exclusively global advertisers or direct marketers. Even companies held up to be global advertisers such as Pepsi, Coke, and Marlboro modify their communications according to the regional/local environment. Furthermore, it is not a new phenomenon. Some advertisers have used the same themes in international campaigns since the 1920s (e.g. Lux).

Another reason for its irrelevance is that most international advertisers would undoubtedly go global if they could. The benefits of going global far outweigh adapted local advertising. Namely, exploiting:

- an excellent creative theme;
- lower production costs;

- media overlap between countries;
- the market of 200m. international travellers.

The real issue is why use regionally or locally adapted campaigns rather than going global? The reasons tend to be good ones: local differences and differences between stages in the international product life cycle.

It seems very unlikely that the number of truly global advertisers will increase dramatically in the next few years. What is more likely is that regionalization will increase. Here, one direct marketing strategy is chosen for the global market but its 'execution' is adapted regionally (or sometimes locally). This is nothing new. For example, Gillette used sports personalities in its 1950s/60s international campaigns with locals used for each market where relevant.

(c) Regulation

A major local difference which has forced many direct marketers to abandon global ambitions has been regulation. The topic is an enormous one of considerable detail. However it boils down to two major aspects: appeals and products. Different countries require the modification of appeals. For example, the Germans prohibit product claims of superiority. Scandinavian countries have extremely strict laws on product claims of all kinds. Many Moslem countries outlaw appeals involving women revealing their bodies (causing particular problems for deodorant/perspirant advertisers). Every country has strict codes relating to advertising to children.

Certain product categories are strictly regulated around the world. The prime examples are cigarettes and tobacco (leading to ever more esoteric appeals where manufacturers literally say nothing in their advertising). Alcohol, medicines, and drugs are also controlled as are miracle cures for such things as baldness.

It is the norm for international direct marketers to seek local professional advice if the legality of an appeal or product direct marketing is in doubt or to seek advice from the local medium or regulatory body.

(e) Attitudes to advertising

Local attitudes towards direct marketing and advertising are also worth bearing in mind. Most local advertising institutions undertake surveys of their public's general views. The Japanese and the British, for example, regard advertising quite favourably and bestow greater value on advertised products. 'As Advertised on TV' is a commonplace slogan in British shops. By contrast, the Germans and North Americans are far more cynical. It is obviously impossible to conclude that direct marketing will work in the UK but not in Germany! But it must be borne in mind that advertising can be seen more negatively in one country compared to another.

10.13 **Summary**

The direct creative brief is central to producing successful work. The brief translates the strategic marketing problem into creative and media requirements with which to frame the tactics. It requires knowledge of the market and the target market as well as the client's objectives and an understanding of how communications work. Another important element in producing creative work is to have an understanding of how to manage the creative process in a direct marketing agency. This in turn needs some knowledge and/or experience of how to motivate creatives and the creative personality. This chapter has also examined some of the key creative philosophies that direct marketers work with and provided an overview to the ethical and international considerations in preparing the creative brief.

Further reading

Andrews J. C., Lysonski S. and Durvasula S. (1991). 'Understanding Cross-cultural Student Perceptions of Advertising in General: Implications for Advertising Educators and Practitioners', *Journal of Advertising*, 20(2), 15–28.

Buttle, F. (1991) 'What Do People Do With Advertising', *International Journal of Advertising*, 10(2), 95–110.

Channon, C. (1981) 'Agency Thinking and Agencies as Brands', *Admap*, March, 116–21.

Corstjens J. (1990) *Strategic Advertising: A Practitioner's Handbook* (New York: Nichols Publishing), ch.4

Dichter, E. (1964) *Handbook of Consumer Motivations: The Psychology of the World of Objects* (New York: McGraw-Hill).

Ehrenberg, A. S. C. (1974) 'Repetitive Advertising and the Consumer', *Journal of Advertising Research*, 14(2), 25–34.

Fletcher W. (1988) *Creative People: How To Manage Them and Maximize Their Creativity*, (London: Hutchinson).

——— (1990) 'The Management of Creativity', *International Journal of Advertising*, 9(1), 1–37.

Frazer C. F. (1983) 'Creative Strategies: A Management Perspective', *Journal of Advertising*, 12(4), 36–41.

Janis, I. and Feshbach, S. (1953) 'Effects of Fear-Arousing Communications', *Journal of Abnormal and Social Psychology*, 48, 78–92

Kover A. J. and Goldberg S. M. (1995) 'The Games Copywriters Play: Conflict, Quasi-Control, A New Proposal', *Journal of Advertising Research*, 35(4), 52–62.

Lannon, J. and Cooper P. (1983) 'Humanistic Advertising A Holistic Cultural Perspective', *International Journal of Advertising*, 2, 195–213.

Levitt, T. (1983) 'The Globalization of Markets', *Harvard Business Review*, May–June, 92–102.

Leymore, V. L. (1975) *Hidden Myths: Structure and Symbolism in Advertising* (London: Heinemann).

Marra J. L. (1990). *Advertising Creativity: Techniques for Generating Ideas* (Englewood Cliffs, NJ: Prentice-Hall).

Moriarty, S. E. (1996) 'Effectiveness, Objectives, and The Effie Awards', *Journal of Advertising Research*, 36(4), 54–63.

Nevett T. (1992) 'Differences Between American and British Television Advertising: Explanations and Implications', *Journal of Advertising*, 21(4), 61–71.

Ogilvy D. (1963) *Confessions of An Advertising Man* (New York: Dell Publishing).

—— (1983) *Ogilvy on Advertising* (London: Orbis).

Osborn A. F. (1963) *Applied Imagination: Principles and Procedures of Creative Problem-Solving* (3rd Edn.) (New York: Charles Scribner's Sons).

Packard, V. (1957) *The Hidden Persuaders* (London: Penguin).

Petty R. E. and Cacioppo J. T. (1983) 'Central and Peripheral Routes to Advertising Effectiveness: The Moderating Role of Involvement', *Journal of Consumer Research*, 10, 135–46.

Reeves, R. (1961) *Reality in Advertising* (New York: Alfred Knopf).

Reid L. N., Whitehill King K. and DeLorme D. E. (1998) 'Top-Level Agency Creatives Look at Advertising Creativity Then and Now', *Journal of Advertising*, 27(2), 1–15.

Reid L. and Rotfeld H. (1976) 'Toward an Associative Model of Advertising Creativity', *Journal of Advertising*, 5(4), 24–9.

Schwartz T. (1973) *The Responsive Chord* (New York: Anchor Books).

Unwin S. J. F. (1974). 'How Culture Affects Advertising Expression and Communication Style', *Journal of Advertising*, 3(2), 24–7.

Vakratsas D. and Ambler T. (1999) 'How Advertising Works: What Do We Really Know?', *Journal of Marketing*, 63(1), 26–43.

Van den Bergh G. B., Reid L. N. and Scherin G. A. (1983). 'How Many Creative Alternatives to Generate', *Journal of Advertising*, 12(4), 46–9.

West D. C. (1988) 'Multinational Competition in the British Advertising Agency Business, 1936–1987'. *Business History Review*, 62(3), 467–501.

West D. C., (1993) 'Cross-National Creative Personalities, Processes and Agency Philosophies', *Journal of Advertising Research*, 33(5), 53–62.

West D. (1994) 'Restricted Creativity: Advertising Agency Work Practices in the US, Canada and the UK', *Journal of Creative Behavior*, 27(3), 200–13.

Williamson, J. (1978) *De-coding Advertising: Ideology and Meaning in Advertising* (London: Marion Boyars).

Chapter 11

Media Planning

Contents

11.1 Objectives

By the end of this chapter you should be able to:

(a) understand the principles of direct marketing media planning,

(b) describe the main media routes available to the direct marketer,

(c) explain how each medium type is purchased,

(d) explain how each medium type is judged and measured,

(e) describe how GANTT and PERT charts are used as an aid in media planning and scheduling.

11.2 **Introduction**

The finest creative work is wasted unless it is presented where it will most effectively influence those people in the target audience. One of the key jobs of a direct marketer is to make sure that the creative message is placed where it will be seen or heard by the right people:

- at the right time,
- in the right environment,
- With the right frequency and weight.

Direct media can include any means employed to communicate a marketing message directly to a consumer with the intention of generating a response. As such, it can include balloons, cans, packets of cereal, parking tickets, and faxes, as well as the more traditional routes of the press and direct mail.

Response to direct media can be one or two-stage—i.e. a consumer completing and returning an order form they have received as part of a mailing is generating a one-stage response. A customer filling in a coupon on a press ad inviting them to send off for more information is generating an enquiry which then has to be fulfilled before the second stage response, the order, can be generated. This obviously has an impact on the cost and efficiency of the campaign (many enquiries are never converted into orders) and is a major factor in the planning of direct response media and creative approaches.

By its nature, direct media is fragmented and fast moving. Some new direct media develop out of necessity. For example, as banks introduced automated teller machines (ATMs) into the high street, they found that customers were less and less likely to go into the branch and so have less opportunity to see the brochures and posters inside. Now the ATM machine has become important medium for direct communications.

Here are some current issues of particular importance to the media industry:

Fragmentation—the huge increase in direct media choices and the division of audiences into smaller and smaller units such as with the explosion of channels on cable and satellite TV (Rust and Oliver, 1994).

Merging of TV/computer/telephones—crossover and multi-access to internet, DVD, videogames, and full motion video.

Data explosion—a wealth of data is now collected and available for use in media planning if it can be marshalled and utilized effectively.

Clutter—the ever-increasing amount of communications and communication routes available leading to a bombardment of messages and choices on an individual level.

IMC—the need to bring direct marketing within the integrated marketing communications remit (Roman, 1995).

11.3 **Direct media strategy**

11.3.1 **Framework**

The simplest approach to setting media planning objectives is the four Ws:

Who—define the exact audience (e.g. 'stationery supply departments').

Where—determine geographic area (e.g. 'London').

When—determine time of decision-making (e.g. 'early May').

What—establish creative material (e.g. '4-page brochure sent to office address').

Direct marketing is about building one-to-one relationships with customers. As such, the effective use of direct media strategy involves the will and capacity to change behaviour towards a customer based upon what they tell you and what you already know about them. Intelligent direct marketers get smarter with each use of a medium and increasingly customize their offerings to a customer. Eventually, even if a rival has the same capabilities, a customer is unlikely to defect, as they would have to teach the rival everything the incumbent has learnt to get the same level of exchange. Preparation for direct media strategy needs careful consideration. Two broad objectives exist: acquisition and retention. With acquisition a medium(s) is used to seek-out new customers whereas with retention a medium(s) is used to build, retain, and extend the customer relationship.

11.3.2 **Acquisition and retention**

In planning media for customer acquisition the need is to locate, identify, and directly contact potential customers in the target market. Campaign targets are likely to involve a core aim to recruit the maximum number of new customers at the minimum cost, and campaign success to be judged on the cost per customer or enquirer acquired. Obviously, there is a balance to be struck between quantity and quality. Many organizations employing relationship marketing techniques are happy to invest in targeted customer acquisition, in the knowledge that they will be able to increase the worth of the customer sufficiently over the lifetime of their relationship with them. Organizations working on a shorter-term transactional basis will be more concerned to minimize the costs of acquisition. Even so, acquisition campaigns usually do not reach break-even point and have to be budgeted as an investment which will self-liquidate over subsequent years as the customer becomes profitable.

Acquisition campaigns involve the recording of customer data. At the start of a new customer relationship the data available is likely to be minimal, just name and address details, information on the media source of the initial order or enquiry, and the date, amount, and type of the initial transaction.

In retention, the relationship with the customer deepens and the organization can begin to record data on preferences and habits, which can be logged at every contact point through drip-irrigation dialogue with customers (asking one or two questions each transaction.) At this stage, the choice of communication media may well be customer-defined (i.e. you may have taken the opportunity to ask them how they would like to be contacted—or this may have become clear through interrogation of past transaction records). The emphasis on media choice for customer retention is on facilitating dialogue with individuals, with communications more likely to be heavily personalized and customized than at the acquisition stage.

The first rule is to invest funds into direct media with efficiency: allocate money on the basis of customer current and potential profitability rather than revenue. Finding the right offer is also important. For example, why should a car company offer everyone £1,000 off through mass marketing, when many would have bought the car without any incentive at all if discretely approached via direct media? Predictive modelling techniques offer the possibility of predicting car-buying behaviour. Coupled with interactive television and web sites, customized print advertisements, e-mail, interactive kiosks, and customer service centres, the opportunities to make more effective communications to particular customers can be increased.

Differentiating customers recognizes their different levels of value and needs. This is invaluable for deciding on the best direct media strategy. This might involve researching your top customers, or isolating customers who have not re-ordered in a while. Use the money saved from contacting lower level customers to target important customers or on 'baby-sitting' them with personal service.

Improving cost-efficiency and effectiveness in interactions with customers is critical. Reduce the customer paper cycle and treat more valuable customers differently by contacting them directly through telemarketing. For example, a company might contact top customers and just talk to them to ensure that they are happy—not using the medium to try and sell to them. Furthermore, all interactions should, like conversations, pick up from where they left off before, so keep data maps to continue the dialogue.

11.4 Media

11.4.1 Telemarketing

(a) Outbound

The telephone brings out a learned reaction in people much like Pavlov's dog. If the phone goes, people will often drop everything (even leap out of the bath) to answer it. Cordless phones, answerphone services, and mobiles have, of course, reduced the effort somewhat, but it remains a communication medium that very few people can ignore. Not surprisingly, using the telephone in direct marketing has grown in significance year-on-year.

Outbound telemarketing is most effective in retention, offering the opportunity for a personal, individually customized, and direct dialogue with the customer. Few companies use the telephone in acquisition to 'cold call' prospects—it is an expensive medium and is viewed as intrusive and irritating if it is poorly targeted.

Often, telemarketing is used in conjunction with direct mail. The mailing may outline an offer with a note that the company will be following up with a telephone call. Alternatively, a call can be used to 'announce' a forthcoming mailed promotion to direct the customer's attention to it.

Any outbound call provides an opportunity for the customer directly to feed back information—which may be a complaint about a product or service, or simply a change in contact details. Telemarketing campaigns are, therefore, often seen as fulfilling a secondary objective of database cleaning additional to the core campaign objective. Telemarketing is also an excellent medium for contacting customers discreetly for test marketing. Outbound telemarketing is costly and time-consuming. Whilst some companies run their own in-house call centres, for most outbound telemarketing is not a constant activity, so a specialist telemarketing agency will be selected and retained to provide the service. Agencies usually charge on a cost per contact/cost per call basis—based on a calculation of overheads (premises, staff, training, and technology) plus call duration. Agencies commonly work to a script which is generated in conjunction with the client. Orders taken may be fulfilled by the agency or transferred to the client, or another fulfilment house, for completion. Telemarketing can generate a one stage or a two-stage response—an order can be taken directly over the phone with payment taken during the call by credit card, or an enquiry can be taken during the call and an arrangement made for further information to be supplied separately. Data is passed from the client to the agency—or the agency may be provided with a direct link to the customer database for the duration of the campaign. Creatively, the core concern when training telemarketing staff is that the dialogue with the customer is undertaken in the correct 'tone of voice' and that the interchange reflects the brand values of the company. The aim is to make the call a positive experience for the customer—and to appear a seamless communication from the company rather than an unlinked and robotic rendition of a standardized script.

Some telemarketing agencies now provide a service whereby the callers can be matched with customers—e.g. if the customer profile is of elderly women, callers matching this description will be used for the campaign. Alternatively, callers may be provided who match the company profile—e.g. a company which perceives itself as young and trendy may be provided with young confident callers. A great deal of research has been undertaken around which sort of 'voice' performs most effectively in outbound selling—e.g. Scottish accents are often used as they allegedly convey values of honesty and prudence!

In considering the use of outbound telemarketing it should also be remembered that it is not a method by which the majority of a database can be reached. Commonly telephone numbers for only 50 per cent of customers can be located/retrieved. Where a telephone number is obtained, answerphones may 'bar the way' in some cases, or the customer may not be available. Typically, a 'contact rate' of around 30 per cent of the customers selected is achieved for any campaign.

(b) **Inbound**

Inbound telemarketing (i.e. the provision of a telephone number to enable calls to be made to a company) is welcomed by customers as it can be quick, effective, and is the preferred communication route of many people. Like outbound calling, it provides the opportunity for dialogue, to make a complaint, request advice, change details, or to seek a repair. Calls can be encouraged by the provision of a freephone number, or a number charged at a reduced or local rate. As with outbound telemarketing, specialist agencies or bureaux tend to be employed unless a company has a permanent need for telephone staff and systems. Increasingly, automated voice-activated systems are used rather than 'live' telephone operators, simply because it is a much cheaper option, and because in many cases the volume of calls which will be generated by a campaign is hard to predict, making staff scheduling a nightmare. This obviously has to be balanced against the advantages of the provision of a 'real voice' at the end of the telephone in terms of customer satisfaction and company image.

Inbound call services are billed on the basis of the technology provided plus the duration and number of calls received. Clients pay for hoax and incomplete calls (which are common with voice-activated systems where the caller hangs up before supplying all details) as well as for completed 'conversations'.

Inbound telemarketing is used in both acquisition (where a telephone number is provided as a response device on a TV ad press ad, direct mail piece, etc.) and in retention, where a 'customer service line' may be promoted on all corporate and marketing literature.

11.4.2 **Direct mail**

In the minds of many people direct mail is direct marketing despite the evidence that companies often spend more of their budgets on telephone. Direct mail is used effectively in both acquisition and retention.

(a) **Acquisition**

Using direct mail as a medium for the acquisition of new customers involves list purchasing, list processing, personalization, and segmentation. Many of these areas have been covered in detail in Chapter 4.

List selection and buying is complex and many organizations employ a specialist list broker to undertake it. There are thousands of lists available to purchase at any time, ranging from simple lists built by other direct marketers (e.g. people who have purchased a product via a newspaper ad) where simple data is available (e.g. what newspaper?, when was the purchase made?, what product was purchased?, what amount was spent?, how was the response made?, customer address details) to the complex lifestyle databases which offer hundreds of pieces of data on millions of people.

Likewise, list selection can involve an enormous level of complexity, with companies using state-of-the-art techniques to profile their customers, and then to match this profile onto the lists available to find the best prospects for mailing. Other companies may be less inventive, merely selecting lists of customers who have responded to the offers closest to their own. As direct mail is a print medium, economies of scale in print production mean that acquisition mailing campaigns tend to be large-scale, as the unit cost of the printed mail package will reduce according to the total number produced. A large number of names will be purchased in order to drive this. Direct mail provides the ability to test—to test the creative treatment, the timing, and the list. A test purchase of any new list will be made (say 10,000 names) and mailed initially. If successful, a further 'rollout' will be purchased and mailed at a later date.

Once lists for a campaign have been selected, they must be data-processed. This commonly involves:

- standardization of data to facilitate matching,
- cleaning,
- de-duplication and suppression.

Lists from different sources will be put into a standard format for processing, and checked one by one for internal duplicates, unmailable addresses, etc. They will then be run against each other to check for duplication—with the ultimate aim being to ensure that each prospect name selected only receives the mailing once. During this process names can also be suppressed from the mailing—usually existing customers will be excluded, as an acquisition offer is unlikely to be a suitable communication for them, and companies may also have a 'stop list' of people who have requested not to receive mailings.

Once the final 'master' list is available, the pack can be mailed. Putting together a direct mail acquisition campaign is a long (and costly) process. However, response rates to effectively targeted and personalized direct mail can be high, and many studies of life-time value find that customers recruited via the mail have a high relative lifetime worth.

List purchase and processing is the only 'media' cost involved in cold direct mail. Other costs relate to design, print, personalization, postage, enclosing, and fulfilment. Cold mail campaigns tend to be judged on campaign ROI, cost per customer recruited, average order value, percentage response rate, or actual versus target.

Cold mail has been an effective medium for customer acquisition for many years, but a downturn in response rates has been reported recently. This may be due to the saturation of the medium—certainly there are many complaints from individuals about the bombardment of direct mail they receive. Whilst still a 'mass' medium to an extent, print and database technology developments mean that direct mail can now be more effectively customized and targeted. However, this may have come too late for consumers who are increasingly choosing to respond through different channels.

(b) Retention

The use of direct mail in communicating with existing customers has been dealt with elsewhere in this book. Again, advances in print and database systems increasingly enable direct marketers to begin to have a dialogue with customers on a more individual level, targeting offers to customers more effectively and working towards the ideal of one-to-one marketing.

11.4.3 **Direct response TV (DRTV)**

There has been a revolution in direct response television in recent years, with the media being adopted by many major companies as a powerful acquisition tool. The explosion of cable and satellite channels both fragmented the market and drove costs of airtime down dramatically.

The majority of TV ads can now be said to be direct response in that they carry an internet address, and the number of ads carrying a telephone number and specifically designed to elicit a direct response has risen substantially. The huge increase in the number of available channels means that TV advertisers can now 'buy' audiences at a decreasing cost, and the increased 'niching' of channels provides opportunities for targeting smaller specialist interest audiences.

(a) **Types of DRTV**

There are several different types of DRTV ad. The most common are:

One stage direct sell—ads which aim to generate an immediate order for a product or service. Creatively such ads tend to be hard-hitting, with a very prominent response device. Such ads will be designed to be self-funding.

Two stage lead generation—ads which aim to begin a dialogue with the respondent but not to sell directly. Frequently, the ad will offer further information rather than pushing the product directly. The enquiry generated will subsequently be followed up with a sales offer.

Product sampling—ads offering a free product sample. Again, these are two stage, and the initial sample request may be followed up by a sales approach at a later stage.

Support for other direct response activity—some DRTV ads are designed to draw attention to other direct response activities—e.g. *Readers Digest* ads 'flagging up' their grand draw mailings.

Promotion of direct brands—there are now a number of companies who deal with their customers exclusively on a direct basis, such as First Direct Bank and Direct Line Insurance. These companies will use DRTV ads both to generate leads and to promote the brand and its direct status—incorporating a brand awareness objective.

Interactive brand differentiation—some companies use DRTV to promote and differentiate their brand through the use of interaction—providing a response device in the ad to facilitate involvement in the brand rather than to generate leads per se. The creative is usually focused on young audiences who traditionally respond well to interactive offers over the telephone.

(b) **Key considerations**

The key measurements determining the success of a DRTV campaign are the cost of airtime, the cost of responses (airtime cost over number of responses generated), and the overall number of responses. The level of response, as with all direct marketing media, is dependent on the choice of the product or service, the offer, the creative execution, the efficiency of the targeting and media selection, and the timing.

Some products are suited intrinsically to promotion on DRTV; some will be suited to one stage, some to two stage or sampling—for others this method of selling will not provide any sort of 'match' between the product and the media at all. The choice and presentation of the offer is paramount. To an extent, the presentation of the offer and the 'rules' for a successful creative execution are the same as with any other media, but the TV medium also requires some special consideration. TV is a linear medium—unlike direct mail the viewer can't start again at the beginning of the communication and re-read. There is not much time—TV ads are typically of 30, 60, or 90 seconds duration. The objective of the ad has to be very clear, and the attention of the viewer must be arrested immediately. Selling statements must be demonstrated and the response mechanism must be clear, simple, and memorable. TV is not a highly targeted medium, though the specialist cable and satellite channels are changing this. However, targeting can be achieved by time slot, channel, or programme.

(c) Buying DRTV

On the costing side of the equation the cost of airtime is critical. The core challenge for media buyers working on TV is to buy audiences for the lowest possible rates. TV buying is a specialist job usually undertaken by specific individuals within media buying agencies. Driving down the cost of airtime often involves the purchase of the least popular parts of a TV schedule—late nights or afternoon, or the purchase of airtime on a 'last minute' basis. Whilst viewing audiences will be smaller at these times, they may be more responsive (people are unlikely to reach for a pen to note a telephone number in the middle of their favourite primetime TV show.) The issue for media planners and buyers is to push the audience cost as low as possible without lowering response levels, maintaining the optimum cost-per-lead generated.

TV production costs can be huge, but need only be a fraction of the cost incurred in the production of an above the line 'image' commercial. Many DRTV ads are simple and feature 'real' situations and people rather than exotic locations and celebrities for this reason. Creatively, this is often not seen as a restriction as the simplicity of the offer and communication of the means of response have to be the key factors of the ad.

The cost of airtime is generally governed by the law of supply and demand. If the supply of time remains constant and demand for that time falls, prices will fall. If demand rises, prices rise. TV is a medium where supply and demand fluctuates dramatically.

There are three main ways to purchase airtime:

- cost per thousand audience,
- spot price,
- per response.

(d) Cost per thousand (CPT)

In some respects airtime buying is similar to the purchase of direct mail lists. It is generally bought on a cost per thousand audience impacts. So if a spot delivers 5,000,000 adult impacts at a cost of £10,000 the CPT is £2. All TV advertising negotiations are based on the assumption that the ad duration is 30 seconds. If a different length of ad is to be used, the cost should simply be multiplied by the relevant time-length factor, as shown in Table 11.1. It should be noted that costs are not linear (i.e. 10 seconds does not cost a third of the rate for 30 seconds).

(e) Spot price

TV spots can be bought and sold on a spot price basis. This usually happens when the audience is so small that they cannot be accurately measured and so the CPT pricing method cannot be used. Spot prices are usually offered when the seller has a problem—a very small audience or very limited demand from other advertisers.

(f) Per response

These offers are based on the advertiser paying the TV contractor a fixed price for each enquiry they receive. This developed in the US as a 'per inquiry' cost and is therefore referred to as a 'PI' deal. PI deals tend to be offered only when demand is light.

(g) Testing and evaluation

DRTV efficiency and performance can be compared and analysed in a number of ways, the main areas being by region/geographical area, by media, and by creative. Some TV channels offer geographical options for testing. Cable companies can increasingly offer targeting by district. Satellite channels offer only national options.

The media options are numerous—selection can be offered by:

- channel,
- programme,
- day of week,
- time of day,
- end break,
- centre break,
- position in break,
- proximity pairing (i.e. the placing of ads close together, in breaks of the same programme, etc.),
- short or long term frequency or 'weighting' over a period.

Table 11.1 Costs of airtime

Time length	Factor
30 seconds	X1
10 seconds	X0.5
20 seconds	X0.85
40 seconds	X1.33
60 seconds	X2.0

From a creative standpoint there are obviously a number of options to test—completely different executions or amendments/variations. Production costs commonly prohibit creative 'playing' to an extent.

(h) **Fulfilment**

The fulfilment of a DRTV ad is enormously important. Many campaigns fail because the 'back end' of the process has not been thought through or managed efficiently, leading to lost enquiries or long delays in the processing of response.

Response to a TV ad comes in very quickly, within minutes of the end of the ad being broadcast. Often, call centres/call centre technology is not sufficient to deal with thousands of calls at the same time, and enquirers are 'lost' in the system, cannot get through or are put on hold for long periods. Also, fulfilment materials may be hastily put together or poorly designed, so the expectation generated by the TV ad is disappointed when the materials reach the potential customer.

Planning for and predicting likely fulfilment volumes and timing is therefore a key part of the TV planning process.

11.4.4 **Direct response radio**

In the UK alone there are more than 200 commercial stations to choose from for acquisition. In recent years, radio has become a more viable option for direct response advertisers as radio audiences have increased, the number of stations has grown, and targeting options have improved. It is still the case that generating a direct response from a radio ad is difficult—radio is most effectively used as a support medium in an integrated direct marketing campaign, generating a desire to respond which is then fulfilled through other media.

Radio is 'consumed' differently to other media. Like TV, it is broadcast into homes and intrudes into the lives of consumers, but the similarities end there. Radio tends to be listened to alone, allowing the advertiser to speak to the listener as an individual rather than as part of an audience. It is listened to in a 'personal space'—the kitchen or the car. Most listeners habitually tune in to the same station and are loyal to certain programmes—the phenomenon of 'channel-hopping' does not occur as it does on TV. Listening to radio is a passive activity—nine out of ten people listen whilst doing something else; cleaning, working, or driving. Radio is not likely to receive their full attention at any time.

Creatively, radio ads can be developed which take account of the way that radio is received by the listener. Like TV, radio is linear, so it works best when the offer is very simple. Ads can be repeated to build awareness of the offer. Many commercial stations encourage listener participation, asking listeners to write in, to fax, phone, or to e-mail the radio station. Listeners may therefore be 'educated' to think of radio as a response medium. Radio operates at an emotional level—many listeners refer to it as a 'friend'. Creative executions can take account of this, being designed to appeal at an emotional level.

(a) Targeting and evaluation

Radio offers the ability to target by station content/style, by time of day, and by listener location. In the UK, audience demographics can be obtained through RAJAR, the radio audience survey operated jointly by the BBC and commercial radio.

The success of a solus direct response radio ad is judged on percentage response—i.e. the number of calls divided by audience size, expressed as a percentage. Audience size can be obtained from the radio station. In a mixed media schedule, where the radio ad is playing a support role, success or failure is harder to judge. Post campaign research can be undertaken amongst respondents, or testing with and without radio in similar regions can be run.

(b) Buying direct response radio

Radio is low cost—both in terms of production and media. Radio ads can be made very quickly, so it is an excellent medium for testing and for topical or time-sensitive promotions. Airtime is bought from the radio stations advertising sales departments, and can be bought directly or through a media-buying agency. As with DRTV, costs rise and fall according to demand, and space is usually sold per 30-second spot.

(c) Fulfilment

As with DRTV, response handling is all important—many successful radio campaigns fall foul at the fulfilment stage with responders unable to get through on a telephone number, receiving the 'busy' signal or being kept on hold for too long. Radio campaigns have to be briefed bearing this stage in mind, with response materials developed in line with the ad creative and in good time.

11.4.5 Press advertising

National and local newspapers and magazines cater for a variety of interests, lifestyles, and audiences; direct marketers can target titles selectively which harmonize with their offers. Regular readers generally form extremely strong bonds with their journals and the medium can be very effective in acquisition. Most people have to scan for items of interest, as it is impossible for them to find the time to read everything, given that each edition often has 10,000s of words. High circulation/readership newspapers, such as the *Sun*, are extremely effective when a direct marketer is looking to generate a large number of leads in the absence of a list (though at a cost commensurate with the large circulation.) More focused journals can be chosen for closer targeting.

(b) Press space

As with other media, the cost of space in the press is subject to market forces of supply and demand. Typically, the ratio of space in a publication is 50 : 50 between editorial and advertising, but it can vary wildly. Whether you choose one publication over another requires a complex assessment of the qualitative (e.g. 'style' and tone of the journal) and quantitative factors (e.g. size and cost of readership).

When purchasing press space for direct response advertising several 'practical' considerations come into play. If the ad carries a coupon it needs to be placed where the reader will be able and willing to cut the coupon from the publication. Thus, direct response press ads will commonly be placed on the outside right-hand edge of the page. As cutting the ad will mutilate the publication, it not advisable to place the ad in a glossy colour section, or amongst editorial content which the reader may wish to preserve.

Newspapers and magazines will offer standard ad space sizes which correspond to the editorial space allocations of the publication. Any size outside this portfolio will only be sold at a large premium. Creative work is therefore restricted to the page, half page, or column sized spaces available.

Page allocation can be specified, but again, only at an extra cost. Many direct response advertisers, for instance, are happy to pay a premium to locate their ad in 'high traffic' sections of the paper, such as next to the crossword.

Creative consideration also needs to address issues of colour—colour is not always available as an option and is always more expensive (because the reproduction costs are higher). Colour ads (and larger ads) do increase response levels, but not always by a big enough margin to offset the additional costs. As with most media, testing and refinement are necessary.

Media space can be bought direct from publications, or via an agency. A standard 'rate card' can be provided by each publication, which will list prices by space (i.e. £XX for a full page, YY for a half page). However, rate cards are only used as a baseline—press space buying, in reality, is a very volatile business based on supply and demand. Press buyers will pride themselves on 'never paying ratecard'. Short term or 'distress' space is also cheaply available to advertisers prepared to supply ads on a very short-term basis when space has become available at the last minute. Charities, for instance, place many of their 'emergency appeal ads' in this way.

Press and magazine ad campaigns can test many variables, such as publication, publication section, distribution region, day of week, colour, size, position, response mechanism (i.e. phone, internet, coupon), plus creative treatment. Many newspapers offer the opportunity to 'A/B test' ads—i.e. to run two different creatives in the same publication in the same position on the same day—the publication will organize the switching from one version to the next part way through the print run. A/B testing attracts an extra payment from the advertiser, but is an effective test mechanism.

11.4.6 Inserts

Many publications also offer to place flyers, cards, and inserts for direct marketers and in some cases, samples of the product. Some readers claim to find these inserts irritating, but many respond well as they are often the first things in the journal that they see and thus have an effective impact. Most inserts out-perform press advertisements, but they can be three to six times more expensive depending on the quality of production. For the direct marketer it means that your message is isolated from the run of the journal and has the opportunity to stand out more effectively. Pre-paid reply cards make it easy for people to respond, as do free phone response numbers. Mini-test markets are also available. The publisher, IPC, will add an extra page to a normal issue in a way that is undetectable to readers. Treated copies are then distributed in special areas to test the pulling power of the direct offering.

Response patterns are often similar between different journals, however, there can be dramatic differences between different types of journals such as gardening and cooking magazines. Bear in mind that journals with a greater deal of frequency such as daily newspapers and weekly magazines will have a shorter lifespan

Insert media is purchased on a cost per thousand basis. Marketers commonly test an initial insertion of, say, 10,000 and evaluate response before committing to a rollout of a larger quantity, or of the full run of the publication. Most publications offer the opportunity to test inserts by region, or the marketer may test different creatives at random within a single publication, tracking response by coding each of the creative treatments differently on the response device.

(a) Qualitative issues in choice of publication

(i) Editorial environment

- percentage of editorial devoted to various lifestyle interests related to product on sale,
- specific editorial content related to product,
- graphics and/or editorial excellence,
- political stance,
- past experience on positioning and editing.

(ii) Competitive environment

- advertising to editorial ratio,
- number of competitor advertising pages,
- promised separation from competitors,
- past experience of proximity to rival advertisers.

(iii) Advertising reproduction

- consistency through the press run,
- quality control in regional editions,
- consistency, match, and balance of colour,
- past experience of adjustments for misprints.

(iv) Perceived reader involvement

- circulation/audience trend and forecast
- percentage renewal of subscriptions,
- number of copies sold at full rate,
- cover price/subscription cost,
- time spent by readers,
- experience of involvement: coupon redemption, recipe, or reprint requests.

(v) Audience matching

- Correlation of publication audience with target audience,

- Reader profile and similarity to customer profile.

(i) Quantitative issues in choice

- Frequency of issue (daily, weekly, monthly or bi-monthly and quarterly),
- Reach of selected audience,
- Cost.

(b) **Cost comparisons**

When making cost comparisons across media titles care should be taken to ensure that the cost per thousand is calculated using the same units, e.g. a page versus a page—note that total audience and target audience may give different CPTs. When comparing journals it is often best to provide a CPT table (see Table 11.2) :

- Here the vehicles are sorted in ascending order with each vehicle being allocated an index number starting from 100.,
- It makes cost comparisons easier.

11.4.7 **Door-to-door**

Door-to-door delivery is becoming increasingly popular as a direct response route. It involves the delivery of unaddressed mail (often marked 'to the occupier') to home addresses. In the UK, the service is offered by the Royal Mail and by a number of other distribution companies, including the distributors of local free sheet newspapers. In the US, the service is offered by the US Postal Service (USPS).

Distribution via the national postal service in both countries offers the advantage of delivery with 'real' post, by a uniformed postman. The service is thus of guaranteed reliability, and the post delivered is likely to be viewed with more interest by the recipient. In the past, other suppliers of door-to-door in the UK have been accused of unreliability and unaccountability.

Door-to-door is a comparatively cheap medium. Creatively, many companies will simply amend an existing successful direct mail acquisition pack to use in an unaddressed format. It is also an ideal medium to use for sampling. One other advantage is that the medium can, in theory, reach people who do not usually respond to direct mail, do not appear on available mailing lists, and are therefore not generally 'available' to the direct marketer for personal approaches.

Table 11.2 CPT table

Vehicle	Page (£)	Audience (000)	CPT (Pence)	Index
X	33,000	600	55	100
Y	18,000	200	90	163 *
Z	13,000	50	260	473 **

* = 90/55
** = 260/55

The 'downside' of door-to-door is that the only targeting available is by postcode/ zipcode. Companies can take this to fairly sophisticated levels, by profiling existing (or best) customers by code, adding demographic indicators (like ACORN codes), and modelling the list against available post/zipcodes to find the closest matches. Generally, a Postcode Sector Ranking (PSR) is provided showing which codes 'look most like' the postcodes of existing customers, and are therefore more likely to be good prospects.

11.4.8 **Internet**

The Internet offers enormous potential, but it takes some figuring out how to do it. What will demand be like for Internet services? Demand is a function of three factors: (1) the number of people using the Net, (2) the characteristics of those users, and (3) most importantly, their purchasing behaviour. The next chapter will look at the growth of the Internet and at the way Net is used in commerce.

There is little doubt that the Internet will have a significant impact on commerce in the coming years. However, many of the surveys are overblown, unrealistic, and misleading. It looks likely that the Net will remain a largely North American and Western European phenomenon for at least the next five years reaching about a third of households, with younger, more affluent, and male users spending within a narrow range of products. Companies are increasingly using e-mail to communicate with customers and such electronic 'direct mail' will undoubtedly grow. It has to be handled sensitively and should always be the result of a customer's agreement. Each e-mail should include the opportunity for the customer to cancel.

The direct business to business dimension of the Internet is where most of the current 'action' is. For example, General Electric has largely shifted over from a physical business community to an electronic model using its Trading Process Network. The system enables GE to trade $1billion worth of business with around 1,400 suppliers all over the world. Simplifying the previous time-consuming manual contract bidding and award processes, the system has begun to push out to not only GE's suppliers, but to their suppliers' suppliers. As a consequence, a multi-tiered business community has been formed. There is little doubt that Electronic Data Interchange (EDI) is set to transform business to business direct marketing.

However, EDI requires substantial investment with hardware, software, messaging, and connection fees to link to a finite number of suppliers. The costs of connecting different participants to a web browser, in contrast, are virtually zero. This is why companies of all sizes are shifting away from proprietary EDI networks to relatively inexpensive and more flexible Extranet technologies.

The so-called 'Extranet' has been built on the Internet for private direct business to business communication. Traditional EDI is complex and has cost barriers of entry for smaller firms, whereas the Extranet has no such problems. Expanding electronic services out to many more and smaller firms is precisely what is fuelling the growth of Extranet communities. A recent example is the Automotive Network Exchange (ANX) founded by General Motors, Ford, and Chrysler. ANX establishes a communications protocol between vehicle parts suppliers and the procurement of order information from the big car companies and direct communications. The potential result is a hoped-for much lower cost structure in the industry.

The biggest obstacle to electronic business communities realizing their direct potential is concerns over security and privacy, and management resistance to the new paradigm. However, competitive market pressure and the continued squeeze on margins will force the adoption of new electronic operating methods. Electronic business communities will undoubtedly have a profound impact on direct marketing.

(a) Buying Internet advertising

There are a number of factors that must be considered when buying advertising space on the Internet. These include:

(i) Historical effectiveness
Some sites will perform better than others. Whilst this might often be a matter of trial and error, there are an increasing number of quantitative indicators that can be used to judge success. What is the site's average click through rate? How often are key words clicked? Is their audience growing or contracting?

(ii) Cost
In comparing various sites where banner ads might be placed it would also be helpful to identify how targeted each site can get. Some sites may charge a premium for enhanced targeting, with costs being a function of each target criterion employed. Whilst costs will therefore rise with increased targeting so too will advertising effectiveness and efficiency.

Other factors that drive cost include reach and frequency. Many sites provide data on the average frequency of visit using cookies (see next chapter) or some other method. Some sites can even provide data on the length of a given visit to a site and this may often be sub-divided by page. Reach (the total audience size) is typically obtained from third party sources such as MediaMetrix or Relevant Knowledge. These organizations specialize in audience definition and measurement.

(iii) Context
Whilst reach, frequency, and targeting are all fairly straightforward criteria, there are also a number of qualitative criteria that might need to be considered. Where might the banner ad appear on the website? As a general rule—the closer it is to the home page, the more likely it is that the banner will be seen.

There are also issues surrounding placement within a page. Banners at the top tend to out-perform those at the bottom and banners cited towards the left outperform those cited towards the right (reflecting the fact that people read from left to right).

Just as with print advertising, the degree of clutter must also be considered. If there are many banners on a single page, the likelihood that much attention will be paid to a single banner ad diminishes accordingly.

It is also worth noting that the advent of frames, where users view one part of the screen continually and can only scroll down a second component, means that banner advertising placed in a framed component is likely to be more effective. This is simply because it is on display for longer and the user cannot simply scroll down to escape it.

(iv) The banner itself

Larger banners are more effective than smaller banners, although as in print, the relation-ship is not a linear one. Doubling the size of a banner will tend typically to generate only a 50 per cent improvement in attention.

Modern technology also means that advertisers can include high quality graphics, or movement in their banner ads. These tend to generate higher levels of attention than those that only offer stills.

(v) Control

Some sites will charge more if the advertiser wants a greater degree of control over the ads placed. Advertisers often want to change the creative treatment on an ongoing basis—somewhere between 200–400,000 impressions would be normal—and the costs of per-mitting this flexibility will vary considerably. This should be considered from the outset and an appropriate degree of flexibility built in.

Finally, it is worth considering the degree of reporting that will be provided by specific sites. Do they report on traffic daily, weekly, or monthly. How detailed will this reporting be? How is it delivered and will the data be audited? These are all key considerations.

11.4.9 **Trade fairs**

International trade fairs are one of the best means for a company to direct market abroad. About 2,000 trade fairs are held a year in 70 countries. Many are booked up several years ahead. The main functions of trade fairs are to:

- meet potential customers,
- develop databases,
- make distributor contacts,
- demonstrate products,
- see what your competitors are doing,
- save time and money in making contacts.

There are several horizontal trade fairs around the world. The biggest is the Hanover Trade Fair held in April which attracts around 500–550,000 industrial buyers and sellers from around the world. Others worth mentioning are Leipzig, Canton, and Milan. Verti-cal trade fairs are held all over the world several times a year from the Paris Air Show to the Earls Court (London) Toy Fair. These are often more technical in nature and normally do not allow entrance to the public (although the Paris Air Show does). It is quite com-mon for exhibitors to 'cocoon' themselves and to insist that conference attendees wear badges to identify who they are. In this way rival companies are restricted in the ease in which they can see products and pick up brochures—only distributors and customer attention is sought!

Personal contacts are of key importance at trade fairs. For this reason it is important for exhibitors of offer a small hospitality area with refreshments.

The main ways to participate in a trade fair are:

- pay yourself (gives most freedom in what you do but is most expensive),

- accept an invitation (still pay yourself, but normally with reduced rates),
- by government aid (cheapest, but space may be standardized).

The costs are usually a function of the following:

- the size of the exhibition space a company might book,
- the nature of the exhibition or fair.,
- the additional facilities that might be required (e.g. telephone lines, power points),
- the nature of the display material,
- the design of the stand,
- transport to and from the venue,
- hospitality provision (if any),
- the opportunity cost of NOT using sales-staff elsewhere.

11.5 **Factors in choice of direct classes**

Direct media can be divided into two categories: classes and vehicles. Class relates to the general choice and vehicles to the specific. For example, a direct marketer might choose television as the class and Carlton as the specific vehicle. What factors should be considered?

Reach—the issue with reach is to what extent the direct medium class will reach the intended audience. For example, direct appeals on commercial radio will obviously not reach loyal BBC 1, 2, 3, 4, or 5 listeners.

Creative scope—*Communication quality* of the medium (sound, colour, still picture, printed word, movement) will vary between different direct media and are important considerations in choice. *Context* relates to the context in which the direct communication will be received. For example, direct TV is likely to be viewed in the home environment whereas e-mails are more likely to opened at work. A company offering a new business software package would be advised to choose e-mail over DRTV simply on a context basis. *Timing* is an important issue. The question is who determines the amount of time spent on a communication? With several direct media, e.g. direct mail and Internet, the receiver is in control. Whereas with direct TV and radio, the sender decides how long the receiver has, e.g. 10 or 30 seconds. Conventionally, it is advisable to choose media that allow the receiver to determine the time if the offer is seen to be of considerable interest. But if it is not of great interest to many people then it would be best for the sender to take control and choose media classes accordingly.

Direct marketing history—this is a simple point. If you have evidence from previous campaigns, what has worked before and what has failed? Learn from past efforts.

Competitors—their activities also need to be considered. Where are they advertising? Perhaps they have got it right? Maybe your advertising should be close to theirs or maybe a different medium class altogether will enable you to dominate the space?

Size of budget—another important consideration. DRTV may require a greater investment than direct mail to undertake effectively.

11.6 **Timing**

There are a variety of factors that might impact on the timing chosen for particular campaigns (Mesak, 1992; Feinberg, 1992). Many organizations would like to dominate with their communications all year round, but there is rarely enough money (Ostrow, 1987). Instead, organizations need to make choices in respect of whether to concentrate the promotional activity at certain times of the year, or whether to spread their media expenditure throughout.

11.6.1 **Sales and media patterns**

- Sales of your product and rivals are the key to timing.
- Examine how sales are spread out over the year.
- Remember that the decision to buy may be made considerably earlier than the sale.
- Use seasonal discounts to effect.

11.6.2 **Launches and sales peaks**

- There is little doubt that product launches need a concentrated burst.
- Most regular advertisers schedule in line with the sales curve.
- However, some try contra-cyclical advertising: Advertising in slack periods to boost demand.

11.6.3 **Arguments for bursts**

- To be effective ads need a *threshold*.
- Ads that generate lots of interest help to generate retail orders.
- 'Concentrate and Dominate' is a widely held conventional wisdom.
- An advertiser with several brands with a house name can benefit from bursts for each brand (e.g. Pepsi or Sony).

11.6.4 **Arguments for continuity**

- Many brands are bought frequently.
- Simple reminding is generally OK.
- If the response is convex, then it will be best to space ads adequately: bursts may lead to rapid diminishing returns.
- Irritating effects may be more noticeable and even harmful with bursts.

11.6.5 **Compromise**

- May be best to continue with at least some advertising rather than end abruptly with a burst.

11.6.6 **A word on decay**

- Response decay rates should also be considered in scheduling.
- Some advertisers can stop advertising and continue to have high awareness (so bursts are OK).
- Others may find awareness rapidly decays and so continuity must be used.

11.7 **Response functions**

Thus far, we have looked at the specific media that can be used for direct marketing and the factors that can drive the selection thereof. In this section, we will examine the specific pattern of response that might be engendered. An example of a response function is provided in Table 11.3. In this example the bulk of the response is attracted immediately following the advertisement with a fairly rapid tailing off in evidence thereafter.

11.7.1 **Kinds of response function**

Response functions such as the one in Table 11.4 can also be presented graphically. Four different types are illustrated in Figure 11.1. It should be noted that response functions can be generated for awareness, sales, enquiries, or indeed any of the specific objectives

Table 11.3 Example of a response function

Impressions	1	2	3	4	5	6
Cumulative response	50	75	90	100	100	100
Additional responses	50	25	15	10	0	0

that might be set for marketing communications. Thinking about the nature of the response that might be received, perhaps on the basis of past experience, can greatly assist marketers in planning for the fulfilment of the orders/requests that are received when a given campaign is run.

(a) **Linear (Fig. 11.1a)**

- Starting at 0 and reaching 100 at a constant rate.
- Several studies have supported linear responses.

(b) **Step-function (Fig. 11.1b)**

- Response remains the same until a critical number of impressions, then it jumps.

(c) **S-shaped response (Fig 11.1c)**

- Low response at the beginning, gradually increasing to a steep slope, then flattening off again.
- Has the most appeal—but the argument is entirely intuitive. There is no evidence to support its existence.

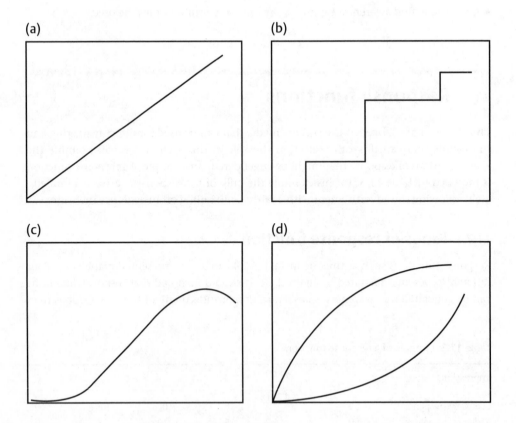

Fig. 11.1 Response functions presented graphically

(d) Convex and concave response functions (Fig. 11.1d)

- The right hand end of an S-shaped response function is either convex or concave.

- In the convex function, each additional impression causes a smaller additional response than the one before. In the concave function, each additional impression causes a larger response than the one before.

- Convex is the shape that research generally supports. That is, that you are likely to get the biggest response from the first direct impression and thereafter it will diminish.

(e) Difficulties in using response functions

There are, of course, difficulties inherent in the use of such functions for planning purposes. These include:

- Rarely does a campaign have a single objective (often has short and long-term objectives).

- All individuals do not respond identically.

- Response functions will vary according to time period (weeks, months, years).

- Competitors' ads will affect response.

11.8 International media

11.8.1 Availability

International advertisers must be prepared to modify their use of advertising media. Not all countries offer such widespread access to media as in the US or UK. Many countries, for example, have limitations on the proportion of time allocated to commercial television. Countries such as Greece also place severe limitations on the nature of advertising that might be undertaken and the groups that might be targeted.

The increasing penetration of satellite/cable television in North America and in Europe (e.g. Murdoch's Sky Channel) is forcing countries to open up to commercial television media as national stations lose a share of their audience to the satellite channels. Many well-known names are getting involved such as NEC, Nikon, Nissan, Gillette, and Polaroid, and it will certainly grow in importance.

11.8.2 Media usage

Media usage varies in different countries. On the whole, the wealthier a country the more likely people are to use electronic media, the Web, and regularly read newspapers and magazines. As would be expected, lack of resources and illiteracy adversely affect media usage (e.g. literacy rate in US and UK = 99 per cent compared to Kenya 47 per cent and India 36 per cent).

Measured as a proportion of GNP, there is relatively little advertising in poorer nations. Many of the markets are sellers' markets in which promotion is unnecessary. Electronic media are scarce. Newsprint is restricted owing to exchange shortages. Thus, outdoor and in-store promotions are more common than TV and press advertising. Advertising in poorer nations is often to teach new consumption behaviour rather than gaining market share. Postal services to deliver direct marketing can be hopeless and unreliable, as in Poland.

11.8.3 Timing

International direct marketers must be cognizant of the seasonality of their country markets and schedule activities accordingly. Obviously, the northern and southern hemispheres have different winters/summers. Vacations in Europe tend to be longer than in North America and in more concentrated periods. Sweden virtually closes in July, as do France and Italy in August. No advertising can be placed in Moslem countries during Ramadan. Also, business to business advertisers need to consider fiscal years and government planning cycles.

11.9 Summary

In this chapter, we have examined how direct marketers might employ a wide range of media to meet their stated communications objectives. We have outlined specifically the advantages and disadvantages of each medium and the factors one might consider in looking to purchase. We have also examined the pattern of likely response that might be generated.

Discussion questions

1   You have a limited budget with which to reach an audience of 40–60 year old males living in the South East of England. Which media might you consider using to reach them? How would you justify this choice?

2   In your role as the marketing director of an organization selling insurance products, prepare a brief for a telemarketing agency that you have selected to deal with incoming responses to a DRTV ad (i.e. specify what the agency would need to know to fulfil the enquiries that come in).

3   You are a nationwide supermarket chain opening a store in a new area. Your aim is to appeal to potential customers within a 15 mile radius of the store. Which direct media would you use to promote the opening of the store?

4   As the marketing director a children's toy manufacturer prepare a briefing for your team indicating what you see as the advantages and disadvantages of each direct marketing medium and how the organization might make use of these to promote and sell its products.

5   As the marketing director of an organization specializing in the manufacture of specialized machine tools for industrial use, specify the media that you feel would be of most use to your organization in promoting and selling its products.

Further reading

Feinberg F. M. (1992) 'Pulsing Policies for Aggregate Advertising Models', *Marketing Science*, summer, 221–34.

Mesak H. I. (1992) 'An Aggregate Advertising Pulsing Model with Wearout Effects', *Marketing Science*, summer, 310–26.

Ostrow J. W. (1987) 'Setting Frequency Levels: An Art or Science?', *Market and Media Decisions*, 19.

Roman E. (1995) *Integrated Direct Marketing: The Cutting-Edge Strategy for Synchronizing Advertising, Direct Mail, Telemarketing, and Field Sales* (Lincolnwood, IL: NTC Business Books).

Rust R. T. and Oliver R. W. (1994) 'Notes and Comments: The Death of Advertising', *Journal of Advertising*, 23(4), 71–7.

Case study: The Indianapolis Colts

In 1984, the Colts football team moved from Baltimore to a new home in Indianapolis, Indiana. The team's arrival caused a huge stir in sports-loving Indy, and initially demand for season tickets was sky high. The season-ticket base grew to 54,000 within the first year.

Season-ticket holders received no special treatment from the Colts, who at this point employed no marketing staff. The sole communication received by these loyal fans was an annual invoice for payment renewal. By 1996, the base had shrunk to just 36,000. A poor performance on the football field added to the team's woes, and by early 1997 they were experiencing real problems in selling out the stadium.

At this point the Colts woke up, and took on some marketing advisers. Early analysis of the customer base showed that the Colts had some very special fans. Some 20 per cent had held season tickets since 1984, which meant that they had spent over $20,000 each to support their team. Priority number one was the development of a personalized programme to keep these top customers happy and loyal. From this point on, existing season ticket holders received communications throughout the year, thanking them for their ongoing support and encouraging them to continue and deepen their relationship with the Colts. These included special gifts, handwritten letters from the owner of the team, access to exclusive events, and a regular newsletter update. Every communication stressed the importance of continuing support, and expressed the gratitude of the team for the support of their fan base.

Further examination of past transaction records showed that fans were offered only one payment option for season tickets—a single lump sum payment at an allocated date.

A more flexible payment plan was conceived and implemented enabling fans to pay for their tickets in two instalments.

The new communications programme and the offer of a more customer-focused payment option reaped rewards very quickly for the Colts. Renewal rates increased and the attrition of existing ticket holders was effectively halted. The Colts were now ready to move on to the recruitment of new season-ticket customers.

The database did not hold details of lapsed ticket-holders, so the marketing team had to look to recruit new customers from a 'cold' audience. First, they returned to the database for more information on existing fans with which to power the search for more people like them.

With the aid of an outside database supplier, demographic, and psychographic data were collected and a profile of profitable customers was established. Other data sources were rifled, including information available on fans from the NFL and from local radio stations. The problem was not a lack of fans—research indicated that over 75 per cent of adults in the Indy area considered themselves Colts supporters!

So the fans were out there, but the Colts weren't filling their stadium. They did more research.

Season ticket holders were older and wealthier than the average fan. They lived within 90 miles of the stadium, and they rated themselves as passionate about their team. Those fans who bought tickets on a more occasional basis were very different. They tended to be younger, less well off, and to have less time available to them. They didn't subscribe to the current season-ticket offer because it was too expensive, and because they really couldn't commit to attending ten games every season. However, they too felt strongly about the team—passion wasn't the issue.

The Colts' marketing team rejected the idea of simply lowering the price to attract these fans. Profitability was key, and they really couldn't afford to lower prices substantially enough to make a sufficient difference. They set out instead to package the offer of their season ticket in a way that would attract this very different new audience.

A new product was developed and tested successfully, offering a half-season five game mini package. This offered reserved seating at a much lower cost than the existing season ticket, though the seating available was restricted to the upper levels of the stadium, which were not considered the 'best seats in the house'. This, the Colts felt, successfully addressed fan's concerns about both costs and time.

Flushed with the success of the early tests, the Colts hired an ad agency and spent $150,000 on a media launch of the mini package product. Although this involved a splash in radio, TV, and press, sales trickled in at a poor rate.

Dismayed at the lack of response, the Colts' marketers reviewed the creative approach that had been taken. In hindsight, it was clear that the ads had relied too heavily of the profile of existing season ticket holders, and as a result, though the product was sound, the campaign had been targeted at the wrong market.

A long-form direct response newspaper ad was created which addressed this problem. A free Colts' highlights video was offered to incentivize early response. By the end of the first week sales had quadrupled, and within two weeks the allocated 1,500 mini-packages had sold out.

The successful mini-package product was promoted again the following year—this time with no limit on numbers. The video incentive had proved powerful but expensive, and the Colts had also received complaints from existing ticket-holders that they were missing out and that new supporters were being rewarded unfairly. Colts' marketers accepted this as a very valid point.

The decision was taken to test the product offer on radio. Desk research on previous sales patterns showed that the window of opportunity for selling season tickets was small. Preseason games begin in August, by which time ticket purchasing decisions have been made for the season. Early summer promotions hit holiday time, and consequently attracted low response.

The first radio campaign was therefore scheduled to break just after the 4 July holiday. Radio had been selected because:

(a) it is low cost,

(b) the listener base of local stations, whilst broader than the Colts' prospect customer profile, included the target audience they were pursuing,

(c) local radio stations perform a community function. Indiana fans are loyal to their home state—and hopefully to their local football team!

(d) local radio personalities are very popular. By creating the impression that the offer was 'recommended' by such icons the Colts hoped to increase response rates to the ticket offer.

Playing on the 'community' aspect of the promotion, the Colts' marketing team asked local radio stations to take an active role in developing the advertising. They requested that each station add their own incentive to encourage their listeners to buy the season ticket package. In return, the Colts committed to buying a proportion of airtime.

WNAP (a classic rock station) came back with a creative proposal. The station was owned by a media company which had car-parking space near to the Colts' stadium. It offered listeners the season-ticket promotional package for the standard Colts' price—plus a free parking space and a free, catered tailgate party for each game. The offer was restricted to 200 fans (which was the number of car parking spaces available). It sold out very quickly, producing a four to one return on investment.

WFMS (a country music station) offered a VIP backstage pass to an all-day country music concert to every listener who purchased the Colts' package. This offer fell completely flat.

Two further stations were tested. One lost money and the other produced a small return.

Whilst radio had proved a mixed success for the Colts' marketers, they had learned from the campaign. New, younger season ticket holders could be recruited if a way could be found to add interest and value to the product. The radio testing had been tracked carefully, the Colts had received extra value by involving the stations, and the 'ownership' by the radio stations of the promotions meant that existing season-ticket holders were not likely to accuse the Colts of mistreating them. Overall, the radio tests bought in a net ROI of three to one.

The product was also tested in press advertising. A new direct response ad featuring the mini-package, but without any gift incentive, was run in the sports section of the state's main newspaper. The ad was written by Dean Rieck, an experienced copywriter and direct marketing expert. The creative was developed as an 'advertorial' style, with a dramatic headline and long copy presented as a news story about the football team. The ad worked tremendously well, generating a five to one return on investment. Subsequent 'tweaks' of the ad proved unsuccessful—these later versions improved the aesthetics, but damaged response—this particular ad worked, and sold season tickets, without looking beautiful.

The Colts rolled out the profitable parts of the radio and press campaigns—and by the end of 1998 had added 2,500 new season-ticket holders to their supporter database. Once on the base, ticket holders continue to receive the personalized communication programme which has increased fan loyalty and has successfully arrested the flow of ticket-holders from the database.

A more recent addition to the marketing programme is the Colts' website (see Figure 1). The site allows fans to purchase tickets (selecting their own seat in the process), to buy Colts' merchandise and to read up on team history and news. The site provides opportunities for interaction including online video footage of the last game, a recorded broadcast of the latest press conference with the coach and a chatroom where fans can exchange views.

The marketing of the Colts is now as, or more, successful than the football team itself.

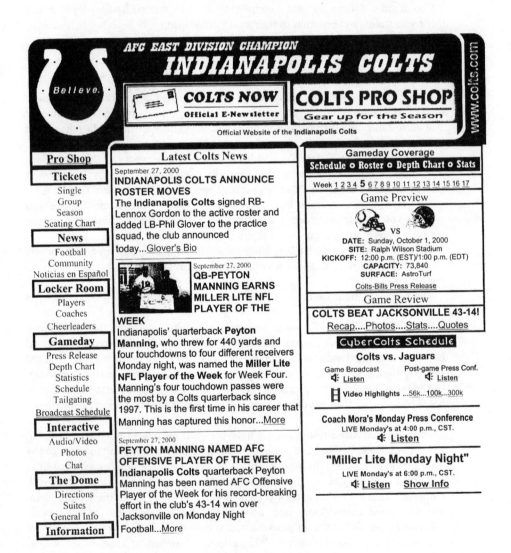

Case Study Fig. 1 Indianapolis Colts' Website

The season ticket base still grows, even when the team experiences the disappointment of a losing season on the playing field.

Discussion questions

1   How have the Colts achieved a major increase in audience numbers? What factors have contributed to their success?

2   Develop a direct marketing plan for both recruitment and retention for the upcoming 2000 season.

3   How might the new website be integrated with other direct communications that potential and existing fans receive?

4   Suggest two other forms of media that the Colts might use to extend the ongoing recruitment campaign.

Chapter 12

Budgeting

Contents

12.1 **Objectives**

By the end of this chapter you should be able to assess and understand the relative merits and applicability of the key methods available to marketers to set their direct marketing budgets.

(a) allowable cost per sale

(b) break-even cost per sale

(c) percentage of sales

(d) Competitive absolute

(e) Competitive relative

(f) Objective-task

(g) Decision models

As well, you should appreciate the process and organizational issues involved in budgeting that can affect choice. The overall discussion is related to companies and organizations for which marketing is a part of their marketing activities as well as for those for which direct marketing is the sole activity. As such the wider methods of setting budgets are reviewed and discussed as well as ones used specifically by direct marketers.

12.2 Introduction

Marketing and advertising budgeting strategies have received substantial academic and practitioner attention over the years starting with Borden's pioneering work in 1942. The direct marketing budget is generally a component of the overall marketing and communications budget, but may be the marketing budget if the company or organization concerned uses only direct marketing. There are two kinds of direct budgets involving the short term and long term. The long term might relate to the lifetime and life cycle of the product or service, but in reality for most organizations relates to two to five years. The short term budget tends to be set annually with shorter time periods for reporting, scheduling, and control. Internet companies tend to have reduced time frames with the short term being around 60 days and the long term, one year.

The high degree of attention devoted to the subject is evidenced by the large number of papers published on it, which totals well over several thousand over the last 40 years (Piercy, 1986). The diligent analysis of the theory and practice of budget methods has improved significantly our understanding of the problems and issues involved. There are three main areas of investigation in these studies: prescriptive writings on how to set the advertising budget, analyses of the methods used related to one or two main explanatory variables, and analyses of the budgeting process. This chapter begins with an assessment of the different available methods to set budgets.

12.3 Methods

There are a number of ways in which companies set their direct marketing budgets.

12.3.1 Allowable cost per sale

The allowable cost per sale is a derivative of the well-known affordable method which is based on what the organization feels it can afford. There is no science, no examination of effects, and no analysis. But it is practical. The budget is linked to the short-term vision of the company or institution and direct marketing budgets will be applied after all the other investments and costs in running the business. If the year is going badly then the direct marketing budget will be cut and if things are going well it will be increased accordingly. Given advertising expenditure reduces taxable profit, there is some incentive, from a fiscal perspective, to follow this method. Though perhaps the very idea of calling the 'affordable' a method is overstating the case. In most respects it is a product of behaviour. The affordable method has been translated by direct marketers into the 'allowable cost per sale' or the 'pre-set allowable marketing spend' (McCorkell, 1997). The question posed is simply: how much are you prepared to spend to bring in a new customer (acquisition) or to make a subsequent sale (retention)? A great deal will depend upon the lifetime value of a customer. In the case of acquiring a new customer it might be decided to spend up to £40 on each new one. The net revenue per sale might only be £10, but the supposition is that having acquired the customer, their gross revenue lifetime value will more than repay the investment. With retention, it might be decided to spend £6 per person and, if possible, there might be some variability in spend according to where someone is considered to be on their life cycle. The spend is below the £10 revenue per sale, because at the retention stage you can no longer afford to subsidize the spend (but there might be some variability depending on where a customer might be in their life cycle). Its main advantage is that companies can control total expenditures on direct marketing, but as it is pre-set it has no regard for sales. The allowable cost per sale is linked to the break-even method.

12.3.2 Break-even cost per sale

The break-even method attempts to link budgeting to direct marketing's profitability threshold. Absolute increases in unit sales and gross sales are related to incremental increases in the direct budget in order to establish the levels of spending necessary to recoup expenditures. The formula is quite simple—you divide direct marketing expenditures (dm) by the absolute 'a' (or percentage 'p') gross revenue:

To apply this successfully, direct marketers need to be at least reasonably sure as to the relationship between direct marketing spending and the likely response of prospects. The idea is to spend to the point where the incremental cost per sale equals the incremental revenue achieved. It sounds fine in principle, but is hard to apply (McCorkell, 1997).

---

break-even unit sales = dm/a
break-even sales = dm/p

where:

dm = direct marketing expenditure
a = absolute gross profit margin
p = pecentage gross profit margin

For example if the gross profit margin per unit is £5 (or 20 per cent of the unit price), the absolute increase in sales to recoup a £2 million direct marketing budget would be:

2,000,000/5 = 400,000 units

and in terms of total sales:

2,000,000/0.20 = £10,000,000

Fig. 12.1 Break-even cost per sale

12.3.3 **Percentage of sales**

There are three ways to apply the percentage of sales method by:

Anticipated sales—a set percentage of expected sales in a forthcoming time period.

Past sales—a set percentage of past sales in a defined time period.

Unit sales—a set amount levied for each anticipated or past unit sold, e.g. a car company might decide that for every car sold £150 would be used for direct marketing. It is part of the percentage of sales approach because as the budget is grossed-up it represents a fixed percentage of sales.

This method basically treats direct marketing as a cost. Treating the direct marketing budget as a percentage of past sales is the easiest way to apply it. So, for example, if you had a set ration of 5 per cent and achieved sales of £30 millions last year, then this year's direct budget would be £1.5 millions. The percentage of sales method is easy to apply and cost. Its main advantage is that companies can control total expenditures on direct marketing and other related marketing expenditures quite easily and relate levels of spending to that of competitors. Unfortunately, this makes the size of the direct marketing budget a function of sales! If sales were high last year or are anticipated to be higher then the direct marketing budget will rise when it might not need to. Similarly, if sales fell or are anticipated to fall, then the direct marketing budget will be smaller when it might be prudent to maintain it or even increase it. However, it can be a good starting point to get a common-sense feel for what should be spent on direct marketing.

12.3.4 **Competitive absolute**

With this method an organization sets it direct marketing budget in line with its closest rival. The argument is that 'maybe they have got it right?'. The problem is that a competitor(s) is bound to have different objectives and use of direct marketing within their marketing mix. This makes comparison somewhat spurious. However, perhaps they have got it roughly right?

12.3.5 **Competitive relative**

This is where an organization sets its budget in line with its market share:

Company	Mkt. Share %	Budget %
A	60	60
B	30	30
C	10	10

Fig. 12.2 Competitive relative

Such an arrangement is rare and would be seen as anti-competitive. It sometimes happens to save direct marketing 'wars'. Each organization roughly spends in line with each one's market share. This maintains the status quo. In the example above, company C may remain small unless it can do something highly impactful and creative with its smaller budget.

12.3.6 **Objective task**

With this method the budget is set in accordance with direct marketing objectives. There are three stages to the process:

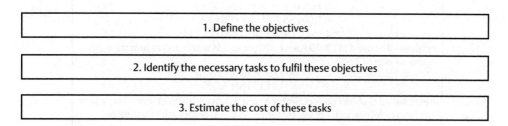

Fig. 12.3 Objective task

This is the only method that relates the budget to objectives. However, the problem is that the organization might not be able to afford the tasks required. Here is an example of its implementation:

Define objectives—a direct marketer sets out to reach men and women in the age range 25–34 with a new money-back/free travel insurance credit card. The profile is business and middle-managers living in the South East. The aim is to acquire 5,000 new customers.

Tasks—research and past experiences points towards the combined use of direct mail and DRTV. Controlled tests reveal that the optimum frequency OTS (opportunity to see) per prospect is two for direct mail and three for DRTV. The OTS is so-called because all that you are doing in direct marketing is providing the opportunity for prospects to see, read, or listen. You cannot be sure that they will do so. Research may indicate that direct mail will require a letter, a brochure, application form, and paid-reply envelope. DRTV will require two alternative 30 second commercials of a high quality and the 10 second condensed reminders.

Costs—it now remains to cost-out the proposed direct campaign. The allowable cost per acquisition has been set at £60, based on revenue per sale of £25. Therefore, the direct budget would be £300,000. The return on investment can be calculated by multiplying the number of responses by the lifetime value of each acquired customer minus £60 plus the costs of retention. The initial investment costs can be calculated by multiplying the revenue per sale (£25) by the number of customers acquired by the campaign and subtracting this sum from the direct budget.

12.3.7 **Response functions**

The great advantage of setting direct marketing budgets over other marketing budgets is the ability to link direct marketing spending to response. By linking direct marketing to response it is possible to analyse the effects of various levels of expenditure on sales, market share, and profits. If for example:

---

acps = allowable cost per sale per 1,000 is £2,000
r = response rate is 1.5 per cent
u = revenue per acquisition is £90 per annum

Then,

outcome = (acps x r)/100 x u
= (1,000 x 1.5)/100 x £90 = £1,350
= a loss on spend of −£650 per 1,000

However if a spend of £3,000 per 1,000 prospects was found to provide a response rate of 3.5%:

= (1,000 x 3.5) x 90 = 3,150
= gain of £150 per 1,000

Bear in mind that loss on acquisition is commonplace in direct marketing where the future lifetime value of the customer may outweigh such initial losses

---

Fig.12.4 Response functions

(a) **Decision models**

Over time, direct marketers can test different historic levels of expenditures and response rates to estimate the optimum level of direct expenditures. Regression analysis can be used to compute the relationship between spending and response. If levels have been varied over time it becomes possible to develop multiple regression equations to take account of other variables such as price changes and frequency in addition to the direct spend levels. It can never be 100 per cent accurate because a variety of factors may affect response and make it very difficult to be able to predict the outcomes. Obviously, historic response rates cannot be computed for new products or services. Another problem is that it assumes continuity with the past so that direct spend and response is assumed to remain constant, which is risky, especially in volatile markets.

There are three main decision models available to direct marketers: adaptive control, competitive share, and sequential.

(i) **Adaptive control**

This method takes control regions and compares results from using different sized budgets in each region. For example, a direct mail campaign might be launched targeted at 5,000 households in Brighton with the frequency of three mailings over two weeks and compared to a mailing of another targeted at 5,000 similar households in Oxford with a frequency of one. The markets need to be closely matched and different levels of spend and frequency allocated to each. These levels should be experimental and best set at higher or lower than last year's overall spend. The idea, of course, is that the sales in the different markets can be compared. Choice is then made based on the market and spend providing the best return for the investment.

If it is clear that differences between test markets can be averaged out, leaving the direct spend as the key variable, then it can be a very useful method. Against the method is the high cost of testing. Furthermore, few companies are willing to take radical risks by setting extremely low budgets for fear of losing sales in the test markets chosen. Competitive sabotage may also be a factor if news of the test leaks. A rival might attempt to cast doubt on the result by targeting the test areas with their own direct activities in the test markets chosen. However, the biggest danger is that test markets are never entirely comparable and so the results must always be regarded with some caution.

(ii) Competitive Share

This model examines the likely reaction of a competitor or competitors to a change in an organization's budget given that decisions by rivals can affect the impact of your budget. For example, if a company increases its spend on direct marketing by 25 per cent, might a rival company choose to match this increased spend or is it likely to spend the same as originally planned? The idea is to try and figure out a rival's likely response and bear this in mind when setting your own budget.

(iii) Sequential

This model sets the direct budget through a series of sequences based on the objective-task method (Lake, 1979). The first part is to establish a hierarchy of objectives. For example, objective 1 might be to make 40 per cent of the target market aware of an offer, objective 2 to have 30 per cent develop the attitude that it is 'a good deal', and finally, objective 3 to motivate 15 per cent to make an enquiry. The next stage is to establish the cost of the tasks to fulfil these objectives by the best direct medium and frequency. Having estimated, the pivotal question is quite simply: can we afford this? If the answer is 'yes' then there is no problem. However, if the budget will not stretch to meet these tasks, the model suggests you go back to your original objectives and start to pare-down until until it meets your allowable cost per sale. Perhaps, in this case, you might need to reduce the initial objective to making 25 per cent of the market aware of the offer and not the hoped-for 40? Now that you have a direct marketing budget that is affordable, the question is 'what is our closest rival spending?'. If this figure is wildly different to our budget, the idea is to go back and re-evaluate our objectives as a check. You still might stay with the budgeted figure even if it was significantly different, but it is worth

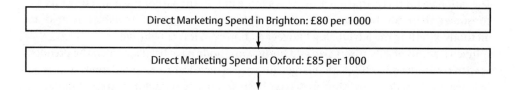

Fig. 12.5 Adaptive control

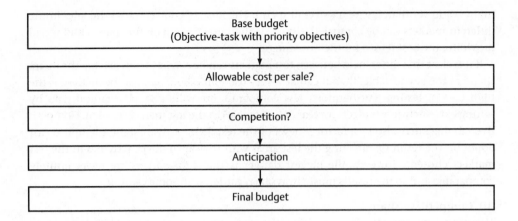

Fig. 12.6 Sequential model

considering. The final stage is to set aside some funds as a 'contingency' in case the direct campaign is a failure and some additional funds are required for remedial actions.

12.4 **Evidence**

Research on companies' advertising budgeting methods has shown conclusively that methods were prevalently unsophisticated. Studies of advertisers in the US have generally found that advertising budgets were set mainly by art rather than by science. Their collective findings were that some variation of the percentage of sales method or the affordable tended to prove most popular. More recent studies have indicated that the gap between theory and practice has narrowed. There is now a broad measure of support to the increasing use of more complex methods, namely the objective-task, particularly amongst large companies.

Four distinct explanatory variables have been identified as having an affect on the choice of budgetary methods: **product type**, **budget size**, **company performance**, and **country**.

Product type approaches have questioned whether consumer advertisers are more sophisticated than non-consumer advertisers and have generally concluded that they are. The rationale for this is that advertising is a more important part of the marketing mix for consumer than for business advertisers. Other assessments of variables related to methods of setting the advertising budget are, however, less conclusive.

Investigations of advertisers **size** and **budget methods** have been based on the premiss, as with consumer advertisers, that larger advertisers have a greater vested interest in good practice than smaller ones. Time may have been an important factor, as studies found no significant difference in the mid-1970s (San Augustine and Foley, 1975; BIM, 1970; Gilligan, 1976 and 1977; and Permut, 1977) whereas the more recent studies (Patti and

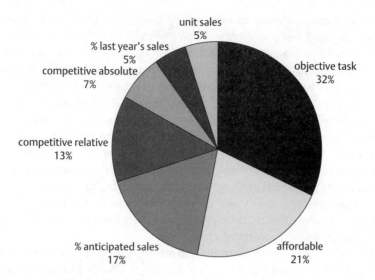

unit sales
5%

% last year's sales
5%

competitive absolute
7%

objective task
32%

competitive relative
13%

% anticipated sales
17%

affordable
21%

Fig.12.7 Methods selected in the UK, US, and Canada
Source: Hung and West (1995)

Blasko, 1981; Blasko and Patti, 1984; Hooley and Lynch, 1985; Hung and West, 1991) have given broad support for this proposition. Despite this, the case remains unproven. A similar supposition that companies that perform better will use more sophisticated methods than worse performers, also remains to be confirmed. There is some indication that more sophisticated methods are used by more profitable firms, but this is not definite.

Studies examining methods by **countries** amongst leading brand advertisers have found that there were significant differences (Synodinos et. al., 1989). Explaining such observed variances in budgeting practices, however, is a complex problem. Utilizing the suppositions applied on firms to countries, it might be argued that sophisticated methods will be found more generally in countries where the economy is predominantly consumer-orientated; where industry is highly concentrated amongst relatively few producers, and where average profitability is high. However, it is extremely difficult to provide valid aggregated data to test this and the ability to examine this issue is further muddled by the widespread centralization of international advertising decisions by multinationals.

12.5 Organizational influences

A much neglected aspect of the budgeting literature is the nature and importance of organizational influences and processes in determining budgeting sophistication. The main issue raised is whether or not top-management can reconcile the differing interests of the various parties involved in establishing the direct marketing budget, without imposing a rigid top-down budgeting solution (Piercy, 1986).

The size of the direct budget can affect several departments within an organization, and is often accompanied by a lot of departmental haggling before the final budget is set. In large companies where the marketing budget may amount to millions of pounds, direct marketing is an important budget item, as well as a resource for departmental development. From this perspective the direct budgetary process may be perceived as an instrument of power and politics in organizational decision-making. The literature on organizational decision-making often begins with the proposition that organizational power plays and politics have adversely affected a firm's performance (in which marketing and advertising play a vital part). Nevertheless, in general, their findings provide little support to this proposition. At any rate, all such studies have methodological problems in that it is generally recognized that power and politics are so pervasive as to be difficult, if not impossible, to isolate from other factors.

There have been many empirical studies on advertising budgeting methods, but little attention has been paid to the link between the organizational decision-making process and the advertising budgetary process. Studies have shown that the sales forecast is pivotal in all marketing plans and budgeting; but the forecasts are often biased because of reward systems, reporting systems, and departmental relations.

Other work has examined the risk avoidance practices and information bias of product managers. In terms of risk, it has been discovered that most managers tended to cope with high risk by ensuring that someone else took the responsibility for success or failure. It was also found that many managers manipulated sales targets in order to raise their budgets and increase the performance of their brands. It has also been questioned as to whether or not advertising and financial executives communicated effectively over budgeting. Associated research on the importance of the organizational process in budgeting in the UK from an organizational perspective has suggested that the advertising budgetary process could be categorized into one of three types: bottom-up, bottom-up/top-down, and top-down/bottom-up. Bottom-up budgeting, where brand and product managers primarily initiate the process and determine the requirements, was found to be the least popular. While used by some companies, it has been argued the popularity of bottom-up had steadily declined over the years owing to the increased need to consider corporate objectives and the rapid turnover of product and brand managers. In bottom-up/top-down budgeting the process was initiated by the product manager, but the final budget was set only after careful scrutiny by top management, which sometimes resulted in some substantial changes to budget allocations. Finally, top-down/bottom-up budgeting is when the initiative as well as the final authority for resource allocation rests with top management and the product manager participates mainly in the phases of implementation and execution.

Furthermore, it has been discovered that the type of budgetary process can affect the method of advertising budgeting. Where top management power is pre-eminent in the process (i.e. in top-down and top-down/bottom-up processes), the budgeting method tends to be less sophisticated and the affordable method the most often used. Conversely, where the marketing executive power is strongest (i.e. in bottom-up and bottom-up/top-down processes) the budgeting method is relatively more sophisticated, and the objective-task method most popular. The general explanation given is that marketing executives are usually required to justify their allocation of resources and to give details of their targets and tasks, whereas top management simply allocate according to what it believed the company could afford. After all, they have the power to generally 'ride-out' the consequences of any mistaken budgetary decisions.

12.6 **Key issue: lifetime value**

Having reviewed the general area of budgeting and its relationship to direct marketing, there are several issues to consider in setting direct marketing budgets:

- If the plan relates to a continuing direct marketing campaign, then the best approach would be to use previous experience linked to future forecasts. Response rates, competitive activities, forecasts of future market activity, and affordability can all be combined to reach a budget. Thus, the best approach would be to combine and compare budgeting methods.

- If the plan relates to a new product launch then the best approach would be to combine test market results with competitive activities and forecasts of future market activity as used with established products.

- However, the key issues for direct marketers to consider is whether the budget is for acquisition or retention or a combination of both.

12.6.1 **Acquisition**

- The starting point for the acquisition budget is to estimate average lifetime value. This may be based on historic projections for existing products or services or test markets (or simple forecasts) for new products and services.

- What tasks are required to acquire a customer?

- What is the allowable cost per sale? Can the company afford these tasks? If so, continue with the process. If not, can the tasks be modified and thereby reduced in cost to acquire a customer? If the answer to this is still 'no' the whole acquisition plan will need to be re-thought.

- However, once affordable tasks to acquire one customer have been agreed, estimate the size of the potential market and calculate the acquisition budget (a) by multiplying market size (m) by cost per sale of acquisition (cpsa): $a = m \times cpsa$

12.6.2 **Retention**

- The starting point for the retention budget is again to estimate average lifetime value.

- What tasks are required to retain a customer per year?

- What is the allowable cost per sale? Again, can the company afford these tasks? If so, continue with the process. If not, can the tasks be modified and thereby reduced in cost to acquire a customer? If the answer to this is still 'no' the whole retention plan will need to be re-thought.

- Once affordable tasks to retain one customer have been agreed, the retention budget (r) can be calculated by multiplying market size (m) by cost per sale for retention (cpsr): r = m x cps

12.7 **Summary**

Budgeting is an issue of central importance in direct marketing. There are seven approaches to setting budgets and in applying them there are a number of factors relating to firms, their markets, and organizations that may affect choice. Firms often get the budgeting methods they deserve rather than the most appropriate to their circumstances! Retention and/or acquisition motives will affect the application of different budgetary approaches as linked the allowable cost per sale.

Discussion questions

1. A mail order clothing company currently sets its budget by the affordable method linked to a set 5 per cent of past sales ratio. What would you consider to be the strengths and weaknesses of the approach?

2. Is it ever possible to use a single budgetary method in isolation or do companies inevitably use combinations?

3. Incorporating your general knowledge, develop a plan, with explanations, for your ideal method to set the direct marketing budget for Marks & Spencer.

4. In what budgeting method is the main problem that one or some of the companies using it will always remain relatively small? What budgeting method leaves you with the problem that you might not be able to afford the end result?

5. In the percentage of sales method approach to direct marketing appropriations which one of the following applies?:

   (a) the advantage is that sales determine the expenditures;

   (b) the appropriation represents the optimal amount set by a logical step-by-step analysis of all relevant factors;

   (c) fluctuations in sales have no effect, as these average out over time;

   (d) it fails to recognize that it is direct marketing that should contribute to sales, and not vice versa;

   (e) the marginal rate of direct marketing effectiveness is an essential element.

6. How might the choice by a company of a bottom-up or top-down approach to budgeting affect the method applied?

7   In what ways might the retention or acquisition motives affect the direct marketing budget?

Further reading

BIM (April, 1970) *Marketing Organization in British Industry*, Information Summary 148.

Blasko V. J. and Patti, C. H. (1984) 'The advertising budgeting practices of industrial marketers', *Journal of Marketing*, 48, 104–10.

Borden N. H. (1942) *The Economic Effects of Advertising* (Chicago).

Gilligan C. (1976) 'How Advertising Budgets Are Arrived At', *Advertising Quarterly*, 46, 32–5.

Gilligan C. (1977) 'How British Advertisers Set Budgets', *Journal of Advertising Research*, 17, 47–9.

Hanmer-Lloyd S. and Kennedy S. (1981) *Setting and Allocating the Marketing Communications Budget: A Review of Current Practice* (Cranfield: Marketing Communications Research Centre).

Hooley G. J. and Lynch J. E. (1985) 'How UK Advertisers Set Budgets', *International Journal of Advertising*, 4, 223–31.

Hung C. L. and West D. C. (1991) 'Advertising Budgeting Methods in Canada, the UK and the US, *International Journal of Advertising*, 10(3), 239–50.

Lake J. (1979) 'Setting The Company Budget Using a Sequential Approach', *Advertising and Marketing*, autumn, 47–50.

Patti C. H. and Blasko V. J. (1981) 'Budgeting Practices of Big Advertisers', *Journal of Advertising Research*, 21, 23–9.

Permut S. (1977) 'How European Managers Set Advertising Budgets', *Journal of Advertising Research*, 17, 75–9.

Piercy N. (1986) *Marketing Budgeting* (Dover, New Hampshire: Croom Helm).

San Augustine, A. J. and Foley, W. J. (1975) 'How Large Advertisers Set Budgets', *Journal of Advertising Research*, 15, 11–16.

Synodinos N. E., Keown C. F., and Jacobs, L. W. (1989) 'Transnational Advertising Practices: a Survey of Leading Brand Advertisers in Fifteen Countries', *Journal of Advertising Research*, 29, 43–50.

West D. C. and Hung C. L. (1993) 'The Organizational Budgeting Processes of Top Advertisers in Canada, the U.K. and the U.S.A.', *Journal of Euromarketing*, 2(3), 7–22.

Chapter 13

E-Marketing

Contents

13.1 **Objectives**

By the end of this chapter you should be able to:

(a) understand the significance of the Internet as part of an integrated communication mix;

(b) describe the design features of a typical webpage;

(c) develop a strategy for website development;

(d) explain how site design can facilitate relationship marketing;

(e) describe how the success of an Internet site might be measured;

(f) describe the media opportunities offered by interactive television/radio.

13.2 **Introduction**

No text on direct or interactive marketing would be complete without a consideration of the opportunities offered by the Internet. Since its introduction in 1991, the use of the Internet has grown faster than any other electronic medium, including, historically, the telegraph. In 1993, when the first web browser became available, only 130 Websites existed and only 1 per cent of these were commercial (or '.com') sites. By 1996, almost 75 per cent of the then 610,000 sites were .com (pronounced 'dot com') in nature. By the turn of the millennium, the number of organizations trading on-line numbered in the millions with many times that number of consumers seeking to do business. At the time of writing, growth rates are still so rapid that quoting more specific statistics is fraught with difficulty. They would almost certainly be out of date by the time the data was published.

Of course, the current growth rates are not sustainable. It seems likely that the exponential growth currently being recorded will reach a plateau within the next decade as the numbers of consumers and commercial organizations likely to benefit from a Web presence begin to reach the optimum. Indeed, it seems likely that the most significant growth over the next few years will occur in Asia where countries such as China are opening up web access for the first time.

The current statistics on internet growth are astounding. The US Internet Council estimates that the capacity of the Internet to handle traffic is doubling every 100 days. With over 13 million unique domain names (e.g. Amazon.com) registered worldwide at the end of 1999, the number continues to grow by 500,000 per week (NetNames Statistics 12/28/99). There are presently 1.6 billion pages of data, 350 million images and 29.4 trillion bytes of text (Censorware Project, January 26, 1999). What is all the more amazing is that a typical Webpage remains current for only around 44 days (Censorware Project, 26 January 1999). This means that to keep up with all the changes taking place it would be necessary for a user to download 873,000,000,000 bytes of information per day and have a connection capable of downloading over 10 million bytes per second!

In the US there are estimated to be over 159 million computer users, 135 million in the EU and 116 million in all of the Asia Pacific region (AEA CyberNation—April 2000). E-Marketer estimates that some 81 per cent of computer users go online and that the percentage is rapidly increasing (eMarketer/Harris Interactive February 2000). In the US in 1995 a mere 15 million households were online. That climbed to 46.5 million in January 2000 and is estimated to climb to 90 million by the end of 2004 (The Strategis Group—February 2000). A typical American spends 35 per cent of his/her working day on the computer and 23 per cent of their workday on the Internet (Heldrich Center for Workforce Development, Rutgers University—February 2000).

The value of the market created by this explosion in the number of internet users is estimated to be immense. Online consumer sales in Europe alone are expected to exceed $115 billion in 2003—a considerable increase from the figure of $5.4 billion recorded in 1999 (Dataquest October 1999). European business to business sales are also expected to experience dramatic growth, worth $1.27 trillion in 2004, up from $76 billion in 2000 (Durlacher—March 2000).

13.3 **Changing user profiles**

In total, 41 per cent of adults in Europe and the US are estimated to utilize the Internet. In just a few years, the profile of a typical user has shifted from a white middle class, educated male, aged 29–34, to become gradually more representative of society as a whole. As Figure 13.1 illustrates, a wider spread of ages are now represented by webusers with

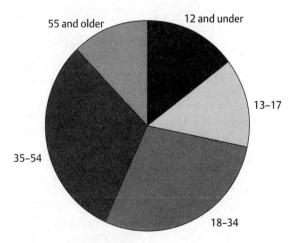

Fig. 13.1 Age profile of Internet users

more recent growth accounted for by both younger and older individuals. As the costs of access continue to decrease it seems likely that this trend will continue.

The demographic is also softening by gender. There has been a particularly sharp increase in recent years in the numbers of females using the Internet with the balance now only marginally in favour of males. There has also been a rise in the number of lower income or more poorly educated families connecting to the web for the first time and a sharp increase in the number of connections established purely for pleasure usage. Table 13.1 illustrates these differences.

It is interesting to note that some differences in behaviour have been reported between new and existing users. Those individuals who connected to the Internet two years or more ago tend to spend longer on line that those who have only recently connected. The former tend to spend 10.5 hours per week on line, whilst the latter spend only 6.6 hours (NUA/Roper Starch, November 1999)

It also appears that differences in behaviour exist between the various demographic categories, notably gender. Men, it seems, tend to visit rather different sites from women, concentrating on product categories such as electronics, entertainment, and home/office

Table 13.1 Changes in profile of Internet user

	Started using in the past year	Used more than a year ago
% of all Internet users	46	53
Gender		
Male (%)	48	55
Female (%)	52	45
Age		
18–29	25	30
30–49	52	50
50–64	16	15
65+	4	4
Income		
$50,000+	35	45
$30,000–$49,999	23	22
Under $30,000	23	16
Education		
University education	29	46
Some university	32	30
High school	33	19
< High school	6	3
Usage		
Work	24	30
Pleasure	52	39
Mix	22	31

Source: Pew Research Centre (2000)

Table 13.2 Top e-commerce sites by gender–percentage of users identifying as a favourite site

Men		Women	
Site	%	Site	%
Amazon.com	55	Amazon.com	49
Barnesandnoble.com	31	Barnesandnoble.com	30
CDNow.com	30	CDNow.com	24
Buy.com	25	EToys.com	21
Egghead.com	22	Drugstore.com	20
OfficeMax	16	JC Penney	18
Best Buy	15	Buy.com	17
Office Depot	14	Disney	17
eToys.com	13	PlanetRX.com	17
Reel.com	13	Bluemountainarts.com	15

Source: Ernst and Young 2000

supplies. Women, in contrast, tend to visit sites specializing in health, beauty, apparel, and on-line greetings. Table 13.2 illustrates this difference in preference.

Despite the almost exponential growth in the number of consumers going on-line, fewer than 40 per cent of web users are estimated to have actually made a purchase on-line, although it is worth noting that many consumers would appear to search for information on-line about products and services that they later acquire through more traditional channels. The power of the Internet to generate sales either directly, or indirectly should therefore not be underestimated.

Key barriers to on-line purchasing would appear to be concerns over the security of credit cards, privacy issues, and the perceived problem of returning defective or inappropriate merchandise. Consumer concerns in respect of security, in particular, have received considerable publicity in recent years, although the incidence of actual credit card theft over the Internet is estimated to be minimal and many times smaller than would occur in a traditional retail environment. As always, however, it is the perception that matters and many sites now go to great lengths to offer consumers secure connections where, they claim, the security of credit card information is assured.

Another major concern is privacy. Many consumers worry that by sharing information with a site perhaps to receive confirmation of an order, or a more tailored environment when they next visit the site, that they will, as a consequence, receive a high volume of unsolicited mail or e-mail. They also worry that their personal data might be shared with other organizations without their consent being sought. For many individuals the issue of privacy is thus a major concern and sites are increasingly compelled to offer some reassurance in this regard, by posting an easily accessible privacy statement which maps out exactly how personal information will be used (if at all).

Central to the issue of privacy is the cookie. A cookie is a small, encrypted data string that website servers write to the hard drive of a user's computer. It contains that user's unique User ID for the Web site. It can be accessed on subsequent visits to a site by the host computer and interrogated to eliminate the need for a user to log in. In effect, the cookie allows a site to recognize a returning visitor and, if appropriate, tailor the environment to suit their needs. Cookies can thus be used to deliver web content specific to visitor interests, keep track of their orders, and to control access to premium content. Cookies cannot be used to access or otherwise compromise the data on a user's hard drive.

Many users object to sites storing data on their hard drive and consider the practice an invasion of their privacy. The use of such mechanisms can therefore deter many potential visitors from returning once they discover the practice is in operation. For this reason many privacy statements make it clear whether cookies will be used and the aims of so doing. Indeed, many websites now offer the user the facility to disable the site cookies if they so desire.

13.4 Site design

The costs of setting up a web site for the first time can vary considerably. At the time of writing a typical business looking to create its own site can expect to pay anywhere between $300,000 and $3.4 million for the privilege. Such costs are clearly a function of the complexity of the site, the number of pages, the amount of information that will be posted and the degree of interaction that will be offered to visitors 'surfing' the site. Costs can also be a function of the quality of design undertaken and the degree of integration that will take place with other existing computer systems such as stock control and financial management.

Smaller businesses can find the costs of start-up considerably lower, with a number of Internet service providers (ISPs) now offering flexible design and hosting packages for only a few hundred dollars. For most businesses, however, the costs associated with establishing an Internet operation for the first time can be very considerable. It is therefore important that the design be carefully thought through to achieve its stated objectives

In designing a site the following points should be considered:

(a) Determine precise goals

The organization should be clear from the outset what the specific goals of the website will be. These might range from simply providing information about the organization to consumers or potential buyers, to specific sales targets for each of the organizations product or service lines. Only by specifying clear achievable objectives will an organization be able to subsequently design and monitor a web strategy that will adequately meet its needs.

(b) Keep the site simple

Whilst it might be tempting to adopt the most modern up-to-date graphic presentations and offer users complex levels of interaction and routes through the site, the most successful sites are undoubtedly those that are simple and easy to use. Many consumers who access a site for the first time will leave the site again after only a few seconds if it is not immediately apparent that the site will both meet their needs and be easy to navigate. If it takes an age to download complex graphics, potential visitors may be deterred and simply move on to the next site before the process is completed. Similarly, if a complex path must be navigated to find the pages that are of most interest, many users will lose interest before reaching their desired target. For this reason many homepages contain a simple navigation guide. Figure 13.2 illustrates an example—the WebMD homepage. The right-hand side of the screen contains a menu offering each class of user their own unique gateway into the site

Striving for simplicity in use, should therefore be an over-riding design specification and it would not be unusual for site designers to develop a series of flow charts that illustrate the route it is proposed that various classes of users will take through the site. These can subsequently be edited to ensure that navigation is as smooth, direct, and simple as possible.

(c) *Develop content that is both beneficial and pertinent to visitors*

Great care should be taken to ensure that the needs of the various target segments are reflected in the site. Of particular relevance here would be a consideration of the specific benefits that will be sought by potential users. These benefits might be either product related or category related. In the case of the former it might be sensible to group certain categories of product together that fulfill common needs. Amazon, for example, groups

Figure 13.2. WebMD home page

access to books, videos, and other product categories. In the case of the latter it might be more practical to group together products that fulfil certain lifestyle categories such as motoring, fishing, gardening, etc. Potential users could then have easy access to a range of very different products that might be related in some way to their unique interests.

It is also important to edit proposed content from a consumer's perspective. Whilst many sites may contain detailed information about the host organization and its products, much of the information may not be of direct relevance to potential purchasers and simply serve to lengthen download times and slow down access to pertinent material. At a simple level one should therefore be asking, 'what information do potential users really need?'

(d) Use caution in developing links to other sites

There are two primary reasons for offering this caveat. Firstly, organizations can find themselves in considerable legal difficulty if they suggest to those visiting their site that the site is in some way endorsed by a third party. Establishing links from a host site to another organization is therefore something that should be undertaken with considerable care. Indeed, it is good practice to seek the permission of any organization to which it is proposed to forge a link.

Aside from the legal difficulties that might be encountered in including links, a second major concern is the degree of encouragement that might be offered users to exit. Internet research has consistently shown that there are two major types of readers inhabiting the Web: Browsers and Seekers. Seekers are those that have a specific information need in mind and work their way methodically through sites to achieve their goal. Browsers, by contrast are using the web almost as one might drive a car for recreational purposes. They move from place to place looking for the next exciting experience or tranche of useful information. They keep one hand on the virtual doorknob (Johnston, 1999) and pay more attention to hyperlinked text on a page than to any other.

In attempting to retain this second category of user it is therefore somewhat ironic that many organizations are intent on providing as many possible exits as they can on a given screen. Clearly, one would wish to provide as friendly and useful an environment as possible for users, but providing higher numbers of links merely increases the likelihood that someone will be tempted away even before they have glanced at the content of the host organization's site.

(e) Aim for a middle ground between quick intelligible communication and strong graphics

Mention has already been made of the need for simplicity in site design. It is worth emphasizing, however, the role that the choice of graphics can play in the accessibility of a site. Until higher speed access to the web such as that offered by broadband technology (see Chapter 15) becomes the norm site designers need to be wary of the lowest common denominator in internet access technology. As was noted above, users faced with a lengthy time to download a given site will quickly tire of the process and move on.

On the other side of the coin, there is an expectation amongst consumers that big name companies and brands will offer sites that both impress the eye and give at least the impression of being technologically advanced. Such organizations thus face something of a trade off in the design of their sites and in particular their homepage (i.e. the gateway to a particular site).

The way around this problem is to offer users a choice. The Silicon Graphics web page, for example, tells users that a text only version of certain pages is available, thereby speeding access for those that desire it. Bell Atlantic, by contrast, offers three levels of access to its CyberLibrary; highspeed, medium speed, and text/minimal graphics.

Other sites show small versions of a picture first and allow the user to decide whether they wish to enlarge it. This can also work well in the case of video clips, with the size of the window greatly impacting on the time taken to download.

(g) Keep contact information in front of the visitor at all times

At any stage in visiting a website or perusing the data that is available, visitors may identify a need for further information. Users may also decide part-way through visiting a site that they do indeed want to make a purchase, or at least initiate a contact with a salesperson. Given the plethora of choices available in respect of potential suppliers, users are unlikely to take long to track down a companies contact information. It is thus good practice to ensure that the contact information for an organization is available at all times, perhaps following a convention such as providing it at the bottom of each page provided.

(h) Publicize your site in every medium possible

Designing an attractive and user friendly site will not in itself guarantee success. Potential customers and users still need to be made aware of the on-line presence. The launch and ongoing operation of a website should therefore be reflected in other forms of marketing communication an organization might generate. Business cards, advertising, and other forms of direct marketing communications should all feature the web address and seek to make it available at times potential customers might require it for access.

(i) Test and measure results

Once operational, it is essential that an organization review the performance of its site. There are a variety of different measures that can be employed for this purpose and an equal variety of measurement tools each with slightly different outputs and modus operandi. Some of the more common measurements undertaken are provided below:

Ad views (or impressions)—the number of times a WWW ad banner is downloaded by visitors.

Reach—the total number of users that a vehicle reaches—calculated by deriving the number of persistent, unique cookies present in a site's log files over a period of time.

Frequency—a measure of how often a unique user interacts with a site over a period of time—calculated as a series of requests by a unique visitor without 30 consecutive minutes of inactivity.

Visit—users' interaction with a site within a specified time period. The visit includes all the pages seen on the same site during one session. It is now common practice to consider a visit terminated when new pages are not consulted for more than 15–30 minutes dependant on the country in which the website is located.

Visit duration—the period over which a visit is undertaken. Most measurement software provides a range of data on this variable including mean, median, and modal durations.

Visitors—the number of individuals consulting the same site in a given period. The total number of visitors thus takes account of visit duplication. It should be noted that some systems refer to visitors as users.

Measurement software is also capable of tracking the movement through a particular site. By tagging each web page with a unique identification number it is possible to trace the typical way in which visitors, or specific segments of visitors, interact with the material presented. It can also track the typical duration that visitors spend viewing each individual page.

Clearly, all this data can be used to great effect in refining ineffectual aspects of the site and improving the quality of a visitor's experience.

13.5 Browser features

The software designed to allow a user to access, organize, and make sense of the web pages they visit is known as a browser. Such software allows the user to access various sites and to tailor their environment to suit their own requirements. Consider Figure 13.3. A typical browser will offer the following features:

13.5.1 Menu bar

The figure shows a home page accessed by Microsoft Explorer Software. The menu bar operates in an identical way to that present in any software application. The production of various editions of Windows software has created an expectation amongst consumers that they will be able to control their working environment from the top of the screen. Drop down functions include the ability to access and save files, editing functions, and the facility to jump directly to favourite web pages on-line.

13.5.2 Button bar–tool bar

The button or tool bar is to be found on most Internet browsers. It provides a more convenient and immediate access to a range of commands also found in the menus. Typical functions include:

Back—which allows the user to retrace their steps, either back through a particular site, or back to other sites visited previously. It should be noted that many companies are now

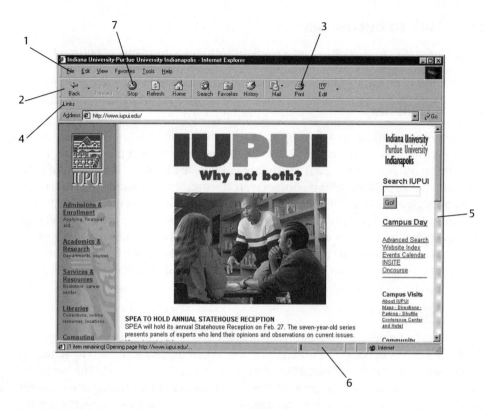

Fig. 13.3 Web browser

able to block (with their own software) the ability of a user to use the back key to exit from their site. This crude method for delaying exit serves only to irritate consumers and should be studiously avoided by ethical marketers.

Home—which takes the user back to a designated start page. This may be the website of their employer, Internet service provider, or another favourite site that they wish to access regularly.

Favourites (or bookmarks)—this provides access to a list of favourite web sites. In Microsoft explorer it is characterized by a file with an asterisk on the front. In Netscape, it is a tagged folder with 'Bookmarks' written above it.

13.5.3 **Uniform Resource Locator–URL**

This component of the display illustrates the address or Uniform Resource Locator of the Website the user is currently viewing. Each page on the web has a unique address and may be accessed by typing the detail in this box. Ideally, organizations should look to choose URLs that are easy to remember and have a clear link to the name of the organization or the nature of its work. In the case of amazon.com, the URL is simply the company's name whilst for the WWF Global Network the URL is panda.org.

13.5.4 **Link to button bar**

By clicking on this icon, a visitor can replace the URL area with a range of buttons linking to websites the visitor has been to recently.

13.5.5 **Scroll bar**

This button allows the user to move up or down the web page currently displayed. On the occasions when a scroll bar is absent, the user is already looking at the full page. When the material will not fit on one screen, the user must use the scroll bar to move around the page and read its content. Website designers are in effect working with a page that is 10–11 inches wide and 7–8 inches long. They have the facility to extend the page length, but doing so will extend the download time and visitors may lose interest before the full page appears on their screen. It is also important to note that where a longer page is created, the initial content presented (i.e. the top of the page) should be of sufficient quality and interest to encourage the user to use the scroll facility to read the whole page.

13.5.6 **Status bar**

When users first type in a new address and attempt to visit the site, the status bar updates them on progress in respect of finding that site. When the site is found, the status bar also provides users with an indication of the progress of the download. The bar to the right of the status bar indicates progress toward completing the download of the current page. Users experiencing difficulty, can often cease the download and revisit the site at a time when web traffic is less heavy.

13.5.7 **Stop**

The stop button simply allows the user to stop downloading a particular website. In Microsoft Explorer the STOP symbol is a stop light, whilst in Netscape it is a stop sign.

13.6 **Writing on-line**

Before a web page can be satisfactorily created a number of issues must be considered.

13.6.1 **Flow chart/site map**

When organizations prepare off the page advertising, or put together a product brochure, information is laid out in a linear format. Each paragraph of the document leads logically to another. In essence the designers have provided a logical sequence that guides the reader through each section of the information presented.

When writing for the web, however, a complex non-linear format replaces this simplistic framework. Websites generally consist of a maze of interlocking decisions and directions. For larger sites the easiest way of opening up access for visitors to the site is to consider offering a flowchart or site map which makes it very clear how the material within the site will be divided.

A flow chart such as the one in Figure 13.4 performs a number of functions. It:

- gives the users the freedom to create their own experience rather than be guided through pages that the organization feels might be appropriate;
- can highlight those aspects of the site that are most important and likely to be visited regularly;
- provides a useful pictorial overview of the information that the site contains.

13.6.2 **Inclusion of links**

Links such as item (i) in Figure 13.4 move the user to a new web page. In most versions of browser the cursor is pointing at a link when the arrow changes to a pointing finger. Pretty much any object can be designed as a link, but the five more common kinds are described below.

(a) **Text based links—hypertext links**

These are usually very easy to identify as they appear in a different colour to the rest of the text and are often underlined. The web page illustrated has a number of these links and they helpfully change colour after a visit to remind the user that they have already explored that link.

Most common browsers can also be set to remember pages that the users have visited. Microsoft Explorer, for example, allows users to set the colours of visited and unvisited links by accessing the View menu and clicking on Options. They then click the General tab and on the right of the screen will view a box illustrating the colour of visited and unvisited links. A colour palette allows the user to chose the colour they prefer in each case.

(b) **Images**

Links can also be also be created by graphics, icons, or photographs. As usual with a link, the cursor will change to a hand and pointed finger when directed at such an image. Clicking on the image will transfer the user to the new site or page.

(c) **Image maps**

Some of the more complex sites on the web have a number of different links embedded in a single picture or map. Such maps can be a very powerful way of illustrating the design and layout of the site. Figure 13.5 shows one such example. The links are usually obvious as in this example and users will see the cursor change into a hand as they move over various aspects of the map. A glance at the bottom of the browser will confirm that the destination URL changes as each part of the image is run over with the mouse. Clicking on any one item will move the user to that part of the site.

EGGHEAD.COM™

Valentine's Day
is Serious Business

MyEgghead | Help | **Home** | **Hardware** | **Software** | **Networking** | **Accessories** | **Office** | **Electronics** | **Clearance**

Register | Buy on Account | Order Status | Customer Service | Reference | Business |

SEARCH
• Search Tips
• Advanced Search

Merchandise Site Map

Resources

Help & Info   SuperStore Best Seller's   Shop by Brand   Manufacturer Rebates   Bid and Order Questions

| Hardware | Software | Accessories | Electronics |

Hardware

CD-ROM/CDRW/DVD
• CD-ROMs IDE
• DVD-ROM Drives
• CD-RW Drives

Desktop / Servers
• Cases / Chassis
• Intel Powered Servers
• Intel® Celeron™
• Intel® Pentium® III

Hard Drives / Storage
• IDE 10GB to 20GB
• IDE Over 20GB
• IDE Under 10GB
• Notebook HD
• SCSI 10GB to 20GB
• SCSI Over 20GB
• SCSI Under 10GB
• Tape Drives
• Zip & Removable

Mac Peripherals

Memory
• Apple Memory
• Flash Memory
• Laptop Memory

Modems / Fax-Modems
• PC Cards

Monitors / Display
• 17 inch
• 19 inch
• 21 inch
• LCD Flat Panel
• Projectors

Multimedia/Audio/Video
• Headphones & Mics
• CD-ROM/CDRW/DVD
• Sound Cards
• Speakers
• AGP Graphics Cards
• PC Video Cameras
• PC Video Cards
• Projectors
• Video Capture/Tuners
• Joysticks / Gamepads

Notebooks / Laptops
• Laptops Accessories

Printers / Multifunction
• Color Laser Printers

Software

Accounting & Finance

Business
• Office Suites
• Software Licensing
• Speech Recognition

Communication

Developer Tools
• Internet / Web Dev.

Games
• Action / Adventure

Graphics
• CAD / Drawing
• Desktop Publishing

Hobbies
• Home & Garden
• Home Publishing

Intra / Inter / Extranet

Kids & Education

Networking

OS Enhancements

Reference & Books
• Book Based Training

Utilities

Networking

Cables / Switch Boxes

Ethernet Switches

Faxes / Phones
• Phones

Hubs

Modems / Fax-Modems

Networking Business

Networking Software

NIC/Ethernet Adapters

Accessories

Adaptors / Connectors

Cables / Switch Boxes

Headphones & Mics

Input Devices
• Graphic Tablets
• Joysticks / Gamepads
• Keyboards
• Mice & Trackballs

Power/UPS/Batteries

Speakers

Ink & Toner

Media / Diskettes
• 4mm/DAT Tape
• CDR / CD-RW
• Zip & High Capacity

Laptops Accessories

Monitor Accessories

Printer Accessories
• Printer Cables

Office

Art / Drafting

Binders / Binding

Breakroom / Janitorial

Business Machines
Supplies

Calendars / Briefcases

Files / Filing

Labels

Mailing / Shipping

Office Basics

Office Forms / Records

Paper Products

Electronics

Audio Systems

Camcorders

Camera Accessories
• Power/UPS/Batteries

Digital Cameras

DVD/DVR/VCR

Flash Memory

MP3 Players

Multifunction Machines

PDAs / Handheld PCs

Phones

Power/UPS/Batteries

Projectors

Clearance

Desktop Computers

Home Office
• Copiers & Fax
• Cordless Phone
• PDA Organizers

Monitors / Displays

Multimedia

Laptops / Notebooks

Printers/Multifunction

Software

After Work

Country Market Foods

Cruises & Vacations

Electronics
• Digital Camera

About Us | Advertise With Us | Contact Us | Site Map | Investor Relations | Legal Notices | Work For Us

Fig. 13.4 Egghead site map

(d) **Blind links**

Blind links are becoming increasingly more common on the web. They are a somewhat devious attempt to bring additional users into a site. Users could, for example, be invited to click on an icon suggesting a free picture or download. Rather than either of these they are immediately directed to a new site. Unscrupulous webmasters have utilized this technique to great effect in uplifting traffic to particular sites. Of course, consumers have a habit of remembering such devious behaviour and it seems likely that they will avoid offending sites in the future.

13.6.3 **Long versus short copy**

When writing for the web many writers feel that long copy should be avoided. As direct marketers know all too well from their experience with direct mail this is not necessarily the case. The test is always whether the text is relevant and whether all the key information and reasons why a purchase should be considered are included. If extraneous information is provided, the text is too long, if it covers the key essentials, it is probably about right.

It should be remembered that many visitors will have 'self-selected' their visit. They will have determined that the site has relevance to their needs and will not necessarily be put off by longer copy. The key in writing text for the web, however, lies in breaking it up into manageable chunks. Copy should not fill one long page. If individuals have to continue scrolling down one page to reach the desired information they are considerably more likely to tire of the experience and leave.

Instead, web authors can compact the text by user a series of hypertext links. This allows the user to skip those sections of the text that are of no relevance and to jump immediately to those that are. Her Majesty's Stationery Office (hmso.govt.uk), for example, make many statutes, such as the Data Protection Act, available online. Rather than present the whole document as an extended page, the table of contents is offered as a menu and users can jump through a hypertext link to those sections of the Act which are of most interest.

13.6.4 **Bullets**

Whilst few organizations would choose to make an extensive use of bullet points in most of their corporate communications, bullet points and the Internet are a match made in heaven. Not only are they a convenient means of summarizing information, but bullet points can also be authored as hypertext links steering users from one section of the site to another. Bullet points can also be made an attractive feature of a given page.

13.6.5 **The power of words**

In designing copy for a web page many of the same rules apply as would be the case in direct mail, direct response press advertising, or indeed any other direct marketing media.

Image Map for the Racecourses of Ireland

Map of Ireland showing all the large Race Courses

To find out about any of the Race courses click on the Image Map or click on the links below

Curragh Derby Festival: June 28th-June 30th

Galway Festival: July 29th-Aug 3rd

Tralee Festival: Aug 25th-Aug 30th

Galway Autumn Festival: Sep 9th-Sep11th

Listowel Festival: Sep 23rd-Sep 28th

Leopardstown Christmas Festival: Dec 26th-Dec 29th

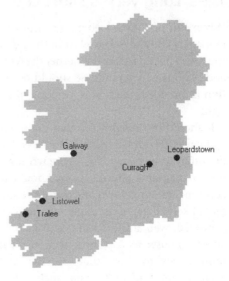

 Return to the M.R. Management home page.

Fig. 13.5 Image map

(i) Use short sentences and vary the length

In writing copy nothing matters except the meaning. Short sentences are OK. Verbs are not necessarily required. Not really. Nor is it necessary to create long verbose sentences that simply demonstrate one's dexterity in the use of punctuation. To quote George Smith (1996, p. 87):

'A (sentence) need not be long, need not defer to the Johnsonian tradition of the periodic sentence that ran to perhaps 200 words complete with subclauses and the full complement of colons and semi-colons to separate the various constructs; a tradition that continues to this day in the hands of writers such as Bernard Levin a journalist who rarely deploys 20 words when 200 can fulfil his sense of personal grandeur, a quality that some may admire but which most would resist on the basis that there are only so many hours a day in which one can read a newspaper.'

As Smith later notes—hands up those who fell asleep during that last sentence!

(ii) Use short paragraphs and vary the length

Paragraphs can consist of only one sentence.
There is nothing wrong with that.
But if a writer consistently engages that technique it can become boring.

Far better to group the ideas and ensure that the length of paragraphs is varied. This will not only look more visually appealing, the text should also be easier to read.

(iii) Talk benefits not features

Writing good copy requires that the text, particularly if it is designed to sell something, actually relates to the reason the reader might be viewing the page. It thus makes little sense to simply concentrate on regurgitating product features. Instead, the benefits that will accrue from using the product (or service) should be made apparent. If this sounds like a play on words consider the following example:

Power steering	Easy handling
Air bags	Improved safety
Greater interior volume	Increased comfort
Increased trunk capacity	Greater storage space
Faster acceleration	Safer overtaking

(iv) Use 'I' and 'you' not 'we' and 'one'

The difficulty in using words such as 'we' is that text can very quickly appear very pompous. A phrase such as 'we at the Oxford University Press' conveys a certain arrogance, where the use of 'I' makes the text more intimate, personal, and unassuming.

It is also good practice to allow potential buyers to 'rehearse' the benefits of ownership through the text. Phrases such as 'you will experience' put the buyer in the position of already owning the product and suggest to them how they will feel thereafter.

(v) Avoid clichés

Whilst the Internet is still comparatively new there are already words which are suffering from over-use. Words or phrases such as:

Cutting edge
Check it out

Cool

Hot

are not particularly helpful and will only serve to irritate the reader. Sites with original language stimulate the eye and gain additional attention.

(vi) Avoid polysyllables

Long words are rarely more impressive than shorter ones. They create the impression of a bureaucratic, inhuman organization that is distant from the needs of its customers. Smith (1996, p. 89) uses the following examples to make the point.

Approximately	About
Participate	Take part
Establish	Set up
Utilize	Use

13.7 Marketing on-line

Of course, authoring and presenting a site is only one way in which an organization might utilize the web for the purposes of marketing. A number of other opportunities are presented by this new medium. These include web rings, reciprocal links, e-mail, and news groups.

13.7.1 Web rings

These are a comparatively recent phenomenon and are, in essence, an association of related sites. They are designed to link together in a way that creates the impression of a single community, with a single focus in mind. There are many thousands of these presently in existence and the number continues to grow daily. Organizations could thus consider joining a ring currently established or form one of their own. Thus, in consumer markets it may make sense for organizations offering products/services pertinent to one life-style category to get together and form an alliance in this way. Ring World is a helpful central index of such rings and information in respect of starting up a new Web ring can be found at *www.webring.com.*

13.7.2 **Reciprocal links**

Even if it does not prove possible to establish the more formal exchange of customers that would typically be a feature of a web ring, it may still be possible to forge alliances with specific individual organizations who offer services or products complementary to those of a given organization. Links could be provided to the website of this complementary supplier in return for them providing a similar link offering customers a route in the opposite direction.

This is by far the most common kind of web marketing strategy. Almost all commercial websites now contain some kind of reciprocal links to other organizations. These might be to sites offering related products or services, or to sites that the host believes will be of wider interest.

To encourage such links it would be normal for webmasters from commercial sites to talk to those responsible for the management of other sites to see whether some form of collaboration might be possible. If agreement can be reached it would be usual for a short description of the site to be provided, together with an icon or graphics which can be inserted in the reciprocating site, containing a hyperlink which will then direct the user to the new site. This site would reciprocate by having a similar link to the partnering site.

Those organizations wishing to maximize the opportunity for reciprocal links would be advised to maintain a short description of this site and an icon that can be used for the purpose of developing a link on their site. Interested parties could then copy this and provide a link.

Of course, whilst this might maximize links, there is also the danger that links might appear on inappropriate sites, suggesting an arrangement that does not in fact exist. The webmaster responsible for a site needs, therefore, to be clear up front in respect of the degree to which the creation of links will be encouraged.

It should be noted that there are ways to identify whether any reciprocal links might already be in place. One need only visit *www.altavista.com* and search for its own site typing link: www.your.domain. The results of the search will then reveal those organizations that have already established a link to the site.

13.7.3 **Link exchanges**

Small organizations, or those operating on limited web budgets may draw some benefit from another comparatively recent phenomenon—the link exchange. These act somewhat like cooperatives, in that organizations join a number of other link members in promoting each other's sites. Each member must prepare a graphic banner for display on other sites containing their link and agree to display the links of partner organizations. A monitoring system for each link exchange keeps track of how often a banner appears on member sites and how often that particular member shows the banners of other members. The number should roughly equate, to ensure a fair distribution of benefit. There are a number of companies that specialize in fostering this kind of link exchange–the most obvious being *http://www.linkexchange.com*.

13.7.4 **e-mail**

E-mail can be a very cost effective tool for marketing over the web. It can be particularly effective where a relationship already exists between a customer and supplier and where, as a consequence, permission will have been given for the organization to make contact in this way. More thoughtful users of e-mail communications attempt to tailor the content of the communications to the specific needs of the individual and offer a very clear 'opt-out' facility where the customer can delete themselves from the list and therefore decline to receive subsequent communications.

13.7.5 **News groups**

There may be some occasions when an organization is engaged in activities or presenting products that might in some sense be newsworthy. If this is the case it may be worth an organization considering the use of Internet news groups. There are many thousands of these, each of which is focused on a specific issue or topic. On-line press releases can be targeted at any news groups it is felt might have an interest in the subject matter of the item. Infinite Ink offer a useful service for locating news groups on specific issues: *http:// www.ii.com/internet/messaging/newsgroups/*.

13.7.6 **Announcement sites**

With so many new sites appearing on the web every day, a new category of web directory has appeared—that of the announcement site. Such sites provide links to the newest additions to the web. Unlike search engines they don't have robots searching for data and thus rely on manual postings. Listings are typically only for a short period and usually a maximum of two to four weeks. Some announcement sites focus exclusively on new sites, whilst others are more flexible and willing to consider new additions to an existing site. Submit-it has a useful directory which might be helpful in identifying appropriate announcement sites. It can be found at *www.directoryguide.com*.

13.8 **Search engines**

Table 13.3 presents a summary of the most visited sites on the web. It is no accident that a number of search engines make it onto this list. A search engine is, in essence, a site that provides a gateway for users to those sites on the web most likely to match their interests or information needs. The user simply types in key words or phrases that reflect their needs and the search engine searches the web (or rather its memory of the web) to retrieve page listings which are normally sorted by relevance.

No one search engine yet covers the whole web, but a large number of sites are typically recorded in the search engine's database. The task for an internet marketer is to ensure that their site is listed on as many search engines as possible and that the listing

Table 13.3 Top sites—January 2000

Rank	Web site	Unique visitors (000)
1	Yahoo.com	36,820
2	Aol.com	36,691
3	Geocities.com	28,492
4	msn.com	26,746
5	Lycos.com	21,251
6	Angelfire.com	18,124
7	Passport.com	17,991
8	Netscape.com	17,629
9	Microsoft.com	17,331
10	Tripod.com	17,226

adequately reflects the content of the site. Position Agent (*http://www.positionagent.com*) allows users to identify what each search engine has as a listing for their organization. Various combinations of key words that researchers might use can be input and the site will then report back and tell the enquirer on what page and in what position its URL occurs in each category in each of the major search engines. If the site is not listed on the first page in a given category the chances of a user actually accessing the site through the search engine rapidly diminish. Few users scan beyond three or four pages of URL listings before choosing to open a site.

So how do search engines gather data about sites on the web? They actually run software programs called robots or spiders that continually crawl around the web looking for new pages. They record information about every new page they encounter and add it to the engine's database. The robot records all of the text of the page and the search engine then analyses it ready to include it in its index.

Thus, one really need do nothing to have a company website recorded on a search engine. However, in practice, the robots spend a lot of time crawling around sites they have already visited updating the material on file by looking for changes. It could take considerable time for a new site to be identified. It is thus better for a marketer to be proactive, approach the engines directly and give them the information first hand.

There are many search engines on the web. The most common are listed in Table 13.4. On each of the sites hosted by these engines, it should be possible to find a link entitled ADD A SITE or ADD YOUR URL. The webmaster responsible for a particular new site could therefore visit the key search engines and rapidly update them in respect of their site's existence. What happens from there is that the website is added to the list of sites for a robot to visit. The site will only be added to the search engine's database after it has been visited by a robot. Manual registration along the lines described merely allows the organization concerned to queue jump.

Of course, visiting all the key search engines can be somewhat tedious. The reader will therefore not be surprised to learn that there are a number of specialist companies that will undertake this work on behalf of an organization. The fee is usually less than $100

Table 13.4 Major Internet search engines

- Infoseek *http://www.infoseek.com*
- AltaVista *http:// www.altavista.com/cgi-bin/query?pg=aq&what=web*
- LiveLink Pinstripe *http://pinstripe.opentext.com/*
- Excite Search *http://www.excite.com*
- Google (Beta) *http://www.google.com/*
- HotBot *http://www.hotbot.com/*
- Microsoft Network Search *http://www.msn.com/*
- Webcrawler *http://www.webcrawler.com*
- Lycos *http://www.lycos.com*
- Savvy Search Multi-Search *http://guaraldi.cs.colostate.edu:2000/*
- Savvy Search Form *http://guaraldi.cs.colostate.edu:2000/form*
- Yahoo! *http://www.yahoo.com*
- Yahoo Search Options *http://search.yahoo.com/bin/search/options*
- Magellan *http://www.magellan.com*
- DogPile *http://www.dogpile.com/*
- Highway 61 Multisearch *http://www.highway61.com*
- Mamma Mother of All Search Engines *http://www.mamma.com/*
- WebSearch MetaSearch *http://www.web-search.com:80/*
- CNETs Search.com Multi-Search Page *http://search.cnet.com/*
- EDirectory search engines from around the world *http://www.edirectory.com/*
- EuroFerret European Site Search *http://www.euroferret.com/*
- International Regional Search Engines *http://searchenginewatch.com/regional/*
- Inquiry Com Information Technology Search *http://www.inquiry.com/*
- Mediafinder *http:www.mediafinder.com/custom.cfm*
- NameSpace Whois Domain Information *http://whois.namespace.org/?*
- Domain Name Search *http://www.ibc.wustl.edu/ibc/domain form.html*
- Study Web Research Site *http://www.studyweb.com/*
- Library of Congress Search *http://lcweb.loc.gov/harvest/*
- FindLaw Legal Search *http://www.findlaw.com/index.html*
- Legal Search Engines *http://www.uklaw.net/lawsearch.htm*
- InfoMine Government info search *http://lib-www.ucr.edu/search/ucr govsearch.html*
- MedScape *http://www.medscape.com/*
- HealthGate Free Medline *http://www.healthgate.com/HealthGate/MEDLINE/search.shtml*
- Medical Matrix Medline Search *http://www.medmatrix.org/info/medlinetable.html*
- Liszt Mailing Lists *http://www.liszt.com*
- Companies *http://www.companiesonline.com/*
- Edgar *http://www.sec.gov/edaux/searches.htm*
- Open Directory Project *http://dmoz.org/*
- Galaxy Professional Directory *http://www.einet.net/*
- Galaxy Adv. Search *http://www.einet.net/cgi-bin/wais-text-multi*
- Lycos A2Z Internet directory *http://a2z.lycos.com/*
- Infoseek Directory *http://www.infoseek.com/*
- Nerd World Subject Index *http://www.nerdworld.com*
- Jump City (Plus Newsgroups) *http://www.jumpcity.com/list-page.html*
- Starting Point *http://www.stpt.com/*

- Suite 101 *http://www.suite101.com/*
- Brint: A Business Researchers Interest *http://www.brint.com/interest.html*
- Martindale's Reference Center *http://www-sci.lib.uci.edu/~martindale/Ref.html*
- About.com (Formerly The Mining Company) *http://www.about.com/*
- Netguide Live (Best of the Web) *http://www.netguide.com*
- Librarian's Guide: Best Info on the Net *http://www.sau.edu/CWIS/Internet/Wild/index.htm*
- Computer Currents Interactive Links of the Week *http://www.currents.net/magazine/reviews/webrevws.html*
- Digital Librarian Best of the Web *http://www.servtech.com/public/mvail/home.html*

and for this sum, the company will usually register the site with over 200 search engines, directories and announcement pages on the web. Examples of companies offering this service are submit-it.com and acclaimweb.com

The search engines will not treat all the content of a web page as being equally significant. Certain sections of the page receive more weight than others. It is therefore essential that webpages are designed to maximize the opportunity to achieve a good listing.

13.8.1 **TITLE key words**

Each web page should be given a title. By title, we do not mean the section of bold text that appears across a visitors screen. Rather we mean a specific chunk of hidden code that helps to identify the page, but which visitors are unaware of. The <HEAD> section of each page should contain a <TITLE> section which in turn contains a description of the content of the page. Search engine robots will scan the data stored in the <TITLE> section. This is the text that is displayed by the search engine, when it generates its list of 'hits' for the user.

13.8.2 **<META> tags**

Meta tags are also codes that the user will not be aware of. They can be read by special programmes, however, and in particular by robots as they attempt to refine the profile of each page in their respective database. Information in the META tags will be used to inform the way in which a particular page is indexed.

13.8.3 **<ALT> image tags**

Organizations employing a lot of images on their site, may well make the site attractive to visitors, but they can also make them invisible to search engines. Organizations, for example, depicting their company's logo or name in a fancy graphic may well find that the name is invisible to robots since they search text not graphics. The way around this problem is for the web page designer to use Image Tags which contain a brief description of each of the pictures on a page. These are again invisible to a standard browser, but they can be read by robots making the listing of a company's site all the more effective.

13.9 **Web directories**

The search engines listed in Table 13.4 have an enormous task. They attempt to list every site on the web. Users visiting a search engine can therefore quickly find themselves swamped with masses of relevant and—importantly—not so relevant material. For this reason a site that would actually be of great interest to a user can be buried under a list of spurious citations of only limited appeal. To get around this problem some users now employ the services of a web directory. These consist of nothing more than a list of sites known to be of relevance to a particular topic. Web directories can be very general (e.g. travel) or highly focused (e.g. fly fishing). Many of the larger, which can often contain the details of many thousands of sites are divided into sub-categories and are designed to be searched by key-word.

Web-directories rely on manual submission as they do not run robots to collect site data. The owners of such sites review paper or electronic notifications of new sites and then decide for themselves whether it is appropriate to forge an additional link to this site. Anyone new to the task of 'hunting down' new directories may find the site (// ds.internic.net/ds/dsdirofdirs.html) helpful. It is a Directory of Directories and users can use the site to identify those that are likely to be of relevance to their product or service category.

13.10 **Relationship marketing on the web**

Writers such as Brondo and Moore (2000) advocate that good websites should treat different constituents differently. They suggest that websites should identify, differentiate, interact, and customize if they are to build relationships with consumers successfully. Each of the facets they suggest is briefly described below:

13.10.1 **Identify**

Websites should capture information in respect of users. This involves much more than simply gathering the name and address of visitors, but rather gathering information about their habits, preferences and interests. Of course, there is a trade-off here. Web users are increasingly being asked for their details when they visit specific sites. The most effective way to encourage completion appears to be in tying it to specific benefits such as a tailored environment or home page, or specific promotional offers.

Some sites have recognized user reticence to supply information and have adopted a 'build' policy in the sense that only a few details are recorded each time a user visits a site. Over time a detailed profile is built up, yet users perceive that the data collection process is minimal and inoffensive. The method is known as 'drip irrigation' dialogue.

13.10.2 **Differentiate**

To build a relationship strategy in the web one needs to understand the relative worth of each user. In some circumstances, it can thereafter be appropriate to tailor the content to reflect relative worth. At its most simple level this may involve prioritizing the effort of designers to offer the greatest utility to higher value customers.

It is also possible to differentiate content by the needs of particular users, using a technique known as 'collaborative filtering'. This involves comparing the interests of a specific user with those of a larger cohort of visitors with a similar profile. In essence, the organization can demonstrate to a user they know what he/she might be interested in and offer a list of pertinent suggestions for purchase. Aside from engendering a feeling of relationship this technique can also provide substantial added value, by suggesting resources that the user might not otherwise have been aware of. The Amazon site, for example, when a purchase is made, prompts the user with a list of other books that people who bought that specific book in the past also purchased.

13.10.3 **Interact**

The most effective websites engage the potential purchaser in a dialogue and add value by being seen to interact with the user. Many examples of successful interaction abound. The Fedex website for example allows users to input a consignment number and to track the progress of a particular package. This has greatly reduced the telephone traffic to the organization's call centre and thus allowed the organization to cut costs, whilst actually enhancing the service provided. Similarly, e-Trade.com allows users to specify information that they might receive from the site. They may, for example, wish to be notified when the price of a stock reaches a certain level. The company will then e-mail them and provide a link to the site should the user wish to buy or sell as a consequence.

13.10.4 **Customize**

The final aspect of implementing a relationship strategy lies in customizing some aspect of the service based on a particular user's needs. Many of the newer sites allow users to visit a site and to tailor the nature of the product to their own specific requirements. You can for example, now specify the characteristics that a new car will have on delivery, or pick and mix the features that will be added to a new computer before it is shipped from the factory.

In many ways, this fourth dimension follows from the first. Having gathered information about users it is important that the organization then uses that knowledge to add value for consumers, by customizing the offering as a result. This may involve offering the facility to tailor the product (as above) or it may involve tailoring the aftersales service, or the manner in which the organization stays in touch. The World Wildlife Fund, for example, sends out regular updates on specific issues that it knows a number of visitors to the site will find of interest.

In using the Internet as a relationship building tool, therefore, organizations should pay particular attention to the four dimensions listed above and perhaps appraise their performance against the best performing sites on the web. They may also find it instructive to conduct an analysis of the performance of related sites (perhaps those of firms in the same product category) to develop a benchmark of their own performance and delineate scope for potential improvement.

13.11 Interactive television

Interactive television has been offered since 1999 in the UK and for a similar period of time in selected pilots in the US. It represents the first real attempt to engage viewers equipped with modern digital technology to engage in a two-way conversation with advertisers and/or programme makers. The earliest attempts to offer interactive TV (iTV) linked the digital decoder (which unscrambled satellite or cable broadcasts) to the subscribers own telephone line. The use of a modem allowed the box to communicate with the system operator when subscribers wished to make a purchase, request additional information about a product or access an interactive service, such as e-mail.

Most early systems allowed the viewer to enter the interactive section of their channel package by selecting it just as they would any of the traditional viewing channels. They were then faced by a menu very similar to that they might encounter on the Internet. By highlighting and clicking on a range of icons, the user could very quickly enter and play a range of computer games, or look to make a number of purchases from one of a number of on-line stores. In these early pilots, however, the interactive environment was held largely separate from the 'normal' television environment and the opportunity to directly interact with specific broadcasts was very limited. Early versions of iTV were very limited and offered access to only a small range of goods and services. As the technology improves and begins to offer full integration with normal television viewing radical changes to the way in which television is enjoyed will shortly be forthcoming.

13.12 eTV

Many organizations are now beginning to recognize the potential of an emerging medium termed 'Enhanced TV' or eTV for short. It is really an advanced form of interactive television and looks set to transform traditional mass media such as broadcast television and the Internet.

eTV allows certain technologies to deliver graphics and information content to the same screen as a video programme. These elements thus appear on top of video programming viewed on traditional television sets. See Figure 13.6 for an example. The additional elements can be opaque or transparent or semi-transparent. They tend to be icons,

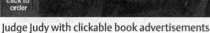

| Judge Judy with clickable book advertisements | Navigation Bar over lawsuit participant |

Fig. 13.6 Judge Judy

banners, labels, menus, information about the programme, data that may be printed, open text fields (e.g. for a user to send an e-mail address), or even forms that may be completed in order to buy a product.

Swedlow (2000) argues that 'what was once . . . a passive, linear, absorbing-only, viewing experience for millions of people around the world can now become a participatory, non-linear viewing and communications medium as well'. People will be empowered to develop a dialogue with the producers and/or characters of shows and to e-mail their friends/relatives immediately about a particular channel's content. They will also be able to join in games, clubs, or to purchase related merchandise, as the Judge Judy example shows.

It is expected that news, sport, game shows, and children's programmes will fare particularly well in this new environment as viewers are offered increasing opportunities to interact with the programme. It is also expected that 'video-on'demand' which the digital environment offers will prove immensely popular as will the facility to engage in home shopping, or special promotions that are designed to link the consumer with paid advertising (See Figure 13.7).

Of course, the cost of providing eTV services is likely to be initially very high. At the time of writing it is likely that these will be offset by some combination of the following:

- fee per subscriber;
- revenue sharing (between the channel owner and advertisers);
- advertising;
- transaction revenue;
- sponsorship.

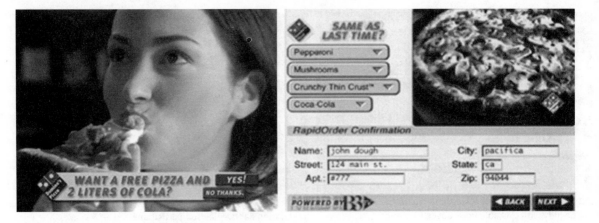

Fig. 13.7 Domino Pizza ads

13.13 **Digital radio**

Just as television is currently undergoing a revolution, so too is radio. In the UK it was as long ago as 1995 that the BBC began offering its first digital broadcasting. In 1999, the corporation offered its first digital-only radio service, although consumer awareness of the new medium is still relatively low. This has largely been due to the fact that digital radio cannot be received on traditional radio receivers.

When radio made the quantum leap from AM to FM over a generation ago, listeners were offered a revolution in the quality of the broadcasts they could receive. Gone were the hisses and crackles of medium and long wave. In came the stereo sound and greater bandwidth afforded by frequency modulation. Digital radio will offer a similar quantum leap offering listeners a completely interference-free environment, a facet that should prove particularly attractive to listeners on the move in cars, etc. It will also offer CD quality sound a much wider choice of programmes and, ultimately, text and data services.

In the future, radio will thus be capable of offering interactive services much in the same way as television, alluded to above. This represents a significant opportunity given that in the UK, the radio audience measurement organization (RADAR) estimates that 91 per cent of the population listen to the radio at least once a week. Radio is felt to be particularly pervasive since it can be regarded as a secondary medium (i.e. it is usually consumed whilst the listener is doing something else).

The ability to broadcast scrolling text alongside the programme content is already exciting some advertisers. It can be used to cite dedications, the details of competitions, or even to provide additional information to supplement advertising or programme sponsorship.

The contemporary hit station Core, for example, offers listeners an enhanced range of services. 'Core Control' allows listeners to pick a song and dedicate it to someone they know. The system then informs the user exactly when it will run and illustrates the dedication in text. The station has also run a promotion with Warner Music to run a text line credit informing users when the track is featured on a new CD.

It should also be possible to arrange the content of digital radio broadcasting like a website in the sense that users enjoying a particular track might be afforded the opportunity to hear news and/or an interview with the pertinent artist, purely by clicking an icon or pressing a particular button. Doubtless, the accompanying text will appraise future listeners of these opportunities.

Of course, all these applications do not presently offer a return path. It does seem likely, however, that PC manufacturers will shortly offer a digital radio facility thereby facilitating the development of an appropriate return path. The manufacturer Psion, for example, launched its first digital radio 'Wavefinder' device for connection to a PC in October 2000. It seems likely that such digital technology will also be included in mobile phones in the near future. It is particularly interesting to note that digital radio is an 'addressable' technology, allowing stations to address specific content to specific users. One can therefore easily imagine a scenario in which lifestyle information is collected in respect of new subscribers and then used to drive the specific nature of the advertising they receive. The adaptive nature of the technology would also make it possible to improve the nature of this targeting as the user's pattern of response is recorded and analysed.

13.14 **Summary**

In this chapter, we have reviewed briefly a number of the new e-media which can be employed for the purposes of marketing. In particular we have examined the role of the Internet, the opportunities created by the medium and a number of the key facets of doing business in this arena. It was argued that a sequential development process be adopted and that at the page level, many of the same design concerns arise as would be the case with traditional print media. We have suggested how some of these issues might best be dealt with. We have also reviewed the techniques that can be employed to promote a site and encourage visits. Of particular note was the use of search engines and the techniques that could be employed to attract the attention of their spiders to new sites or the amended pages of existing ones.

It seems clear that the use of electronic channels for both consumer and business to business marketing will continue to grow over the next decade. The pace of technological change makes it essential that organizations continue to appraise themselves of the opportunities available and to plan innovative new ways of developing the level of interaction and customization they offer to customers as a consequence.

Discussion questions

1   You are the marketing manager of Leeds United Football Club. Suggest how the Internet could be used by the club to promote the team.

2   What factors might you bear in mind in designing a website for a florist offering delivery of bouquets, etc. across the country? How might the site be laid out? What advice would you offer designers?

3   How might a small nonprofit organization setting up a web presence for the first time publicize the existence of its site?

4   You work in the life insurance industry. Your managing director believes that interactive TV might offer your company a new and exciting sales channel. She has asked you for some guidance in a report outlining what you consider to be the key advantages and disadvantages of the medium.

5   In your role as the marketing manager of a large multinational firm you are preparing a presentation to a visiting group of students about recent developments in e-media. Outline the points that you would cover in this presentation.

Further reading

Brondo H. P. and Moore G. (2000) *The Engaged Customer: The New Rules of Internet Direct Marketing* (New York: Harper Business)

http://www.netnames.com/template.cfm?page = statistics&advert = yes

http://www.censorware.org/web_size/

http://www.aeanet.org/aeanet/research/ordercybernation.asp

http://www.emarketer.com/ereports/econsumer/welcome.html

http://strategis.commnow.com/

http://gartner11.gartnerweb.com/dq/static/dq.html

http://www.durlacher.com/fr-pub.htm

http://www.nua.ie/surveys/

Johnston M. (1999) *The Fund Raisers Guide to the Internet* (New York: NSFRE, Wiley).

Smith G. (1996) *Asking Properly: The Art of Creative Fundraising* (London: White Lion Press).

Swedlow T. (2000) http://www.itvt.com/etvwhitepaper.html   Interactive TV Today.

Case study: Vietnam National Administration of Tourism (VNAT)

The scenario

Pat Lim snapped shut the lid of her briefcase and gazed out the window. Her train was just passing the district of Phu Yen, possibly one of the most unspoilt regions of the country, on its journey south towards Ho Chi Minh City. The view from the carriage was astounding—mile after mile of unspoilt sandy beach, punctuated only by an occasional cluster of palms. It was simply impossible to ignore the natural beauty of the coastline as it glided slowly past the carriage. 'How could I ever fail in this role?' she thought to herself.

A graduate from Assumption University in Thailand, with several years' business experience, Pat had recently been appointed as the Marketing Director of the Vietnam National Administration of Tourism (VNAT). Her success in achieving this new position had come as something of a shock to her, because although she had desperately wanted to take on the role, she was slightly surprised that the Vietnamese government had seen fit to appoint a foreigner. Perhaps, she mused, they had wanted to get an outside perspective on what was proving to be a very unique problem.

Gazing at the array of paperwork strewn across the table in front of her, she wondered quite where to start. Forty eight hours was not long in which to consider the primary issues and as the train journey was likely to continue for some time yet, this seemed like a good opportunity to think through the problem once more.

Two days from now she would be expected to make a presentation to the government representatives on the VNAT board in respect of the potential new marketing strategies that VNAT could pursue. 'We need to attract 10 per cent more visitors per annum, for each of the next five years' she had been told. That was her target. Just how she was going to recommend accomplishing this however, when the data she had been supplied with was of such poor quality, was quite another matter.

She had already spent what seemed like an eternity reviewing the material she had been given and was beginning to lose track of all she had read. Unfortunately, most of the data she had received seemed to consist of meaningless figures relating to new hotel developments or details of the personnel involved in one or more of the government's new initiatives. A small number of documents were, however, somewhat more illuminating and, in particular, the briefing document written by her predecessor was proving to be invaluable. She remembered having had a few ideas when she last read through it at the start of her journey in Hanoi. Perhaps it was time to glance through it again.

The Briefing Document

Introduction

The travel and tourism industry continues to increase in importance for Vietnam. Identified as one of a small number of strategic priorities to aid in the economic regeneration of the country, moves are already afoot to heighten the profile of the country as a major international destination. The Vietnamese government has already begun to allow its national airline greater independence from the state, and foreign access has been greatly facilitated through a progressive relaxing of immigration regulations. Visas are now much easier to obtain and the VNAT organization is already beginning to promote Vietnam in a number of markets across the globe.

The real aim of these initiatives is to enable the country to regain the position it held in the world travel market prior to the war with the United States. This is not likely to be an easy task. Many other Asian countries have long since entered the tourism market and carved out unique identities for themselves on the world stage. Nevertheless, VNAT officials remain optimistic about the potential for growth and feel that the reforms of the past 10 years and a new era of relations with the United States will greatly facilitate the necessary strategic actions.

History of Vietnamese Tourism

The Vietnamese economy was devastated by thirty years of war. Even when the conflict was brought to an end in 1975, widespread mismanagement and the effects of the US boycott combined to stifle any fledgling signs of recovery. Indeed, the communist government operated a very traditional command style of economy and it was not until 1986 that real change began to be instituted. In a bid to revitalize the economy the government introduced a policy of 'doi moi' (the Vietnamese equivalent of perestroika), involving widespread market reforms and a push towards privatization. The measures clearly had the desired impact as the economy has recently seen a rapid increase in its pace of growth.

This, combined with improving relations both with the West and with other members of the ASEAN (Association of South East Asian Nations) organization which Vietnam joined in 1996, have combined to strengthen the country's overall position.

The Tourism Potential

Of course, it will be a while yet before Vietnam can reap the full benefit of the changes described above. Whilst external perceptions of the country are improving, the creation of an infrastructure which would support a sustained growth in the tourism sector is still proving somewhat problematic. The key to this is undoubtedly the attraction of foreign investment, but there remain many administrative hurdles that must be removed before this can really begin to happen. Corruption, for example, remains a major problem. Difficulties have also been encountered in disposing of the last remnants of the old communist bureaucracy and some foreign investors have been actively discouraged from putting money into tourism initiatives by what is increasingly seen as unnecessary 'red-tape'. Government systems are, however, beginning to change and a very real effort is now being made to encourage as much inward investment as possible.

Indeed, the potential for tourism is immense, if only because the country has so much to offer its visitors. Vietnam's natural resources include delightful sandy beaches, caverns, spas, marine islands, many places of unique and unconventional beauty, and a rich variety of plants and animals. Moreover, the population of the country is culturally diverse with some 60 distinct ethnic groups represented. Vietnam thus has much to offer in terms of both its physical beauty and the rich cultural history of its people.

The attempts to exploit these natural advantages are currently centring on three key zones, namely:

(a) Northern
The Northern Centre comprises Hanoi-Haiphong-Quang Ninh and its precincts. The area has two airports, one domestic and one international (Hanoi). It also has two seaports.

Hence, the region is easily accessible. This area has been earmarked for the development of business, conference, and leisure tourism, particularly commercial, mountain and seaside tourism.

(b) Central

The central zone consists of Hue-Danang-Nha Trang Quang Tri provinces and precincts. This area has two airports at Danang and Hue, the international border gate and Lao Bao which gives access from the Lao People's Democratic Republic and Thailand, and seaports at Hue and Danang. This centre is particularly concerned with developing projects in cultural and historical heritage preservation and conservation.

(c) Southern

The Southern Centre includes the Ho Chi Minh City—Bien Hoa—Vung Tau provinces and precincts. The area has a relatively good transport infrastructure and is easily accessible from abroad with an international airport and road network access from Cambodia and Thailand, and 11 waterways connecting to the Mekong river. The Southern Centre has been earmarked for the development of business centres and tourist resorts. Eco-Tourism will be a particular feature.

The cool, damp winter (October to April) and a hot humid summer (May to September), allow the tourist season to be spread out over the year, i.e. three to five months in the North: October-December and May/June; and four to eight months in the Centre: January-August—thus creating a substantial window of opportunity.

The first steps

The first key step forward undoubtedly came in the late 1980s when the decision was taken by the government to designate 1990 as 'Visit Vietnam Year'. A general lack of promotional effort and (at that time) a lack of supporting infrastructure doomed the project to failure (only 250,000 tourists were recorded). However, a wide-ranging reform of many tourism management structures was initiated in preparation for this year, including a law allowing private companies to enter tourism markets for the first time and certain pubic sector companies to gain three year international tour operating licences. Finally, a fledgling infrastructure was beginning to emerge.

In June 1993, a decision was issued by the prime minister's office for state ministries and government offices to transfer all guest houses and rest-houses under their control into 'business units' under the supervision of VNAT. The aim was to give them their financial independence and to encourage an entrepreneurial management, whilst retaining some control over the standards thereof. Indeed, in December 1993, the government specified a licensing system for hotels, guest houses, and other accommodation units and in mid-1995 began implementing a hotel classification system.

Major strides forward have been made in the attraction of other hotel operators to the country. International hotel groups such as Sofitel, New World, and Century now have a presence in Vietnam, whereas only six years ago the Vietnamese had to resort to towing in ships and converting them to hotels that were berthed on the banks of the Saigon river. The first such property, the Saigon Floating Hotel, has now had its licence revoked and will be towed out, allegedly to improve the landscape.

Most of the early construction of hotels was concentrated in the commercial capital, Ho chi Minh City, which has placed the city in the grip of an over-supply of quality hotel rooms. No redress is expected for at least another two years by which time another 3,000 hotel rooms are expected to open. Occupancy levels have dropped to about 45 per cent and there is increasing pressure on room rates.

According to Travel Trade Report, Saigontourist estimates that 300,000 international tourists stayed in its hotels in 1996, an increase of 6 per cent on 1995.

While the urban capitals are expected to continue to see growth in the five star hotels, coastal areas such as Ha Long, Hue, Danang, Nha Trang and Ba Ria-Vung Tau will also see the development of supplementary hotels and resort properties. The government's aim is to secure about 10-15 tourism resort projects by 2002. Indeed, Danang is already set to become the first beach resort in Vietnam to get an international hotel since the war, with the opening in mid-1997 of the 200 room Furama Resort on China Beach.

VNAT estimates that by 2002 the country will need to build an additional 25,270 guest rooms, with demand fluctuating between various regions of the country.

Promotion/new markets

VNAT is clearly about to embark on a major new promotional effort, capitalizing on the country's ancient and contemporary histories. In recent years, the lifting of Vietnamese government restrictions and the increase of budget travel have enabled more con-temporary and relevant portraits of the country to gain currency world-wide.

However, Vietnam is currently focusing on attracting tour groups which spend an average of US$75 per day per head and stay at top-end hotels, in contrast to budget travellers who spend, on average, at most US$20 per day, per head. Other potential target segments include:

(a) overseas Vietnamese (Viet Kieu) who have settled abroad, predominantly in the USA, Canada, Australia, and France;

(b) foreign business people, investors, and researchers seeking business opportunities;

(c) the 2.7 million US war veterans and their families;

(d) travellers from the West in search of an 'adventure holiday'; and

(e) holiday travellers visiting at certain periods of the year.

In line with the country's airline links, Vietnam is focusing its priorities on the countries of South East Asia and the Pacific region, followed by western Europe and North America. There are co-operative promotional agreements in place with both Singapore and Thailand.

Although the country has held one travel trade fair, its main regional tourism event will come in 2001 when it will host its first ASEAN Tourism Forum. The country also regularly has a presence at major international trade shows such as ITB in Berlin and is making strong efforts to get the maximum out of its membership of the ASEAN Tourism Association.

Over the next few years, VNAT is also working at diversifying the tourism product base in order to segment the marketing efforts more effectively. Two priority areas are:

(a) creating original and special tourist products with national character, especially those related to the country's culture, history, art, traditions, and customs; and

(b) creating particular tourist products such as tourism for health improvement, sea resort treatment (thalassotherapy), cave tourism, golf tourism, sport, fishing, river entertainment, tourism for handicraft and art lovers, traditional village tourism, wild-life tourism, and celebrations and festivals.

In 1997/8, Vietnam is also planning to open its first overseas tourism offices in Singapore, Japan, and France. The plan, which was mapped out as part of a tourism strategy announced in a conference on tourism sponsored by the European Union in March 1997, must first be approved by the Prime Minister, Vo Van Kiet.

Problems and constraints

Although the outlook for the future of the Vietnam tourism industry is positive, several obstacles have been identified. The primary ones are as follows:

(a) the absence of any distinctly recognizable characteristics of Vietnam as a destination;

(b) the poor image of Vietnam in world travel markets;

(c) a general reputation for poor standards of service;

(d) no clearly identifiable link between quality and price. The quality of service at even the most expensive of hotels is known to be variable;

(e) poor general development of tourism 'products'.

A number of recent media reports have claimed that many travellers are leaving the country earlier than scheduled, complaining of the high cost and low quality of services. The poor performance was attributed to bad tourism management, specifically the lack of qualified guides, dull travel itineraries, and unscrupulous competition between travel agencies.

The train whistle blew, distracting Pat's attention from the report for a moment. What was she going to recommend? The Board had asked for suggestions in respect of the marketing strategy that could be adopted for the next three to five year period, but they had been relatively vague in respect of what they perceived as the key dimensions of this strategy. It was therefore clear to her that she was going to receive little help from them in the actual design of the strategy. Any new ideas were likely to have to come from her and her alone.

Discussion questions

1   On the basis of the information presented in the case develop a communications plan for VNAT to pursue over the next three-year period.

2   Pat Lim has decided to develop a new website for VNAT—decide on the information that the site should contain and develop a site map which illustrates how the material might best be grouped.

3   Design and present an appropriate home page for VNAT.

4   To which other websites should Pat look to develop links? What are the implications of creating these links for the overall image of VNAT?

Chapter 14

Print, Production, and Fulfilment

Contents

14.1 **Objectives**

By the end of this chapter you should be able to:

(a) outline a process by which direct response communications are produced and printed.

(b) distinguish between different forms of printing.

(c) understand the advantages and disadvantages of each form of printing.

(d) understand the significance of the fulfilment function.

(e) outline the primary considerations in the fulfilment process.

14.2 **Introduction**

Designing a strategy that includes the use of print media for either customer development or retention is only one part of the direct marketing equation. The materials it is intended to use have then to be designed, printed, and dispatched. The organization has also to think about the implications for fulfilment, including how orders/enquiries will be handled, the time it will take for orders to be fulfilled/dispatched and how returns and after-sales queries will be handled and managed. In this chapter, it is our intention to concentrate on these issues beginning with the question of printing.

14.3 **Print production**

Moreland (1999) recommends that the sequential process outlined in Figure 14.1 be adopted. The timings the author provides should best be thought of as minimums, the exact duration depending on the nature of the work and the complexity involved.

14.3.1 **Estimate**

The first stage of the process is the estimate. It is advisable to contact the printers that will tender for the work at the earliest possible opportunity. Some printers will require the materials presented in a specific way which might add to the delay prior to dispatch if the originator is not aware of them. Some printers may also be able to suggest ways in which the job might be handled more cheaply, by perhaps altering the format in some way, specifying different qualities of paper, or changing the nature of the materials that will be dispatched. It is useful to know all this at an early stage so that if necessary modifications can be made to the original design specification.

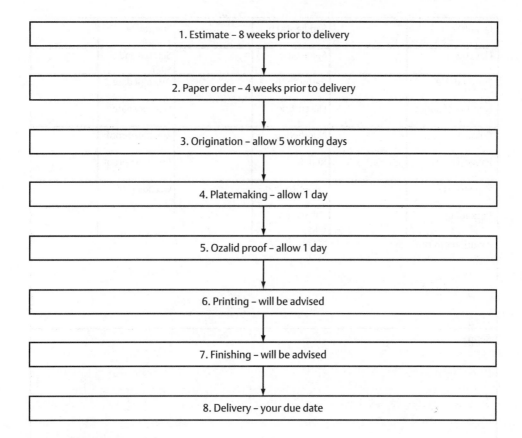

Fig. 14.1 The print process

To provide costings, printers will require detailed information in respect of each item that will be included in a mailing. The specifications for each item are likely to vary considerably. Typically, mailpacks consist of envelopes, order forms, leaflets, price lists, and a reply mechanism such as an envelope. A suggested print enquiry form is provided in Figure 14.2.

Costs will likely be a function of:

Quantity—where the printer will offer a discount for higher volume print runs.

Paper—the weight of the paper to be used.

Size—whilst it may be appropriate to be innovative and present a pack in a non-standard size this could greatly add to the cost.

Finishing—a general term which includes such additional processes as folding, gluing, varnishing, etc.

Print process—e.g. whether laser printing or offset litho will be used. This is a matter that will be returned to in more detail below.

Quantity		Saddle stitch		Fragrance burst	
Flat size		Spine glue		Scratch and sniff	
Finished size		Perforations		Artwork date	
Number of pages		Die cutting		Delivery date	
Colours		Numbering		Machine proof	
Paper (cover)		Run on		Cromalin proof	
Paper (text)		Ink jet coding		Ozalid proof	
Packaging		Silk screen inks			

Additional Information

Repro

Diagram

Fig. 14.2 Suggested print enquiry form

Dates—the greater the degree of flexibility that can be offered, the greater the likelihood that a discount may be negotiated.

The printer will also require some idea of how the artwork will be presented since different formats require differing degrees of effort on their behalf. Typically, the presentation of such material may take one of two forms:

Conventional—a solid baseboard on which would be mounted a bromide indicating the degree of enlargement or reduction required for illustrations or photographs. These would be positioned on the board as they would be intended to appear in the final work. The text of the article would then be overlaid on the bromide in the position in which it is intended to appear. A second overlay would typically include the colour mark-up, specifying the colours and tints that should be used. Finally, each transparency would be labelled so that it is immediately clear where each will be used in the finished article and in what order they will appear.

Digital artwork—is rapidly becoming the norm in artwork presentation. Desktop publishing systems are used to digitally represent the design that will be printed. This would typically be provided on disk or sent via an ISDN line and would be accompanied by a proof detailing the exact nature of the colours to be used.

Having been furnished with the requisite data, the printer should be in a position to develop a quote or estimate of the likely costs of the job. This in tandem with other considerations such as a printer's reputation and experience can help guide the final choice of which supplier will be used.

14.4 **Paper order**

In cases where very large mailings will be undertaken a 'making' of paper will typically be purchased. This is simply a reel or sheet format delivery of the required size and weight. They can typically take up to six weeks to manufacture and large volume mailers may therefore need to allocate time to allow this process to happen. Most print shops keep smaller quantities of paper in stock, although they may not necessarily fit the desired specifications.

There are six grades of paper in common use. They range in weight from as little as 45 grammes per square metre (gsm) to well over 200 gsm. From a direct marketing perspective it is important to note that weight is often taken as a proxy for quality, yet heavier papers will cost considerably more and possibly add significantly to the weight of the pack resulting in higher postal charges. The six most common types of paper are:

WSOP (Web sized offset paper)—this is really the bottom of the range and is low cost and hence perfect for long run weekly publications such as consumer magazines.

BCM—blade coated mechanical—off white, mid-range and coated to make it suitable for colour work such as fliers, brochures, etc.

Matt coated part mechanical—off-white matt coated. This can be used for work where quality might be an issue such as in letters or application forms.

Near woodfree—whiter than the preceding and of a higher quality. It may be used for some high-quality reproduction work such as brochures or magazines.

Woodfree—matt coated—this is the top of the range. It is extra white and of a very high quality. It may thus be used for application forms, letters, and brochures for higher-value products.

Woodfree-art—high gloss paper with high reflective properties. Used largely for prestige reproductions such as company reports and prospectuses.

14.5 Origination

When the designer has completed the artwork and any photographic work has been supplied, this material is separated into four printing colours for final reproduction. These are

- black;
- yellow;
- cyan;
- magenta.

When pictures finally appear in a completed piece they are an amalgam of these four basic printing colours. To assess the correct mix to use, each piece of artwork is typically scanned electronically and filtered sequentially to allow the presence of only one of these colours at a time to be detected. This results in one of four 'positive films', one for each of the production colours.

14.6 Platemaking

To be in a position to reproduce the desired images on paper it is necessary to transfer them to a printing plate or cylinder. The type of plate that will be used will depend on the nature of the printing process. This is therefore detailed in a later section.

14.7 **Proofing**

To check the accuracy of positive films the printer will normally generate one of four different types of proofs.

14.7.1 **Wet proofs**

These are produced on a small colour press capable of printing each colour separately. Each colour is generated and allowed to dry before the next one is applied. The overall effect is to mirror that which will be generated by the actual printing process.

14.7.2 **Cromalin proofs**

This is a method of photomechanical proofing. A light sensitive laminate is applied to a base material. A film positive is then laid on top and exposed to a bright light. The laminate is dusted with a powder, one for each process colour and excess removed. The process is then repeated until each colour has been laid down.

Generally speaking this type of proof is quicker and less expensive than wet proofs under circumstances where only a few proofs are required.

14.7.3 **Ozalid proofs**

These are proofs taken at the platemaking stage and are a black and white representation of the images presented. This is usually the last opportunity to pick up any errors before the job goes to press.

14.7.4 **Digital proofs**

Digital proofs are now widely used to check the position of text, photographs, etc. on a document. The low cost means that they can be employed as a check right throughout the production process. On the downside, digital proofs are only as good as the display or printing technology employed to produce them. Thus, they may, or may not be, an accurate portrayal of the colours that will appear. As technology improves so too will the colour accuracy of these proofs.

14.8 **Printing**

There are six printing processes currently in commercial use:

14.8.1 **Letterpress**

The technology for this method of printing dates back to the time of Caxton. The image is created in relief and ink applied the image. The image is then pressed onto the paper. Hence this form of printing is also known as impact printing. The nature of the process gives the resultant print a very fresh crisp look, but is very rarely used today because of the costs associated with it. It is also not as flexible as the other forms of print described below.

14.8.2 **Photogravure**

Image areas are engraved on the surface of large printing cylinders. These rotate in reservoirs of ink before having surplus ink removed from the surface by a 'doctor blade'. The effect is to retain ink in the cells of the cylinder rather like a honeycomb. When the paper makes contact the ink is transferred. The process takes place at a very high speed and all four colours are dealt with simultaneously. It is typically used for magazine production and for items with a very long print run. Smaller runs would prove prohibitively expensive since the cylinders take a long time to prepare.

14.8.3 **Silk screen**

A material with a fine weave is stretched across a frame. On top of the frame would be placed a stencil which blocks the areas where ink is not required. Ink is then poured into the frame and the frame lowered onto the material to be printed. Ink is squeezed through the weave forcing ink through those areas not protected by the stencil. The process is repeated for each colour.

The process can be used to great effect to print onto difficult surfaces such as metal, plastic, and fabric. It can also be used on timber and glass. It is best suited to short print runs (typically under 2,000 copies) and is often used in circumstances where a high density of colour is required. It is thus suitable for signs, point of sale material, notices and posters.

14.8.4 **Lithography**

This is undoubtedly the most widely used of the all the print processes and would be a common choice for the purposes of direct mail. The volume of the printing to be undertaken would normally drive the form of lithography that will be utilized—sheet fed or web offset.

These two systems both operate on the same principle. An image is created on the surface of a plate. The image is made grease receptive whilst the non-image area or background is made water receptive. A film of water is then applied to the plate and is thus attracted to the background areas. The water is repelled by the image areas of the film. A greasy ink is then applied to the plate and is repelled by the moisture in the background areas, being attracted only to the images on the plate. As the moisture evaporates only the ink is left behind to form the image. This is then transferred to a rubber blanket and from there to the paper to be printed. This is repeated for each of the printing colours. The fact that the printing takes place via the rubber blanket leads to the term 'offset' litho.

Sheet fed litho—This type of press prints onto flat cut sheets of paper. They operate at speeds capable of handling up to 18,000 sheets per hour. They are typically most suitable for print runs of up to 50,000 impressions.

Web offset litho—This prints from a continuous reel of paper and can print in 4 colours on both sides of the paper simultaneously. The ink is dried with hot air giving rise to a high gloss finish. The fact that hot air is used also means that the drying process is rapid. This allows the printer to include additional applications at the end of the printing process such as folding, gluing, perforating, etc. A completed product can often be generated as the output from this machine. The speed of operation is extremely rapid nearing 40,000 impressions per hour and print runs of several million items may be possible.

14.8.5 **Laser printing**

Laser printing involves an electronic process offering great flexibility. It is used frequently in direct mail to produce letters because it can easily be linked to a list permitting personalization of printed items such as letters. Laser printing and ink jet printing can often be used to 'fill-in' details on pre-printed items that have been produced by other means, such as forms, etc. Laser printing is currently quite costly and the availability of large laser printing machines is relatively limited, so printers who own them will limit their usage to specific types of job. However, the industry is moving quickly towards a point when laser print will become 'standard'.

14.8.6 **Digital offset**

Modern technology also permits digital printing using wet ink. A laser is used to create a new latent image on the image cylinder with EVERY revolution that takes. This image is lifted from digital information taken from the input source. The colour of the ink will vary for each rotation and the paper being printed is retained on the impression cylinder until each of the four colours has been imprinted. The advantage of this technology is that colours can be personalized, as can the content of the communication.

14.9 **Finishing**

As items complete the printing process they often have to have a number of additional operations performed before they are ready for dispatch. These can often be completed at the print shop or they may be undertaken by a mailing house (see below). Typical operations include:

• folding: to fit size of envelope;

- saddle stitching: stapling multiple pages together;
- numbering;
- creasing;
- perforating: where a tear-off response device is to be used;
- punching;
- trimming: cutting leaflets of brochures to a specific size;
- plastic comb binding;
- wire binding;
- gluing.

Ample time needs to be added to the production schedule for the completion of each of these processes. Some machines will enable the printer to accomplish two or more of these tasks simultaneously.

14.10 **Mailing houses**

Mailing houses are specialized agencies that prepare a mailing for dispatch and place it in the postal system. The more typical functions provided by a mailing house are given below:

Sorting for delivery by the postal carrier—mailing houses will place items in Mailsort order (i.e. by postcode or zip code) which attracts a discount from the postal carrier as they do not have to undertake the first stage of sorting themselves.

Letter and leaflet printing—some mailing houses are also able to offer limited printing and production facilities. In those instances where print quality is not a particular issue it may be appropriate to ask a mailing house to take over this aspect of a mailing.

Collation—where packs are to contain multiple items such as a reply envelope, letter, and catalogue for example, mailing house technology can be used to collate the materials that will ultimately be inserted in each envelope.

Folding and insertion—many mailing houses will also offer to fold and insert items into dispatch envelopes. This is usually undertaken mechanically. Hand insertion can also be undertaken, but is time consuming and therefore expensive. The inclusion of items in mailpacks such as pens which cannot be inserted by machine therefore adds substantially to costs and extends the required production timescale.

Personalization of letters—many companies require the covering letter to be personalized using technology such as mailmerge. The details of recipients are provided to the mailing house on disk and names, addresses and salutations are added by the mailing house to each letter as it passes through the system. Other data can also be mailmerged, e.g. customer account details can be added to forms to provide information to the customer and/or to save them time and effort in form-filling. In each case variable data has to be supplied to the mailing house with instructions as to where the data is to appear in the finished item.

Addressing of envelopes—in cases where personalization has not taken place and where as a consequence window envelopes cannot be used for dispatch it may be appropriate for the mailing house to address the envelopes. Addresses can be printed manually or inkjetted on each envelope, or sticky address labels can be provided and affixed.

14.11 **Fulfilment**

14.11.1 **Overview**

The trade press uses the term 'fulfilment' to describe a plethora of different activities. Ask any two direct marketers to define it and you will likely get two very different perspectives. It can include list maintenance, promotional mailings, customer relations, and what are referred to as 'back-end' operations such as order fulfilment.

Such consensus as does exist would seem to suggest that fulfilment should best be regarded as the distribution aspect of direct marketing. It thus describes what happens after an order or request for further information is initiated by a customer.

When a mailing, or indeed any other direct marketing communication has been initiated, orders or enquiries that result must thereafter be dealt with promptly. At this point there are four primary areas of concern:

Shipping—the goods or services ordered need to be packaged and shipped in a timely fashion.

Enquiries—these may take the form of requests for further information, or in cases where an order has already been placed, requests for advice on the status of that order.

Returns—customers may return goods for credit or a refund.

Exchanges—some customers may also find that the product did not suit their needs, or in the case of clothing products did not fit as expected. They may, therefore, request an alternative product.

Complaints—a (hopefully!) small number of customers may also be dissatisfied with the service or products and require a mechanism whereby they can air their grievances.

Each of these elements is a component of the fulfilment function. To illustrate just how important the fulfilment function is Fenvessy (1988) notes the breakdown of major problems experienced by in-home shoppers. These are presented in Table 14.1. It should be noted that of all the problems typically cited by customers, well over 90 per cent of them would typically relate to the fulfilment function.

Table 14.1 Breakdown of customer complaints

Major complaints	%
Delivery-daily/damage	57.8
Credit and billing	13.7
Unsatisfactory service	11.8
Failure to provide refunds	10.9
Sub total	*94.2*
Selling practices	2.0
Product quality/performance	1.7
Advertising practices	1.1
Guarantee/warranty	0.6
Unsatisfactory repair	0.3
Discontinued business	0.1
Total	*100*

It is perhaps in the nature of direct marketing that complaints about this aspect of the service would tend to predominate. After all, customers will not have had the opportunity to try out the goods or inspect them before they are finally dispatched. That is not to say, however, that direct marketers should be complacent. Complaints of whatever nature should be minimized and the exact reasons for dissatisfaction plotted and attended to.

The activities involved in fulfillment will vary greatly from one organization to another. In the case of publishing houses the publication and distribution of magazines to subscribers is a fairly routine process. Demand can be plotted a long time in advance and production schedules are cyclical and regular. In the realm of catalogues however, fulfilment is relatively complex. There are often many thousands of products each of which may be ordered at irregular intervals and in conjunction with any one of a thousand other products. Each order has typically to be picked, either by machine or by hand from a warehouse containing the complete assortment of products.

Fenvessy (1988) outlines what he regards as the ten steps in the fulfilment cycle. These are depicted in Figure 14.3. Key aspects of this process are described below:

14.11.2 **Order receipt**

As the diagram makes clear, the fulfilment process begins with the receipt of an order. These might typically come in from a variety of direct channels including the mail, telephone, fax, or Internet. When communications are received they are generally streamed to separate payments, orders, and general enquiries. It would also be normal in the case of mail or telephone receipts to record at this stage the media that generated the order. This information can be fed back directly to the marketing department to facilitate future accuracy in the targeting of specific campaigns. It is for this reason that many direct response press ads contain code numbers that identify the journal and date of publication.

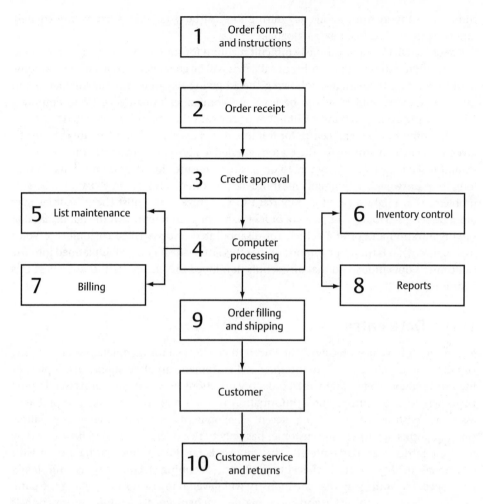

Fig. 14.3 Ten steps in the fulfilment cycle
Source: Fenvessy, S. J. (1988), *Fenvessy on Fulfillment* (New York: Cowles Business Media).

14.11.3 **Telephone responses**

Companies involved in a high volume of transactions can sometimes find that purchasing fulfilment technology such as mechanical devices to open envelopes can save a great deal of time and effort. Other machinery can be employed to imprint cheques with data which subsequently facilitate processing by accounts and/or the organization's bank.

Toll free or reduced rate telephone lines are increasingly being provided to customers to place orders. It is estimated that up to 65 per cent of catalogue orders are now received over the phone. Direct marketers offering this facility are advised to plan for the volume of calls that might be expected over the duration of a campaign. Often, specialized agencies are retained for this purpose with the client paying for all the calls received. Some of the larger catalogue companies employ their own telemarketing staff and contract out additional support from an agency during forecast busy periods (such as immediately following the release of a new catalogue).

The use of DRTV is a notoriously difficult medium for subsequent fulfilment planning. It is difficult to estimate the volume of calls that will be generated and what calls do come tend to come in immediately following the ad giving rise to enormous fluctuations in call volumes. It would therefore be usual for companies utilizing DRTV to employ a telemarketing agency to handle fulfilment of any calls that might be generated.

In planning to use a call centre for fulfilment it is essential that adequate thought be given to capacity planning for the reasons alluded to above. An efficiently run call centre should make it easy for customers to do business, ensure that they do not have to wait long to be answered, encourage repeat orders, and offer to resolve any customer service problems that might arise. It is important to recognize that whilst these facilities may often be designed for the purposes of order taking they often represent the public 'face' of the organization and offer a vehicle for disappointed or dissatisfied customers to voice their concerns. It is therefore important that this latter category of call is planned into the call centre's operations and that any scripts developed for agency staff to use reflect this additional objective.

14.11.4 **Data entry**

When orders have been received they need to be checked for completeness and clarity. Handwriting may be difficult to interpret and customers can often supply incomplete or incorrect product codes. Many mail order organizations now generate forms that require customers to enter only limited information in each box to minimize the problems associated with poor handwriting. Recent developments in scanning technology allow standard forms (i.e. where the customer has only to tick or cross boxes) to be scanned by machine rather than data-entered. This process is far quicker and cheaper, even with additional quality control checking built in. Scanning technology is still being developed, but is the way that the industry will develop in the future, making the data-capture process much faster and more highly mechanized. Bar-coding information is another similar aid to fast data capture. Additional information such as the page number on which an item appeared in a catalogue may also be collected, allowing the cross-referencing of incorrect or incomplete product codes.

As orders are input to the system, it would then be normal to sift the customer details and to perform a check on bad credit risks. Those with whom it is preferable not to do business can then be dealt with accordingly. More sophisticated systems allow the comparing of customer data with existing records to identify whether someone is a returning customer, whether they have been reactivated after a period of lapse, etc. Clearly, all this is useful information in segmenting the way in which those customers are dealt with subsequently. In the case of new customers a check might also be performed to verify that the zip or postal code information that has been supplied is valid.

Some systems also allow the organization to protect themselves against fraud, checking the details of credit cards used for payment and running balance checks on cheques received over a certain amount, typically £50, automatically.

When the respective customer files have been updated with the details of the order it would then be normal to generate acknowledgements and system paperwork such as picking instructions for the warehouse, shipping documents, etc.

14.11.5 **List maintenance**

Whenever a new communication is received it is important that customer records be updated. The database, as we have established in previous chapters, is fundamental to direct marketing activity and it is imperative that this be maintained as studiously as possible. Recording accurate data makes it possible for direct marketers to then decide when a customer should be mailed again, with which specific offer, etc. Information such as category, recency, frequency, and monetary value are central to future segmentation strategy.

Regular updating is not only essential for future planning, it can also ensure that in the short term the customer does not receive further follow-ups encouraging them to purchase a product or service for which an order has already been made. The lists to be used for subsequent marketing activity can be checked carefully against data held on the database to prevent the generation of such inappropriate communications.

Of course, the converse is also true. Recording the detail of those who responded can also assist administrators in identifying non-respondents who might be targeted with a fresh communication or follow-up. Indeed, if it has been a long time since they were last activated, it may be appropriate to reclassify some individuals as lapsed.

14.11.6 **Shipping orders**

The time elapsed between sending out the mailing or calling in an order and the receipt of that order is known as the delivery time. The mailing industry prides itself that the majority of consumer products ordered via direct means are delivered with two weeks of order. Enhanced customer expectations and the plethora of shipping methods now available ensure that in most cases the customer can now specify the form of delivery and shorten the time taken should they so require. Many Internet outlets now offer customers the choice of special courier, priority mail, or standard surface delivery.

Companies such as J. C. Penney make a point of offering superior service and aim to process 85 per cent of orders on the day that they are received. Delivery is then scheduled to take place in around 72 hours if the item is held in stock. Indeed, as consumers look to the web to make more routine purchases such as food items, expectations of delivery are likely to shorten even further.

In the context of physical products, once a customer order has passed through the various checks alluded to above, the details of the order will be passed to the warehouse for fulfilment. The manner in which material is stored varies greatly from context to context. In some cases, it may be appropriate to store the whole quantity of each item held together in one location. Whilst this reduces the time necessary to restock each location it can also be inefficient in the sense that the order picker could then have to traverse the whole warehouse to pick out the components of any one order. An alternative is for small quantities of the most popular items to be held near the dispatch bay for easy picking as required.

Once the order has been assembled, the completed order is sent to a packer. It would be usual for the packer to check the order against the shipping document and if correct to place it in a bag or carton. The address label is then affixed and the carton sealed for transport. The package would then be weighed and an appropriate postal rate assigned.

14.11.7 **Inventory**

The percentage of orders completely shipped is known as the fill ratio. Inevitably, customers will only be satisfied if their complete order is dispatched. Delays in shipment (back-orders) and product substitutions can be a great source of dissatisfaction. Higher completion rates also ensure that shipping and handling can be kept to a minimum and cancellations of orders are minimized as customers see their orders through to completion.

Customer demand will determine the outflow of stocks from the warehouse. The management of fulfilment requires that an adequate stock level is maintained so that stockout situations do not occur and customer's orders are left unfulfilled. Of course, no direct marketing organization will wish to hold vast levels of stock of each item because of the working capital that would then be tied up in stock (or inventory). The goal has, therefore, to be to achieve an adequate balance. For this reason, considerable time and effort in the catalogue industry is typically devoted to planning purchases from suppliers.

Indeed, all resellers have to be concerned with what are termed economic order quantities. The order quantity directly affects the size of the stockpile. If twelve months' requirements arrive in one lot, average stock over the whole year is equivalent to six months' requirements. But if only one month's requirements arrive, average stock over the whole year is equivalent to only half a month's supply. Frequent small orders for such regular requirements, instead of large orders, can result in substantial reductions in the size of stocks. Unfortunately, this can also result in increases in paperwork and administrative effort.

Analysis of the costs involved lead to formulae which enable the economic order quantity (EOQ) to be derived for any combination of the variables, price, rate of usage or demand, and internal costs. The EOQ is the quantity that results in the lowest total variable costs. It should not be surprising to note that if the annual usage value is low in relation to the costs of ordering and processing deliveries, the formula indicates that orders should be placed infrequently, whereas if it costs appreciably more to hold a month's supply in stock than it does to order it, the formula indicated that frequent orders should be placed. For non-mathematicians, it is worth noting that order quantity is proportional not to the annual usage value, but to its square root, so that if demand doubles, the order quantity should be increased by about 40 per cent.

The basic EOQ formula is:

$$EOQ = \sqrt{\frac{2 \times auq \times oc}{uc \times sc}}$$

Where

auq = annual usage quantity
oc = ordering cost

uc = unit cost

sc = stockholding cost

The beauty of this formula is that it is simple to calculate and may safely be attempted on any pocket calculator! In practice, however, most stock control systems will generate EOQs automatically and prompt re-orders at the time most suited to the organization's needs.

It should be noted, however, that EOQ calculations should not be attempted where the price fluctuates or where the rate of demand is not approximately constant, or where the lead time is long and uncertain. A constant rate requirement is really the only category of demand where the EOQ will be useful.

(a) Service level and stock turn

Two common measures of stock control are the service levels and stock turn rate. The service level is a measure of how successfully the organization has been in meeting demand off the shelf. If every customer order for an item can be met immediately from stock the service level is 100 per cent. If only seven out of ten requests can be met immediately the service level is 70 per cent.

The stock turn rate measures not the effectiveness of stock control in meeting demand, but rather its efficiency in doing so economically. The measure relates the amount of money needed to invest in stock to the use that is made of it. Achieving a high service level by maintaining high stock levels would result in a low stock turn rate. At the other extreme, a high stock turn rate could be achieved by carrying hardly any stock. Of course, the further one moves towards the latter model the more likely it is that stock out situations will occur and that the level of service provided to customers will fall as a result.

The stock turn rate is calculated as follows:

$$\frac{\text{Total usage for period}}{\text{Average stock for period}}$$

e.g. if the level of stock at the beginning of October is $100,000 and the stock at the end of the month is $110,000, the average stock for the month will be $105,000. If the cash value of sales for the month is $52,500 then the stock turn rate becomes:

$$\frac{52,500}{105,000} = 0.5$$

In other words, we can say that the stock is turned 0.5 times a month or six times a year.

(b) Re-order levels

Aside from the EOQ, some companies utilize reorder levels of stock control. In these circumstances a purchase is triggered when the stock of an item falls to a quantity known as the reorder level (or order point). The order level is the average quantity required in the lead time plus buffer stock. Buffer stock is the reserve quantity required to take care of demand should delivery be delayed. Regrettably, there is no scientific way of deciding on an appropriate buffer stock and it is likely that many companies will have built up a picture of what is an acceptable level drawing on experience over time.

14.11.8 **Fulfilment reports**

There are a number of reports which might be generated in respect of the fulfilment function. These include:

(a) **Response record**

This report includes the number of responses received. It is particularly useful to know how many phone, mail, and internet responses are generated each day. This allows planners to forecast the likely number of enquiries/sales that might be generated in the future and to plan the response capacity accordingly.

It is also important to identify the nature of the responses. Are they coming in from certain parts of the country, from certain ads, or mailshots? Are certain types of customers responding? All this information will be invaluable to direct marketers in tracking the success of each media vehicle or campaign.

(b) **Inventory data**

This report would contain details of the orders placed in a given period with suppliers, what additional stock is required, what is overstocked, etc. Some companies may also employ measures such as the rate of stock turn alluded to above.

(c) **Returns**

This report would contain details of returned or refused merchandise during the period. It is invaluable as the data it contains will have a major impact on cost. The costs of returns and complaint handling are often significant and often unanticipated. A detailed analysis of returns by product line could yield data in respect of over-selling on the part of direct marketers. Perhaps the quality has been misrepresented, or the marketing materials are not a fair reflection of the nature of the product on offer. Catalogue marketers, for example, are careful not to make the items at the lower end of their range appear to be of too high a quality in the manner in which they are presented on the printed page of their catalogue.

(d) **Work in progress**

This report contains details of the orders awaiting entry, correspondence requiring answers, and the shipments awaiting dispatch in the warehouse. These reports are therefore designed to measure the efficiency of operating departments and likely levels of customer satisfaction.

(e) **Customer service reports**

These might include details of complaints, enquiries, incomplete orders, and damage claims. They highlight errors where improvements might need to be made in the future.

(f) **Credit and billing information**

As the name suggests, companies selling on credit will need to track the percentage of customers who are turned down and the percentage of those that are proving to be a bad debt, etc.

(g) **Other reports**

It may also be appropriate to generate reports which identify the quality of the work undertaken by the fulfilment operation. Dummy orders may thus be placed in the system and checked for their subsequent accuracy at the point of dispatch. Error rates are particularly crucial data.

Reports may also be generated in respect of matters such as productivity and the output of particular employee groups. Quantitative and qualitative measures can be employed for this purpose.

14.12 **Summary**

In this chapter, we have reviewed the printing and fulfilment aspects of a direct marketing operation. We have examined the various forms of printing that might be undertaken and presented a framework that might be used for the purposes of print planning. We have also alluded to the role that print houses and mailing houses might typically perform and the nature of the overlap in services between these two agencies. We then moved on to consider the fulfilment function and to consider key aspects of that operation such as order receipt and processing, credit approval, list maintenance, and the generation of key management reports.

Discussion questions

1   As a Product Manager for a clothing company, put together a briefing to enable a printer to provide a quotation on a mailpack to be sent to your 200 best customers. Outline the contents of the pack, and provide guidance on the high-quality production you will require.

2   Map out instructions for your mailing house on the enclosing, collation, and mailing of a catalogue. The mailing will include a personalized covering letter and response envelope for orders.

3   You are the Marketing Manager for a Christmas sales catalogue. What steps should you take to ensure that you run no risk of running out of stock on your most popular Christmas cards?

Further reading

Fenvessy S. J. (1988) *Fenvessy on Fulfillment* (New York: Cowles Business Media).

Moreland P. (1998) 'An Introduction to Direct Mail Printing', *The Direct Marketing Guide* (Teddington: Institute of Direct Marketing), 3. 4–2–3.4–24).

Chapter 15

Towards the Future

Contents

15.1 **Objectives**

By the end of this chapter you should be able to:

(a) identify a number of the key challenges facing the direct marketing industry;

(b) describe how recent developments will impact on the future of the industry;

(c) understand the marketing implications of broadband technology;

(d) distinguish between disintermediation and meta-mediation;

(e) understand the marketing implications of VEMI technology.

15.2 **Introduction**

'It was the best of times, it was the worst of times.'

The opening words of Dickens' 'A Tale of Two Cities' are probably a fair description of the position of direct marketing at the turn of the century. Direct and interactive marketing is experiencing rapid growth and appears to be prospering in almost every sector and country the world over. Yet the picture is not all rosy. The pace of change makes it difficult for organizations to keep up with the latest developments in their sector. There continues to be a pattern of large capital investment in new technology, particularly in the realm of information technology increasing the power of organizations to store and process vast quantities of consumer information. Whilst this may be a golden opportunity for direct marketers to hone the precision of their activity, they are doing so at a time when consumer concerns over the use of their personal data are at an all-time high.

In this chapter, we will review some of the key changes that are taking place in the direct marketing sector and speculate how these developments might impact on the industry from both positive and negative perspectives. Whilst the majority of the technological developments we will discuss can only serve to enhance the quality and precision of direct marketing, they will only be effective as long as consumers can be kept on board and convinced that the changes taking place are to their mutual advantage. In this chapter, we shall therefore be considering a number of the most pressing consumer concerns and how these might best be managed by the sector.

Of course, in any chapter written ostensibly about the future, there will always be an element of 'crystal ball gazing' involved. We can never be 100 per cent sure of the direction that direct marketing will take. Speculation, however well informed, remains exactly that—speculation. We would, therefore, encourage readers to think through for themselves the impact of the changes described in this chapter and to consider the likely relevance for their own organization as they plan for the future.

15.3 **Privacy issues**

15.3.1 **SPAM**

The new communication medium opened up by the Internet is attracting ever greater interest on the part of commercial organizations. Growth in both the number of sites and the number of consumers accessing these sites, continues almost exponentially. Communication is inexpensive and can reach millions of customers much more cost effectively than would hitherto have been the case with more traditional media.

The growth in opportunity has also been coupled with rising concerns amongst Internet users about the manner in which such communication takes place. Indeed, there are many interesting parallels with the development of direct mail in the 1980s and 90s. As the number of consumers connected to the web continues to grow, so too does the volume of unsolicited and often annoying commercial e-mail. Commonly referred to as SPAM, these e-mails advertise goods and services directly to the consumer without their explicit consent. Modern technology has ensured that such communications are easy to send and that practically anybody with a computer and a modem can send them. At the time of writing, it is possible to buy lists of thousands of e-mail addresses for a cost of only circa $100. An advertiser, therefore, has little to lose by bombarding as many individuals as the organization can with the details of their products because the incremental cost of each new communication is miniscule. Even if the response rate is a fraction of a hundredth of 1 per cent, the advertiser will probably still have met their objectives.

What makes these communications particularly irritating, is the fact that, unlike traditional mail, where the cost of the communication is borne entirely by the sender, the cost of receiving SPAM is borne almost solely by the receiver. Aside from the time required to download the material from one's Internet Service Provider (ISP), SPAM can take up valuable storage space, and place additional burden's on the ISPs, forcing them to invest heavily in new technology to cope with the volume of mail created by SPAM. Inevitably, it is the consumer that will ultimately be asked to pick up the tab for this expenditure. *Marketing News* (a publication of the American Marketing Association) estimates that some ISPs have had to charge fees to users that are up to 10 per cent higher than would actually be necessary if SPAM were to be eliminated.

Aside from these cost issues, a matter of increasing concern to regulators, is the significant use of SPAM by fraudsters. Some analysts estimate that up to 50 per cent of SPAM may contain fraudulent information undermining the credibility of the medium still further for those enterprises that may want to use it for legitimate purposes. A high percentage of SPAM promotes illegal or somewhat questionable goods and services, such as adult entertainment, get rich quick schemes or credit repair (see Figure 15.1).

Spammers have also proved difficult to track down as anyone attempting to reply to a piece of SPAM will already be aware. It is not uncommon for a Spammer to conceal their true identity and to disguise their actual e-mail address to avoid the possibility of retaliation. SPAM therefore gets routed via non-existent return addresses, or worse still through the e-mail system of an unsuspecting and perfectly legitimate third party. The ingenuity of the Spammers seems to be keeping pace with the technology now being employed in an attempt to stop them. Many ISPs have now designed filters to keep out unwanted SPAM. Equally, the recent versions of e-mail software now invite consumers to block e-mail from certain specified addresses. Regrettably, more sophisticated Spammers have proved the equal of such devices designing communications that vary the 'origin' address, making it difficult for such filters to isolate the offending communications.

It therefore seems inevitable that in the coming decade legislators will play an increasing role in curbing the excessive and illegal use of this medium. At the time of writing, federal lawmakers in the US have passed legislation in 14 states, to deal with Spammers and the US Congress is currently reviewing six pieces of legislation recently proposed by the federal government. It seems unlikely that anyone will seek to ban SPAM entirely, but

From: U_of_S@osite.com.br
Sent: Tuesday, September 26, 2000 9:30PM
Subject: University Diplomas

UNIVERSITY DIPLOMAS

Obtain a prosperous future, money earning power, and the admiration of all.

Diplomas from prestigious non-accredited universities based on your present knowledge and life experience.

No required tests, classes, books, or interviews.

Bachelors, masters, MBA, and doctorate (PhD) diplomas available in the field of your choice.

No one is turned down

Confidentiality assured.

CALL NOW to receive your diploma within days!!!

1-214-853-5588

Call 24 hours a day, 7 days a week, including Sundays and holidays.

Fig. 15.1 SPAM

legislation looks certain to curtail the worst excesses. The mechanisms for achieving this are numerous. Firstly Congress could require ISPs to keep a list of individuals who have indicated that they do not wish to receive SPAM. Companies wishing to generate SPAM would then have to check their selected addresses against this list, and delete anyone indicating that they do not wish to receive this material. Heavy fines could then be imposed against offenders. An alternative would be to require Spammers to post accurate routing information, making it possible for recipients to trace the site of origin. It would also seem likely that individual Spammers, could be specifically required to offer an 'opt-out' facility, where recipients can reply and automatically delete themselves from a particular list.

A yet further possibility, would be to tackle the supply side of the equation and for countries to outlaw the use and distribution of software designed to generate SPAM. Amongst the most likely targets for this kind of legislation would be the manufacturers of the so called 'harvesting' software which makes it possible for an organization to collect the e-mail addresses of those using specific Internet facilities, such as chat-rooms.

The pull from Internet users seems likely to generate legislation along the lines indicated above. It also seems likely to generate increased interest on the part of software suppliers who will undoubtedly design ever more sophisticated methods of filtering SPAM automatically before it reaches a particular mailbox. The advent of broadband and the enhanced speed of communication that it will offer, should make it possible for e-mail software to check the origin of e-mail from addresses not presently listed in the address book of a particular user. As an attempt is made to send SPAM, the software could check the origin address against the address book and where the origin address is not recognized, an attempt could be made to verify the identity of the sender. If the origin address proves false, the mail could simply be deleted, without the user ever being aware a communication had taken place.

As the reader will by now appreciate, the e-communication environment seems set to generate increasing interest on the part of both legislators and consumers. As the framework of what constitutes acceptable communication looks set to undergo frequent change, anyone seeking to use e-mail as a means of contacting prospective customers would be well advised to check the laws governing both the country or state of origin of communications **AND** the laws governing communication in the country or state in which it will be received. Ethical users of SPAM would also be advised to consult any voluntary codes of conduct that may be in existence in each case and ensure that they work to the highest common denominator.

15.3.2 **Wider privacy issues**

Aside from the daily irritation that can be caused by SPAM, direct marketers look set to have to grapple with an increasingly 'hostile' public that will demand ever stricter controls over the way in which their personal information is stored and manipulated.

One of the most enduring consumer concerns appears to the anxiety over the extent to which information held by direct marketers might fall into the wrong hands. A number of widely publicized examples of such abuses have only served to fuel public concern. In the mid-1990s, a group of reporters in the US was, for example, able to obtain a list of video tapes rented by a Supreme Court nominee, Robert Bork. Although, in the case, none of his choices were at all controversial, the US Congress was spurred to pass a bill, forbidding video stores from releasing such information in the future. Also, in the US, an ice cream parlour by the name of Farrell's sold a list of children's birthdays to the Selective Service, enabling the organization to make sure that young men attaining the age of 18 were registered for the draft.

Of particular concern to consumers is the extent to which their information is stored by one organization and then swapped or sold to another, leading to a proliferation of marketing communications of one form or another. Whilst this remains a common practice, consumer influence within the EC on legislators has led to strict new rules governing the storage and usage of personal data. Those companies now wishing to sell customer details to other organizations must explicitly seek the permission of those customers before such details are exchanged. Returning and new customers to an organization are therefore now routinely asked whether they are willing to have their details shared with other organizations whose products/services are likely to be complimentary and therefore of interest.

Consumers within the EU have also been given new rights to object to the processing of their personal data for the purposes of direct marketing. Consumers can now request that their personal data should not be input to any subsequent form of marketing analysis designed to facilitate personal targeting. They may also request copies of the data held about them on file and object to any errors that they find therein. The new legislation also distinguishes between personal data and what should be regarded as sensitive personal information, such as data concerning an individual's health. The rules concerning how each category of information might be used and the extent to which the explicit consent of the individual might be required, now vary depending on the nature of the data.

The new EC legislation constitutes the tightest operating framework that direct marketers must adhere to currently in existence anywhere in the world. At the time the European Commission were considering privacy issues, there was much debate and opposition from the industry in respect of these measures. In the final analysis, this opposition was almost certainly self-defeating as consumers were found to have many legitimate concerns. Industry attempts at self-regulation designed to curb the abuses of a few unscrupulous direct marketers had proved largely ineffective. Those organizations willing to subscribe to a code of conduct were generally not those that had given the public cause for concern in the first place.

The lesson for direct marketers outside Europe is clear. Get your house in order. A failure to take account of consumer concerns and pressure voluntarily will ultimately result in the same somewhat Draconian legislation being implemented progressively across the globe.

15.4 **Broadband**

Perhaps one of the most exciting developments of the late 1990s was the design of a completely new means of accessing the web. Traditionally, the majority of home Internet users have sat at their computer terminal, dialled in to their Internet Service Provider and waited often considerable periods of time for their browser to move from one Internet page to the other. With the advent of broadband technology all this will change. Offering connection to the web at an amazing pace, it will quite literally revolutionize the way in which we interact with e-business. Broadband can be provided through a satellite, cable, modem, or a telephone line. It offers connection to the web at speeds in excess of 50 times what can currently be achieved with a 56K modem. In practice, this means that downloading files that currently take up to an hour will be accomplished in a matter of seconds using broadband. Waiting time will be eliminated and the quality of the consumer experience greatly enhanced. Rather than viewing ads, for example on an 18 inch flat screen, consumers will be participating actively in them, experiencing a plethora of sounds and images designed specifically to reflect their individual needs.

The birth of broadband will thus sound the deathknell for the traditional hour glass that so many of us are used to watching whilst we wait for the next page of interest to download. Long standing jokes about the WorldWide Wait will be a thing of the past. To the human eye, connection will appear immediate and transactions will finally happen in 'real-time'.

The sheer speed of transmission allows e-business not only to communicate faster, but also to convey much larger quantities of data. This releases the potential for a genuinely multi-media consumer experience. Sound, video, and even other sensations can easily be conveyed without appreciably lowering the speed with which a given page can be loaded. In preparation for this revolution in sound and experience, direct marketers need to begin considering the range of media they will use in the future to promote their products and services on the web. Graphic quality will be greatly enhanced, audio will be of broadcast quality and real-time chats will prove possible on-line with company representatives. In short, the consumer of the next decade will come to demand a web experience rich in atmosphere and texture.

The ability to be able to employ both sound and video will greatly assist marketers in using the Internet for the purposes of brand building. This is probably one of the last major advantages of television which allows companies to link their brand to particular sounds (e.g. Intel's ping). This hasn't previously been possible on the web because of the nuisance factor of having to sit and wait whilst sizeable files are downloaded. Indeed, the technology is already in place for web-users to enjoy not only sound and video, but also smells. This will allow the manufacturers of perfume, hygiene, and food products a considerable advantage. Indeed, it is a little ironic that on-line retailing may well follow the path recently trod by in-store retailers looking to enhance the ambience offered to visitors. It may, therefore, not be long before we find ourselves buying scent cartridges alongside the more traditional ink cartridges at our local stationers!

Broadband will also offer consumers the luxury of permanent connection. It will no longer be necessary to go through a lengthy dial-up process fraught with frustrations of engaged lines and equipment failures. Consumers will be connected permanently and home access speeds will therefore rival those many consumers are used to in their offices.

By the end of 1999 approximately 2 million US homes were said to have broadband access. Companies such as Road Runner and Home and Herdon estimate that by 2003 at least one quarter of US households will be joining them. It seems likely that such access will initially be provided through the cable decoder already present in many North American homes. This is now all the more likely following the acquisition of Time Warner's cable system by America Online.

Catalogue companies will stand to draw particular benefit from the broadband revolution. The technology currently available to consumers has limited the desirability for many catalogue organizations to showcase the full breadth of their product range. In the interim, whilst broadband penetrates the market it is likely that many organizations will be compelled to develop two versions of their website. Boo.com, a company which specializes in sportswear, for example, currently offers two sites. The first showcases a limited product range, projecting still photographs of the available items. The second site, designed for broadband users, allows shoppers to zoom in on products, rotate them, and to view three-dimensional images.

Catalogue companies will also gain from the richer graphics broadband will permit. Fashion retailers, in particular, will be in a position to reflect accurately the true nature of the colours available. Indeed, they will be able to achieve the same degree of accuracy that is currently possible with traditional printed media. Users should ultimately be able to compare a product they already have at home with what they are seeing on their screens and be confident that the two items will ultimately match. Not only does this provide a much higher quality of service to the customer, it also greatly reduces the number of returns and, therefore, a typical company's transaction costs.

The experience of shopping will come to resemble that of a traditional store. E-salespersons will 'cruise' the site offering help and advice to consumers, both proactively and reactively. Consumers desiring advice will be in a position to have a real-time chat with someone qualified to deal with their enquiry. Using 'voiceover' and 'video-over', Internet protocol sites will allow their customers to talk to a sales representative simply by clicking a button.

The technology already exists to track the movement of consumers both within a site and from one site to another. Marketers are already able to use this facility to personalize the experience they offer. With broadband consumers already known to view 130 per cent more web pages per month, the accuracy with which personal interests can be captured and profiled improves greatly. Neilson also estimates that broadband users access the Internet more frequently, indeed 83 per cent more than those with traditional modem driven access.

In short, broadband offers so many advantages to both e-business and e-consumers that it is likely that traditional forms of Internet access will all but disappear in the next ten years. Consumers will no longer be prepared to put up with delays and will come to expect an Internet experience that more closely resembles that of the High Street.

15.5 Disintermediation versus cyber/meta-mediation

When the authors first started teaching Internet marketing some five years ago, there was much talk in the popular marketing press of so-called 'disintermediation'. It was felt that the worldwide web would offer manufacturers an unprecedented opportunity to deal direct with their customers and to eliminate the need for traditional intermediaries such as agents, distributors, wholesalers, or retailers. To a large extent, this disintermediation does appear to have happened. Consumers can now access suppliers of goods/services irrespective of where they might be in the world, greatly expanding individual choice.

Moreover, it has also become more attractive for suppliers to conduct business directly with their customers. Traditional intermediaries offered suppliers the benefit of high volume, low cost. For many, it would not have been economic to deal with a large number of low volume clients because they did not have the infrastructure necessary to deal with people on this basis. Instead, they preferred to ship large volumes to intermediaries who would then conduct the marketing on their behalf to end-users. The fact that such intermediaries often carried a large number of complementary items, meant that the size of the average order placed by a consumer made the transaction economic. Consumers would typically buy several different items from different manufacturers making it possible for the intermediary to make a profit where individual manufacturers would not. Indeed, the profit from multiple transactions made it attractive for intermediaries to make outlets available wherever concentrations of customers were found to exist, offering the manufacturers whose lines they carried a geographical coverage they could never hope to have achieved on their own.

The Internet has changed this dynamic. It is no longer prohibitively expensive for a manufacturer to deal directly with consumers. The costs of establishing a website are minimal and bear almost no comparison to the expenditure that would previously have been necessary to reach consumers directly through more conventional channels. A supplier need only meet the costs of establishing a web presence and an appropriate fulfilment operation. Indeed, the fact that both of these can now be adequately out-sourced makes dealing direct an increasing attractive option.

Rather than remove intermediaries from the distribution channel completely, many organizations have attempted to implement the direct contact a consumer might have with the manufacturer into their overall marketing strategy. Companies such as Jeep (see Figure 15.2) now allow consumers to specify the type of product they wish to buy, the features it should have, and the site at which they wish to collect it. Consumers accessing the Jeep site, for example, can specify the model of the vehicle they wish to purchase, the colour, engine size, seat colour, interior fittings, etc. The specified vehicle is then priced and if the consumer wishes to proceed the vehicle made available at an appropriate local outlet.

As the number of sites continues to grow, however, consumers are being faced with an increasingly bewildering number of potential suppliers through whom they could make a purchase. Anyone conducting a search on a standard Internet search engine on the word 'car' will know this all too well. In many ways Internet trade appears to have followed the model of traditional trade since the industrial revolution, albeit at an accelerated rate. When consumers had only a few alternatives from which to buy their goods or services, which was largely the case until the early nineteenth century, it made sense to deal directly with local suppliers for each specific category of goods demanded. It was not difficult to identify the players in the market, nor was it a chore to compare prices between the available alternatives and to maximize the available utility as a consequence. As the pattern of trade changed and the alternatives available to consumers began to proliferate a new model of retailing began to emerge. Department stores, with their impressive range of goods, are a comparatively recent phenomenon, dating only from the latter half of the nineteenth century. They arose because consumers were faced with a plethora of alternative products/services that could potentially have met their needs. The aim of the department store was to showcase these alternatives and to allow the shopper to make an informed choice as to the product most suited to their needs.

It is possible to draw many parallels from this experience to the current state of the Internet trading environment. In the early days of the web, there were comparatively few outlets available on line and only a small percentage of these were interactive in the sense

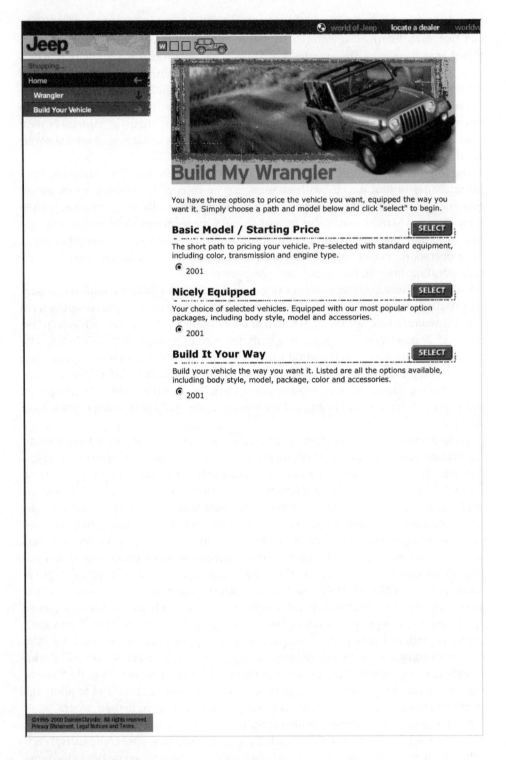

Build My Wrangler

You have three options to price the vehicle you want, equipped the way you want it. Simply choose a path and model below and click "select" to begin.

Basic Model / Starting Price

The short path to pricing your vehicle. Pre-selected with standard equipment, including color, transmission and engine type.

⊙ 2001

Nicely Equipped

Your choice of selected vehicles. Equipped with our most popular option packages, including body style, model and accessories.

⊙ 2001

Build It Your Way

Build your vehicle the way you want it. Listed are all the options available, including body style, model, package, color and accessories.

⊙ 2001

Fig. 15.2 Build your Jeep

Source: http://www.jeepunpaved.com/international

that it was possible to make a purchase. It was therefore not difficult to isolate the few suppliers with whom one could practically conduct business, compare the nature of the respective offers and place an order with the most attractive supplier. The proliferation of web sites has made this problematic—and rather than disintermediation we are now seeing a trend to cyber or meta mediation, where a new generation of intermediaries are being created to make it easier for customers to compare the alternatives available to them in a given product category. Those pundits that forecast the end of the intermediary, may therefore have been premature in their predictions. Both types of intermediary are defined below:

Cyber-mediaries—cyber-mediaries are simply commercial organizations that have been created on the web with the express purpose of selling a range of products from an equally diverse range of manufacturers. These are often catalogue based and centred on a

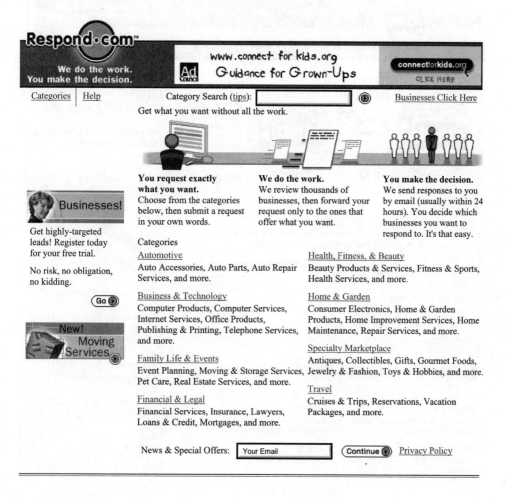

Fig. 15.3 Respond.com

particular product category. There are many sites that specialize in clothing, home furnishings or white goods for example (see figure 15.3) where the consumer can easily compare between different product offerings.

Metamediary—the metamediary takes this idea one stage further and offers the consumer choice, not only in respect of one product category, but also the related product categories that could potentially be of interest. Moreover, they will take the details of the product/service that the consumer is looking to purchase and search both their own database and even other websites to locate the best possible price for the consumer on that item. Figure 15.4 shows one such example. Edmunds.com will find pretty much any car the consumer might demand liasing with distributors and manufacturers to locate the

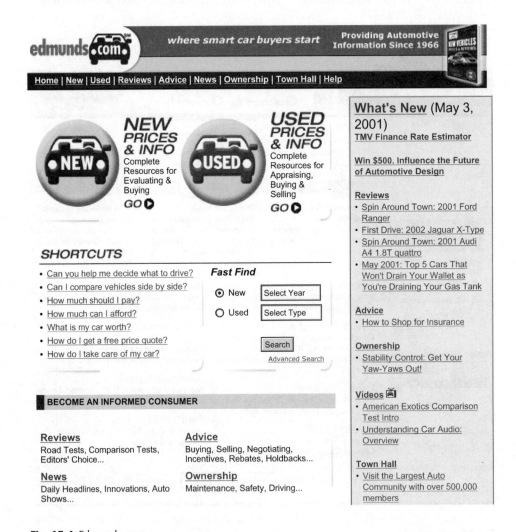

Fig. 15.4 Edmunds.com

desired item. Edmunds adds considerable value for the consumer, however, by acting as a one stop shop for a vehicle, insurance and even finance should that be required.

Authors such as Mohan Sawhney argue that the rise of metamediaries was inevitable since in effect suppliers are being compelled to think of markets in the same way as consumers. Consumers tend to see markets in terms of activities, whilst sellers have tended to think of them in terms of products. Metamediaries organize themselves around serving consumer needs in respect of the former. They put together a collection of 'cognitively related activities that consumers engage in to satisfy a distinct set of needs'. We are therefore now seeing a rise in the number of sites catering for metamarkets such as:

- home ownership;
- parenting;
- wedding;
- cooking;
- healthy living;
- active travel.

And in the business to business context

- corporate travel and entertainment;
- logistics management;
- procurement;
- human resource management.

Sawnhey argues that new metamarkets will arise when.

- there is a sufficient number of cognitively related activities that appeal to an economically viable segment of the population;
- the activities are intensive, complex and high involvement—allowing a metamediary to add value by simplifying the process;
- the activities, span diverse, fragmented and on the face of it, unrelated industries and markets;
- the experience of buying these products/services is typically inefficient and unpleasant.

The metamarket for healthy living is illustrated in Figure 15.5. As the reader will appreciate, the product categories listed are diverse and would traditionally have had to be purchased separately necessitating considerable time and expense on the part of the purchaser. By using a metamediary, the consumer is in effect offered a one-stop shop that deals with everything they need to indulge their particular lifestyle interest. Given the financial success of metamediaries, the trend towards distribution of this type looks set to continue, with the manufacturers of goods and services likely to become increasingly reliant on such sites for referrals and sales. It is interesting to note that in the early days of these sites, manufacturers were reluctant to have any direct association with such organizations, fearing that many might not be reputable, or were operating on a shoestring out

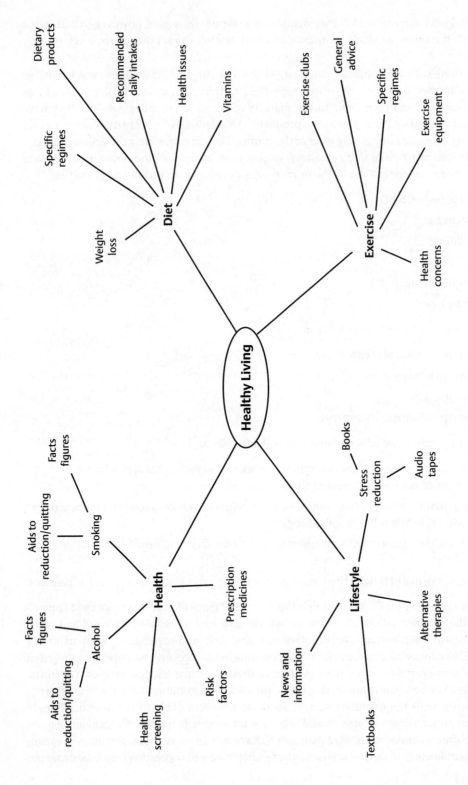

Fig. 15.5 Healthy living metamarket

of someone's attic. The smarter organizations recognized the potential and exchanged access for equity ensuring that as the metamediary began to grow in power, their link to the site could be assured. Metamediaries are now so significant in some markets that the owners of such sites are able to charge healthy sums of money to allow suppliers access to their clients.

15.6 Channel integration

With web TV now a reality and cable and satellite companies now integrating access to the Internet in their own portfolio of services, it seems increasingly likely that a new generation of home entertainment system will emerge. Consumers will be offered a plethora of different television and radio channels and search engines will scan for the most desirable programme given the history of viewing/listening that an individual might have. On returning home of an evening the consumer of the early 2000s will be welcomed by a menu of activities that their new home entertainment units believe will be appealing.

This additional choice will also be available to advertisers. As viewers/listeners tune in to particular channels, data in respect of their specific interests will likely be captured and used to inform the nature of the commercials that they receive. Increasingly, advertising content will be developed on an almost one to one basis, with products and messages uniquely tailored to the perceived needs of the individual.

The nature of television and radio will also change. Home entertainment systems will integrate a variety of different media, making it possible, for example, for someone watching the news to click an icon on the screen and visit a web site with further information on a topic they find of particular interest. Channels will also be capable of being viewed simultaneously, thus, those interested in the performance of particular shares will be able to track movements in their portfolio at the same time as doing their shopping or watching a favourite film.

Nor will this integration be limited to the home. Internet access will be possible from palmtop, cordless receivers, almost certainly integrated with mobile telephony. In-car entertainment systems will be integrated with satellite navigation systems and open Internet access. The technology now exists to integrate these systems making it possible for auto-manufacturers to augment the nature of the services they provide for their clients. It will shortly be possible to drive listening to one's favourite radio station, wherever in the world that station happens to be based, decide that it is time to eat, and ask the e-terminal on the dashboard to display the nearest location offering, say, an Indian takeaway. It will then be possible to examine the menu and place an order whilst satellite navigation equipment provides a map indicating the best possible route to take to get there.

Indeed, it is not inconceivable that this new technology will alter the economics of transport. When one considers the utility that such systems could offer consumers—and thus the manufacturers serving the needs of those consumers, the providers of such systems could afford to charge manufacturers/service providers for the right to become a part thereof. The fact that a charge might be made for this would give automotive manu-facturers an incentive to lower the cost of their vehicles to entice consumers to use information systems where, ironically, the margin may soon be higher than could ever be achieved on the car itself. This may particularly be the case for vehicles that are leased from the manufacturer. Lease costs could therefore decrease as car manufacturers discover a further source of revenue.

It would be a mistake to believe that any of these 'predictions' reside in the realm of science fiction. The technology exists to provide many of these services today. It is only a matter of time before home, car, and office information systems are capable of integrating all of the diverse information sources that we presently have access to. As consumers begin to derive value from this process, the pace of change can only accelerate.

15.7 Changing demographics

In the late 1990s, the typical Internet user was classified as a white male, in his mid-thirties, and earning an above average income. With the passing of each year this profile is changing dramatically. The gender balance has now been redressed with Internet users as likely to be female as male. Interestingly, this shift has particularly manifested itself in the profile of consumers making purchases on line. Some 60 per cent of consumer purchases are currently being initiated by women, bringing on-line retailing into line with trad-itional in-store retailing.

The income profile of the Internet user is also softening. In 1999, the average annual income of an individual making their first purchase over the Internet had decreased to c. $60,000, from well over $80,000 just a few years previously. All the signs are that this profile will now undergo an accelerated decline, matching ever more closely the income of a typical income earner in society at large. The only groups who may enjoy less ubiquitous access are likely to be the lowest income earners in society, although even these latter groups may ultimately be served with developments such as web TV. It seems likely that within the next ten years it will be difficult to obtain a television set that does not provide this additional technology as standard.

15.8 Some specifics

15.8.1 More direct marketing

The days of mass marketing, or as it has come to be affectionately known 'crass market-ing' are severely numbered. With the proliferation in media channels already alluded to above, the mass audience of 20 years ago will simply cease to exist. Brand advertising will therefore become increasingly expensive as it becomes increasingly necessary to main-tain a presence across a wide range of different media. Whilst a few major global players, such as Coca Cola and Microsoft, may well be capable of rising to this challenge, it seems more likely that a larger percentage of brand building will take place below the line and be highly targeted at those consumers that match the target profile. Brand advertising may well take place, but the selection of those media where communication is deemed optimal will become an ever more sophisticated operation.

With the end of mass marketing now being trumpeted, it seems likely that all marketing will be capable of classification as 'direct marketing' within the next ten years. DRPA and DRTV are becoming ever more popular, as are other direct media such as direct mail, door to door distribution, and telemarketing. These trends look set to continue to the foreseeable future, although it is increasingly less likely that any one medium will be used in isolation. A steady trend towards the integration of marketing communications is already in evidence and creative direct marketers are taking advantage thereof.

15.8.2 **Place based media**

The late 1990s saw the creation of a succession of new place based media. These media are designed to be available in strategic locations, keeping you informed about products/ services right at the time when you are likely to be most interested in the category. The Six Flags Promotion Network is an effective multimedia channel designed to attract the attention of visitors to one of the numerous Six Flag Theme Parks that pepper the United States. The audience is captive whilst they wait in line for new rides and attractions—and can be kept up to date with Six Flags developments and products whilst at the same time being entertained and thus shortening the perceived waiting time for the ride.

Anyone visiting their local airport in the United States will also be familiar with the Airport Channel. Audiences can view the channel whilst they wait at the gate for the departure of their aircraft. Programming and advertising content reflects the perceived needs of the target audience.

Even retailers are now creating their own place-based media. Virgin and HMV now pipe their own radio stations around their stores, featuring topical tracks that shoppers may well be interested in purchasing. The travel group Granada provides a similar service to visitors to its motorway service station, promoting the range of services it provides and providing a timely mixture of entertainment and travel information.

The current proliferation of place based media looks set to continue, particularly given the synergy between it and the latest retailing trend—destination retailing. In a bid to claw back sales lost to the Internet and other home shopping channels, retailers are increasingly looking to provide an entertaining experience for shoppers that will entice trial and encourage subsequent revisits and purchases. August 1999, for example, saw the opening of a new destination retail Levi's store in San Francisco. Displays are interactive, products are offered from all over the world and a range of customization services are offered such as fabric painting and a shrink to fit hot tub. Place based media include interactive displays and a showcase of new art and music felt likely to be of interest to those visiting the store. Sites such as this are designed to reflect a brand's image and to offer shoppers a hitherto lacking sense of fun. One of the more entertaining examples of this the authors discovered in 2000 was a Bass Pro shop in Illinois where shoppers could even try out new fishing equipment in an in-store trout stream!

15.8.3 **Infomercials**

The proliferation of media channels has both widened the scope for, and lowered the cost of, so-called infomercials. The infomercial has been around since the 1950s and consists of a programme length commercial. Whilst traditionally it was used to promote kitchen implements and long playing records, it now seems to be breaking into the mainstream with many Fortune 500 companies now looking to invest in the opportunity. In the last four years of the twentieth century the number of infomercials aired on commercial television increased by 76 per cent. Sales via this medium are currently estimated to be of the order of $1.6 billion and the total continues to grow. Whilst today sales enquiries are typically dealt with via a toll free telephone number aired regularly on screen, it seems likely that web TV will allow consumers to place an order directly by simply clicking a button on their remote. Doubtless the ease with which such purchases can be made will entice yet more manufacturers into the medium.

15.8.4 **Home shopping**

Allied to the above, there has been a parallel increase in the use of home shopping. Infomercials are but one notable example of a wider trend. Although the forecast growth in home shopping predicted in the mid-1990s has yet to materialize, as the number of Internet users grows, the more attractive the market becomes for producers of goods and services. In the UK even supermarkets which have traditionally offered a large selection of low value items are now able to offer a home shopping service, although most are geographically concentrated in the south east of the country where the concentration of consumers makes home delivery a practical option. Stores such as Iceland have cast their net somewhat wider, although there are typically minimum order values to ensure that the stores offering this service lose no money on the transaction.

There has also been a growth in home shopping television channels such as QVC; channels devoted to nothing other than selling their merchandise to consumers. Even more amazing is the audience that such channels are able to draw. It is not at all unusual for many hundreds of thousands of individuals to be viewing a home shopping channel at any given time. The reader will appreciate that if only a small percentage of viewers decide to make a purchase, the revenue so generated is likely to be (and is!) substantial.

15.8.5 **The rise and fall of telemarketing**

Since the heady days of 1962, when a network of 13,000 American housewives pioneered the use of telemarketing in generating leads for Ford salespeople selling the Ford Mustang, the industry has come a long way. The use of telemarketing by firms in almost every sector has mushroomed. In the early days, the emphasis was firmly on sales, generating leads which would then be followed up by more traditional channels. As time went on, the potential of telemarketing to generate inbound calls was noted and even used for the purposes of fundraising. It was, for example, used to raise the monies necessary to restore the Statue of Liberty in the early 1980s. The fact that almost every home in the developed world now has a phone and it is comparatively easy to access the desired profile of individuals have combined to make this medium an attractive candidate for investment. Regrettably, however, the activities of less scrupulous operators have acted to generate considerable hostility towards the industry. Few consumers object to placing inbound calls to an organization of their own choosing, but many are now objecting to what they see as the invasion of their privacy by unwelcome telemarketers. Indeed, the industry must shoulder much of the blame for this perception as many firms have targeted houses at random with little or no thought for the interests of those they were calling. Others employed gimmicks; 'congratulations Dr Sargeant you've been selected. . . .' was a phrase one author found all too common in the 1980s and 90s.

The resultant consumer hostility should therefore come as little of a surprise to an industry that has long resisted regulation. Indeed, so hostile have consumers become that other telecommunications sectors are now 'cashing in' on the hostility and offering consumers new technology designed to filter unwanted calls. The advent of caller display and the flashing signal indicating 'number withheld' provided the first hint of a telemarketing call. More recently, telephone service providers have taken steps to provide a service for clients that specifically screens calls, diverting away unwanted telemarketing to an operator. Amazingly, consumers in many countries feel so strongly about 'intrusive' telemarketing' they are willing to pay for the provision of this service.

As the availability of this technology spreads it seems increasingly likely that cold outbound telemarketing will wither on the vine. Few companies will be able to access the desired targets and the cost per sale will climb to the point where it appears uneconomic in relation to other media.

It isn't all gloom for the telemarketing industry, however, as both inbound and warm use of the medium look set to continue their growth. Warm telemarketing, where organizations have specifically asked if they might from time to time call with relevant offers causes little offence and can be genuinely welcomed by the consumer. As with so much of direct marketing, the key undoubtedly lies in moving away from intrusion as the basis for strategy to invitation.

15.9 Summary

In this chapter, we have briefly reviewed a number of the key changes currently impacting on the direct marketing industry. The pace of technological change is opening up a wealth of new creative opportunities, particularly in the realm of the Internet where the rise of broadband will revolutionize the quality of the consumer experience. We have also noted that the rapid growth in companies using the Internet to conduct business has given rise to a proliferation of consumer choice. To assist consumers in dealing with this burgeoning mass of information a new generation of intermediary is being born. Metamediaries such as Web-MD and Edmunds.Com now add considerable value for consumers by providing an integrated service that reflects a lifestyle interest rather than a simple product category per se.

Whilst consumers seem in general to have welcomed the changes taking place, both in technology and the way in which that technology might be exploited to service their needs and number of critical concerns remain. Notable among these is the issue of individual privacy. Consumers are reported as being increasingly wary of the manner in which organizations might use the information stored about them and their purchasing behaviours. We have examined the concerns of consumers in this regard and identified how organizations might best respond to the challenge of being seen to deal fairly with personal information. The approach of different countries to controlling this process has been contrasted and it seems clear that the only way that direct marketers may ultimately avoid the draconian legislation now in existence throughout Europe, is voluntarily to curb what are regarded as the worst excesses and actively to promote any corrective action that might be taken.

Discussion questions

1   You are the marketing director of a leading manufacturer of children's toys. Prepare a presentation to your board outlining the challenges posed by Broadband technology and how you believe your organization should respond.

2   Distinguish between metamediation and cybermediation. What examples can you find of each category of intermediary on the web? What would you say were the strengths and weaknesses of the sites you find?

3   What is a metamarket? For one of your own choosing identify the products/ services that might be provided by a metamediary serving that market.

4   For a country of your own choosing, outline what you see as being the primary consumer concerns over the use of personal information. What steps are being taken by both the direct marketing industry and government to manage these concerns? How effective do you think these steps might be?

Further reading

Sawhney M. (2001) *Techventure: Sustaining Value and Profit in a Techology Ecosystem* (Chichester: John Wiley & Sons).

Index